Collins

The Shanghai Maths Project

For the English National Curriculum

Teacher's Guide 6A

Teacher's Guide Series Editor: Amanda Simpson

Practice Books Series Editor: Professor Lianghuo Fan

Authors: David Bird, Linda Glithro, Paul Hodge, Richard Perring and Paul Wrangles

Collins

William Collins' dream of knowledge for all began with the publication of his first book in 1819.

A self-educated mill worker, he not only enriched millions of lives, but also founded a flourishing publishing house. Today, staying true to this spirit, Collins books are packed with inspiration, innovation and practical expertise. They place you at the centre of a world of possibility and give you exactly what you need to explore it.

Collins. Freedom to teach.

Published by Collins
An imprint of HarperCollins*Publishers*
The News Building
1 London Bridge Street
London
SE1 9GF

Browse the complete Collins catalogue at
www.collins.co.uk

10 9 8 7 6 5 4 3 2 1

978-0-00-819724-7

Teacher's Guide Series Editor: Amanda Simpson

Practice Books Series Editor: Professor Lianghuo Fan

Authors: David Bird, Linda Glithro, Paul Hodge, Richard Perring and Paul Wrangles

British Library Cataloguing in Publication Data

A catalogue record for this publication is available from the British Library.

Publishing Manager: Fiona McGlade and Lizzie Catford
In-house Editor: Mike Appleton
In-house Editorial Assistant: August Stevens
Project Manager: Karen Williams
Copy Editors: Catherine Dakin and Tracy Thomas
Proofreaders: Steven Matchett, Amanda Dickson, Brian Speed and Karen Williams
Cover design: Kevin Robbins and East China Normal University Press Ltd.
Internal design: 2Hoots Publishing Services Ltd
Typesetting: Ken Vail Graphic Design Ltd
Illustrations: Ken Vail Graphic Design Ltd
Production: Sarah Burke

Printed and bound by CPI Group (UK) Ltd, Croydon, CR0 4YY

MIX
Paper from responsible sources
FSC
www.fsc.org
FSC® C007454

This book is produced from independently certified FSC paper to ensure responsible forest management.

For more information visit:
www.harpercollins.co.uk/green

Contents

The Shanghai Maths Project: an overview

The Shanghai Maths Project is a collaboration between Collins and East China Normal University Press Ltd. adapting their bestselling maths programme, *One Lesson, One Exercise*, for England, using an expert team of authors and reviewers. This carefully crafted programme has been continually reviewed in China over the last 24 years, meaning that the materials have been tried and tested by teachers and children alike. Some new material has been written for The Shanghai Maths Project, but the structure of the original resource has been preserved and as much original material as possible has been retained.

The Shanghai Maths Project is a programme from Shanghai for Years 1–11. Teaching for mastery is at the heart of the entire programme, which, through the guidance and support found in the Teacher's Guides and Practice Books, provides complete coverage of the curriculum objectives for England. Teachers are well supported to deliver a high-quality curriculum using the best teaching methods; pupils are enabled to learn mathematics with understanding and the ability to apply knowledge fluently and flexibly in order to solve problems.

The programme consists of five components: Teacher's Guides (two per year), Practice Books (two per year), Shanghai Learning Book, Homework Guide and Collins Connect digital package.

In this guide, information and support for all teachers of primary maths is set out, unit by unit, so they are able to teach The Shanghai Maths Project coherently and confidently, and with appropriate progression through the whole mathematics curriculum.

Practice Books

The Practice Books are designed to serve as both teaching and learning resources. With graded arithmetic exercises, plus varied practice of key concepts and summative assessments for each year, each Practice Book offers intelligent practice and consolidation to promote deep learning and develop higher-order thinking.

There are two Practice Books for each year group: A and B. Pupils should have ownership of their copies of the Practice Books so they can engage with relevant exercises every day, integrated with preparatory whole-class and small-group teaching, recording their answers in the books.

The Practice Books contain:

- chapters made up of units, containing small steps of progression, with practice at each stage
- a test at the end of each chapter
- an end-of-year test in Practice Book B.

Each unit in the Practice Books consists of two sections: 'Basic questions' and 'Challenge and extension questions'.

We suggest that the 'Basic questions' be used for all pupils. Many of them, directly or sometimes with a little modification, can be used as starting questions, for motivation or introduction or as examples for clear explanation. They can also be used as in-class exercise questions – most likely for reinforcement and formative assessment, but also for pupils' further exploration. Almost all questions can be given for individual or peer work, especially when used as in-class exercise questions. Some are also suitable for group work or whole-class discussion.

Basic questions

1. What number does each ● in the following number sentences represent?

   (a) ● + 2.8 = 17.2   (b) 10.3 − ● = 4.7

   ● = _____   ● = _____

   (c) ● × 6 = 120   (d) 1260 ÷ ● = 9

   ● = _____   ● = _____

   (e) ● × ● = 81   (f) ● + ● + ● = 96

   ● = _____   ● = _____

   (g) ● + 1.3 + 7.7 = 14   (h) 15.2 − 3.4 − ● = 1.6

   ● = _____   ● = _____

2. The ▲ in each calculation represents the same digit. Find its value.

   (a) 6 ▲   (b) ▲ 8   (c) 5 ▲
      + ▲   − ▲   − ▲ 8
      ─────   ─────   ─────
       7 2   ▲ 5   1 5

   ▲ = _____   ▲ = _____   ▲ = _____

Challenge and extension questions

5. What digits do the ▲ and ● stand for?

   ▲
   ●
   + ● ▲
   ─────
   8 9

   ● = ☐   ▲ = ☐

6. Look for patterns and then fill in the ○ with suitable numbers.

   | 12 | 35 | 38 | 25 | 78 | 49 | 64 | 71 |

   47   63   127   ○

   11   9   10   ○

All pupils should be given the opportunity to solve some of the 'Challenge and extension questions', which are good for building confidence, but they should not always be required to solve all of them. A general suggestion is that most pupils try about 40–60 per cent of the 'Challenge and extension questions'.

Unit tests sometimes include questions that relate to content in the 'Challenge and extension questions'. This is clearly shown in the diagnostic assessment grids provided in the Teacher's Guides. Teachers should make their own judgments about how to use this information since not all pupils will have attempted the 'Challenge and extension questions'.

Teacher's Guides

Theory underpinning the Teacher's Guides

The Teacher's Guides contain everything teachers need in order to provide the highest quality teaching in all areas of mathematics, in line with the English National Curriculum. Core mathematics topics are developed with deep understanding in every year group. Some areas are not visited every year, though curriculum coverage is in line with Key Stage statutory requirements, as set out in the National curriculum in England: mathematics programmes of study (updated 2014).

There are two Teacher's Guides for each year group: one for the first part of the year (Teacher's Guide 6A) and the other for the second (Teacher's Guide 6B).

Lessons are a mixture of teacher-led, peer and independent work. The Teacher's Guides set out subject knowledge that teachers might need, as well as guidance on pedagogical issues – the best ways to organise activities, to ask questions and to increase difficulty in small steps. Most importantly, the Teacher's Guides contain, threaded throughout the whole book, a strong element of professional development for teachers, focusing on the way mathematics concepts can be enabled to develop and connect with each other.

The Shanghai Maths Project Teacher's Guides are a complete reference for teachers working with the Practice Books. Each unit in the Practice Book for each year group is set out in the corresponding Teacher's Guide over a number of pages.

Most units will need to be taught over more than one lesson – some might need three lessons. In the Practice Books, units contain a great deal of learning, densely packed into a few questions. If pupils are to be able to tackle and succeed with the Practice Book questions, they need to have been guided to learn new mathematics and to connect it to their existing knowledge.

This can only be achieved when teachers are able to break down the conceptual learning that is needed and to provide relevant and high-quality teaching. The Teacher's Guides show teachers how to build up pupils' knowledge and experience so they learn with understanding in small steps. This way, learning is secure, robust and not reliant on memorisation.

The small steps that are necessary must be in line with what international research tells us about conceptual growth and development. The Shanghai Maths Project embodies that knowledge about conceptual development and about teaching for mastery of mathematics concepts and skills. The way that difficulty is varied, and the same ideas are presented

in different contexts, is based on the notion of 'teaching with variation'. 'Variation' in Chinese mathematics carries particular meaning as it has emerged from a great deal of research in the area of 'variation theory'. Variation theory is based on the view that, 'When a particular aspect varies whilst all other aspects of the phenomenon are kept invariant, the learner will experience variation in the varying aspect and will discern that aspect. For example, when a child is shown three balls of the same size, shape, and material, but each of a different color: red, green and yellow, then it is very likely that the child's attention will be drawn to the color of the balls because it is the only aspect that varies.' (Bowden and Marton 1998, cited in Pang and Ling 2012)

In summary, two types of variation are necessary, each with a different function; both are necessary for the development of conceptual understanding.

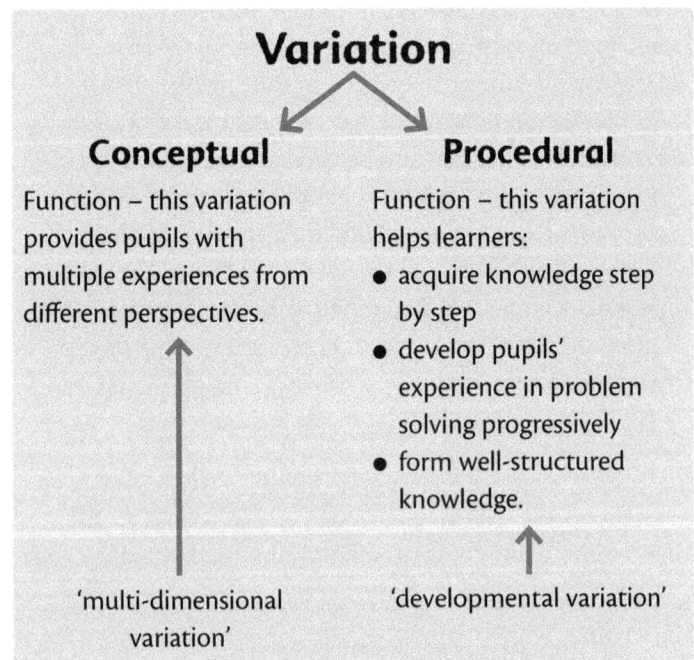

Variation

Conceptual

Function – this variation provides pupils with multiple experiences from different perspectives.

'multi-dimensional variation'

Procedural

Function – this variation helps learners:

- acquire knowledge step by step
- develop pupils' experience in problem solving progressively
- form well-structured knowledge.

'developmental variation'

Teachers who are aiming to provide conceptual variation should vary the way the problem is presented without varying the structure of the problem itself.

The problem itself doesn't change, but the way it is presented (or represented) does. Incorporation of a Concrete–Pictorial–Abstract (CPA) approach to teaching activities provides conceptual variation since pupils experience the same mathematical situations in parallel concrete, pictorial and abstract ways.

CPA is integrated in the Teacher's Guides so teachers are providing questions and experiences that incorporate appropriate conceptual variation.

Procedural variation is the process of:
- forming concepts logically and/or chronologically (i.e. scaffolding, transforming)
- arriving at solutions to problems
- forming knowledge structures (generalising across contexts).

In the Practice Book, there are numerous examples of procedural variation in which pupils gradually build up knowledge, step by step; often they are exposed to patterns that teachers should guide them to perceive and explore.

It is this embedded variation that means that when The Shanghai Maths Project is at the heart of mathematics teaching throughout the school, teachers can be confident that the curriculum is of the highest order and it will be delivered by teachers who are informed and confident about how to support pupils to develop strong, connected concepts.

Teaching for mastery

There is no single definition of mathematics mastery. The term 'mastery' is used in conjunction with various aspects of education – to describe goals, attainment levels or a type of teaching. In teaching in Shanghai, mastery of concepts is characterised as 'thorough understanding' and is one of the aims of maths teaching in Shanghai.

Thorough understanding is evident in what pupils do and say. A concept can be seen to have been mastered when a pupil:
- is able to interpret and construct multiple representations of aspects of that concept
- can communicate relevant ideas and reason clearly about that concept using appropriate mathematical language
- can solve problems using the knowledge learned in familiar and new situations, collaboratively and independently.

Within The Shanghai Maths Project, mastery is a goal, achievable through high-quality teaching and learning experiences that include opportunities to explore, articulate thinking, conjecture, practise, clarify, apply and integrate new understandings piece by piece. Learning is carefully structured throughout and across the programme, with Teacher's Guides and Practice Books interwoven – chapter by chapter, unit by unit, question by question.

Since so much conceptual learning is to be achieved with each of the questions in any Practice Book unit, teachers are provided with guidance for each question, breaking down the development that will occur and how they should facilitate this – suggestions for teachers' questions, problems for pupils, activities and resources are clearly set out in an appropriate sequence.

In this way, teaching and learning are unified and consolidated. Coherence within and across components of the programme is an important aspect of The Shanghai Maths Project, in which Practice Books and Teacher's Guides, when used together, form a strong, effective teaching programme.

Promoting pupil engagement

The digital package on Collins Connect contains a variety of resources for concept development, problem solving and practice, provided in different ways. These include an 'Image Bank' for each Book. All images in the Teacher Guides, including pictorial representations and many word problems, are provided in the Image Bank so that teachers can share these with their class easily and quickly. Other resources, for pupils to work with directly, are provided as photocopiable resource sheets at the back of the Teacher's Guides, and on Collins Connect. These might be practical activities, games, puzzles or investigations, or are sometimes more straightforward practice exercises. Teachers are signposted to these as 'Resources' in the Unit guidance.

Coverage of the curriculum is comprehensive, coherent and consolidated. Ideas are developed meaningfully, through intelligent practice, incorporating skilful questioning that exposes mathematical structures and connections.

Shanghai Year 6 Learning Book

Shanghai Learning Books are for pupils to use. They are concise, colourful references that set out all the key ideas taught in the year, using images and explanations pupils will be familiar with from their lessons. Ideally, the books will be available to pupils during their maths lessons and at other times during the school day so they can access them easily if they need support for thinking about maths. The books are set out to correspond to each chapter* as it is taught and provide all the key images and vocabulary pupils will need in order to think things through independently or with a partner, resolving issues for themselves as much as possible. The Year 6 Learning Book might sometimes be taken home and shared with parents: this enables pupils, parents and teachers to form positive relationships around maths teaching that is of great benefit to children's learning.

---

* Note that because Chapters 5 and 10 in Year 6 are Consolidation and Enhancement Chapters, there are no Chapters 5 or 10 in the Year 6 Learning Book.

How to use the Teacher's Guides

Teaching

Units taught in the first half of Year 6:

Contents

Teacher's Guide 6A sets out, for each chapter and unit in Practice Book 6A, a number of things that teachers will need to know if their teaching is to be effective and their pupils are to achieve mastery of the mathematics contained in the Practice Book.

Each chapter begins with a chapter overview that summarises, in a table, how Practice Book questions and classroom activities suggested in the Teacher's Guide relate to National Curriculum statutory requirements.

Chapter overview

Area of mathematics	National Curriculum statutory requirements for Key Stage 2	Shanghai Maths Project reference
Algebra	Year 6 Programme of study: Pupils should be taught to: ■ generate and describe linear number sequences ■ express missing number problems algebraically.	Year 6, Unit 1.1
Number – addition, subtraction, multiplication and division	Year 6 Programme of study: Pupils should be taught to: ■ perform mental calculations, including with mixed operations and large numbers ■ identify common factors, common multiples and prime numbers ■ use their knowledge of the order of operations to carry out calculations involving the four operations ■ solve addition and subtraction multi-step problems in contexts, deciding which operations and methods to use and why ■ solve problems involving addition, subtraction, multiplication and division.	Year 6, Units 1.2, 1.3
Number – fractions (including decimals and percentages)	Year 6 Programme of study: Pupils should be taught to: ■ solve problems which require answers to be rounded to specified degrees of accuracy	Year 6, Units 1.4, 1.5

It is important to note that the National Curriculum requirements are statutory at the end of each Key Stage and that The Shanghai Maths Project does fulfil (at least) those end of Key Stage requirements. However, some aspects are not covered in the same year group as they are in the National Curriculum Programme of Study – for example, end of Key Stage 1 requirements for 'Money' are achieved in Year 2 and 'Money' is not taught again in Year 2.

All units will need to be taught over 1–3 lessons. Teachers must use their judgment as to when pupils are ready to move on to new learning within each unit – it is a principle of teaching for mastery that pupils are given opportunities to grasp the learning that is intended before moving to the next variation of the concept or to the next unit.

All units begin with a unit overview, which has four sections:

Conceptual context – a short section summarising the conceptual learning that will be brought about through Practice Book questions and related activities. Links with previous learning and future learning will be noted in this section.

Conceptual context

This unit introduces the use of symbols to represent unknown numbers. This will be developed in Chapter 3, Introduction to algebra.

Learning pupils will have achieved at the end of the unit

- Pupils will have explored solving addition and subtraction equations containing an unknown represented by a symbol, by using their inverse relationship (Q1)
- Pupils will have explored solving multiplication and division equations containing an unknown represented by a symbol, by using their inverse relationship (Q1)
- Pupils will have solved calculations containing symbols to represent numbers by reasoning and applying their mathematical knowledge (Q2, Q4)
- Arithmetic number sequences, where the numbers increase and decrease in different intervals, will have been revisited (Q3)
- Pupils will have been introduced to number sequences composed of two alternating number patterns (Q3)
- Different types of number sequences will have been explored, including geometric sequences, square numbers, cube numbers, Fibonacci numbers (Q3)
- Pupils will have explained the pattern of number sequences using full sentences (Q3)

This list indicates how skills and concepts will have formed and developed during work on particular questions within this unit.

These are resources useful for the lesson, including photocopiable resources supplied in the Teacher's Guide. (Those listed are the ones needed for 'Basic questions' – not for 'Challenge and extension questions'.)

This is a list of vocabulary necessary for teachers and pupils to use in the lesson.

Resources

mini whiteboards; 1–100 number cards; 0–6 dice; **Resource 6.1.1a** Number sequences; **Resource 6.1.1b** Number sequences with unknowns

Vocabulary

symbol, unknown, number sequence, term, natural numbers

The Shanghai Maths Project: an overview

After the unit overview, the Teacher's Guide goes on to describe how teachers might introduce and develop necessary, relevant ideas and how to integrate them with questions in the Practice Book unit. For each question in the Practice Book, teaching is set out under the following headings:

What learning will pupils have achieved at the conclusion of Question X?

This list responds to the following questions: Why is this question here? How does this question help pupils' existing concepts to grow? What is happening in this unit to help pupils prepare for a new concept about …? This list of bullet points will give teachers insight into the rationale for the activities and exercises and will help them to hone their pedagogy and questioning.

What learning will pupils have achieved at the conclusion of Questions 1 and 2?

- Pupils will have explored solving addition and subtraction equations containing an unknown represented by a symbol, by using their inverse relationship.
- Pupils will have explored solving multiplication and division equations containing an unknown represented by a symbol, by using their inverse relationship.
- Pupils will have solved calculations containing symbols to represent numbers by reasoning and applying their mathematical knowledge.

Activities for whole-class instruction

- Show pupils the following equation.

  $6 + 7 = 13$

  Give pupils mini whiteboards. Ask them to draw a bar model to illustrate this equation and to write the other number facts that can be deduced from this.

13	
7	6

Activities for whole-class instruction

This is the largest section within each unit. For each question in the Practice Book, suggestions are set out for questions and activities that support pupils to form and develop concepts and deepen understanding. Suggestions are described in some detail and activities are carefully sequenced to enable coherent progression. Procedural fluency and conceptual learning are both valued and developed in tandem and in line with the Practice Book questions. Teachers are prompted to draw pupils' attention to connections and to guide them to perceive links for themselves so mathematical relationships and richly connected concepts are understood and can be applied.

The Concrete–Pictorial–Abstract (CPA) approach underpins suggestions for activities, particularly those intended to provide conceptual variation (varying the way the problem is presented without varying the structure of the problem itself). This contributes to conceptual variation by giving pupils opportunities to experience concepts in multiple representations – the concrete, the pictorial and the abstract. Pupils learn well when they are able to engage with ideas in a practical, concrete way and then go on to represent those ideas as pictures or diagrams, and ultimately as symbols. It is important, however, that a CPA approach is not understood as a one-way journey from concrete to abstract and that pupils do not need to work with concrete materials in practical ways if they can cope with abstract representations – this is a fallacy. Pupils of all ages do need to work with all kinds of representations since it is 'translating' between the concrete, pictorial and abstract that will deepen understanding, by rehearsing the links between them and strengthening conceptual connections. It is these connections that provide pupils with the capacity to solve problems, even in unfamiliar contexts.

In this section, the reasons underlying certain questions and activities are explained, so teachers learn the ways in which pupils' concepts need to develop and how to improve and refine their questioning and provision.

Usually, for each question, the focus will at first be on whole-class and partner work to introduce and develop ideas and understanding relevant to the question. Once the necessary learning has been achieved and practised, pupils will complete the Practice Book question, when it will be further reinforced and developed.

Same-day intervention

Pupils who have not been able to achieve the learning that was intended must be identified straight away so teachers can try to identify the barriers to their learning and help pupils to build their understanding in another way. (This is a principle of teaching for mastery.) In the Teacher's Guide, suggestions for teaching this group are included for each unit. Ideally, this intervention will take place on the same day as the original teaching. The intervention activity always provides a different experience from that of the main lesson – often the activity itself is different; sometimes the changes are to the approach and the explanations that enable pupils to access a similar activity.

Same-day intervention

- Pupils work with a partner. Each chooses two 1–10 number cards. They use the cards to write four different number sentences with an unknown and then find the unknown. They then solve each other's number sentences.
- For example, if one pupil chooses the number cards 3 and 9, they could write the following number sentences:

  $3 + \square = 9$
  $3 \times \square = 9$
  $3 \times 9 = \square$
  $9 \div \square = 3$

- Or for number cards 5 and 8:

  $5 + \square = 8$
  $5 \times \square = 8$
  $5 \times 8 = \square$
  $8 \div \square = 5$

Same-day enrichment

- Pupils work with a partner. Each pupil chooses two different two-digit numbers and uses them to write four different number sentences with an unknown. They then find the unknown. They then solve each other's number sentences.
- For example, for the digits 15 and 75, they could write the following number sentences:

  $15 + \square = 75$
  $75 \div \square = 15$
  $15 - 75 = \square$
  $75 + 15 = \square$

- Pupils will find that statements are easier to write if they choose related numbers, doubles or other multiples.

Same-day enrichment

For pupils who do manage to achieve all the planned learning, additional activities are described. These are intended to enrich and extend the learning of the unit. This activity is often carried out by most of the class, while others are engaged with the intervention activity.

Lessons might also have some of the following elements:

Information point

Inserted at points where it feels important to point something out along the way.

The final example in the Practice Book uses Fibonacci numbers. In this number series, each number is the sum of the two preceding numbers: (0), 1, 1, 2, 3, 5, 8, 13, 21, ... Pupils can explore Fibonacci numbers which occur in many areas of mathematics and also in nature.

All say ...

Phrases and sentences to be spoken aloud by pupils in unison and repeated on multiple occasions whenever opportunities present themselves during, within and outside of the maths lesson.

All say ... 5.162 rounded to two decimal places is 5.16.

Look out for ... pupils who muddle 'sum' and 'product'.

Look out for ...

Common errors that pupils make and misconceptions that are often evident in a particular aspect of maths. Do not try to prevent these, but recognise them where they occur and take opportunities to raise them in discussion in sensitive ways so pupils can align their conceptual understanding in more appropriate ways.

Within the guidance there are many prompts for teachers to ask pupils to explain their thinking or their answers. The language that pupils use when responding to questions in class is an important aspect of teaching with The Shanghai Maths Project. Pupils should be expected to use full sentences, including correct mathematical terms and language, to clarify the reasoning underpinning their solutions. This articulation of pupils' thinking is a valuable step in developing concepts, and opportunities should be taken wherever possible to encourage pupils to use full sentences when talking about their maths.

Ideas for resources and activities are for guidance; teachers might have better ideas and resources available. The principle guiding elements for each question should be 'What learning will pupils have achieved at the conclusion of Question X?' and the 'Information points'. If teachers can substitute their own questions and tasks and still achieve these learning objectives, they should not feel concerned about diverging from the suggestions here.

Planning

The Teacher's Guides and Practice Books for Year 6 are split into two volumes, 6A and 6B, one for each part of the year.

- Teacher's Guide 6A and Practice Book 6A cover Chapters 1–5.
- Teacher's Guide 6B and Practice Book 6B cover Chapters 6–10.

Each unit in the Practice Book will need 1–3 lessons for effective teaching and learning of the conceptual content in that unit. Teachers will judge precisely how to plan the teaching year, but, as a general guide, they should aim to complete Chapters 1–3 in the autumn term, Chapters 4–7 in the spring term and Chapters 8–10 in the summer term.

The recommended teaching sequence is as set out in the Practice Books.

Statutory requirements of the National Curriculum in England 2013 (updated 2014) are fully met, and often exceeded, by the programme contained in The Shanghai Maths Project. It should be noted that some curriculum objectives are not covered in the same year group as they are in the National Curriculum Programme of Study – however, since it is end of Key Stage requirements that are statutory, schools following The Shanghai Maths Project are meeting legal curriculum requirements.

A chapter overview at the beginning of each chapter shows, in a table, how Practice Book questions and classroom activities suggested in the Teacher's Guide relate to National Curriculum statutory requirements.

Level of detail

Within each unit, a series of whole-class activities is listed, linked to each question. Within these are questions for pupils that will:

- structure and support pupils' learning,
- aid teachers' assessments during the lesson.

Questions and questioning

Within the guidance for each question are sequences of questions that teachers should ask pupils. Embedded within these is the procedural variation that will help pupils to make connections across their knowledge and experience and support them to 'bridge' to the next level of complexity in the concept being learned.

In preparing for each lesson, teachers will find that, by reading the guidance thoroughly, they will learn for themselves how these sequences of questions very gradually expose more of the maths to be learned, how small those steps of progression need to be, and how carefully crafted the sequence must be. With experience, teachers will find they need to refer to the pupils' questions in the guidance less, as they learn more about how maths concepts need to be nurtured and as they become skilled at 'designing' their own series of questions.

Is it necessary to do everything suggested in the Teacher's Guide?

Activities are described in some detail so teachers understand how to build up the level of challenge and how to vary the contexts and representations used appropriately. These two aspects of teaching mathematics are often called 'intelligent practice'. If pupils are to learn concepts so they are long-lasting and provide learners with the capacity to apply their learning fluently and flexibly in order to solve problems, it is these two aspects of maths teaching that must be achieved to a high standard. The guidance contained in this Teacher's Guide is sufficiently detailed to support teachers to do this.

Teachers who are already expert practitioners in teaching for mastery might use the Teacher's Guide in a different way from those who feel they need more support. The unit overview provides a summary of the concepts and skills learned when pupils work through the activities set out in the guidance and integrated with the Practice Book. Expert mastery teachers might, therefore, select from the activities described and supplement with others from their own resources, confident in their own 'intelligent practice'.

There is more material in the Teachers' Guide than most teachers will need. This is because there are enrichment and intervention activities designed to match each question in the Practice Book. Teachers might find that they are able to deliver the programme, keeping their whole class focused on the same content at all times. This means that all pupils receive teaching input, then complete particular Practice Book questions, before returning for teaching related to the next part of the lesson together. This would look like this:

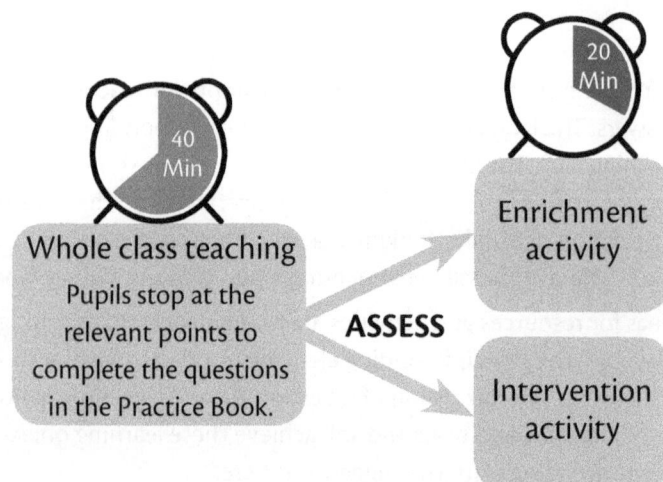

40 Min

20 Min

Whole class teaching
Pupils stop at the relevant points to complete the questions in the Practice Book.

ASSESS

Enrichment activity

Intervention activity

Following this model, at the end of the first session of the day, teachers will use pupils' attainment, evident in class interactions and Practice Book exercises to assess which pupils require intervention. Teachers then select which of the enrichment and intervention activities, linked to the content taught, are most relevant for their class that day. Usually, more than one question will have been covered during the lesson so some activities will not be used.

There is also scope for teachers to be more flexible if they find it difficult to keep the whole class working at the same pace. If there is a disparity among pupils in the time taken to complete Practice Book questions, teachers can select one enrichment activity for all early finishers to move on to if they complete the Practice Book questions quickly. The enrichment activity might be something that pupils work on in two or three 'bites' following completion of successive Practice Book questions at different stages in the lesson.

All pupils should come together for the second and consecutive teaching inputs. Following the next input, all pupils should complete the relevant practice questions and, if appropriate, return to their enrichment activity.

The enrichment activity selected to be used would be the same for all pupils and would not then be available for use in the second part of the maths input later in the day (or next day).

As with the previous, simpler, model, at the end of the first session of the day, teachers will use pupils' attainment, evident in class interactions and Practice Book exercises to assess which pupils require intervention and which should go on to complete other enrichment activities.

Assessing

Ongoing assessment, during lessons, will need to inform judgments about which pupils need further support. Of course, prompt marking will also inform these decisions, but this should not be the only basis for daily assessments – teachers will learn a lot about what pupils understand through skilful questioning and observation during lessons.

At the end of each chapter, a chapter test will revisit the content of the units within that chapter. Attainment in the text can be mapped to particular questions and units so teachers can diagnose particular needs for individuals and groups. Analysis of results from chapter tests will also reveal questions or units that caused difficulties for a large proportion of the class, indicating that more time is needed on that question/unit when it is next taught.

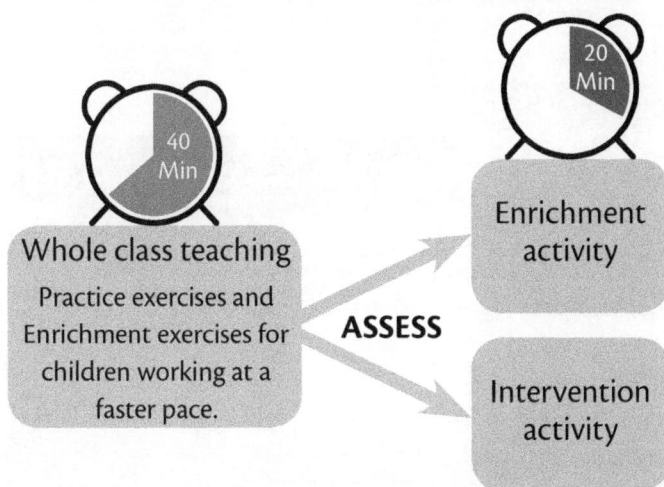

40 Min

20 Min

Whole class teaching
Practice exercises and Enrichment exercises for children working at a faster pace.

ASSESS

Enrichment activity

Intervention activity

The Shanghai Maths Project: an overview

Shanghai Year 6 Learning Book

As referenced on page vii, The Shanghai Maths Project Year 6 Learning Book is a pupil textbook containing the Year 6 maths facts and full pictorial glossary to enable children to master the Year 6 maths programmes of study for England. It sits alongside the Practice Books to be used as a reference book in class or at home.

Maths facts correspond to the chapters in the Practice Books for ease of use.

Chapter 8: Geometry and measurement (2)

Cuboid

A cuboid is a 3-D shape that is a rectangular prism.
All six faces of a cuboid may be rectangles, or four faces rectangles and two faces squares.

vertex (8)
edge (12)
face (6)

The net of a cuboid is made up of three different pairs of rectangles (or four rectangles and two squares).

rectangle B
rectangle A
rectangle C

The volume of a cuboid is length × width × height.

height
width
length

Nets of other 3-D shapes

Triangular pyramid   Square pyramid   Triangular prism   Cone   Cylinder

Key models and images are provided for each mathematical concept.

Glossary

acute angle: An angle that is smaller than a right angle. It is greater than 0 degrees and less than 90 degrees.

adjacent sides: two sides that meet to create an angle

adjacent sides   adjacent sides

algebra: The use of letters to represent numbers in combination with numbers and operators. For example, $3x + 2$ is an expression that uses letters, numbers and operators.

area: the amount of space occupied by a 2-D object

average: a middle or typical value of a dataset

bar chart: a graphical display of data in which the height of each bar relates to quantity or measurement

Types of trees in a park

Number of trees
oak   holly   ash   birch   pine
Type of tree

base: the side of a shape that forms a right (90 degree) angle with the height of the object

height
base

brackets: Symbols used in pairs to group numbers and symbols together; they show which calculation to do first, for example $3(x + 2)$ means 'consider $x + 2$, then multiply it by 3'.

centi: Used in units, it means 'one hundredth' of a unit. So, 1 centimetre is $\frac{1}{100}$ metre and 1 centilitre is $\frac{1}{100}$ litre.

centre (circle): the point equidistant from all points on the circumference of a circle

A visual glossary defines the key mathematical vocabulary pupils need to master.

Homework Guides

The Shanghai Maths Project Homework Guide 6 is a photocopiable master book for the teacher. There is one book per year, containing a homework sheet for every unit, directly related to the maths being covered in the Practice Book unit. There is a 'Learning Together' activity on each page that includes an idea for practical maths the parent or guardian can do with the child.

Homework is directly related to the maths being covered in class.

2.8 Adding two 2-digit numbers (4)
Add 2-digit numbers using a formal written method

1. Use the column method to help complete these addition walls.
One has been completed for you.
The two bottom numbers are added to find the number directly above.

81
46   35

(a)
59   27

(b)
35   38

(c)
64   27

(d)
38   49

(e)
56   36

(f)
49   45

2. Try these addition walls.
(a)
16   28   18

(b)
28   19   27

Tin totals
Choose some tins of soup, beans, rice pudding, etc. from your kitchen cupboard. Stick some paper as price labels on the top of each tin, with any price values from 20p up to 50p. Your child can then choose different pairs of tins and work out their total cost using a written method. Set them a challenge, 'Can you find me two tins with a total between 80p and 90p?'

You need:
at least 6 tins of food (e.g. soup, beans, rice pudding and so on), paper, pen and scissors

An idea for practical maths the parent or guardian can do with the child.

Collins Connect

Collins Connect is the home for all the digital teaching resources provided by The Shanghai Maths Project.

The Collins Connect pack for The Shanghai Maths Project consists of four sections: Teach, Resources, Record, Support.

Teach

The Teach section contains all the content from the Teacher's Guides and Homework Guides, organised by chapter and unit.

- The entire book can be accessed at the top level so teachers can search and find objectives or key words easily.
- Chapters and units can be re-ordered and customised to match individual teachers' planning.
- Chapters and units can be marked as complete by the teacher.
- All the teaching resources for a chapter are grouped together and easy to locate.
- Each unit has its own page from which the contents of the Teacher's Guide, Homework Guide and any accompanying resources can be accessed.
- Teachers can record teacher judgments against National Curriculum attainment targets for individual pupils or the whole class with the record-keeping tool.
- Units from the Teacher's Guide and Homework Guide are provided in PDF and Microsoft Word versions so teachers can edit and customise the contents.
- Any accompanying resources can be displayed or downloaded from the same page.

Resources

The Resources section contains 35 interactive whiteboard tools and an image bank for front-of-class display.

- The 35 maths tools cover all topics, and can be customised and used flexibly by teachers as part of their lessons.
- The image bank contains the images from the Teacher's Guide, which can support pupils' learning. They can be enlarged and shown on the whiteboard.

Record

The Record section is the home of the record-keeping tool for The Shanghai Maths Project. Each unit is linked to attainment targets in the National Curriculum for England, and teachers can easily make records and judgments for individual pupils, groups of pupils or whole classes using the tool from the 'Teach' section. Records and comments can also be added from the 'Record' section, and reports generated by class, by pupil, by domain or by National Curriculum attainment target.

- View and print reports in different formats for sharing with teachers, senior leaders and parents.
- Delve deeper into the records to check on the progress of individual pupils.
- Instantly check on the progress of the class in each domain.

Support

The Support section contains the Teacher's Guide introduction in PDF and Word formats, along with CPD advice and guidance.

Chapter 1
Revising and improving

Chapter overview

Area of mathematics	National Curriculum statutory requirements for Key Stage 2	Shanghai Maths Project reference
Algebra	Year 6 Programme of study: Pupils should be taught to: ■ generate and describe linear number sequences ■ express missing number problems algebraically.	Year 6, Unit 1.1
Number – addition, subtraction, multiplication and division	Year 6 Programme of study: Pupils should be taught to: ■ perform mental calculations, including with mixed operations and large numbers ■ identify common factors, common multiples and prime numbers ■ use their knowledge of the order of operations to carry out calculations involving the four operations ■ solve addition and subtraction multi-step problems in contexts, deciding which operations and methods to use and why ■ solve problems involving addition, subtraction, multiplication and division.	Year 6, Units 1.2, 1.3
Number – fractions (including decimals and percentages)	Year 6 Programme of study: Pupils should be taught to: ■ solve problems which require answers to be rounded to specified degrees of accuracy	Year 6, Units 1.4, 1.5

Measurement	Year 6 Programme of study: Pupils should be taught to: ■ solve problems involving the calculation and conversion of units of measure, using decimal notation up to three decimal places where appropriate ■ use, read, write and convert between standard units, converting measurements of length, mass, volume and time from a smaller unit of measure to a larger unit, and vice versa, using decimal notation to up to three decimal places.	Year 6, Units 1.2, 1.4
Geometry – properties of shapes	Year 6 Programme of study: Pupils should be taught to: ■ illustrate and name parts of circles, including radius, diameter and circumference and know that the diameter is twice the radius ■ recognise angles where they meet at a point, are on a straight line, or are vertically opposite, and find missing angles.	Year 6, Unit 1.6

Pre-requisite knowledge

For pupils to be successful with the work in this chapter, they will need to have achieved mastery in their learning in previous relevant units. Teaching there will have introduced and developed concepts and skills that are necessary to work with the content in this chapter. A summary of pre-requisite knowledge is set out in the table below. If you believe that some pupils need to revisit particular areas, the units in which they were taught are also shown in the table so that you can locate appropriate guidance in the Teacher's Guides and Practice Books. Guidance provided for Chapter 1 on the following pages will therefore focus on new learning.

Pre-requisite knowledge, understanding or skill	Where this was taught in The Shanghai Maths Project
Pupils can solve problems in four operations with an unknown	Years 1–5
Pupils can identify missing numbers in linear number sequences	Year 4, Unit 2.2 Year 5, Unit 10.3
Pupils are able to solve equations and inequality statements containing unknowns	Year 5, Chapter 7 (all units)
Pupils can illustrate and name parts of circles, including radius, diameter and circumference and know that the diameter is twice the radius	Year 5, Units 8.1, 8.2, 8.3
Pupils can recognise angles where they meet at a point, are on a straight line, or are vertically opposite, and find missing angles	Year 5, Units 8.4, 8.5, 8.6, 8.7, 8.8
Pupils can round numbers to the nearest 10, 100, 1000	Year 4, Units 2.3, 2.4, 2.5
Pupils understand place value and decimal notation	Year 4, Chapter 6 (all units)
Pupils can add and subtract decimal numbers	Year 5, Chapter 6 (all units)

Unit 1.1
Using symbols to represent numbers

Conceptual context

This unit introduces the use of symbols to represent unknown numbers. This will be developed in Chapter 3, Introduction to algebra.

Learning pupils will have achieved at the end of the unit

- Pupils will have explored solving addition and subtraction equations containing an unknown represented by a symbol, by using their inverse relationship (Q1)
- Pupils will have explored solving multiplication and division equations containing an unknown represented by a symbol, by using their inverse relationship (Q1)
- Pupils will have solved calculations containing symbols to represent numbers by reasoning and applying their mathematical knowledge (Q2, Q4)
- Arithmetic number sequences, where the numbers increase and decrease in different intervals, will have been revisited (Q3)
- Pupils will have been introduced to number sequences composed of two alternating number patterns (Q3)
- Different types of number sequences will have been explored, including geometric sequences, square numbers, cube numbers, Fibonacci numbers (Q3)
- Pupils will have explained the pattern of number sequences using full sentences (Q3)

Resources

mini whiteboards; 1–100 number cards; 0–6 dice; **Resource 6.1.1a** Number sequences; **Resource 6.1.1b** Number sequences with unknowns

Vocabulary

symbol, unknown, number sequence, term, natural numbers

Questions 1 and 2

1 What number does each ● in the following number sentences represent?

(a) ● + 2.8 = 17.2

(b) 10.3 – ● = 4.7

● = _____

● = _____

(c) ● × 6 = 120

(d) 1260 ÷ ● = 9

● = _____

● = _____

(e) ● × ● = 81

(f) ● + ● + ● = 96

● = _____

● = _____

(g) ● + 1.3 + 7.7 = 14

(h) 15.2 – 3.4 – ● = 1.6

● = _____

● = _____

2 The ▲ in each calculation represents the same digit. Find its value.

(a)
```
    6 ▲
  +   ▲
  ─────
    7 2
```
▲ =

(b)
```
    ▲ 8
  –   ▲
  ─────
    ▲ 5
```
▲ =

(c)
```
    5 ▲
  – ▲ 8
  ─────
    1 5
```
▲ =

(d)
```
      ▲
    2 ▲
  + ▲ ▲
  ─────
    9 8
```
▲ =

(e)
```
    ▲ 3
  ×   ▲
  ─────
  3 7 8
```
▲ =

(f)
```
    ▲ ▲
  ×   ▲
  ─────
  1 7 6
```
▲ =

(g)
```
      4 8
  ×   ▲ 7
  ─────
  ■ ■ ■
  ■ ■ ■
  ─────
  1 7 7 6
```
▲ =

(h)
```
  ▲ ) 2 7
      2 ▲
      ───
        2
```
▲ =

What learning will pupils have achieved at the conclusion of Questions 1 and 2?

- Pupils will have explored solving addition and subtraction equations containing an unknown represented by a symbol, by using their inverse relationship.
- Pupils will have explored solving multiplication and division equations containing an unknown represented by a symbol, by using their inverse relationship.
- Pupils will have solved calculations containing symbols to represent numbers by reasoning and applying their mathematical knowledge.

Activities for whole-class instruction

- Show pupils the following equation.

  6 + 7 = 13

  Give pupils mini whiteboards. Ask them to draw a bar model to illustrate this equation and to write the other number facts that can be deduced from this.

13	
7	6

Agree that, because addition and subtraction are inverse operations, we can deduce three further number facts.

7 + 6 = 13   13 – 6 = 7   13 – 7 = 6

Thus, any addition or subtraction equation with an unknown can be rearranged to find the unknown. Ask pupils to draw a bar model to represent 17 – ☐ = 6.5.

Agree that the missing value is one of the addends, so by subtracting the given addend from the sum, the missing value is revealed.

- Solve some more examples of this type, showing unknowns in all positions, for example:

  ☐ + 34 = 80

  17.8 – ☐ = 12

  34 = ☐☐☐

  675 = 74 + ☐

- Write: 6 × 7 = 42. Ask: *What is the relationship between multiplication and division?* Confirm that they are inverse relationships. Record three further number facts from this equation. 7 × 6 = 42   42 ÷ 6 = 7   42 ÷ 7 = 6

  Thus, any multiplication or division equation with an unknown can be rearranged to find the unknown.

- Solve some examples of this type, for example:

  ☐ × 8 = 320, ☐ ÷ 7 = 12.

- Display these calculations:

```
      A
      4 ★
  +     ★
  ───────
      5 6
```

```
      B
      6 ◆
  ● ◆ 8
  ───────
      1 6
```

```
      C
        ♥ ♥
  ×       ♥
  ─────────
    3 9 ♥
```

```
      D
  1♣6 ÷ ♣ = 63
```

Ask pupils to discuss with a partner how to solve these problems to find the value of ★, ◆, ♥, ● and ♣.

Invite pupils to share their explanations. For A, they could say: 'The two doubles that make 6 in the ones place are 3 and 8. The tens place has increased from 4 to 5 so ★ must be 8.' Encourage pupils to check that the solution is correct: 48 + 8 = 56.

For C, they might say: '55 × 5 = 275 which is too small, 88 × 8 = 704 which is too big so ♥ must be 6 or 7. 66 × 6 = 396 which is correct.'

- Pupils should complete Questions 1 and 2 in the Practice Book.

Same-day intervention

- Pupils work with a partner. Each chooses two 1–10 number cards. They use the cards to write four different number sentences with an unknown and then find the unknown. They then solve each other's number sentences.
- For example, if one pupil chooses the number cards 3 and 9, they could write the following number sentences:

  $3 + \boxed{} = 9$

  $3 \times \boxed{} = 9$

  $3 \times 9 = \boxed{}$

  $9 \div \boxed{} = 3$

- Or for number cards 5 and 8:

  $5 + \boxed{} = 8$

  $5 \times \boxed{} = 8$

  $5 \times 8 = \boxed{}$

  $8 \div \boxed{} = 5$

Same-day enrichment

- Pupils work with a partner. Each pupil chooses two different two-digit numbers and uses them to write four different number sentences with an unknown. They then find the unknown. They then solve each other's number sentences.
- For example, for the digits 15 and 75, they could write the following number sentences:

  $15 + \boxed{} = 75$

  $75 \div \boxed{} = 15$

  $15 - 75 = \boxed{}$

  $75 + 15 = \boxed{}$

- Pupils will find that statements are easier to write if they choose related numbers, doubles or other multiples.

Question 3

> **3** Look for patterns and then write the missing numbers.
>
> (a) 1, 5, 9, 13, ★, 21, 25, 29, ▧, 37, …
>
> ★ = ☐, ▧ = ☐
>
> (b) 0.3, 7.7, 0.5, 7.4, 0.7, ●, ★, 6.8, 1.1, 6.5, …
>
> ● = ☐, ★ = ☐
>
> (c) 2, 4, 8, 16, ▧, 64, 128, ★, …
>
> ▧ = ☐, ★ = ☐
>
> (d) 0.1, 0.2, 0.3, 0.5, 0.8, ▲, 2.1, …
>
> ▲ = ☐

What learning will pupils have achieved at the conclusion of Question 3?

- Arithmetic number sequences, where the numbers increase and decrease in different intervals, will have been revisited.
- Pupils will have been introduced to number sequences composed of two alternating number patterns.
- Different types of number sequences will have been explored, including geometric sequences, square numbers, cube numbers, Fibonacci numbers.
- Pupils will have explained the pattern of number sequences using full sentences.

Activities for whole-class instruction

- Display the following number pattern. Ask pupils to discuss, with a partner, how it is constructed and how it would continue by writing the next four terms.

  1, 0.1, 4, 0.3, 9, 0.5, 16, 0.7, 25, 0.9, 36, 1.1, __, __, __, __

  Agree that the pattern is composed of two number sequences with alternating terms.

- 1,　4,　9,　16,　25,　36, … The terms in this series are square numbers.
- 0.1,　0.3,　0.5,　0.7,　0.9,　1.1, … The rule for the second sequence is + 0.2 starting from 0.1. The next four terms are: 49, 1.3, 64, 1.5.
- The examples in the Practice Book have symbols representing missing numbers. Here is an example.

  1, 2, 10, 4, 100, ★, 1000, 8, ◆, 10

  Ask pupils to discuss, with a partner, what ★ and ◆ represent.

- Challenge pupil pairs to write their own number pattern that is composed of two alternating number sequences. Share some of the pupils' examples.

(i) The final example in the Practice Book uses Fibonacci numbers. In this number series, each number is the sum of the two preceding numbers: (0), 1, 1, 2, 3, 5, 8, 13, 21, ... Pupils can explore Fibonacci numbers which occur in many areas of mathematics and also in nature.

● Pupils should complete Question 3 in the Practice Book.

Same-day intervention

● Give pupil pairs **Resource 6.1.1a** Number sequences to complete.

Resource 6.1.1a

Number sequences

Here are some number sequences. Deduce the value of each symbol.
Tip: Work out the differences.

1. 1, 7, 13, ☆, 25, 31, ✦, ...

   ☆ = ☐   ✦ = ☐

2. 0.2, 0.4, ◇, 0.8, 1.0, 1.2, ✧, ...

   ◇ = ☐   ✧ = ☐

3. 1, 4, ✕16, ♥, 36, 49, ...

   ✕ = ☐   ♥ = ☐

4. 3, 4, 6, 9, ○, 18, 24, ✦, 39, 48, ...

   ○ = ☐   ✦ = ☐

Tip: In these number patterns, there are two number sequences.

5. 7, 100, 10, 98, ☆, 96, 16, ✦, 19, 92, 22, ...

   ☆ = ☐   ✦ = ☐

6. 5, 5, ◇, 10, 125, 15, 625, ✧, ...

   ◇ = ☐   ✧ = ☐

© HarperCollinsPublishers 2018

Answers: **1.** 19, 37; **2.** 0.6, 1.4; **3.** 9, 25; **4.** 13, 31; **5.** 13, 94; **6.** 25, 20

Same-day enrichment

● Give pupil pairs **Resource Sheet 6.1.1b** Number sequences with unknowns

Resource 6.1.1b

Number sequences with unknowns

Here are some number sequences. Deduce the value of each symbol.

1. 6, 18, ☆, 162, 486, ...

   ☆ = ☐

2. 1, ○, 27, 64, ✧, ...

   ○ = ☐   ✧ = ☐

3. 2, 0.3, 4, 0.6, ✕, 0.9, 16, ♥, 32, 1.5, ...

   ✕ = ☐   ♥ = ☐

4. 10, 0.4, 5, 0.8, 0, ○, –5, 1.6, ✦, 2.0, –15, ...

   ○ = ☐   ✦ = ☐

Sequences that have the rule 'add the previous two numbers' are known as Fibonacci sequences. Deduce the value of each symbol.

5. 0.1, 0.1, 0.2, 0.3, ✦, 0.8, 1.3, ✧, 3.4

   ✦ = ☐   ✧ = ☐

6. 2, 2, 4, ◁, 10, 16, 26, ✦, 68

   ◁ = ☐   ✦ = ☐

Find out about Fibonacci numbers.

© HarperCollinsPublishers 2018

Answers: **1.** 54; **2.** 8, 125; **3.** 8, 1.2; **4.** 1.2, –10; **5.** 0.5, 2.1; **6.** 6, 42

Question 4

4 Complete each statement. (Note: 'natural numbers' are positive integers, that is, 1, 2, 3, ...)

(a) In ☆ × 71 + ☆ < 500, the greatest natural number that can be filled in the ☆ is ☐.

(b) In 100 > ▦ × 9 > 30, the natural numbers that ▦ can stand for are ....

(c) If 125 ÷ ● = 10 r 5, then the number that ● stands for is ☐.

(d) If 12 + ◆ = 3 × ◆, then the number that ◆ stands for is ☐.

What learning will pupils have achieved at the conclusion of Question 4?

● Pupils will have solved calculations containing symbols to represent numbers by reasoning and applying their mathematical knowledge.

Activities for whole-class instruction

● Remind pupils that natural numbers are 1, 2, 3, 4, ... Some of the problems in Question 4 involve inequality symbols. For these, there is a range of possible answers.

● Display the following number statement.

★ × 40 + ★ < 400

Ask pupils to discuss, with a partner, how to find the possible values for ★.

Agree that 10 × 40 = 400, so ★ = 10 would be too big because the statement would be 410. Therefore, the possible natural numbers that make the statement true are 1–9. ★ = 1, 2, 3, 4, 5, 6, 7, 8 or 9.

- Pupils should complete Question 4 in the Practice Book.

Same-day intervention

- Ask pupils to choose one 0–50 number card and one 51–100 number card, and to then roll a 1–6 dice.

  ☐ < (dice roll) × ♠ < ☐
  (smallest number)   (largest number)

- Pupils put the chosen numbers into the statement above and find possible solutions for ♠. For example, number cards 23 and 88, and a dice roll of 3, gives 23 < 3 × ♠ < 88.

- Solutions for ♠ are 8, 9, 10, 11 … 29. Pupils can then repeat with new numbers.

Same-day enrichment

- Ask pupil pairs to look at the four parts of Question 4 and to write similar questions, incorporating the following numbers.
  a) 250   **b)** 7   **c)** 9   **d)** 13

Challenge and extension questions

Question 5

5   What digits do the ▲ and ● stand for?

```
        ▲
        ●
    +  ● ▲
    ───────
      8 9
```

● = ☐   ▲ = ☐

This challenges pupils to solve a number calculation composed only of symbols.

Question 6

6   Look for patterns and then fill in the ◯ with suitable numbers.

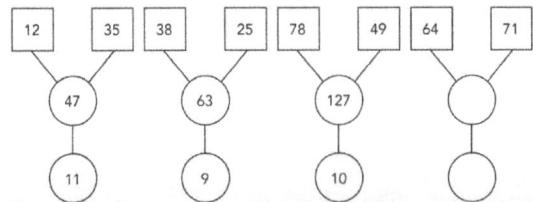

| 12 | 35 | 38 | 25 | 78 | 49 | 64 | 71 |

47   63   127   ◯

11   9   10   ◯

Pupils need to look for number patterns, adding numbers and adding digits.

Unit 1.2
Addition and subtraction of decimals (1)

Conceptual context

This unit revisits addition and subtraction with decimal numbers, focusing on calculating mentally and using the column method.

Throughout this unit, pupils will be using their understanding of place value to multiply and divide by 10, 100 and 1000. In some instances (such as when working with metric units), this will be explicit in the question. Where it is not explicit (such as with the informal calculation strategies), it is important to draw pupils' attention to this strategy.

Look out for ... pupils who talk about 'moving the decimal point'. This can be an efficient strategy to keep track of the position of the digits when calculating. However, ensure pupils understand that it is the relative movement of the point and the digits that is important. Each digit is increasing or decreasing in value by a factor of 10 for each place that it moves relative to the point.

Learning pupils will have achieved at the end of the unit

- Pupils will be able to extend informal calculation strategies using their understanding of place value to mentally carry out calculations with decimal numbers (Q1, Q2, Q3, Q4)
- Pupils will be able to extend column methods for calculation to calculate with decimal numbers (Q1, Q2)
- Pupils will be able to use place value to convert between metric units of measure (Q5, Q6, Q7)
- Pupils will understand the prefixes milli, centi and kilo and the relationships between them (Q5, Q6, Q7)
- Pupils will be able to calculate using metric units (Q5, Q6, Q7)

Resources

place value sliders; mini whiteboards

Vocabulary

sum, difference, decimal point, decimal number, whole number

Questions 1 and 2

> **1** Work these out mentally. Write the answers.
>
> (a) $0.2 \times 100 =$ ☐   (b) $6.3 \div 10 =$ ☐
>
> (c) $1.8 + 8.2 =$ ☐   (d) $1 - 0.08 =$ ☐
>
> (e) $9.6 + 3.04 =$ ☐   (f) $25.2 - 5.2 =$ ☐
>
> (g) $3.3 + 7.7 =$ ☐   (h) $8.8 - 1.5 - 6.5 =$ ☐
>
> (i) $9.8 + 0.3 + 9.7 =$ ☐   (j) $1 - 0.25 + 0.75 =$ ☐
>
> (k) $7.6 \times 10 \div 100 =$ ☐   (l) $8.2 - 3.1 + 0.9 =$ ☐
>
> (m) $1.2 + 0.18 - 1.2 + 0.18 =$ ☐
>
> (n) $0.36 + 0.9 + 0.64 + 8.1 =$ ☐
>
> **2** Choose the column method to calculate the following. (Check the answer to the question marked with *.)
>
> (a) $98.27 + 2.73 =$ (b) $*2.3 - 0.23 =$

What learning will pupils have achieved at the conclusion of Questions 1 and 2?

- Pupils will be able to extend informal calculation strategies using their understanding of place value to mentally carry out calculations with decimal numbers.

- Pupils will be able to extend column methods for calculation to calculate with decimal numbers

Activities for whole-class instruction

- Write a familiar multiplication such as $7 \times 8 = 56$ on the board and ask pupils to write other facts that they can work out using this product, and without having to calculate.

  Share ideas. Ensure that some division calculations are identified, and that some of the calculations involve decimals. If decimals are not used, then ask pupils: *How could I use this to calculate 7×0.8?*

- Explain to pupils that the focus for this task is to work with decimals, and that you'd like them to now use $7 \times 8 = 56$ to write other related calculations using decimals. Share ideas, recording results on the board.

- Write $7 + 8 = 15$ and ask pupils to write other related calculations using decimals. Share ideas, recording them alongside the previous list.

  Look at both sets of results. Discuss with pupils what is the same and what is different about the two sets of calculations.

Agree that informal strategies that are used with whole numbers can also be used with decimal numbers, but that place value has to be understood too.

- Write $71.92 + 78.02$ and $7192 + 7802$ on the board and ask pupils to use the column method for addition to calculate both sums.

  Again, ask: *What's the same and what's different?* Discuss the ways in which methods used for whole numbers can also be used for decimal numbers.

- Pupils should complete Questions 1 and 2 in the Practice Book

Same-day intervention

- Provide pupils with place value sliders. Ask them to write calculations that they feel able to answer (challenge them to work with at least two digits when working additively), either using mental strategies or using a column method.

- Once pupils have calculated the result of their calculation, work with them, using place value sliders to convert their calculations to decimals. Point out the links between the calculation strategies used with whole numbers and decimal numbers.

Same-day enrichment

- Ask pupils to work in pairs to solve the following problem. If time permits, they should make up a similar problem for another pair to solve.

> **Without calculating**, decide which is **larger**.
>
> 5.19×4
>
> or
>
> 5×4.19
>
> Explain how you know.
>
> **Without calculating**, can you work out what the difference is between the two results?

Questions 3 and 4

3 Work out the answers to the calculations. Do they give the same answer?
(a) 92.8 − 52.6 + 27.4

(b) 92.8 − (52.6 + 27.4)

4 Calculate smartly.
(a) 5.78 + 4.5 + 4.22

(b) 4.82 + 7.9 − 1.82

(c) 84.67 − (14.67 + 15.3)

(d) 31.2 + 24.58 − 11.2 + 16.42

What learning will pupils have achieved at the conclusion of Questions 3 and 4?

- Pupils will be able to extend informal calculation strategies using their understanding of place value to mentally carry out calculations with decimal numbers.

Activities for whole-class instruction

- Write these calculations on the board.

  A: $0.2 + 0.8 \times 2.5$

  B: $(0.2 + 0.8) \times 25$

  C: $(2 + 8) \times 2.5$

  Ask pupils, working in pairs, to find reasons why each calculation might be the odd one out. Suggest an example – that C is the odd one out because it's the only calculation to contain two integers.

  Accept any reasonable answers (for example, A is the odd one out because it doesn't contain brackets; A is the odd one out because the result is not 25; B is the odd one out because it's the only calculation to include one integer).

- Draw pupils' attention to the effect of brackets on the order in which the result is calculated, and discuss their strategies when tackling the questions.

  Ask pupils to look at the way in which the numbers in the brackets add to a number that is easy to calculate with. Agree that a useful strategy when calculating is to look for these combinations.

- Write the calculation $13.2 + 0.73 + 1.8$ on the board and discuss any useful combinations of numbers that can be found within the calculation by changing the order in which the additions are carried out.

- Pupils should complete Questions 3 and 4 in the Practice Book.

Same-day intervention

- Display the following.

  Shopping for pencils

  Stanley wants to buy at least 45 pencils (but doesn't mind a few extra).

  What's the cheapest way to buy 45 pencils?

1 × pack of 12 pencils	1 × pack of 4 pencils	1 × pack of 1 pencil
£1.36	£0.45	£0.15
1 × pack of 10 pencils	1 × pack of 6 pencils	1 × pack of 5 pencils
£1.20	£0.69	£0.55

- Work with pupils to identify which of the calculations will give a whole-number answer to the calculation. Find the solution.

  Answer: 9 packs of 5 pencils, £4.95.

Same-day enrichment

- Tell pupils that there are two decimal numbers. Their sum is 5.56 and one of the numbers is 1.86 greater than the other. Ask: *What are the two numbers?*

  Answer: 1.85 and 3.71

Questions 5, 6 and 7

---

5 Multiple choice questions. (For each question, choose the correct answer and write the letter in the box.)

(a) When '0' is added to the end of each number, the number that will change value is ☐.

    A. 0.24   B. 2   C. 2.4   D. 24.00

(b) When calculating $8.06 \div 100 \times 10$, the result is ☐.

    A. 0.806   B. 8.06   C. 80.6   D. 806

(c) In 20.01, if all of the digits are first moved three places to the right across the decimal point and then one place to the left across the decimal point, the result is ☐.

    A. 0.020 01   B. 0.2001   C. 2.001   D. 20.01

(d) Put 5600 m, 5 km 60 m, 5.006 km, 5 km 660 m in order, from the greatest to the least. The second number is ☐.

    A. 5600 m   B. 5 km 60 m   C. 5.006 km   D. 5 km 660 m

6 Convert these units of measurement.

(a) 1.35 kg = ☐ g   (b) 780 kg = ☐ t

(c) 15.4 l = ☐ ml   (d) 30 000 ml = ☐ l

(e) 0.08 m = ☐ cm   (f) 8080 m = ☐ km

(g) 4.2 km² = ☐ m²   (h) 0.5 kg = ☐ g

(i) 1000 cm² = ☐ m²   (j) 150 cm² = ☐ m²

7 Solve these problems.

(a) A rope was originally 10 m long. First, 2.8 m of the rope was cut off and then another 4.2 m was cut off. What is the length of the rope remaining?

(b) Tom had £580 in savings. After he spent £60 on stationery and £42.80 on books, how much money did he have left?

What learning will pupils have achieved at the conclusion of Questions 5, 6 and 7?

- Pupils will be able to use place value to convert between metric units of measure.
- Pupils will understand the prefixes milli, centi and kilo and the relationships between them.
- Pupils will be able to calculate using metric units.

Activities for whole-class instruction

- Write the lengths 8.2 mm, 8.2 cm and 8.2 m on the board. Agree that they are written in order of length, from shortest to longest. Ask: *How many 8.2 cm long strips of paper would be needed to make one 8.2 m long strip?*

Discuss that there are 100 cm in 1 m, which means that one hundred 8.2 cm strips would be needed, so 8.2 m is 100 times longer than 8.2 cm.

- Discuss how 'kilo' means thousand, so a kilometre is 1000 metres and a kilogram is 1000 grams. Remind pupils that 't' stands for tonnes. There are 1000 kilograms in 1 tonne. Record these on the board.

- Discuss how 'milli' means thousandth, so there are 1000 millimetres in a metre, 1000 milligrams in a gram and 1000 millilitres in a litre. Record these values on the board.

- Finally, discuss how 'centi' means hundredth, so there are 100 centimetres in a metre and 100 centilitres in a litre. Record these on the board.

- Now ask pupil pairs, on their whiteboards, to write:

  7 mm in cm

  7 cm in m

  7 m in km

  7 m in cm

  7 cm in mm.

  Gather responses and discuss strategies. Ensure that the discussion covers multiplication and division by 10, 100 and 1000 and remind pupils that the digits move around the decimal point.

- Pupils should complete Questions 5, 6 and 7 in the Practice Book.

Same-day intervention

- Use a place value slider to show pupils how the digits change their value when multiplying and dividing by 10, 100 and 1000.

- Leave pupils to work with the slider as they tackle the questions in the Practice Book.

Same-day enrichment

- Display the following:

> The world record for the men's 100 m race is 9.58 seconds.
>
> Using this information, what would you expect the world record for the men's 10 000 m to be? Explain why.
>
> The world record for the women's 10 000 m is 29:17.45 minutes.
>
> Using this information, what would you expect the world record for the women's 100 m to be? Explain why.
>
> The world record for the men's 10 000 m race is 26:17.53 minutes.
>
> The world record for the women's 100 m race is 10.49 seconds.
>
> How far away were your estimates?

- Suggest pupils discuss the questions in pairs and then give a written justification for their answers.

Challenge and extension question

Question 8

8 Given $\textcircled{x}$ stands for $x + x + x$, and $\boxed{y}$ stands for $y - 0.25$, calculate the following.

(a) $\textcircled{0.95} + \boxed{0.8}$

(b) $\textcircled{0.8} - \boxed{0.95}$

This question uses non-standard notation to ask pupils to calculate with decimal numbers.

Although the calculations are complex, it is making sense of the notation that is likely to challenge pupils. You may like to suggest that pupils rewrite the calculations using standard notation to make the questions more accessible.

Unit 1.3
Addition and subtraction of decimals (2)

Conceptual context

This unit challenges pupils to solve problems involving decimal numbers. A diagrammatic representation of the problem (tree diagram) is introduced and then related to some word problems.

Tree diagrams support pupils in identifying the route through a problem and help them to determine the order of operations needed. Pupils are then required to work backwards through a problem, using inverse operations to reach a solution.

(i) The order of operations is key to success in this unit. The acronym BIDMAS (or BODMAS) is commonly used to describe this, but can also introduce misconceptions as it implies that division must take place before multiplication, and that addition must take place before subtraction. This is not necessarily the case and so is best avoided.

Learning pupils will have achieved at the end of the unit

- Pupils will be able to calculate using tree diagrams (Q1, Q2)
- Pupils will be able to model word problems using tree diagrams and number sentences (Q1, Q2)
- Pupils will have used the order of operations and inverse operations to identify missing values in tree diagrams and number sentences (Q1, Q2, Q3, Q4, Q5)

Resources

mini whiteboards; **Resource 6.1.3a** Working forwards and backwards; **Resource 6.1.3b** Tree stories

Vocabulary

inverse operations, order of operations

Questions 1 and 2

1 Fill in the missing numbers on the tree diagrams. Write the order in which you completed the calculations below.

(a)

(b)

First calculate: _____

_____

then calculate: _____

_____

First calculate: _____

_____

then calculate: _____

_____

2 Draw a tree diagram and then use backward reasoning to find the answer to the following:

Guess the age: Jay and his family were celebrating his grandma's 80th birthday. One guest asked Jay: 'How old are you?' Jay replied with a riddle for the guest to work out: 'If you multiply my age by 6 and then add 8 to it, you will get my grandma's age. How old am I?'

Tree diagram:

Number sentence:

What learning will pupils have achieved at the conclusion of Questions 1 and 2?

- Pupils will be able to calculate using tree diagrams.
- Pupils will be able to model word problems using tree diagrams and number sentences.
- Pupils will have used the order of operations and inverse operations to identify missing values in tree diagrams and number sentences.

Activities for whole-class instruction

- Display this diagram and complete it together.

- Display the following. Pupil pairs should copy and complete the tree diagram.

● Now display this diagram. Discuss how to calculate the missing values.

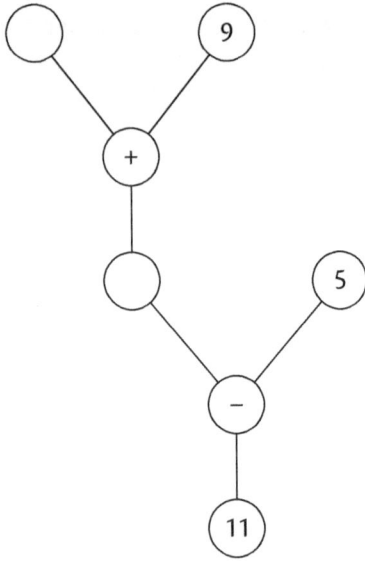

Complete the diagram together, emphasising the 'reverse' order aspect of the calculations where appropriate.

● Pupils should complete Question 1 in the Practice Book.

● Show pupils these diagrams and stories.

Sadie   Fatima   Jack

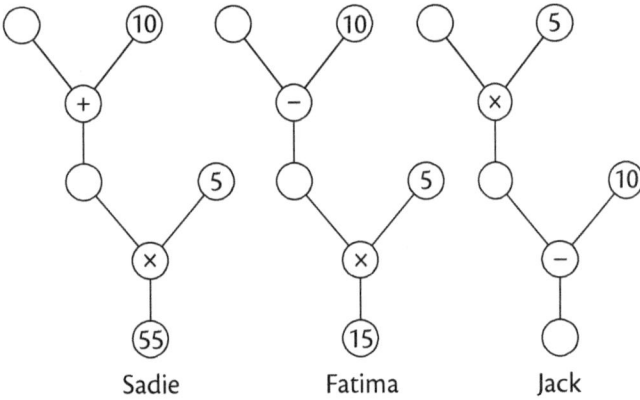

Sadie says, 'I think of a number and add 10 to it. I multiply the answer by 5 and I get 55. What was my number?'

Fatima says, 'I think of a number and take 10 from it. I multiply the answer by 5 and I get 15. What was my number?'

Jack says, 'I think of a number and multiply it by 5. I take 10 from my answer and I get 15. What was my number?'

Ask pupils: *What is the connection between the diagrams and the stories? What is the same and what is different?* Allow time for discussion and share ideas.

● Pupils should complete Question 2 in the Practice Book.

Same-day intervention

● Use **Resource 6.1.3a** Working forwards and backwards, which offers prompts for pupils to work through the tree diagrams.

Answers: 4, 20; 9, 6.

Same-day enrichment

● Give pupils **Resource 6.1.3b** Tree stories, which offers two tree diagrams and ask pupils to write a story (as in Question 2 in the Practice Book) that the tree diagram might represent.

Answers: 5, 4; 10, 5

Questions 3, 4 and 5

3 Find the missing number.

(a) ☐ − 5.37 + 1.73 = 9

First calculate: _____ then calculate: _____ .

Write the complete number sentence: _____

(b) 19.9 − (☐ + 5.45) = 10.1

First calculate: _____ then calculate: _____ .

Write the complete number sentence: _____

4 Use an efficient method to find out the numbers in each box.

(a) 15.25 + ☐ − 0.75 = 18.65

(b) 29.6 − (☐ − 18.7) = 9.3

5 Solve these problems.

(a) Some workers were measuring the depth of a river with a 4 m bamboo pole. They put it vertically into the river and found that the part in the mud measured 0.58 m and the part above the water measured 1.27 m. What was the depth of the river?

(b) John is 0.03 m taller than Sanjit. Emma is 0.05 m shorter than Sanjit. Emma is 1.42 m tall. How tall is John?

(c) A flour mill produced 85.6 tonnes on the first day. It produced 2.56 fewer tonnes on the second day. On the third day, it produced 6.47 fewer tonnes than on the second day. How many tonnes did it produce on the third day? How many tonnes did it produce in the three days altogether?

What learning will pupils have achieved at the conclusion of Questions 3, 4 and 5?

- Pupils will have used the order of operations and inverse operations to identify missing values in number sentences.

Activities for whole-class instruction

- On the board, write the calculation 3.51 + 0.21 = 3.72.

  Ask: *What three other number sentences can we make straight away, using these numbers?* Pupils should offer:

  0.21 + 3.51 = 3.72

  3.72 − 3.51 = 0.21

  3.72 − 0.21 = 3.51

  Pupil pairs should repeat this task for 8.27 + 7.92 = 16.19 on their whiteboards.

Ensure pupils understand that these number sentences must be true and that there is no need for them to calculate to check.

- On the board, write ___ + 3.61 = 8.92. Ask: *What three other number sentences can we make straight away without actually calculating the missing value?* Pupils should offer:

  3.61 + ___ = 8.92

  8.92 − ___ = 3.61

  8.92 − 3.61 = ___

  Ask: *Which of these four calculations is the best for finding the missing value?* Agree that the one that has the missing value on one side of the equals sign on its own is the best.

- Now write on the board:

  ___ + 3.81 = 5.97

  ___ − 3.81 = 5.97

  Ask: *How will you find the missing decimal numbers?* Agree that one number needs to be subtracted from the other in the addition and that two numbers must be added together in the subtraction question.

- Write ___ + 3.31 − 2.11 = 8.85. Ask: *What calculation needs to be done to find the missing value?* Write it down.

  Share ideas. Pupils should suggest 8.85 + 2.11 = 10.96, then 10.96 − 3.31 = 7.65. Agree that 3.31 − 2.11 = 8.85 − ___ is also correct.

- Pupils should complete Questions 3, 4 and 5 in the Practice Book.

Same-day intervention

- Work with pupils to represent the calculations pictorially. The tree diagram used in Questions 1 and 2 may be a useful image. Pupils may prefer to access the calculations by using a bar model or a flow chart to help them understand the order in which the number sentence needs to be carried out.

- Relate images used to the number sentences, asking pupils to represent the number sentences with their chosen representation, before going on to find the missing value.

  If necessary, work with whole numbers at first, so that pupils are able to understand the structure of the relationships being worked on and then, once this structure is understood, reintroduce decimals to the number sentences.

Same-day enrichment

- On the board, show:

  A: ____ − 4.31 + 2.7

  and

  B: 15.71 − (3.1 + ____)

  Tell pupils that the same decimal number is missing from each of these number sentences.

  Ask: *What is a missing decimal number that could be inserted in the number sentences so that:*

  - *the result of A is greater than the result of B*
  - *the result of B is greater than the result of A*
  - *the result of A and B is equal?*

Challenge and extension question

Question 6

> 6 There are 48 kg of apples in two baskets. If 4.2 kg of apples are removed from one basket and put into the other basket, the apples in both baskets will have the same weight. How many kilograms of apples does each basket have?

Encourage pupils to represent the situation described diagrammatically, to help them make sense of what is happening.

Pupils are likely to think that the initial difference in weight between the two baskets is 4.2 kg. Ask pupils to think first about what the initial difference in weight between the two baskets must be if moving 4.2 kg makes the baskets equal.

Unit 1.4

Decimals and approximate numbers (1)

Conceptual context

This unit revisits rounding decimal numbers to whole numbers, and to one and two decimal places. The use of a number line is key to help pupils understand the process of rounding.

Learning pupils will have achieved at the end of the unit

- Pupils will be able to round a decimal number to one or two decimal places (Q1, Q2, Q3, Q4, Q5)
- Pupils will be able to round a decimal number to the nearest whole number (Q2, Q3, Q4, Q5)
- Pupils will be able to carry out calculations and write the result to a given number of decimal places (Q2, Q3, Q4, Q5)

Resources

place value slider; mini whiteboards; **Resource 6.1.4a** Rounding numbers; **Resource 6.1.4b** Number lines; **Resource 6.1.4c** Rounding first or last?

Vocabulary

round, round off, decimal place, approximate, tenths, hundredths

Question 1

> **1** Fill in the spaces to make each statement correct.
>
> (a) When rounding a decimal number, keeping the whole number means
> the result is correct to the ones place.
>
> Keeping one decimal place means it is correct to the
>
> _____ place.
>
> Keeping two decimal places means it is correct to the
>
> _____ place, and so on.
>
> (b) When 'rounding off' (or simply 'rounding') a decimal number to a
> certain place, if the digit in the value place to its right is
>
> _____ than 5, just drop off all the digits to its right.
>
> So, rounding 5.545 to the tenths place, the result is _____ .
>
> If the digit is greater than or equal to 5, increase the digit in it by
>
> _____ and drop off all the digits to its right.
>
> So, rounding 10.257 to the hundredths place, the result is
>
> _____ .
>
> (c) The '0' in 6.0 should not be dropped when it is rounded to the
>
> _____ place.

What learning will pupils have achieved at the conclusion of Question 1?

- Pupils will be able to round a decimal number to one or two decimal places.

Activities for whole-class instruction

- Display this number line on the board.

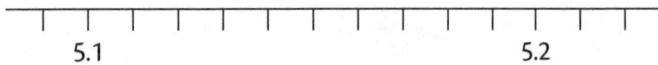

5.1   5.2

Together, count up and back in 0.01s from 5.1 to 5.2. When reaching 5.2, continue on to 5.21, 5.22, ... When counting back again, count past 5.1 to 5.09, 5.08.

- Display this number line.

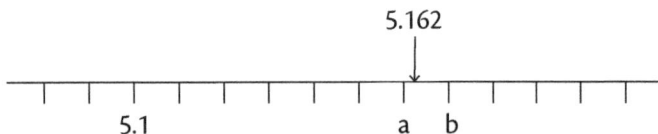

5.162
↓

5.1   a   b

Ask pupil pairs to identify the two decimal numbers either side of 5.162, marked a and b. Ask: *Is 5.162 nearer to 5.16 or 5.17?* Agree 5.16.

(All say...) *5.162 rounded to two decimal places is 5.16.*

Agree that the third digit after the decimal point is important when rounding to two decimal places.

Ask pupil pairs to:

- find another decimal number between 5.16 and 5.17 that will round to 5.16 when rounded to two decimal places, and another, and another …

- find a decimal number between 5.16 and 5.17 that will round to 5.17 when rounded to 2 decimal places.

Agree that the number exactly between 5.16 and 5.17, which is 5.165, rounds to 5.17.

Ask: *Is 5.162 is nearer to 5.1 or 5.2?* Agree 5.2.

(All say...) *5.162 rounded to one decimal place is 5.2.*

Agree that the second digit after the decimal point is important when rounding to one decimal place.

- Ask pupil pairs to find:

- another decimal number between 5.1 and 5.2 that will round to 5.2 when rounded to one decimal place, and another, and another …

- a decimal number between 5.1 and 5.2 that will round to 5.1 when rounded to one decimal place.

- Pupils should complete Question 1 in the Practice Book.

Same-day intervention

- Work with pupils to complete **Resource 6.1.4a** Rounding numbers, using number lines to round decimal numbers to one and two decimal places.

Answers: 5.15, 5.1; 5.22, 5.2; 1.52, 1.5; 1.57, 1.6; 1.57, 1.6.

Same-day enrichment

- Tell pupils that you're thinking of a number. Say:

  When the number is rounded to two decimal places, it is 3.00.

  When the number is rounded to one decimal place, it is 3.0.

- Ask how many different numbers they can find that fit your rule.

  You might like to limit pupils to only working with numbers that have three decimal places, or you could encourage pupils to write the number with the most 1s that would fit the rule, or the most 0s.

Questions 2, 3, 4 and 5

2 Round the numbers as required. Fill in the table.

Rounding	1.751	9.995	19.547	23.5023
to the whole number				
to one decimal place				
to two decimal places				

3 The table shows the exchange rates on one day in January 2018. Use this information to answer the questions.

	British Pound (GBP £1)
US Dollar (US $1)	£0.6999
Euro (€1)	£0.7640
Hong Kong Dollar (HK $1)	£0.0898
Chinese Yuan (¥)	£0.1064

(a) €10 = £ ☐

(b) ¥100 = £ ☐

4 Based on the exchange rates in the table in Question 3, use rounding to find out the approximate values.

(a) How many £ is 1 HK $ equivalent to? (Round to two decimal places.)

☐

(b) How many £ is 100 US $ equivalent to? (Round to one decimal place.)

☐

(c) € is worth more GBP £ than US $1. How much more? (Round to two decimal places.) ☐

5 A piece of ribbon was 22.21 m long. 5.9 m was cut off and then the remaining ribbon was cut into 100 equal pieces. How long is each piece? (Keep your answer to the nearest 0.01 m.)

What learning will pupils have achieved at the conclusion of Questions 2, 3, 4 and 5?

- Pupils will be able to round a decimal number to the nearest whole number.
- Pupils will be able to round a decimal number to one or two decimal places.
- Pupils will be able to carry out calculations and write the result to a given number of decimal places.

Activities for whole-class instruction

- Write the following in the board.

  — — . — — — — —

  Tell pupils this represents a number that, when rounded to one decimal place, gives 13.3. Ask: *What might the number be?* Share ideas.

  Agree that the effect of rounding digits in the 3rd and 4th column must all be considered because sometimes the digit in the 0.01 column will change in a way that means the tenths digit will change.

- Again, write the following on the board.

  — — — . — — — — —

  Tell pupils this number, when multiplied by 10, gives a result that is 162.3 to one decimal place. Ask: *What might the number be?* Share ideas.

  Ask: *What is the largest number you could write in the frame that, having been multiplied by 10, will round to 162.3? What is the smallest number?*

- Pupils should complete Questions 2, 3, 4 and 5 in the Practice Book.

Same-day intervention

- Use a place value slider to work with pupils.
- Set problems to work on such as: 'A number is multiplied by ten and the result, when rounded to one decimal place, is 13.4. What could the number be?' Try different solutions.

If helpful, use **Resource 6.1.4b** Number lines. It offers a series of number lines with different scales, similar to a Gattegno place value chart, to identify the position of the number on the number line and the decimal numbers that are closest to it.

Resource 6.1.4b

Number lines

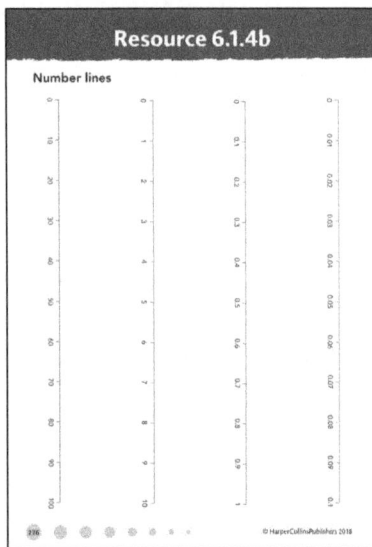

© HarperCollinsPublishers 2018

Same-day enrichment

- Give pupils **Resource 6.1.4c** Rounding first or last? in which they are asked to consider the implications of rounding before and after carrying out a calculation.

Resource 6.1.4c

Rounding first or last?

Zeb and Lindi are working on this maths question.

Calculate 3.988 + 2.855.
Give your answer to 2 decimal places.

Zeb says, 'I'm going to add the numbers first, then round the answer to 2 decimal places.'

Lindi says, 'I'm going to round the numbers to 2 decimal places first to make the addition easier.'

Does it matter whether the rounding is done first or last? _____

Explain how you know.

© HarperCollinsPublishers 2018

Answers: Yes. Both children's strategies give different answers: Zeb: 6.843, 6.84; Lindi: 3.99 + 2.86 = 6.85.

Challenge and extension questions

Question 6

6 Fill in the missing numbers to make each statement correct.

(a) When 0.999 is rounded to the nearest tenth, it is ☐.
The difference between the approximate value and the actual value is ☐.

(b) After a decimal number with three decimal places is rounded to the ones place, it is 30. The least possible decimal number is ☐.

(c) When a decimal number with two decimal places is rounded to one decimal place, it is 2.7. The greatest possible decimal number is ☐. The least possible decimal number is ☐.

This question challenges pupils to reason with rounding. Suggest that pupils draw a diagram, such as a number line, to help them with their reasoning.

Question 7

7 One day in January 2018, Luis went to a bank to exchange €1000 into GBP £ before going shopping. The following were the items, with prices, he wanted to buy.

Headphones: £53.99   Washing machine: £185

Microwave: £64.99   Smart LED TV: £256

Luis is going to buy three items from the above list. How many different ways can Luis buy three items with the money he exchanged? How much money would he have left with each combination? (Refer to Question 3 for the exchange rate.)

This question challenges pupils to work systematically, identifying all possible ways of buying three different items from the selection (there are four possible selections) and to then carry out a calculation with multiple stages, first converting €1000 to pounds, then finding the remaining money after each selection of items has been purchased. Ensure that pupils reflect on their solutions and consider whether they have worked in the most efficient way.

Unit 1.5
Decimals and approximate numbers (2)

Conceptual context

Pupils learned how to round large numbers to varying degrees of accuracy in Year 5. Here, pupils will extend their understanding when rounding decimal numbers.

(i) 'Round off' means 'round to the nearest ...'

'Round up' means 'round to the next ...' (even if it is not nearest)

'Round down' means 'round to the previous ...' (even if it is not nearest)

Learning pupils will have achieved at the end of the unit

- Pupils will be able to identify which two values a decimal number lies between and round up or round down according to the instructions (Q1, Q2, Q3)
- Pupils will know how to round to one or two decimal places (Q2, Q3, Q4, Q5, Q6)
- Pupils will understand that rounding approximates a value and therefore rounding should take place at the end of a calculation, rather than at earlier stages (to preserve some accuracy) (Q5, Q6)

Resources

mini whiteboards; **Resource 6.1.4b** Number lines (from Unit 4)

Vocabulary

round, round up, round down, round off, decimal places

Questions 1, 2, 3 and 4

1 Round the following amounts of money to whole pence using 'rounding down' or 'rounding up'. One result of each method has been given.

£8.215   £12.2316   £7.998   £99.9124   £35.0080

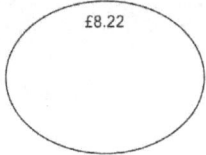

£8.22

£8.21

Rounding up method   Rounding down method

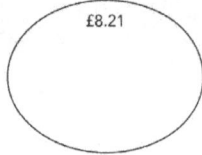

2 Round the following decimal numbers to one decimal place.

(a)   7.895 ≈ [   ]   (by rounding off)

(b)   33.018 ≈ [   ]   (by rounding up)

(c)   102.087 ≈ [   ]   (by rounding down)

(d)   81.955 ≈ [   ]   (by rounding off)

3 Complete the table.

	11.936	2.4895	1.054
Round down to the whole number			
Round off to one decimal place			
Round up to two decimal places			

4 Multiple choice questions. (For each question, choose the correct answer and write the letter in the box.)

(a) Using the rounding off method, the result of rounding 0.6504 to three decimal places is [   ].

A. 0.6504   B. 0.65   C. 0.650   D. 0.651

(b) Using the rounding off method, the result of rounding [   ] to one decimal place is 6.0.

A. 5.946   B. 6.049   C. 6.091   D. 5.899

(c) When comparing 5.0 and 5, the correct statement is [   ].

A. They are the same in value as well as in accuracy.

B. They are the same in value, but different in accuracy.

C. They are not the same in value, but the same in accuracy.

D. They are neither the same in value, nor the same in accuracy.

What learning will pupils have achieved at the conclusion of Questions 1, 2, 3 and 4?

- Pupils will be able to identify which two values a decimal number lies between and round up or round down according to instructions.

- Pupils will know how to round to one or two decimal places.

Activities for whole-class instruction

- Draw a number line on the board.

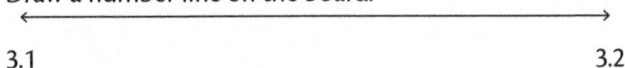

3.1   3.2

Tell pupils that you are thinking of a number that is on the number line. Ask pupil pairs to copy the number line, choose an appropriate number and plot it on the line. Share ideas.

- Now offer a restriction, for example, say that your number has three decimal places, or that it's closer to 3.1 than 3.2. Pupils might want to change their idea.

  Tell pupils that your number was 3.142. Pupil pairs should plot this on their number line. Agree that it should be close to the centre of the line, but closer to 3.1 than 3.2.

- Ask: *What is 3.142 'rounded down' to one decimal place?* Agree that 'rounding down' means the number must go 'down' to the previous significant value, in this case the 0.1 column or tenths. Agree the answer 3.1 and indicate this on the number line.

- Ask: *What is 3.142 'rounded up' to one decimal place?* Agree that 'rounding up' means the number must go 'up' to the next significant value, in this case the 0.1 column or tenths. Agree the answer is 3.2 and indicate this on the number line.

- Ask: *What is 3.142 'rounded off' to one decimal place?* Agree that 'rounding off' means 'rounding to the nearest' so the answer is 3.1.

- Ask pupils pairs to indicate 3.185 on a number line and:

  - round it up to one decimal place

  - round it down to one decimal place

  - round it to the nearest whole 0.1.

  (All say ...) *3.185 rounds up to 3.2 to one decimal place.*

  3.185 rounds down to 3.1 to one decimal place.

3.185 rounds to 3.2 to one decimal place.

- Repeat with 3.992.

- Draw this number line on the board.

5.23   5.24

Repeat activities, rounding up/down and off to two decimal places (nearest whole 0.01 or hundredth).

- Pupils should complete Questions 1, 2, 3 and 4 in the Practice Book.

Same-day intervention

- Use **Resource 6.1.4b** Number lines to support pupils in placing decimal numbers and identifying the values 'on each side'.

Resource 6.1.4b

Number lines

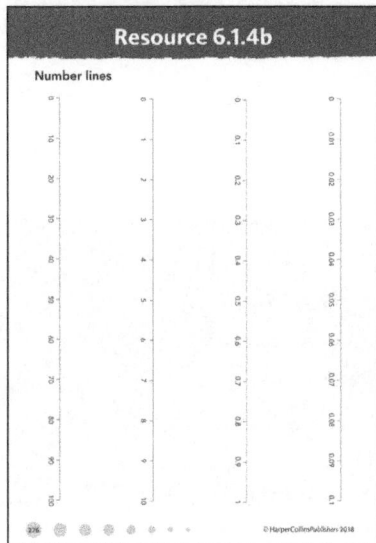

- Give pupils a decimal number, for example 0.37, and select a number line from **Resource 6.1.4b** on which pupils should plot it.
- Support pupils in identifying the decimal numbers 'on each side'.
- Once pupils are confident with this, draw a number line from 4.4 to 4.5, and work with pupils to plot 4.43. Repeat with other similar examples.
- Pupils should practise the vocabulary of 'rounding up to the next', 'rounding down to the previous' and 'rounding off to the nearest'.

Same-day enrichment

- Display the following.

What's my number?

I'm thinking of a decimal number that has three decimal places.

My number rounds to 19.3 to one decimal place.

My number rounds up to 19.4 to one decimal place.

One of the digits in my number is a 2.

My number rounds to 19.33 to two decimal places.

My number contains four different digits.

Answer: 19.329

Questions 5 and 6

5 A school bought a red ribbon that was 200 m long. First, 27.6 m was cut off to make 3 pieces of equal length to decorate the hall. The remaining ribbon was cut into 100 equal pieces and given to choir members for their performance. What was the length of each piece of red ribbon given to the choir members? (Round off to 0.01 m.)

6 A rope 52 m long was cut into four pieces. The first piece was 15.2 m long, 3.7 m longer than the second piece. The second piece was 2.8 m shorter than the third piece. What was the length of the fourth piece?

What learning will pupils have achieved at the conclusion of Questions 5 and 6?

- Pupils will know how to round to one or two decimal places.
- Pupils will understand that rounding approximates a value and therefore, rounding should take place at the end of a calculation, rather than at the earlier stages (to preserve some accuracy).

Activities for whole-class instruction

- Display the following.

A car is 2.82 m long. Ten of these cars are lined up bumper to bumper in a lay-by. How far is it from the beginning of the line of cars to the end, to the nearest tenth of a metre?

- Ask: *Without actually calculating, describe the calculations that you would do and in what order to find the answer.* Agree that there are two possible strategies:
  - round the length of one car and multiply by 10
  - multiply the length one car by ten and round to the nearest 0.1.
- Ask: *Which strategy gives you the most accurate answer, even though it is an approximation?* Agree that it is better for rounding to be done at the end, not earlier.
- Pupils should complete Questions 5 and 6 in the Practice Book.

Same-day intervention

- Display the following.

> Mandy's stride length is 1.2 m. How far will she walk after 10 paces? (Give your answer to one decimal place.)

- Discuss with pupils:

  - the meaning of 'one decimal place' – that is, only decimal tenths (0.1s) showing in the answer

  - that 1.2 could be rounded and then multiplied by 10, or 1.2 could be multiplied by 10 and the product rounded.

  Work through both together and agree that the most accurate answer is obtained when the rounding is done at the end.

Same-day enrichment

- Display the following.

> A number is rounded up to two decimal places.
>
> The same original number is rounded down to one decimal place.
>
> Which gives the greater result in this context? Rounding up or rounding down?

- Ask: *Is this always true and, if not, under what circumstances is it not true?*

- Now adjust the statement slightly – display the following.

> A number is rounded up to two decimal places.
>
> The same original number is rounded off to one decimal place.
>
> Which gives the greater result in this context? Rounding up or rounding down?

- Ask: *Is this always true and, if not, under what circumstances is it not true?*

Challenge and extension questions

Question 7

> 7 Convert these units of measure and round as indicated.
>
> (a) 2340 kg = ☐ t ≈ ☐ t   (Round down to the whole number.)
>
> (b) 31130 ml = ☐ l ≈ ☐ l   (Round up to one decimal place.)
>
> (c) 953 m = ☐ km ≈ ☐ km   (Round off to two decimal places.)

In this question, pupils are challenged to convert between units before rounding. Draw pupils' attention to the distinction between the = and the ≈ signs, ensuring that they are able to write the exact conversion before rounding to an approximate value.

Question 8

> 8 At a book fair, there are 5 different Maths books, 6 different Chinese books and 4 different English books.
>
> (a) Simon wants to buy one of each, a Maths book, a Chinese book and an English book, to make a set. How many combinations can he have?
>
> (b) Simon just wants to buy one resource book from these books. In how many ways can he buy one?

This question does not involve rounding, rather it encourages pupils to think systematically about the different possible combinations of a student choosing books from a selection. Some pupils may find it useful to break the choices down, first considering (for example) how many ways a book could be chosen from the Maths books and the Chinese.

Unit 1.6
Revision for circles and angles

Conceptual context

In this revision unit, pupils are reminded of the parts of a circle: centre, radius, diameter and circumference, and the relationship between the radius and the diameter. They use a compass to draw circles with specified dimensions and use the relationship between radius and diameter to calculate missing measurements in diagrammatic problems. A more challenging circle problem is presented where pupils must determine the correct radius to draw arcs to form a symmetrical pattern.

Other diagrammatic problems are presented that ask pupils to use their knowledge of angles to determine missing angles in a right angle, straight line and around a point.

Learning pupils will have achieved at the end of the unit

- Pupils will have revised and consolidated identification, naming and drawing parts of a circle, including centre, radius and diameter, and understand that the diameter is twice the radius (Q1, Q3, Q6)

- Using a compass, pupils will have practised and consolidated the steps involved in constructing circles of a specified size, marking the centre, radius and diameter (Q1)

- Pupils will be able to identify, draw and label a line between points on a circle (chord), and use this knowledge to solve simple problems (Q2)

- Pupils will have revised and consolidated using knowledge of angles to calculate missing angles for right, straight and full angles (Q4, Q5)

- Using knowledge of the equivalence relationships between angles, pupils will have practised finding missing angles in geometric diagrams including complementary angles (those with a sum of 90°), angles on a straight line (those with a sum of 180°) and angles around a point (those with a sum of 360°) (Q4, Q5)

- Pupils will have applied their knowledge of arithmetic and inverse operations to solving missing angle problems (Q4, Q5)

Resources

compasses; large compasses for teaching; black felt-tip pen; squared paper; cardboard; tape; pencils; rulers; erasers; pupils' 'My geometry notebook' from Year 5; **Resource 6.1.6a** Yin Yang symbol; **Resource 6.1.6b** Missing angle problems

Vocabulary

chord, centre, radius (radii), diameter, circumference

Question 1

> **1** Use a pair of compasses to draw two circles as indicated, marking the centre O, diameter *d* and radius *r*.
>
> (a)　radius = 15 mm　　　　　(b)　diameter = 4 cm

What learning will pupils have achieved at the conclusion of Question 1?

- Pupils will have revised and consolidated identification, naming and drawing parts of a circle, including centre, radius and diameter, and understand that the diameter is twice the radius.

- Using a compass, pupils will have practised and consolidated the steps involved in constructing circles of a specified size, marking the centre, radius and diameter.

Activities for whole-class instruction

- Provide pupils with paper, cardboard, tape, pencils and compasses. Hold up a large compass. Can pupils remember how to load a pencil in the compass? Remind them to insert the pencil into the cam lock and tighten the screw. The tip of the pencil must be at the same height as the sharp point of the compass when the compass is closed. Pupils adjust the pencil height and tighten the cam screw once the pencil is at the correct height.

Ask: *How do we prepare the surface for drawing with a compass?* Remind pupils that we should place a sheet of paper on top of cardboard to prevent damage to the table surface and to keep the needle point from slipping as the pencil is rotated. Pupils follow the instructions and prepare the surface for drawing.

Ask: *Which part of the compass should we turn to draw the circle?* (the knob on top of the compass)

Ask pupils to practise pressing the needle point firmly onto the paper and turning the compass using the knob. Pupils may wish to tape the cardboard down to prevent it from spinning.

Demonstrate how to hold the compass in a vertical position. Rotate the pencil point with one hand while holding the paper in place with the other.

Pupils should draw circles of various sizes and become familiar adjusting the compass pencil to obtain a larger separation.

- Once pupils have re-familiarised themselves with correct use of the compass, ask them to draw circles with a specific dimension, radius or diameter. For example, ask them to use a ruler to set the separation distance of the compass to 25 mm, and draw a circle. Ensure that pupils place the needle point at 0 when measuring the separation distance.

- Say: *I want to draw a circle with a diameter of 20 cm. What separation should the compass be set to?* Give pupils time to consider the problem then accept answers. Confirm that a separation of 10 cm is required as this is the radius that will give a diameter of 20 cm.

Repeat for lines of various lengths representing radii and diameters.

- Pupils should complete Question 1 in the Practice Book.

Same-day intervention

- Repeat the main activity, differentiating methods according to the following needs:
  - When using a compass, some pupils may find it easier to keep the compass still and move the page around.
  - Pupils who are left-handed may find it easier to reverse the direction of the compass rotation.

- Provide guidance for each step and remind pupils of the following specific points:
  - Keep light pressure on the point while drawing with the pencil.
  - Ensure the pencil is secure to prevent it from moving.
  - Take the knob of the compass between the second finger and thumb, and produce a rolling action.
  - Encourage pupils to repeat this several times to get a smooth motion.

Same-day enrichment

- Provide pupils with **Resource 6.1.6a** Yin Yang symbol and compasses. Pupils should recreate the outline of the Yin Yang symbol. Advise pupils that they might need to draw full outlines of some circle sections and then rub them out afterwards.

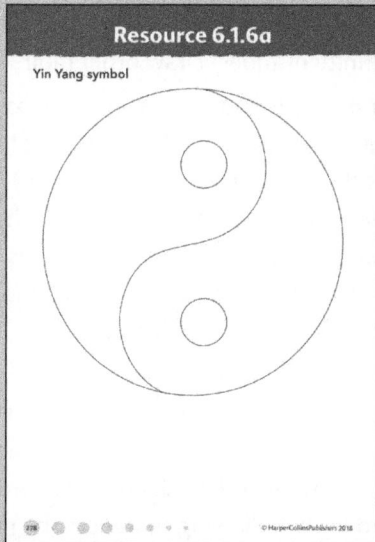

Resource 6.1.6a

Yin Yang symbol

© HarperCollinsPublishers 2016

Question 2

2 The diagram shows a circle with six points.
You can draw ☐ lines by connecting any two of the six points.

What learning will pupils have achieved at the conclusion of Question 2?

- Pupils will be able to identify, draw and label a line between points on a circle (chord), and use this knowledge to solve simple problems.

Activities for whole-class instruction

- Using a large compass, draw a circle on the board. Label two points on the circle, A and B, and use a ruler to connect the points. For example:

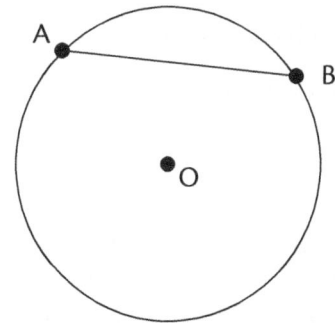

Point out that AB is a line that joins two points on the circle. Pupils should work in pairs, using a compass to draw a circle on paper. They mark two points on the circle, A and B, and draw the line segment AB.

Pupils hold up their papers to confirm they have correctly drawn the line segment.

- Ask: *What do you think is the longest possible line segment that joins two points on a circle?* Accept suggestions. Can pupils see that the diameter is the longest?

Ask pupils to mark and label three more points on the circle, C, D and E.

Ask: *If you were to draw lines between any two points, how many lines would be possible?* Pupils use a ruler to mark lines between the pairs of points. Choose a pair to say how many lines they found in total and demonstrate the joined pairs of points. (They should have 10 lines.)

Ask: *How do you think this number would change if you only had four points? What about six points?* Invite pupils to make suggestions and justify their reasoning. After discussion and predictions, pupils can investigate practically.

- Pupils should complete Question 2 in the Practice Book.

Same-day intervention

- Provide each pupil with a small notebook and ask them to write the title, 'My geometry notebook'. Pupils may have begun a similar notebook in Year 5; if so, they should continue with it.

- Remind pupils that geometry is a subject that requires understanding of many mathematical terms and it is a good idea to write these terms down in one place in order to remember them. Explain that they will be able to refer to their notebook whenever they need to clarify a term. Explain that for most terms, pupils will draw a diagram alongside the written definition in order to clarify its meaning.

- On the board, draw a circle using a large compass. Label two points on the circle, A and B, and use a ruler to connect the points. Write the following below the circle: 'AB is a line that joins two points on the circle.'

- Using a compass, pupils draw a circle in their notebooks. They then mark two points on the circle, A and B, and draw the line AB. Below the diagram, they copy the definition of the line segment from the board. Ask pupils to practise marking other points on a circle and joining them with lines.

Same-day enrichment

- Ask pupils to draw a circle and mark nine points on the circumference. They then draw triangles by joining three dots on the edge of the nine-point circle. Have them draw at least four triangles.

Question 3

> 3 The diagram shows a large circle with two identical small circles inside.
>
> If the diameter of each small circle is 10 cm, then the radius of the large circle is ☐ cm and its diameter is ☐ cm.

What learning will pupils have achieved at the conclusion of Question 3?

- Pupils will have revised and consolidated identification, naming and drawing parts of a circle, including centre, radius and diameter, and understand that the diameter is twice the radius.

Activities for whole-class instruction

- Using a large compass, draw a circle on the board. Mark and label the centre. Mark a point on the edge of the circle and use a ruler to connect the point with the centre. Ask: *What is the name of this line?* (radius) *How do we define the radius?* (It is the distance from any point on a circle to the centre point.) *How many radii does a circle have?* (an infinite number) Draw other radii.

  Place a ruler on the board so that the edge passes through the centre of the circle. Draw the diameter of the circle. Ask: *What is the name of this line?* (diameter) *How do we define the diameter?* (A diameter is the length of any line that joins two points on the circle and passes through the centre.) *How many diameters does a circle have?* (an infinite number) Draw other diameters.

  Highlight one radius and one diameter by using a colour. Ask: *What is the relationship between a radius of a circle and a diameter?* (The diameter is twice the radius.) *Is there another way to express this?* Ask pupils to complete the missing word in the following sentence: The radius is __ the diameter. (half)

  Label the radius '5 cm'. Ask: *What is the diameter of the circle? How do you know?* Agree that since the diameter is double the radius, the diameter of the circle is 10 cm. Label the diameter '48 m'. Ask: *What is the radius? How do you know?* Agree that since the radius is half the diameter, the radius of the circle is 24 m.

- Display the diagram below. Prompt pupils to comment on the vertical diameters of the circles. Agree that they are aligned vertically through the centres.

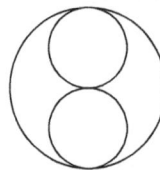

  Ask: *If the diameter of each smaller circle is 40 cm, what is the radius of the larger circle?* Give pupils time to consider the problem, then ask for answers. Establish that since the smaller circles have equal diameters, it follows that each circle must have a diameter equal to the radius of the larger circle (40 cm). Ask: *What is the diameter of the larger circle? How do you know?* (80 cm: twice the radius)

- Pupils should complete Question 3 in the Practice Book.

Same-day intervention

- Ask pupils to draw a circle using a compass. They mark and label the radius of the circle '20 cm'. Can they say what the diameter is? If pupils do not know how to begin, ask scaffolding questions such as:
  - *What properties does every circle have?*
  - *What can you say about the size of the diameter compared to the radius?*
- Give pupils a measurement and the freedom to choose the property measured. For example: *One of the measurements of a circle is 16 centimetres. Draw and show at least one other measurement of the circle.* The freedom to choose the dimension makes the question more accessible to pupils.

Same-day enrichment

- Ask pupil pairs to construct a diagram that comprises circles inside a larger circle. They draw three or four smaller circles that share the same vertical or horizontal diameter as the larger circle.
- Each group writes one or more questions below the diagram that asks for a missing dimension, for example: 'If the radius of the larger circle is x cm, what is the diameter of each smaller circle?'
- Pupils swap papers with another group to answer. They return the papers for marking once complete.

Questions 4 and 5

4   Look at the diagram. If $\angle a = \angle b = 40°$, then $\angle c = \boxed{}$ °.

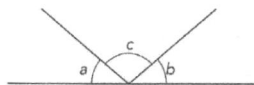

5   In the diagram, $\angle x = \boxed{}$ °.

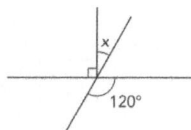

What learning will pupils have achieved at the conclusion of Questions 4 and 5?

- Pupils will have revised and consolidated using knowledge of angles to calculate missing angles for right, straight and full angles.
- Using knowledge of the equivalence relationships between angles, pupils will have practised finding missing angles in geometric diagrams including complementary angles (those with a sum of 90°), angles on a straight line (those with a sum of 180°) and angles around a point (those with a sum of 360°).
- Pupils will have applied their knowledge of arithmetic and inverse operations to solving missing angle problems.

Activities for whole-class instruction

- Display the following image.

Diagram A

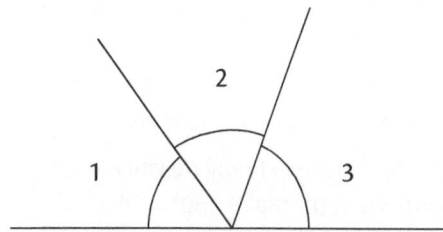

Ask: *If angle 1 is 55 degrees and angle 3 is 80 degrees, what is angle 2?* Give pupils time to consider the problem then prompt them by asking: *What do you need to know about angles on a straight line to be able to solve this problem?* Remind pupils that angles on a straight line add to 180 degrees.

Ask for a volunteer to come to the board to write the calculation that will give angle 2. Expect: $\angle 2 = 180° - 55° - 80°$. *What is the answer?* (45°) Repeat the problem for different sizes of two of the angles, asking pupils to calculate the one unknown angle.

- Display the following image.

Diagram B

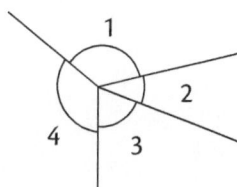

Ask: *If angle 1 is 120 degrees, angle 2 is 35 degrees and angle 3 is 70 degrees, what is angle 4?* Give pupils time to consider the problem then prompt them by asking:

What do you need to know about angles at a point to be able to solve this problem? Remind pupils that angles at a point add to 360 degrees.

Ask for a volunteer to come to the board to write the calculation that will give angle 4. Expect:
$\angle 2 = 360° - 120° - 35° - 70°$. *What is the answer?* (135°)
Repeat the problem for different sizes of three of the angles, asking pupils to calculate the one unknown angle.

- Display the following image.

Diagram C

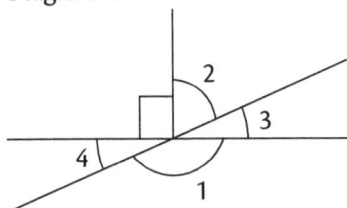

Ask: *If angle 1 is 160 degrees, what are angles 2, 3 and 4?* Give pupils time to consider the problem, then prompt them by asking: *What do you need to know about the other angles in the diagram?* Point to the right angle and ask pupils to identify the size of the angle. (90 degrees)

Ask: *How would we use the size of angle 1 to determine angle 3?* Accept suggestions and praise pupils who identify that angles 1 and 3 are angles on a straight line.

Ask: *What is angle 3?* (20 degrees) *How do you know?* (sum of angles 1 and 3 is 180°; 180° − 160° = 20°)

Point to angle 4. Ask: *What do we know about this angle?* Prompt pupils by asking how the angle is related to angle 3. Praise pupils who identify that angles 3 and 4 are vertically opposite angles and are equal. Ask: *What is angle 4?* (20°)

Ask: *How do we use the angles we have identified to work out angle 2?* Remind pupils that all the angles are at a point and therefore, have a sum of 360 degrees. Invite a pupil to the board to write a calculation that will give angle 2. Expect: $\angle 2 = 360° - 90° - 160° - 20° - 20°$. Give pupils time to calculate the answer. Ask: *What is angle 2?* (70°)

- Pupils should complete Questions 4 and 5 in the Practice Book.

Same-day intervention

- Provide alternative angle measurements for the problems given in the main activity.
  - Diagram A: If angle 1 is 50 degrees and angle 3 is 75 degrees, what is angle 2?
  - Diagram B: If angle 1 is 110 degrees, angle 2 is 40 degrees and angle 3 is 65 degrees, what is angle 4?
  - Diagram C: If angle 1 is 150 degrees, what are angles 2, 3 and 4?

- Go through each question as a guided example and ask pupils to make notes and diagrams in their 'My geometry notebook'. The notes should be made under the titles: 'How to a find a missing angle where the sum of angles is a right angle/straight angle/full angle (angles at a point)'. Pupils should also make a separate definition for vertically opposite angles.

Same-day enrichment

- Give pupils **Resource 6.1.6b** Missing angle problems. They should work out the missing angles for each problem.

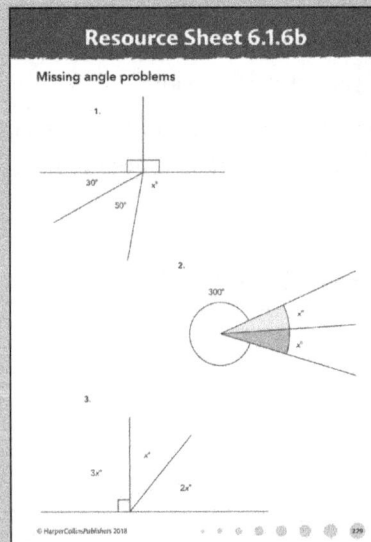

Answers: **1.** 100°; **2.** 30°, 30°; **3.** 90°, 30°, 60°

Question 6

6   Draw the following two figures in the grid below.

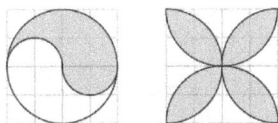

What learning will pupils have achieved at the conclusion of Question 6?

- Pupils will have revised and consolidated identification, naming and drawing parts of a circle, including centre, radius and diameter, and understand that the diameter is twice the radius.

Activities for whole-class instruction

- Pupils should practise drawing arcs to create a flower pattern. Give them squared paper and ask them to follow step-by-step instructions for completing the flower design.

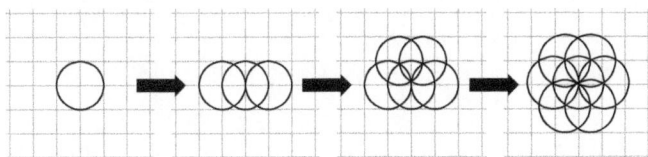

- Display these instructions.

  - Highlight a line horizontally across the centre of the grid paper.
  - Draw a circle with a radius of one square.
  - Use the points where the edge of the circle intersects with two grid lines as centre points, and draw two more circles. The radius is the same all the time, so there is no need to change it on your compass.
  - Use the points where the edges of the circle intersect as centre points, and draw four more circles (two above the centre line of the grid and two below).
  - Erase your original line as the flower arrangement is now complete.

Same-day intervention

- Repeat the compass practice outlines from the section in Question 1.
- Explain that sometimes only a part of a circle is required, called an arc. Point out that when you use a compass to draw an arc, you position the needle point on the centre, set the radius and draw.
- Draw a line on the board and mark each end with a point. Explain that one point will be the centre of the arc, and the other point will be on the circumference of the circle.
- Set a large compass to the length of the line and explain that this will be the radius of the arc. Draw an arc to complete a semi-circle. Repeat for a second line and this time, draw a three-quarter circle.
- Provide pupils with a compass, a ruler and 1 cm square paper. Ask them to draw a semi-circle and a three-quarter circle using the same method.

Same-day enrichment

- Provide each pupil with a compass, a ruler and 1 cm square paper and ask them to construct the following shapes:
  i) a semi-circle with a diameter of 12 cm
  ii) a quarter-circle with a radius of 8 cm
  iii) a three-quarter circle with a diameter of 14 cm.

Challenge and extension question

Question 7

7 Measure and draw.

(a) Measure the side length of the square shown. It is ☐ cm.

A   B

• O

C   D

(b) Starting at the point O, draw a line OE passing through the vertex C of the square. (Point E is outside the square.)

(c) Measure the size of ∠ACO. ∠ACO = ☐°.

(d) Draw a circle with centre O and radius OA.

Pupils practise, draw and measure the angle formed by the side of a square and a line drawn from the centre of the square extended through and beyond a vertex. They draw a circle with a radius equivalent to half the length of the diagonal of the square.

Chapter 1 test (Practice Book 6A, pages 23–29)

Test question number	Relevant unit	Relevant questions within unit
1	Unit 1.2	Q1
2	Unit 1.1	Q1
3	Unit 1.2	Q2
4	Unit 1.2	Q4
5	Unit 1.5	Q2
6	Unit 1.6	Q4
7		
8	Unit 1.1	Q6
9	Unit 1.1	Q3
10	Unit 1.6	Q1
11	Unit 1.6	Q3
12		
13	Unit 1.3	Q5
14	Unit 1.3	Q3
15	Unit 1.3	Q3
16	Unit 1.2	Q7
17	Unit 1.2	Q7
18	Unit 1.1	Q2, Q5

Chapter 2
Multiplication and division of decimals

Chapter overview

Area of mathematics	National Curriculum statutory requirements for Key Stage 2	Shanghai Maths Project reference
Number – fractions (including decimals and percentages)	Year 6 Programme of study: Pupils should be taught to: ■ identify the value of each digit in numbers given to three decimal places and multiply and divide numbers by 10, 100 and 1000 giving answers up to three decimal places	Year 6, Units 2.1, 2.2, 2.5, 2.8
	■ multiply one-digit numbers with up to two decimal places by whole numbers	Year 6, Units 2.1, 2.2, 2.3, 2.4, 2.5, 2.9, 2.10, 2.11
	■ use written division methods in cases where the answer has up to two decimal places	Year 6, Units 2.5, 2.6, 2.7, 2.8, 2.9, 2.10, 2.11
	■ solve problems which require answers to be rounded to specified degrees of accuracy.	Year 6, Units 2.10, 2.11
Measurement	Year 6 Programme of study: Pupils should be taught to: ■ solve problems involving the calculation and conversion of units of measure, using decimal notation up to three decimal places where appropriate.	Year 6, Units 2.1, 2.2, 2.3, 2.4, 2.5, 2.6, 2.7, 2.8, 2.9, 2.10, 2.11

Pre-requisite knowledge

For pupils to be successful with the work in this chapter, they will need to have achieved mastery in their learning in previous relevant units. Teaching there will have introduced and developed concepts and skills that are necessary to work with the Year 6 content. A summary of pre-requisite knowledge is set out in the table below. If you believe that some pupils need to revisit particular areas, the units in which it was taught are also shown in the table so that you can locate appropriate guidance in Teacher's Guides and Practice Books. Guidance provided for Chapter 2 on the following pages will therefore focus on new learning.

Pre-requisite knowledge, understanding or skill	Where this was taught in The Shanghai Maths Project
Pupils can multiply a two- or three-digit number by a two-digit number	Year 4, Units 3.1, 3.2, 3.3, 3.4, 3.5
Pupils can understand and use the laws of operations to evaluate multi-step calculations	Year 4, Units 10.11, 10.12, 10.13, 10.14
Pupils can divide a multi-digit number by a two-digit number	Year 5, Units 3.6, 3.7
Pupils can add and subtract decimal numbers	Year 5, Units 6.5, 6.6
Pupils can understand and interpret decimal notation, connecting it with place value	Year 4, Units 6.5, 6.7, 6.10
Pupils can multiply and divide decimal numbers by 10, 100 and 1000	Year 5, Units 6.1, 6.2

Unit 2.1
Multiplying decimal numbers by whole numbers (1)

Conceptual context

This unit explores the use of place value to work with multiplication of decimal numbers by whole numbers.

Pupils already have a secure understanding of multiplication, the use of place value and of decimal numbers, so it is important that this unit is not seen as introducing a 'new' idea, rather that it is bringing together threads pupils already understand.

Learning pupils will have achieved at the end of the unit

- Pupils will be able to use their understanding of place value to connect multiplication of integers and multiplication of decimals in order to calculate products (Q1, Q2, Q3, Q4)
- Pupils will understand and interpret different approaches to calculating products (Q1)
- Pupils will understand that the product of a decimal and a whole number can be approximated using two whole numbers (Q3)
- Pupils will be able to identify operations in worded problems and calculate with decimal measures (Q4)

Resources

Resource 6.2.1a Place value slider; **Resource 6.2.1b** Which is larger?; **Resource 6.2.1c** Sliding; **Resource 6.2.1d** Matching the questions; mini whiteboards

Vocabulary

tenths, hundredths, whole number, place value, decimal

Question 1

> **1** A toy windmill costs £5.80. How much do 8 toy windmills cost? Use the pupils' strategies below to find the answer.
>
> (a) Jason: 'Let me estimate first.'
>
> $8 \times \boxed{} = £\boxed{}$. So it must be less than £$\boxed{}$.
>
> (b) Tom: 'I do it by converting units.'
>
>   £5.8 = $\boxed{}$ p, and $8 \times \boxed{} = \boxed{}$ p.
>
> (c) May: 'I change it to multiplication of two whole numbers.'
>
> $8 \times 5.8 = \boxed{}$ That is: 8×5.8
>
> $\downarrow \times 10 \quad \uparrow \div 10$ $= 8 \times 58 \div 10$
>
> $8 \times \boxed{} = \boxed{}$ $= \boxed{} \div \boxed{}$
>
> $= \boxed{}$

What learning will pupils have achieved at the conclusion of Question 1?

- Pupils will be able to use their understanding of place value to connect multiplication of integers and multiplication of decimals in order to calculate products.
- Pupils will understand and interpret different approaches to calculating products.

Activities for whole-class instruction

- On the board, write:

  $4 \times 5 = 20$

  $4 \times 6 = 24$

  Now write 4×5.9 on the board and ask pupils to discuss, in pairs, how to use the two given products to estimate the answer.

  Request answers and agree that the product will be nearer, but less than, $4 \times 6 = 24$. Agree also that it will be more than 4×5.

  Ask pupil pairs to write on their whiteboards a multiplication similar to 4×5.9 that will give a product between 20 and 24, but is closer to 20 (an example would be 4×5.1 or 4×5.2). Share ideas.

  Repeat for 22. Encourage pupils to notice that this is half way between 20 and 24.

- Take one of the examples generated by the class, for example 4×5.2, and write it on the board alongside 4×52 (or, if you've chosen 4×5.3, then write it alongside 4×53).

  Pupil pairs should discuss what is the same and what is different about the calculations and predict what will be the same and different about the resulting products. Share ideas.

Now write the result of each calculation, 20.8 and 208, and ask pupils to explain why the results differ in this way.

- Share ideas and ask questions such as:
  - *What do we multiply by to convert 5.2 to 52?*
  - *What do we divide by to convert 52 to 5.2?*
  - *What do we multiply by to convert 20.8 to 208?*
  - *What do we divide by to convert 208 to 20.8?*
- Agree with pupils that the calculation 4×5.2 can be rewritten as $4 \times 52 \div 10$ and that this can be used to find the product of 4×5.2.
- Write $5 \times 3.1 = 5 \times$ __ $\div 10$ on the board. Ask pupils to fill in the gap and to find the product.
- Pupils should complete Question 1 in the Practice Book.

Same-day intervention

- Use **Resource 6.2.1a** Place value sliders to make two place value sliders and use these to work with pupils to draw parallels between calculating with decimals and calculating with whole numbers.

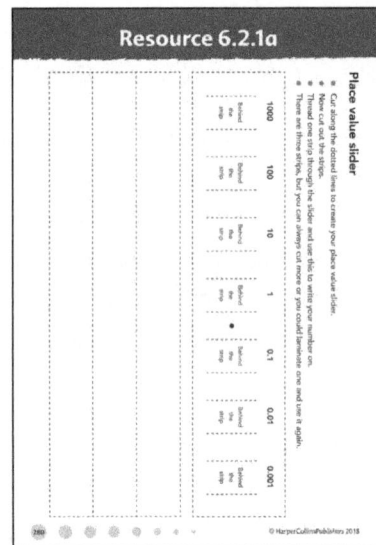

Resource 6.2.1a

- Write 1.2 on one of the place value sliders and, on the board, write $3 \times$.

  Hold up the place value slider next to this so that it completes the number sentence 3×1.2. While holding it, shift the slider so that the calculation reads 3×12 and elicit the answer to this calculation.

  Use the second place value slider to record the answer, 36, holding it in place on the board so you have the complete calculation $3 \times 12 = 36$.

  Now remind pupils that this was not the original question, and move the slider so that the calculation now reads 3×1.2. Again, draw attention to the way the digits move one place across the decimal point.

• Ask pupils to discuss how you could use the second slider to get the correct product and agree that by making the same movement as the first slider, the calculation will again be correct.

Move the second slider so that the calculation reads $3 \times 1.2 = 3.6$, drawing attention to the way that the digits move one place across the decimal point.

• Ask pupils to now work on **Resource 6.2.1b** Which is larger?, using place value sliders to support if necessary.

Resource 6.2.1b

Which is larger?

Which of these calculations gives the greatest product?

| 0.8 × 3200 | 8 × 320 | 80 × 32 | 800 × 3.2 |

Explain how you know.

Write two more multiplications that could be a part of the set.

© HarperCollinsPublishers 2016

Answer: 2560 (they are all the same)

Same-day enrichment

• Give pupils **Resource 6.2.1b** Which is larger? in which they are asked to arrange the results of calculations in order of size.

• All of the products in the question give the same result. Ensure that pupils focus on explaining why this happens.

Questions 2 and 3

2 Calculate the following.

(a) 8×3.2
$= 8 \times 32 \div 10$
$= \boxed{} \div \boxed{}$
$= \boxed{}$

(b) 0.62×4
$= \boxed{} \times 4 \div \boxed{}$
$= \boxed{} \div \boxed{}$
$= \boxed{}$

(c) 9×0.135
$= \boxed{} \times \boxed{} \div \boxed{}$
$= \boxed{} \div \boxed{}$
$= \boxed{}$

3 Estimate first and then calculate the answers.

(a) $8 \times 0.94 =$

Estimation: _____

Calculation: _____

(b) $9.05 \times 7 =$

Estimation: _____

Calculation: _____

(c) $110.7 \times 3 =$

Estimation: _____

Calculation: _____

(d) $284.55 \times 9 =$

Estimation: _____

Calculation: _____

What learning will pupils have achieved at the conclusion of Questions 2 and 3?

• Pupils will be able to use their understanding of place value to connect multiplication of integers and multiplication of decimals in order to calculate products.

• Pupils will understand that the product of a decimal and a whole number can be approximated using two whole numbers.

Activities for whole-class instruction

• Write 3×5.7 on the board. Ask pupils to estimate the approximate product and write it on their whiteboard.

Most pupils are likely to use $3 \times 6 = 18$ or $3 \times 5 = 15$ as estimates. Look out for any that are particularly far from these and ensure that you follow up with these pupils during the lesson.

• Give place value sliders, each showing 57, to three pupils and ask them to come to the front of the class.

Explain that the three sliders all show the same value. Ask pupils to find the total displayed on all three sliders.

Discuss and share strategies. Agree that the calculation that has been carried out is 3×57. Write $3 \times 57 = 171$ on the board.

Pupils should watch you adjust the sliders so that they now show 5.7. Ask: *What have I done to the 57s?* (divided by 10) Can pupils predict what will happen to the product? Share ideas and check to show that 3×5.7 is a tenth of 3×57.

- Display the following image to help pupils understand and visualise comparisons between product and quotient when multiplying (or dividing) numbers that are multiples (or factors) of each other.

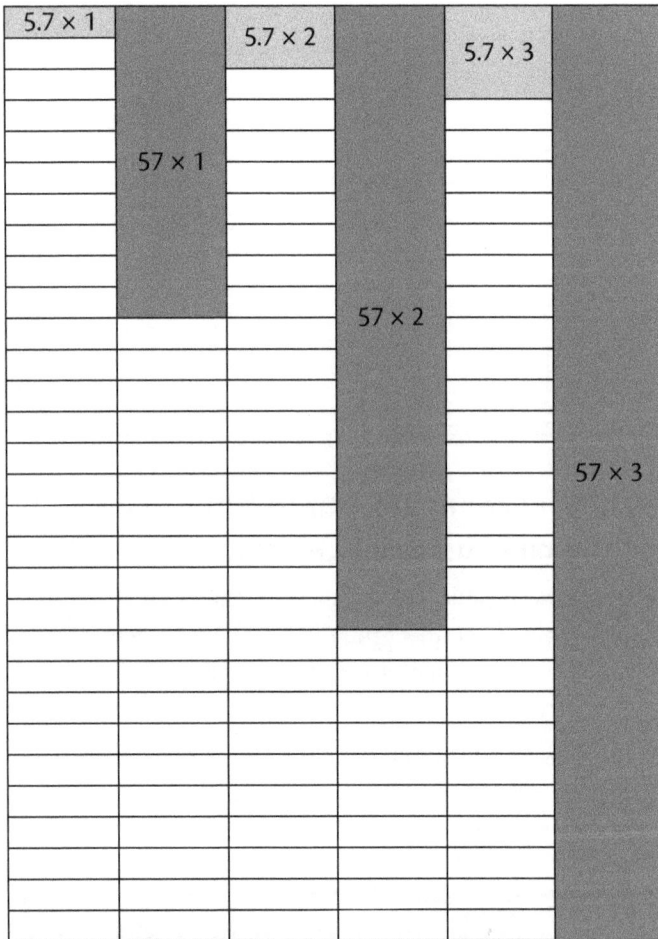

- Each small cell represents 5.7.

3×5.7

$=$ _____

- Display the following:

$3 \times 57 \div$ _____

$=$ _____ $\div$ _____

$=$ _____

- Together, complete the missing values:

3×5.7

$= 3 \times 57 \div 10$

$= 171 \div 10$

$= 17.1$

- Repeat the process used for 3×5.7, drawing pupils' attention to the way that the additional decimal place means that the number has to be multiplied and then divided by 100, rather than 10.

- Display the following:

3×5.71

$= 3 \times 571 \div$ _____

$=$ _____ $\div$ _____

$=$ _____

Together, complete the missing values:

3×5.71

$= 3 \times 571 \div 100$

$= 1713 \div 100$

$= 17.13$

- Pupils should complete Questions 2 and 3 in the Practice Book.

Same-day intervention

- Use **Resource 6.2.1c** Sliding, and two place value sliders.

- Show the first calculation on the resource sheet, using the two place value sliders.

  Now adjust the first slider, moving the digits one place across the decimal point, and discuss with pupils the way that this will affect the result.

  Agree that the slider showing the product must move in the same way.

- Pupils now use the sliders to complete the resource sheet.

Resource 6.2.1c

Sliding

Where needed, fill in the numbers on the place value sliders to show the products.

3 × [2 3] = [6 9]

3 × [2 3] = [6 9]

6 × [1 4] = [8 4]

6 × [1 4] = [ ]

5 × [1 3 5] = [6 7 5]

5 × [1 3 5] = [ ]

4 × [ ] = [9 2 4]

4 × [2 3 1] = [ ]

5 × [1 0 4] = [ ]

5 × [1 0 4] = [ ]

© HarperCollinsPublishers 2018

Answers: $6 \times 1.4 = 8.4$; $5 \times 1.35 = 6.75$; $4 \times 231 = 924$; $4 \times 2.31 = 9.24$; $5 \times 104 = 520$; $5 \times 1.04 = 5.2$

Same-day enrichment

• Display the following challenge.

> **Without calculating**, decide which is larger.
>
> 5.19×4
>
> or
>
> 5×4.19
>
> Explain how you know.
>
> **Without calculating**, can you work out what the difference is between the two results?

• Guide a discussion to share ideas and develop understanding.

Question 4

4 Solve these problems.

(a) The side length of a square flowerbed is 3.68 m. If it is fenced on all its sides, how long is the fence in total?

(b) The price of a pencil is £0.75. James bought 9 pencils. How much did he pay?

(c) The ground level of a 6-storey building is 4 m high, and each of the other five levels is 3.6 m high. What is the height of the building?

What learning will pupils have achieved at the conclusion of Question 4?

• Pupils will be able to use their understanding of place value to connect multiplication of integers and multiplication of decimals in order to calculate products.

• Pupils will be able to identify operations in worded problems and calculate with decimal measures.

Activities for whole-class instruction

• Write $4 \times 3 = 12$ on the board. Tell pupils that this calculation might be described by the story: 'Four people each have three pens. If they put all of the pens in one pot, there are twelve pens in total.'

Ask: *What other stories might describe the calculation?* Share ideas.

It is likely that many of the stories will echo yours and can be considered using repeated addition. This repeated addition image of multiplication is one that can prove problematic when moving on to multiplying decimals.

• Write the multiplication 3.52×4 on the board. Ask pupil pairs to decide on a story to describe this calculation. For example, a story might involve buying 4 items, each costing £3.52, or finding the area of a rectangle with the dimensions 4 m by 3.52 m, or two objects – one with a weight of 3.52 kg and the other weighing 4 times as much.

• Repeat with 4×3.52.

- Discuss with pupils the impact that the order of the numbers might have on the story they use, and agree that the order is not important when multiplying (this is the commutative rule) and that they should write the number sentence to a problem in a way that makes most sense to them.

- Pupils should complete Question 4 in the Practice Book.

Same-day intervention

- Ask pupils to complete **Resource 6.2.1d** Matching the questions, in which they have to match situations, calculations and results.

Resource 6.2.1d

Matching the questions

Cut out the cards and sort them into sets so that each set:
- shows a question
- the calculation needed to work it out
- the answer to the question.
One of the answers is missing, so you will need to make an extra card!

6 × 0.81	8kg of apples are packed in a box that weighs 0.59kg. What's the weight of the apples and the box?	8.59
A calculator costs £4.80. Amanda buys 3 calculators. How much does she spend?	0.3 × 16	4.8
4.72	0.59 + 8	3 × 4.80
A pencil costs £0.59. Fiona buys 8 pencils. How much does she spend?	A ruler is 0.3m long. 16 rulers are set out end to end. How long are they in total?	0.59 × 8
4.86	An elastic band is 0.81 m long and is stretched so that it is 6 times its original length. How long is it?	

© HarperCollinsPublishers 2018

Answers: 6 × 0.81 = 4.86; 0.3 × 16 = 4.8; 0.59 + 8 = 8.59; 0.59 × 8 = 4.72; missing answer 3 × 4.80 = 14.4

- Ask pupils to complete the following challenge.

Pencil shopping

Anik wants to buy at least 45 pencils, but doesn't mind if he has a few extra.

What is the cheapest way to buy 45 pencils?

1 × pack of 12 pencils	1 × pack of 6 pencils	1 pencil
£1.36	£0.69	£0.15

1 × pack of 4 pencils	1 × pack of 10 pencils	1 × pack of 5 pencils
£0.45	£1.20	£0.55

Answer: 9 packs of 5 pencils, £4.95

Challenge and extension question

Question 5

5 Compare the numbers. Fill in the space with 'greater' or 'less'.
Number A ÷ 100 × 10 = Number B × 100 ÷ 10 and both Number A and Number B are greater than zero.

Number B is _____ than Number A.

This question gives pupils an opportunity to reason about the size of numbers when given some information. There are only two options for this question ('greater' or 'less'), so ensure that pupils are able to justify their solution.

Unit 2.2
Multiplying decimal numbers by whole numbers (2)

Conceptual context

In this unit, pupils will extend what they have learned about multiplying whole numbers and decimals with up to two decimal places, to multiplying by decimals with three decimal places.

Pupils will relate what they have learned – about calculating with whole numbers and then adjusting to take account of the decimal they started with – to the way that the written column method for multiplication with decimals actually 'works'.

Learning pupils will have achieved at the end of the unit

- Pupils' recent learning – about calculating with whole numbers and then adjusting to take account of the decimal they started with – will be related to the written method for multiplying. They will have practised converting decimals to whole numbers by multiplying and then dividing the product accordingly (Q1, Q2, Q4, Q5)

- Pupils will have reasoned about related products when the product of two integers is known (Q3)

- Pupils will be able to use place value to find related products when the product of two integers is known (Q3)

- Pupils will have become more fluent when using the column method to multiply a decimal by an integer (Q4, Q5, Q6)

- Pupils will be able to multiply integers by decimal numbers with an integer part that is not zero (Q3, Q4, Q5, Q6)

Resources

place value counters, **Resource 6.2.1a** Place value slider; sticky notes; **Resource 6.2.2a** Points in different places; **Resource 6.2.2b** Missing digits

Vocabulary

tenths, hundredths, whole number, place value, decimal, product, convert

Questions 1 and 2

1 Convert the decimal multiplication into whole-number multiplication and then calculate the answer.

$$\begin{array}{r} 4\ 2 \\ \times\ 0\ .\ 5\ 7 \end{array}$$ → $$\begin{array}{r} 4\ 2 \\ \times\ \ \ 5\ 7 \end{array}$$

2 Use whole-number multiplication first and then calculate the answers to the decimal multiplications.

(a) $$\begin{array}{r} 2\ 9 \\ \times\ \ \ \ 6 \end{array}$$ (b) $$\begin{array}{r} 2\ 9 \\ \times\ 0\ .\ 0\ 6 \end{array}$$ (c) $$\begin{array}{r} 4\ 7 \\ \times\ \ 1\ 5 \end{array}$$ (d) $$\begin{array}{r} 0\ .\ 4\ 7 \\ \times\ \ \ \ 1\ 5 \end{array}$$

What learning will pupils have achieved at the conclusion of Questions 1 and 2?

- Pupils' recent learning – about calculating with whole numbers and then adjusting to take account of the decimal they started with – will be related to the written method for multiplying. They will have practised converting decimals to whole numbers by multiplying and then dividing the product accordingly.

Activities for whole-class instruction

- Display the following:

$$\begin{array}{r} 4\ \ 2 \\ \times\ \ 3\ \ 6 \\ \hline \end{array}$$

Together, work through each step of the written calculation using this image:

This is 42 × 6

This is 42 × 30

- All say … *In this calculation, 42 is being multiplied by 6 ones and then by 3 tens.*

- Describe how, when multiplying by 30 (3 tens), that 2 times 3 tens is 6 tens, so 6 tens counters are placed in the tens column.

- Ask: *What is 4 tens multiplied by 30, or 30 multiplied by 4 tens?* Agree 120 tens or 12 hundreds. Write on the board: $40 \times 30 = 12 \times 10 \times 10 = 12 \times 100$ and discuss. Agree that 10 hundreds are equal to 1000, so they are swapped for a one thousand counter.

- Look together at the right-hand diagram in the image above. Focus on the zero in 1260. Agree that, when multiplying by a number of tens, the product always ends with 0 in the ones column.

- Add to find the total value of the part-products 252 and 1260.

- Now display the calculation:

$$\begin{array}{r} 4\ \ 2 \\ \times\ \ 0\ .\ 3\ \ 6 \\ \hline \end{array}$$

Ask pupils how this calculation is different from the first. Agree that the digits are the same, but the value of each digit is different.

- Work through the calculation step by step using the following image.

- All say … *In this calculation, 42 is being multiplied by 6 hundredths and then by 3 tenths; by 0.36.*

- Display the following:

  42 × 0.36

  = 42 × 36 ÷ 100

  = 1512 ÷ ____

  = ____

  Remind pupils of the strategy used in Unit 2.1, in which they multiplied the decimal number to make a whole number and then divided the product by the same factor at the end.

- Ask: *What's the same and what's different about these two methods?*

- Repeat this with a similar 2 × two-digit multiplication, for example: 52 × 73 and 0.52 × 73.

- Pupils should complete Questions 1 and 2 in the Practice Book.

Same-day intervention

- Ask pupils to complete **Resource 6.2.2a** Points in different places.

- As they work through the calculations, draw pupils' attention to the way in which the whole-number calculation can be used, and then adjusted by dividing, to calculate the product with the decimal numbers.

Resource 6.2.2a

Points in different places

Fill in the blanks for each of these calculations.

1.
```
    3 2
  × 5 9
```
2.
```
    3 2
  × 0 . 5 9
```
3.
```
    3 . 2
  × 5 . 9
```
4.
```
    0 . 3 2
  × 5 9
```
5.
```
    3 . 2
  × 5 9
```

© HarperCollins Publishers 2018

Answers: **1.** 1888; **2.** 18.88; **3.** 188.8; **4.** 18.88; **5.** 188.8

Same-day enrichment

- Display the following challenge.

  Ayesha works out 24 × 0.17.

  ```
          2  4
  ×   0 . 1  7
      1 . 6  8
      2 . 4  0
      4 . 0  8
  ```

  Ayesha says, 'That can't be right. I've multiplied 24 by a number and I've got an answer that's smaller than 24! Multiplying always makes the answer bigger.'

  Joe says, 'It is right. When you multiply a whole number by a decimal, it always gives an answer that is less than the whole number.'

  Do you agree with Joe?

  Do you agree with Ayesha?

  Or do you think they're both wrong?

- Ask pupils to work in pairs to decide who is right – Ayesha, Joe or neither.

Question 3

3. Use the fact that 23 × 75 = 1725 to write the products of these multiplications.

   (a) 23 × 0.75 = ____

   (b) 0.023 × 75 = ____

   (c) 2.3 × 0.075 = ____

   (d) 2.3 × 75 = ____

   (e) 2.3 × 750 = ____

   (f) 75 × 0.23 = ____

What learning will pupils have achieved at the conclusion of Question 3?

- Pupils' recent learning – about calculating with whole numbers and then adjusting to take account of the decimal they started with – will be related to the written method for multiplying. They will have practised converting decimals to whole numbers by multiplying and then dividing the product accordingly.

- Pupils will have reasoned about related products when the product of two integers is known.

- Pupils will be able to use place value to find related products when the product of two integers is known.

- Pupils will be able to multiply integers by decimal numbers with an integer part that is not zero.

Activities for whole-class instruction

- Use three place value sliders set to show pupils an integer multiplication, for example:

$$\boxed{1\ 6\ \ .\ \ \ } \times \boxed{2\ 3\ \ .\ \ \ } = \boxed{3\ 6\ 8\ \ .\ \ \ }$$

Adjust one of the sliders and discuss how the answer should be corrected. Agree that the slider showing the product also must be adjusted in the same way. For example, if the first slider is moved one place to the right, the slider showing the product must also be moved one place to the right.

$$\boxed{\ \ 1\ .\ 6\ \ } \times \boxed{\ 2\ 3\ .\ \ \ } = \boxed{\ 3\ 6\ .\ 8\ \ }$$

Agree that each movement on the sliders on the left of the calculation must be 'reflected' by the slider showing the product – that is, the opposite or inverse operation needs to be carried out.

- Write on the board:

$16 \times 23 = 368$

$1.6 \times 23 = 36.8$

Invite pupils to offer more calculations that they can immediately work out using their knowledge of place value. Ask pupils to explain and show, using the sliders, how their calculation and product are linked to $16 \times 23 = 368$.

- Pupils should complete Question 3 in the Practice Book.

Same-day intervention

- Use place value sliders to explore the family of products given by $13 \times 16 = 208$.
- Pupils work in pairs. One of the pair adjusts one slider and the other then adjusts a different slider to make the calculation correct.

$$\boxed{1\ 3\ .\ \ \ } \times \boxed{\ 1\ 6\ .\ \ \ } = \boxed{2\ 0\ 8\ .\ \ \ }$$

Same-day enrichment

- Tell pupils that $37 \times 42 = 1554$.
- Ask pupils to explain how they can use this calculation to find the answer to 3.7×42, without having to calculate an answer.

Questions 4, 5 and 6

4 Choose the column method to calculate the following. The first one has been done for you.

(a) $7 \times 0.24 = 1.68$ (b) $3.85 \times 13 =$ (c) $14.5 \times 18 =$

```
  0 . 2 4
×       7
  1 . 6 8
```

(d) $25 \times 0.306 =$ (e) $10.2 \times 54 =$ (f) $23.6 \times 50 =$

5 Are these calculations correct? (Put a ✓ for yes and a ✗ for no in each box and make corrections if necessary.)

(a)
```
    4 . 5
×       8
  3 . 6 0
```

(b)
```
    1 . 3 6
×   2 5 0
    6 8 0
  2 7 2
  3 4 . 0 0
```

(c)
```
      3 . 1 4
×   1 0 5 0
    1 5 7 0
    3 1 4
  4 7 1 . 0 0
```

6 Solve these problems.

(a) If an object weighs 1 kg on Earth, it will weigh 0.16 kg on the Moon. Jack weighs 39 kg on Earth. If he was on the Moon, how much would he weigh?

(b) The price of a pen is £12.70 and the price of a notebook is £4.50. Bob wants to buy a pen and two notebooks with £20. Does he have enough money to buy them? Why or why not?

What learning will pupils have achieved at the conclusion of Questions 4, 5 and 6?

- Pupils' recent learning – about calculating with whole numbers and then adjusting to take account of the decimal they started with – will be related to the written method for multiplying. They will have practised converting decimals to whole numbers by multiplying and then dividing the product accordingly.
- Pupils will become more fluent in using the column method to multiply a decimal by an integer.
- Pupils will be able to multiply integers by decimal numbers with an integer part that is not zero.

Activities for whole-class instruction

- Use the column method to calculate 27×2.51. Write it on the board, but cover the digits in the method with sticky notes (see next page).

```
        2   7
  ×   2 . 5   1
```

- Explain to pupils that they are going to play a game. They will be split into teams and each team will take it in turns to say what digit they think is behind a particular sticky note.

  Each sticky note has a different number of points attached to it and, if they are correct then they win those points. If they are incorrect, they lose those points.

  Teams take it in turns to decide which sticky note they want to remove and the team with the most points wins.

- Explain that the sticky notes can have a value of 1, 2 or 3 points, depending on how difficult it is to predict that number. Explain that the first job is to decide which of the sticky notes are hardest to work out (and so should carry the most points) and which are easiest (and so should have the fewest points). Ask pupil pairs to discuss which are the most difficult sticky notes to calculate and gather responses. Write a small 1, 2 or 3 on the corner of each sticky note.

- Play the game together. Repeat with new factors.

- Pupils should complete Questions 4, 5 and 6 in the Practice Book.

Same-day intervention

- Use **Resource 6.2.2b** Missing digits to work with pupils on the column method for multiplication. As you work with pupils, use the calculations to draw their attention to what is the same and what is different as the position of the decimal point changes.

Answers: **1.** 2, 4, 0, 8; **2.** 5, 0, 7, 9, 5; **3.** 5, 8;
4. 4, 8, 6, 9, 7, 0, 5, 8, 2

Same-day enrichment

- Ask pupils to work independently on **Resource 6.2.2b** Missing digits, in which they have to find the missing digits to make a calculation correct.

Challenge and extension questions

Question 7

7 Number A is 9 less than Number B. If all of the digits in Number A are moved one place to the right across the decimal point, it becomes 0.009.

Number B is ☐.

This question challenges pupils to reason about decimal numbers given some information about the relationship between them. Encouraging pupils to represent the situation pictorially may support them in accessing the structure of the problem, rather than using a trial and improvement approach.

Question 8

8 Calculate the product of these decimal numbers.

(a) 2.5×0.8 (b) 1.3×3.6 (c) 10.52×0.25

This question asks pupils to use their understanding of multiplying a decimal by a whole number, to move on to multiplying two decimals. Encourage pupils to estimate an approximate answer to the calculations, then to use their understanding of place value to find a method for calculating the products.

Unit 2.3
Addition, subtraction and multiplication with decimals

Conceptual context

In this unit, pupils will solve decimal problems that include more than one operation. Pupils will become fluent with using brackets to show multiplication of a number that is itself found by operating on others. Multiplicative relationships are explored and revealed, strengthening pupils' conceptual understanding and developing their ability to approach problems with deep understanding; enabling them to interpret and operate with information in different ways.

Learning pupils will have achieved at the end of the unit

- Pupils will be able to use their knowledge about brackets to write a number sentence using decimals with more than one operation (Q1, Q2)
- Pupils will be able to evaluate number sentences combining addition, subtraction and multiplication with decimals (Q1, Q2, Q3)
- Pupils will understand and interpret different ways of describing calculations (Q3, Q4)
- Pupils will be able to evaluate calculations written in both mathematical and real-life contexts (Q3, Q4)

Resources

Resource 6.2.3a Number and word sentences; **Resource 6.2.3b** Place the brackets; **Resource 6.2.3c** Match the calculations; **Resource 6.2.3d** Different ways to say …

Vocabulary

tenths, hundredths, whole number, decimal, product, sum

Questions 1 and 2

1 Combine two number sentences with a single operation into one number sentence with different operations. The first one has been done for you.

(a) $2.5 + 5.6 = 8.1$ (b) $6.2 - 2.6 = 3.6$ (c) $0.45 \times 1.2 = 0.54$

    $11 \times 8.1 = 89.1$ $25 \times 3.6 = 90$ $34 \times 0.54 = 18.36$

    $11 \times (2.5 + 5.6) = 89.1$ _____

2 Work these out step by step.

(a) $4 \times 0.5 \times 4.81$ (b) $57.82 - 1.03 \times 42$

(c) $18 \times (8.14 - 3.64)$ (d) $0.8 \times 50 \times 0.07$

(e) $12.49 - 0.48 \times 25 + 6.3$ (f) $0.75 \times 14 \times 42$

What learning will pupils have achieved at the conclusion of Questions 1 and 2?

- Pupils will be able to use their knowledge about brackets to write a number sentence using decimals with more than one operation.
- Pupils will be able to evaluate number sentences combining addition, subtraction and multiplication with decimals.

Activities for whole-class instruction

- Write a multiplication of a decimal by an integer, for example $7 \times 2.93 = 20.51$, on the board and invite a pupil to the board to work with you.

Each of you takes turns to add a layer of complexity to your side of the equation by breaking down one value to make the number sentence more complex. You might find it easier to keep track of the changes by underlining the value that you're going to change.

For example:

$\underline{7} \times 2.93 = 20.51$ First the 7 is rewritten as $3 + 4$.

$(3 + 4) \times 2.93 = \underline{20.51}$ Then 20.51 is rewritten as $10 + 10.51$.

$(3 + \underline{4}) \times 2.93 = 10 + 10.51$ The 4 is rewritten as 2^2.

$(3 + 2^2) \times \underline{2.93} = 10 + 10.51$ 2.93 is rewritten as $\frac{1}{2} \times 5.86$.

$(3 + 2^2) \times \frac{1}{2} \times 5.86 = \underline{10} + 10.51$ Finally, 10 is rewritten as 2×5.

$(3 + 2^2) \times \frac{1}{2} \times 5.86 = 2 \times 5 + 10.51$

Repeat with new numbers, working through with the whole class. Pupil pairs can then repeat the task, making up their own starting numbers.

Share ideas, focusing on the use of brackets. The intention of this task is to support pupils in feeling confident with greater complexity, and to focus attention on the order of operations. By understanding the way in which complexity is increased, pupils are more likely to be able to approach calculations flexibly and be able to simplify fluently.

- Use an example where the meaning of the number sentence may be seen by pupils to be ambiguous, for example $3 + 4 \times 2.93$.

Discuss with pupils the order in which this calculation must be done, reminding them that multiplication and division always take priority over addition and subtraction, and that calculations in brackets take priority over these.

- Pupils should complete Questions 1 and 2 in the Practice Book.

(i) There are common acronyms to remember the order of operations (BIDMAS and BODMAS are commonly used in the UK) but these should be used with caution as they can appear to suggest that division takes priority over multiplication, and that addition takes priority over subtraction. This means that pupils may, for example, work on $10 - 6 + 3$ by evaluating $6 + 3$ first, then carrying out the subtraction, giving $10 - 6 + 3 = 1$.

Same-day intervention

- Work with pupils on **Resource 6.2.3a** Number and word sentences, a matching activity in which pupils connect calculations and words.

Resource 6.2.3a

Number and word sentences

Cut out and match the number sentences and the word sentences. Two of the number sentences give the same answer. Which two? Can you explain why?

$3 \times (2.1 + 5)$	$3 \times 2.1 + 5$	$3 \times 5 + 2.1$
Multiply 3 by 5 then subtract 2.1	Subtract 2.1 from 5 then multiply by 3	$3 \times 2.1 - 5$
Add 2.1 and 5, then multiply by 3	Add 5 and 2.1, then multiply by 3	$3 \times (5 - 2.1)$
Multiply 3 by 2.1 then subtract 5	$3 \times 5 - 2.1$	$3 \times (5 + 2.1)$
Multiply 3 by 5 then add 2.1	Multiply 3 by 2.1 then add 5	

Answers: $3 \times (2.1 + 5)$ and $3 \times (5 + 2.1)$ give the same answer.

Same-day enrichment

- Pupils work through **Resource 6.2.3b** Place the brackets, in which they are challenged to insert brackets to correct the calculations.

Resource 6.2.3b

Place the brackets

Some of these calculations are missing a pair of brackets.
Find these calculations and add brackets so that the calculations are correct.

1. $3.2 + 5 \times 1.7 = 13.94$

2. $26 \times 3.8 - 1.3 = 97.5$

3. $1.2 \times 2.3 + 1.5 - 0.2 = 4.32$

4. $5 - 1.7 + 3.2 = 0.1$

5. $3.2 + 5 \times 1.7 = 11.7$

6. $26 \times 3.8 - 1.3 = 65$

7. $1.2 \times 2.3 + 1.5 - 0.2 = 4.36$

© HarperCollinsPublishers 2018   387

Answers: **1.** $(3.2 + 5) \times 1.7 = 13.94$; **2.** $(26 \times 3.8) - 1.3 = 97.5$ (using the order of operations, the calculation is already correct without brackets); **3.** $1.2 \times (2.3 + 1.5 - 0.2) = 4.32$; **4.** $5 - (1.7 + 3.2) = 0.1$; **5.** $3.2 + (5 \times 1.7) = 11.7$ (using the order of operations, the calculation is already correct without brackets); **6.** $26 \times (3.8 - 1.3) = 65$; **7.** $1.2 \times (2.3 + 1.5) - 0.2 = 4.36$

Questions 3 and 4

3 Write the number sentences and then calculate the answers.

(a) The sum of 7.8 and 1.2 is multiplied by 0.6. What is the product?

(b) The number that is 1.2 less than 3.2 is multiplied by 3.9. What is the product?

(c) How much more is 10 times 0.44 than 2.5?

(d) Number A is 6.9, which is 0.9 more than twice Number B. What is Number B?

4 Solve these problems.

(a) A textile factory produces clothes for both children and adults. To make one set of children's clothes, it needs 2.08 metres of cloth; to make one set of adult clothes, it needs 3 times as much. To make one set each of children's clothes and adult clothes, how many metres of cloth are needed in total?

(b) A piece of iron rod is 6 m long. It weighs 4.9 kg per metre. How much do 70 pieces of iron rod weigh in kilograms and in tonnes? (Note: 1 tonne = 1000 kg)

(c) Tom bought eight 250 ml bottles of soft drink at £0.32 per bottle. He paid the cashier £4. How much change should he get?

(d) The side length of a square is 0.5 m. Four such squares make one large square. What are the perimeter and the area of the large square?

What learning will pupils have achieved at the conclusion of Questions 3 and 4?

- Pupils will be able to evaluate number sentences combining addition, subtraction and multiplication with decimals.

- Pupils will understand and interpret different ways of describing calculations.

- Pupils will be able to evaluate calculations written in both mathematical and real-life contexts.

Activities for whole-class instruction

- Give pupil groups **Resource 6.2.3c** Match the calculations, and ask them to match the descriptions and number sentences. Tell them that each number sentence might have more than one written description.

- Share solutions. Ensure that the vocabulary used is understood by pupils and encourage them to define words such as 'product' and 'sum'.

Answers: Missing calculations: $(1.4 - 0.7) \times 4$; $4 - (1.4 + 0.7)$.

Look out for … pupils who muddle 'sum' and 'product'.

Same-day intervention

- Work through **Resource 6.2.3d** Different ways to say … with pupils. Listen for and correct misconceptions around the different ways of referring to each operation.

- Discuss 'real-life' situations for each calculation.

Same-day enrichment

- Give pupils a sheet of plain paper and write a decimal number in the centre, for example 2.45.

- Ask pupils to write at least three calculations that give the result 2.45 and then to write as many word problems as they can that describe the calculation.

- For example, the calculation $24.5 \div 10 = 2.45$ might be describing the situation: 'A reel of cotton is 24.5 metres long and is cut into 10 equal pieces. How long is each piece?'

Challenge and extension question

Question 5

5 Insert brackets in the following number sentences to make each equation true.

(a) $15.2 + 2.5 \times 3 - 10.6 = 42.5$

(b) $30 - 11.8 \times 2 - 1.5 = 9.1$

(c) $4.5 \times 6.5 - 2.5 + 1.8 = 19.8$

This question asks pupils to insert brackets to correct a series of calculations. Encourage pupils to use estimation to reduce the time spent on each calculation.

Unit 2.4
Laws of operations with decimal numbers

Conceptual context

Pupils have previously learned about laws of operations in Year 4; here they will extend that knowledge to work with decimal numbers.

In this unit, pupils work with multi-step calculations that can include any of the four operations, and with calculations containing different operations. Pupils revisit the idea that some operations take precedence over others in a calculation, and use this along with the commutative, distributive and associative laws, to calculate efficiently with decimal numbers.

(i) In calculating efficiently, pupils are likely to use the associative property – which is that the order in which some calculations are carried out does not affect their value, for example, $2 \times (3 \times 4) = (2 \times 3) \times 4$, and the distributive property, which is that multiplication is distributive over addition and subtraction, for example, $2 \times (3 + 4) = 2 \times 3 + 2 \times 4$.

Learning pupils will have achieved at the end of the unit

- Pupils will look carefully at calculations and calculate efficiently using the commutative, distributive and associative properties (Q1, Q2, Q3, Q4)
- Pupils will be able to construct equations and calculate with decimals in applied situations (Q4)

Resources

Resource 6.2.4 Which way?

Vocabulary

tenths, hundredths, whole number, decimal, product, sum

Questions 1 and 2

---

1 Draw lines to match the calculations with the same answers. Use a ruler.

4×5.4	$8 \times 1.25 + 8 \times 12.5$
$4.6 \times 9 + 5.4 \times 9$	$6.7 \times (4 \times 2.5)$
$8 \times (1.25 + 12.5)$	$(4.6 + 5.4) \times 9$
$6.7 \times 4 \times 2.5$	5.4×4

2 True or false? (Put a ✓ for true and a ✗ for false in each box.)

(a) $19 \times 0.59 = (19 + 0.1) \times 0.59$ ☐

(b) $12 \times 8.8 = 12 \times 8 \times 12 \times 0.8$ ☐

(c) $10 \times 2.7 - 5.4 = 2.7 \times (10 - 2)$ ☐

(d) $15 \times 2.4 = (15 \times 8) \times 3$ ☐

What learning will pupils have achieved at the conclusion of Questions 1 and 2?

- Pupils will look carefully at calculations and calculate efficiently using the commutative, distributive and associative properties.

Activities for whole-class instruction

- Display the following.

Elinor and Matilda worked out the answer to this calculation in two different ways.

$10 \times 2.8 - 9 \times 2.8$

Elinor's method

> I worked out that 10 lots of 2.8 is 28, and then I used this to work out that 9 lots of 2.8 is 25.2.
> Once I'd got these two, I subtracted 25.2 from 28 and the answer 2.8.

Matilda's method

> I noticed that 9 lots of 2.8 was being taken away from 10 lots of 2.8, which means that there'd be just one lot of 2.8 left, because $10 - 9 = 1$.
> So, I knew that the answer must be one lot of 2.8, which is 2.8.

- Ask pupil pairs to discuss the two methods shown for the calculation. Once pupils have had time to work on the calculations, ask:

- Can you explain why Elinor's method works? Can you explain why Matilda's method works?

- Which of the methods would you use? Why?

- Which method do you think is best? Why?

- Is there a different method that you would use? Why?

- Can you draw a diagram or picture to represent each method?

- Ask pupils to discuss whether both methods would work if the calculation was changed to $10 \times 2.8 - 2.8 \times 9$.

   Discuss and agree that, because of the commutative law, both methods are still appropriate and will give the correct answer. It is likely that Matilda's method is more efficient.

- Ensure pupils understand that it is only because multiples of the same number are being subtracted that Matilda's method works. If the calculation was $10 \times 2.8 - 9 \times 1.9$ then this would not be a useful method and a different strategy would need to be found.

- Display the following.

Sam and Cassidy worked out the answer to this calculation in two different ways.

$2.4 \times 4 \times 6.25$

Sam's method

> I spotted that multiplying 6.25 and 4 together gives a whole number answer, so I did this first and found out that the answer was 25. I then multiplied 2.4 by 100 to get 240 and then halved it and halved it again to get 60.

Cassidy's method

> I worked it out in order. I know that 2.4×4 is 9.6 and then I worked out that 9×6.25 is 56.25. I worked out that 6×6.25 is 37.5, so 0.6×6.25 is 3.75. Adding 56.25 to 3.75 means that the answer must be 60.

- Give pupils pairs time to discuss, then ask:

- Can you explain why Sam's method works? Can you explain Cassidy's method?

- Which of the methods would you use? Why?

– *Which method do you think is best? Why?*

– *Is there a different method that you would use? Why?*

– *Can you draw a diagram to show each method?*

● Ensure pupils understand that looking for multiplications that give an integer is a useful strategy when multiplying decimals.

● Pupils should complete Questions 1 and 2 in the Practice Book.

Same-day intervention

● Display the following.

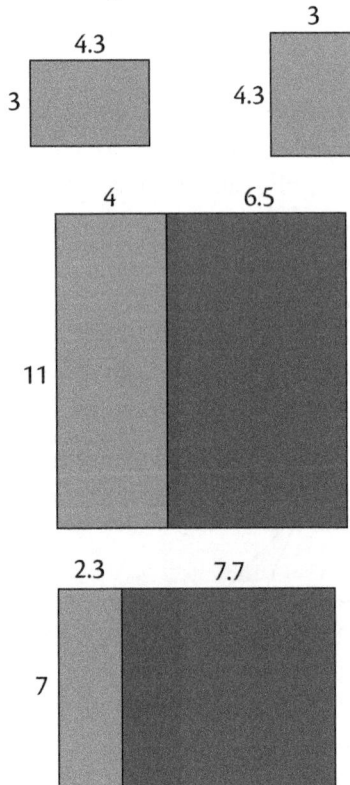

● Together, talk about number sentences that are represented by the diagrams.

● Ask questions, such as (for part 1):

– *Are both rectangles the same?*

– *Which rectangles represent an area that can be found by 3 × 4.3?*

● (for part 2):

– *Where on the diagram can you see 6.5 + 4?*

– *Where on the diagram can you see 11 × (6.5 + 4)*

– *Where on the diagram can you see 11 × 4?*

– *Where on the diagram can you see 11 × 6.5?*

● Agree with pupils that being able to see calculations in different ways can help them to simplify the number of steps needed to reach an answer.

Same-day enrichment

● Tell pupils that you are going to give them a complex calculation that they will be able to simplify and calculate smartly.

● Write 2.01 × 3.7 + 6.4 × 2.01 – 0.1 × 2.01 on the board and ask them to work out an answer, and to draw a diagram or picture to explain their strategy.

● Next, pupil pairs should create their own version of this type of calculation, one which can be simplified to 10 × 3.14.

Questions 3 and 4

3 Use the most appropriate method to find the answer to each calculation.

(a) 12.5 × 3.2 × 8   (b) 7 × 0.25   (c) 0.99 × 11

(d) 6.4 × 6 + 6.4 × 4 – 6.4   (e) 720 × 12.5 ÷ 8

(f) (6.2 × 5 + 1.8 × 5) × 1.25   (g) (2.5 + 2.5 + 2.5 + 2.5 + 2.5) × 88

(h) 5.4 × 4 – 7 × 4.4 + 3 × 5.4   (i) 17.48 × 38 + 1.748 × 820 – 174.8 × 2

4 Solve these problems.

(a) In a school uniform, the blazer costs £12.50 and the trousers cost £10.99. How much do 320 sets of the school uniform cost?

(b) One water pump can pump 12.5 tonnes of water into a swimming pool in one hour. At this rate, how many tonnes of water in total will 16 water pumps pump in 2.5 hours?

What learning will pupils have achieved at the conclusion of Questions 3 and 4?

- Pupils will look carefully at calculations and calculate efficiently using the commutative, distributive and associative properties.
- Pupils will be able to construct equations and calculate with decimals in applied situations.

Activities for whole-class instruction

- Display the following.

Tom and Owen worked out the answer to this calculation in two different ways.

$$(3.42 + 9.71) + 0.58$$

Owen's method

> I worked out the calculation in the brackets first, so 3.42 + 9.71 is 13.13, then I added 0.58 to this which gives 13.71.

Tom's method

> I noticed that 3.42 + 0.58 = 4 and, although there are brackets, all of the calculations are additions so it doesn't affect the answer to change the order. Adding 4 to 9.71 gives 13.71.

- Pupil pairs should discuss the two methods shown. Then, ask:
  - *Is it really all right to ignore the brackets in Tom's method? When else is it acceptable to ignore the brackets?*
  - *Which of the methods would you use? Why?*
  - *Which method do you think is best? Why?*
  - *Is there a different method that you would use? Why?*
  - *Can you draw a diagram to show each method?*
- Remind pupils that looking for additions that give an integer sum is a useful strategy when adding decimals.
- Pupils should complete Questions 3 and 4 in the Practice Book.

Same-day intervention

- Work with pupils on **Resource 6.2.4** Which way? asking pupils to decide which of the calculations from each section they would prefer to work out.
- Use their answers to make explicit the links between the different calculations, that they are different ways to tackle the same calculation and that these methods reduce the need for carrying out several different and complex calculations.

Resource 6.2.4

Which way?

1. Which calculation do you think is easier?
   $3.5 \times 2 + 3.5 \times 8$
   OR
   3.5×10

2. Which calculation do you think is easier?
   $20 \times 2.1 \div 10$
   OR
   $20 \div 10 \times 2.1$

3. Which calculation do you think is easier?
   $25 \times 3.14 \times 4$
   OR
   100×3.14

4. Which calculation do you think is easier? (Fill in the gaps.)
   $7 \times 7.2 + 3 \times 7.2$
   OR
   ___ $\times 7.2$

5. Which calculation do you think is easier? (Fill in the gaps.)
   $2 \times 1.7 \times 5$
   OR
   ___ $\times 1.7$

© HarperCollinsPublishers 2018

Same-day enrichment

- Ask pupils to complete this challenge by finding the missing numbers.

Missing numbers

All of these calculations give the answer 24. What are the missing numbers?

$$2 \times 0.6 \times 2 \times 5 \times \underline{\quad} = 24$$

$$2.4 \times 2.4 + \underline{\quad} \times 2.4 = 24$$

$$(24 \times 2.4 - 4 \times 2.4) \div \underline{\quad} = 24$$

$$4 \times (7 \times \underline{\quad} + 0.1 \times 5) \times 5 = 24$$

$$0.2 \times 0.2 \times 0.3 \times \underline{\quad} = 24$$

Answers: 2, 7.6, 2, 0.1, 2000

Challenge and extension question

Question 5

5 Write a suitable number in each box to make the equation true.

$$4.7 \times 125 + \boxed{} \times \boxed{} = 1000$$

This question asks pupils to find missing numbers.

There are multiple possible correct solutions (any pair of numbers where the product is equal to 1000 – 4.7 × 125 will give a correct answer), but this question implicitly requires pupils to find a 'simple' solution. Key to this is for pupils to notice that 125 × 8 = 1000, which then raises the questions: 'How many 125s are there already in the calculation?' and 'How many more 125s are needed to reach 8 lots of 125?'

Unit 2.5
Division of decimals by whole numbers (1)

Conceptual context

In this unit, pupils will consider division of decimals using a strategy related to what they did when multiplying decimals earlier in this chapter. They will learn to adjust the decimal dividend (converting it to an integer) so they can operate with integers and then reverse that adjustment at the end.

By practising and developing fluency with these adjustments and reverse-adjustments, pupils are able to solve problems using flexible thinking and reasoning about division based on place value.

Learning pupils will have achieved at the end of the unit

- Pupils will be able to convert decimal division to integer division and understand the effect of this, adding the reverse conversion to determine solutions (Q1, Q2, Q3)
- Pupils will have related their new understanding about decimal division to the written method, understanding that adjustments to convert decimals to integers must be reversed at the end of the written procedure to find the solution (Q2, Q3, Q4, Q5)
- Pupils will have identified appropriate operations to represent and solve word problems, calculating with decimals and decimal measures (Q4, Q5)

Resources

place value sliders; place value counters; mini whiteboards; **Resource 6.2.5a** Place value sliders – division; **Resource 6.2.5b** Double digits; **Resource 6.2.5c** Matching the divisions; **Resource 6.2.5d** Best buys

Vocabulary

divisor, dividend, quotient, decimal number, whole number

Question 1

> **1** Fill in the missing numbers.
>
> (a) 8.4 ÷ 6 = ☐
>
> ☐ times 0.1 is 8.4.
>
> 84 ÷ 6 = ☐
>
> ☐ times 0.1 is ☐.
>
> (b) 9.38 ÷ 7 = ☐
>
> ☐ times 0.01 is 9.38.
>
> 938 ÷ ☐ = 134
>
> ☐ times 0.01 is ☐.

What learning will pupils have achieved at the conclusion of Question 1?

- Pupils will be able to convert decimal division to integer division and understand the effect of this, adding the reverse conversion to determine solutions.

Activities for whole-class instruction

- On the board, write: 24 ÷ 3 = 8.

  Ask: *How will the quotient change if :*

  – *24 is doubled to 48*

  – *24 is halved*

  – *24 is multiplied by ten*

  – *24 is multiplied by 0.3?*

  Can pupils see that any multiplicative change to the dividend will result in the same change to the quotient?

- Write one of the examples generated, for example:

  48 ÷ 3 = 16

  24 times 2 is 48

  24 ÷ 3 = 8

  8 times 2 is 16

- Pupils should complete Question 1 in the Practice Book.

Same-day intervention

- Use place value counters to model both 8.4 ÷ 6 and 84 ÷ 6, creating six equal piles of counters for each dividend.

- As you model this, record the procedure as in the Practice Book and stress that, when the dividend has been multiplied to make an integer, the quotient will also be inflated by the same multiple. Ensure that pupils understand that this means the 'solution' they have reached is actually a multiple of what it would have been if the decimal had not been converted to a whole number at the beginning.

- Ask: *So, what should we do to find the actual solution?* Pupils should suggest dividing the number reached by the multiple that was used at the beginning. Refer to this as 'adjusting' or 'converting' and 'reverse-adjusting'.

Same-day enrichment

- Show pupils the following.

  ☐ ☐ . ☐ ÷ ☐

- Use four digits from 2, 3, 4, 5, 6 to make the quotient:

  i) as close to 15 as possible

  ii) as close to 13 as possible

  iii) as close to 10 as possible.

Questions 2 and 3

> **2** Calculate the following. Most of the first one has been done for you.
>
> (a) 22.4 ÷ 14 =
>
> 22.4 is 224 times 0.1.
>
> ```
>       1 6
> 14 ) 2 2 4
>      1 4 0
>        8 4
>        8 4
>          0
> ```
>
> 16 times 0.1 is ☐.
>
> (b) 26.1 ÷ 9 =
>
> (c) 41.04 ÷ 12 =
>
> **3** Use the column method to calculate the answers. (Check the answers to the questions marked with *.)
>
> (a) 43.2 ÷ 4 =
>
> (b) 115.2 ÷ 18 =
>
> (c) *408.8 ÷ 73 =
>
> (d) 38.22 ÷ 7 =
>
> (e) 313.6 ÷ 49 =
>
> (f) *99.32 ÷ 13 =

What learning will pupils have achieved at the conclusion of Questions 2 and 3?

- Pupils will be able to convert decimal division to integer division and understand the effect of this, adding the reverse conversion to determine solutions.

- Pupils will have related their new understanding about decimal division to the written method, understanding that adjustments to convert decimals to integers must be reversed at the end of the written procedure to find the solution.

Activities for whole-class instruction

- Write the calculation 1065 ÷ 5 on the board and ask pupil pairs to use the column method for division to find the quotient. Agree it is 213.

- Write 106.5 ÷ 5. In pairs, pupils should write down the quotient without having to carry out another division calculation. Agree that, because the dividend is ten times smaller than the original calculation, the quotient must also be ten times smaller (21.3).

- Write 1.065 ÷ 5. Agree that, since the dividend is now 1000 times smaller, then the quotient must also be 1000 times smaller.

- Ask: *What whole-number division could you use to calculate 7.47 ÷ 3?* Agree that 747 ÷ 3 uses whole numbers by using a dividend that is 100 times larger. Ask: *What would you need to do to the quotient that you find?* Agree, divide it by 100.

- Together, work out that 747 ÷ 3 = 249. So 7.47 ÷ 3 must be 2.49.

- Pupils should complete Questions 2 and 3 in the Practice Book.

Same-day intervention

- Work with two place value sliders.

- Adjust the sliders to show the calculation set out in the column method in Question 2a, 224 ÷ 14, as follows.

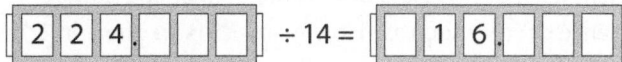

- Adjust the sliders so that they show 22.4 ÷ 14 = 1.6, drawing pupils' attention to the way that changing one slider means the other slider changes by the same factor.

- Together, complete **Resource 6.2.5a** Place value sliders – division, representing division on place value.

Answers: 7, 0.7; 6, 0.6; 107, 1.07; 63, 0.63

Same-day enrichment

- Give pupils **Resource 6.2.5b** Double digits, in which they are asked to investigate the way that digits change when a number is divided by 5.

Questions 4 and 5

> **4** Write the number sentences and then calculate the answers.
> (a) 6 times a number is 128.4. What is the number?
>
> (b) Number A is 2.28. Number A is 12 times Number B. What is the difference between Number A and Number B?
>
> **5** Solve these problems.
> (a) A car travelled from place A to place B in 3.6 hours at a speed of 48 km per hour. When the car travelled back from place B to place A, it took 0.4 more hours. What was the speed of the car on the way back?
>
> (b) A piece of wire can be bent into a rectangle of 1.6 m × 1.2 m. If it is bent into a square, what is the area of the square?

What learning will pupils have achieved at the conclusion of Questions 4 and 5?

- Pupils will have related their new understanding about decimal division to the written method, understanding that adjustments to convert decimals to integers must be reversed at the end of the written procedure to find the solution.
- Pupils will have identified appropriate operations to represent and solve word problems, calculating with decimals and decimal measures.

Activities for whole-class instruction

- Write 30 ÷ 6 = 5 on the board. Tell pupils that this calculation might be described by the story: 'Six people share £30 between them. How much does each person get?' Ask pupils to work in pairs to decide on an alternative story for this calculation.
- Collect some of the stories in and draw together the common ideas.

(i) It is likely that many of the stories will be based on sharing. The concept of sharing is based on repeated subtraction and can be problematic when dividing with decimals. It is important therefore that pupils do not envisage division only as sharing. This has parallels with the way in which repeated addition can be used as an image for multiplication but has limited applications. This is because additive and multiplicative relationships are not the same and so (apart from when first learning about multiplication

and division) pupils should not be encouraged to think additively when working with multiplicative relationships. Alternative images for multiplicative relationships include:

- multiplication as 'scaling' or 'stretching'– think of stretching an elastic band until it is twice as long, or reducing a document on a photocopier
- multiplication as 'rate', for example, 'For every hour worked a person earns £11.50. How much do they earn in an eight-hour day?'

- Write 3.51 ÷ 3 on the board. Ask pupil pairs to decide on a story that this calculation might describe. Share ideas. These could include:
  - 'How many threes are there in 3.51?'
  - 'There are two pieces of wood. The longer piece is 3.51 m long and is three times as long as the short piece. How long is the short piece of wood?'
  - 'An elephant walking at a steady pace travels 3.51 km in 3 hours. How far did it walk in each hour?'
  - 'A pack of 3 pairs of socks costs £3.51. What's the price of one pair of socks?'
- Ask pupils to decide on a new story for 3.51 ÷ 3; one that doesn't include the word 'shared' or 'sharing'.
- Share ideas.

(Look out for) … pupils who do not understand that division is not commutative (that is, 3 ÷ 4 ≠ 4 ÷ 3) and, if the opportunity to raise this misconception does not present itself during class discussion, then offer a number sentence or story such as: 'How many 3.51s are there in 3?' as an option and discuss with pupils why this is not a valid representation for the calculation 3.51 ÷ 3.

- Pupils should complete Questions 4 and 5 in the Practice Book.

Same-day intervention

- Ask pupils to complete **Resource 6.2.5c** Matching the divisions, in which they are able to match situations, calculations and results.

Resource 6.2.5c

Matching the divisions

Cut out the cards and sort them into sets so that each set:
- shows a question
- the calculation needed to work it out
- the answer to the question.

One of the calculations is missing, so you will need to make an extra card.

1.17 ÷ 3	3.51 kg of cherries are put into three bags so that each bag has the same weight of cherries. How much does each bag weigh?	168.3 ÷ 11
15.3	3.51 ÷ 3	0.39
Number A is five times greater than Number B. If Number A is 9.1, what is number B?	9.1 ÷ 5	1.82
1.17	A bottle of water holds 1.17 litres. Three cups of water fill the bottle completely. How much does one cup hold?	11 times a number is 168.3. What is the number?
0.13	An elastic band is stretched so that it is 6 times its original length. The stretched band is 0.78 m long. How long is the band normally?	

© HarperCollinsPublishers 2018

Answer: 0.78 ÷ 6

Same-day enrichment

- Pupils should complete **Resource 6.2.5d** Best buys, in which they are asked to find the cheapest price per litre for orange juice.

Resource 6.2.5d

Best buys

Which of these is the cheapest way to buy 1 litre of orange juice?
Arrange the prices in order, from the cheapest to the most expensive price per litre.

A — One 3-litre bottle for £1.86

B — Buy one 2-litre bottle for £1.68 and get another 2-litre bottle half price

C — One 2-litre bottle for £1.23

D — One 1-litre bottle costs £0.65

E — One 250ml bottle costs £0.30

© HarperCollinsPublishers 2018

Answer: C, A, B, D, E

6   Sam and Alvin went shopping for a class trip. There are 42 pupils in the class and they bought everyone three items: a carton of milk, a can of oat porridge and a muffin. What quantity did they buy of each item? How much did they spend on each item and in total? Fill in the table.

Food	Price	Quantity	Total price
milk	6 cartons in a box; £0.99 per box		
oat porridge	3 cans in a pack; £4.89 per pack		
muffin	£0.36 each		
Total cost (£)			

This question challenges pupils to sort through information to solve multi-stage calculations to reach a solution.

Encourage pupils to use the table to structure their route through the question. It will help them to see the question as a series of smaller problems, making it more manageable. Pupils may find it helpful to use a whiteboard to carry out the calculations needed to find the solution to each step.

Unit 2.6
Division of decimals by whole numbers (2)

Conceptual context

This unit explicitly teaches the column method for dividing a decimal number by a whole number. It is important that pupils do not see this as a 'new' method, but rather understand that it is an extension to their understanding of the column method for dividing a whole number by another whole number.

The images and explanations in this unit echo and build on those used when pupils worked on dividing by two-digit numbers in Unit 3.6 of Year 5.

Learning pupils will have achieved at the end of the unit

- Pupils will be able to use adjustment and reverse-adjustment (learned in the previous unit) to divide a decimal number by a whole number (Q1)
- Pupils will be able to use the column method to divide a decimal number by a whole number (Q2, Q3, Q4, Q5)
- Pupils will be able to construct number sentences to solve word problems (Q4, Q5)

Resources

place value sliders; mini whiteboards; place value counters; **Resource 6.2.6** Division corrections

Vocabulary

dividend, divisor, quotient

Question 1

> **1** Calculate mentally and then write the answers.
>
> (a) $6.9 \div 3 =$ ☐   (b) $8.4 \div 4 =$ ☐
>
> (c) $44.8 \div 7 =$ ☐   (d) $59.4 \div 9 =$ ☐
>
> (e) $4.2 \div 6 =$ ☐   (f) $37 \div 5 =$ ☐
>
> (g) $11.8 \div 2 =$ ☐   (h) $8.68 \div 7 =$ ☐

What learning will pupils have achieved at the conclusion of Question 1?

- Pupils will be able to use adjustment and reverse-adjustment (learned in previous unit) to divide a decimal number by a whole number.

Activities for whole-class instruction

- Use a place value slider to show a whole number. For example, show the following.

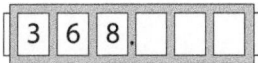

| 3 | 6 | 8 . | | | |

- Ask pupils to divide the number you're showing by 2. Gather their answers and write on the board $368 \div 2 = 184$. On a second slider, write 184.

- Now adjust the first slider to show 36.8.

| 3 | 6 . | 8 | | |

  Ask pupils to divide this number by 2. Gather responses and write on the board $36.8 \div 2 = 18.4$.

- Adjust the second slider showing 184 so that it also shows 18.4. Agree with pupils that, when dividing, whatever is done to the slider showing the dividend, the same must also be done to the slider showing the quotient to maintain the balance.

- Display the following.

| 5 | 3 | 1 . | | | | $\div 3 =$ | | | | | . | | |

| 5 | 3 . | 1 | | | $\div 3 =$ | | | | . | | |

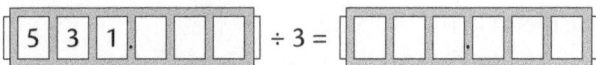

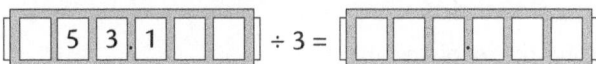

- Pupil pairs should write the missing digits on the sliders.
- Pupils should complete Question 1 in the Practice Book.

Same-day intervention

- Use pairs of sliders to set up and work on the calculations from Question 1 (for example, show the calculation $69 \div 3 =$ and calculate this, recording the quotient on a second slider, then moving the sliders together to calculate the quotient for $6.9 \div 3$).

Same-day enrichment

- Pupils should work in pairs to complete this challenge.

> Billy looks at the calculation
>
> ### $8.19 \div 9$
>
> and says, '$8.19 \div 9$ means "How many 9s are there in 8.19". But 9 is bigger than 8.19 so there are NO 9s in 8.19. The question is impossible!'
> How would you explain to Billy that he is wrong? Write a paragraph for him so that he understands what the calculation means AND is able to get the right answer.

Questions 2 and 3

> **2** Complete the working of the calculation by filling in the blanks.
>
> $$\begin{array}{r} \square \\ 5\overline{)0.95} \end{array} \rightarrow \begin{array}{r} 0 \\ 5\overline{)0.95} \end{array} \rightarrow \begin{array}{r} 0.1\,\square \\ 5\overline{)0.95} \\ \underline{5} \\ 45 \\ \underline{45} \\ 0 \end{array}$$
>
> 4 5 ···· represents 45
> 4 5 times ☐
>
> The whole number part of the dividend is less than the divisor. The ones place of the quotient should be ☐.
>
> The decimal point in the quotient must be aligned with the decimal point in the _____.
>
> The method is the same as the division of whole numbers.

> **3** Use the column method to calculate the answers. (Check the answers to the questions marked with *.)
>
> (a) $6.64 \div 8 =$ (b) $28.95 \div 15 =$ (c) $*1.248 \div 26 =$
>
> (d) $8.64 \div 36 =$ (e) $8.12 \div 7 =$ (f) $*1.11 \div 37 =$

What learning will pupils have achieved at the conclusion of Questions 2 and 3?

- Pupils will be able to use the column method to divide a decimal number by a whole number.

Activities for whole-class instruction

- Write 4215 ÷ 15 = ___ on the board and display the following array.

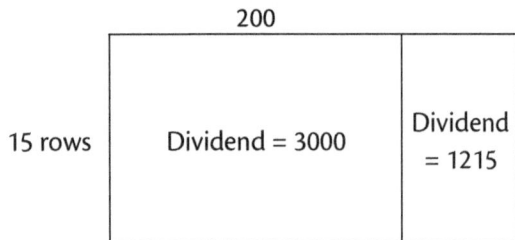

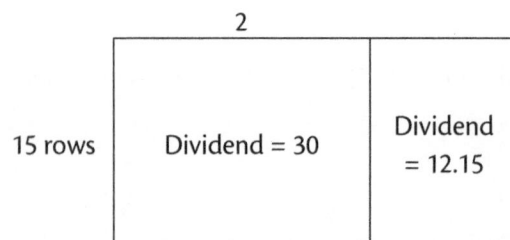

15 rows	Dividend = 4215

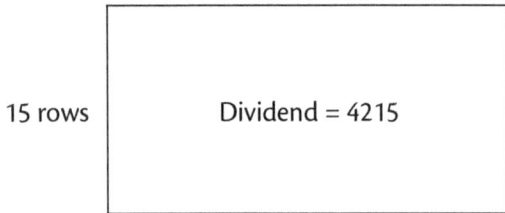

Also, write the calculation using the column method on the board:

```
  1 5 ) 4 2 1 5
```

- Ensure pupils understand that the array represents the calculation, then circle the 42 in the dividend.

  Agree that the quotient must be between 200 and 300 since 15 × 200 = 3000 and 15 × 300 = 4500.

- Display the following array.

```
              200
| 15 rows | Dividend = 3000 | Dividend = 1215 |
```

Agree that the hundreds digit of the quotient is now known to be 2 and record this using the column method.

```
          2
  1 5 ) 4 2 1 5
        3 0 0 0
        1 2 1 5
```

- Circle the 121 and ask: *How many 15s are in 121?* Agree that 15 × 8 = 120 and 15 × 9 = 135.

- Display the following array.

```
           200          80
| 15 rows | Dividend = 3000 | Dividend = 1200 | Dividend = 15 |
```

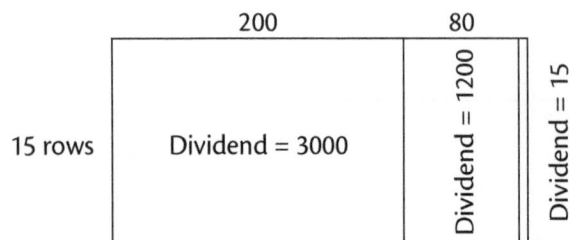

- Agree that the tens digit of the quotient is now known to be 8 and record this using the column method.

```
        2   8
  1 5 ) 4 2 1 5
        3 0 0 0
        1 2 1 5
        1 2 0 0
```

- Agree that the remaining dividend is 15, and that the ones digit of the quotient must be 1.

  Display the array and record this using the column method.

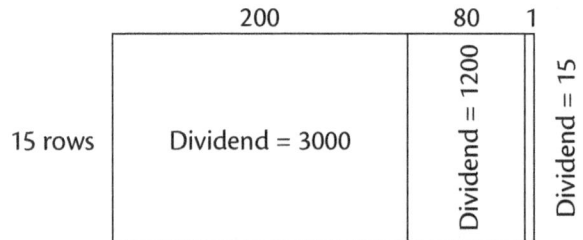

```
         200          80    1
| 15 rows | Dividend = 3000 | Dividend = 1200 | Dividend = 15 |
```

```
        2   8   1
  1 5 ) 4 2 1 5
        3 0 0 0
        1 2 1 5
        1 2 0 0
            1 5
            1 5
```

Complete the original calculation: 4215 ÷ 15 = 281.

- Now write 42.15 ÷ 15 = ___ on the board and display the array.

15 rows	Dividend = 42.15

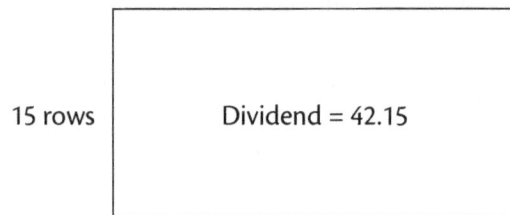

- As with the integer calculation, ensure that pupils understand that the array represents the calculation, then circle the 42 in the dividend.

  Agree that the quotient must be between 2 and 3 since 15 × 2 = 30 and 15 × 3 = 45

- Display the following array.

```
              2
| 15 rows | Dividend = 30 | Dividend = 12.15 |
```

Agree that the ones digit of the quotient is now known to be 2 and record this using the column method.

```
        2 .
1  5 ) 4  2 . 1  5
       3  0
       ‾‾‾‾‾‾‾‾‾‾
       1  2 . 1
```

Circle the 12.1 and agree that it is useful to consider 'How many 15s are in 121?'

Agree that $15 \times 8 = 120$ and $15 \times 9 = 135$ and so $15 \times 0.8 = 12.0$ and $15 \times 0.9 = 13.5$.

Display the array.

	2	0.8	
15 rows	Dividend = 30	Dividend = 12	Dividend = 0.15

Agree that the 0.1s digit of the quotient is now known to be 8 and record this using the column method.

```
        2 . 8
1  5 ) 4  2 . 1  5
       3  0
       ‾‾‾‾‾‾‾‾‾‾
       1  2 . 1
       1  2 . 0
       ‾‾‾‾‾‾‾‾‾‾
          0 . 1  5
```

Agree that the remaining dividend is 0.15, and that the 0.01s digit of the quotient must be 1.

Display the array and record this using the column method.

	2	0.8	0.01
15 rows	Dividend = 3000	Dividend = 12	Dividend = 0.15

```
        2 . 8  1
1  5 ) 4  2 . 1  5
       3  0
       ‾‾‾‾‾‾‾‾‾‾
       1  2 . 1
       1  2 . 0
       ‾‾‾‾‾‾‾‾‾‾
          0 . 1  5
          0 . 1  5
          ‾‾‾‾‾‾‾‾‾
                0
```

Complete the original calculation: $4215 \div 15 = 2.81$.

- Draw pupils' attention to the importance of aligning the decimal points in the dividend and the quotient, then write on the board $43.65 \div 15 =$ ___ . Ask pupils to use the column method to find the quotient.

- Pupils should complete Questions 2 and 3 in the Practice Book.

Same-day intervention

- Work with pupils on the calculation $4215 \div 15$, using place value counters.

- Construct 4215 using the counters and divide it into 15 equal piles (stress that the piles are of equal value), substituting 10 hundreds for 1000 as necessary.

- As you share the counters, use the column method to record your steps.

- Repeat this using 42.15, again recording your steps using the column method.

Same-day enrichment

- Show pupils the calculations on **Resource 6.2.6** Division corrections, and ask them to spot and correct the errors that have been made.

Answers: **1.** 9.57; **2.** 15.8; **3.** 15.7; **4.** 8.6 (correct).

Questions 4 and 5

4 Write the number sentences and then calculate the answers.

(a) 180 times 0.6 is added to the quotient of 62.5 divided by 25. What is the sum?

(b) The difference between 53.8 and 53.26 is divided by 54. What is the quotient?

5 Solve these problems.

(a) An elephant weighs 9.9 tonnes, which is 18 times the weight of a horse. A hippopotamus weighs 3 times as much as a horse. What is the weight of the hippopotamus?

(b) A box of milk has 8 packs and costs £24.80 in total. What is the unit price for one pack of milk? There is a promotion of 'buy 1 box, get 2 packs free' in a supermarket. How much does each pack of milk actually cost? How much cheaper is the promotional price than the original price?

(c) A sugar refinery produced 3.25 tonnes of sugar by using 25 tonnes of sugar cane. How many tonnes of sugar can be produced from every tonne of sugar cane on average? Based on this calculation, how many tonnes of sugar can be produced from 40.5 tonnes of sugar cane?

What learning will pupils have achieved at the conclusion of Questions 4 and 5?

- Pupils will be able to use the column method to divide a decimal number by a whole number.
- Pupils will be able to construct number sentences to solve word problems.

Activities for whole-class instruction

- Display the following.

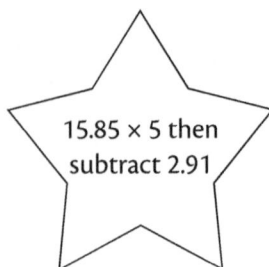

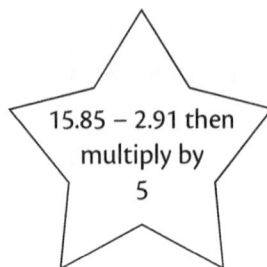

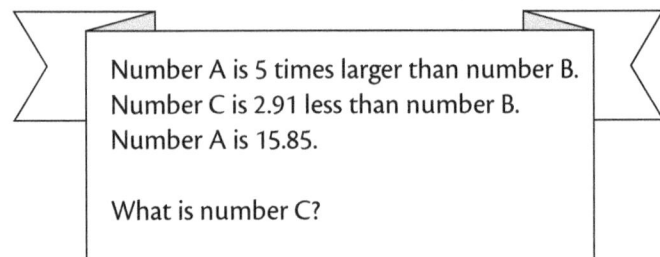

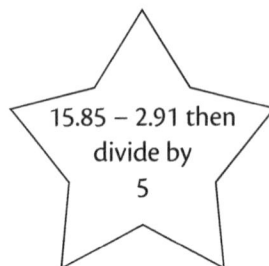

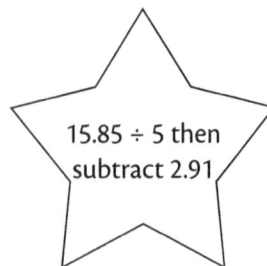

15.85 × 5 then subtract 2.91

15.85 – 2.91 then multiply by 5

Number A is 5 times larger than number B. Number C is 2.91 less than number B. Number A is 15.85.

What is number C?

15.85 – 2.91 then divide by 5

15.85 ÷ 5 then subtract 2.91

Ask pupils to discuss and identify which number sentence fits the word problem in the centre.

- Ask pupils to explain what they looked for when interpreting the word problem.

- **Look out for** … pupils who can calculate accurately but do not fully understand the order of operations. Use images such as tree diagrams or flow charts to support pupils in interpreting the order of operations correctly.

- Now choose a different number sentence from the diagram and ask pupils to write a word problem like the one in the centre for the selected sentence.

- Share some of these word problems and use them to discuss the similarities and differences.

- **Look out for** … pupils who are uncertain about using the column method for dividing a decimal number by a whole number. Use one of the pupils' problems to model the process again if appropriate.

- Pupils should complete Questions 4 and 5 in the Practice Book.

Same-day intervention

- Write on the board: 6 times a number is 43.26. What is the number?

  Discuss how to represent the calculation, and record pupils' ideas. Ensure that an array and a number sentence such as 6 × ___ = 43.26 are two of the representations (others may include bar models and repeated addition).

  Discuss strategies to find the missing number and agree with pupils that division can be used to 'undo' multiplication and find the missing value.

  Use the images and representations that pupils have given to identify the division calculation.

  For example:

  - In an array representation, the dividend is the area of the array and the quotient and divisor are the 2 dimensions.

  - In a multiplication, the reverse of making a value six times larger is to make it one sixth of the size, meaning that the multiplicand becomes the divisor and the product becomes the dividend.

- Now add a context to the calculation, saying that a teacher bought six calculators for her class, costing a total of £43.26. How much does each calculator cost?

  Ask: *Which of the representations fits this situation?* Share ideas and solve.

- Now discuss the problems in Question 4 with pupils and display the following.

  > Some of these calculations are used in Question 4. Use them to help you solve the problems. Which calculations are not used? How many ways can you say those calculations?
  >
  > $$53.8 + 53.26 = 107.06$$
  > $$62.5 \div 25 = 2.5$$
  > $$0.54 \div 54 = 0.01$$
  > $$108 + 2.5 = 110.5$$
  > $$0.6 \times 180 = 108$$
  > $$108 - 2.5 = 105.5$$
  > $$53.8 - 53.26 = 0.54$$

- Work with pupils to identify the calculations that match those in the questions and to find the result.

Same-day enrichment

- Display the following.

  > Close to …
  >
  > ___ ___ . ___ ÷ ___ ___
  >
  > insert the digits 4, 5, 6, 7 and 8 so that the result is as close as you can get to …
  >
  > **a.** 1.5
  >
  > **b.** 2
  >
  > **c.** 0.5

- Challenge pupils to enter the digits to make a calculation as close to 1.5 as they can.

- How close can they get to 2? To 0.5?

Challenge and extension question

Question 6

6 A group of 50 pupils plan to go boating. A 6-seater boat costs £20 while a 4-seater boat costs £15. Propose a few boat renting plans and then complete the following table.

Plan	6-seater boat (No.)	4-seater boat (No.)	Cost (£)
1			
2			
3			
4			

Which renting plan is the cheapest? How much does it cost?

This problem requires pupils to first think about how they can seat 50 pupils in the different boats.

The context means that pupils need to find ways to have at least 50 seats, but some pupils may only consider situations in which exactly 50 seats are taken and will need to be challenged on this. However, practise at representing this sort of real-life situation mathematically is important, so avoid the temptation to intervene too early.

Once pupils have decided on the possible renting plans, the calculations to work out the total cost should be relatively straightforward.

Unit 2.7
Division of decimals by whole numbers (3)

Conceptual context

This unit continues to focus explicitly on the use of the column method for division, but extends the method to consider situations where the dividend is considered as having several decimal places (by adding zeros) to be able to complete the calculation.

Key to this method is the understanding established in Year 4, Practice Book Chapter 6, that extra zeros can be added to the end of a decimal number without affecting the value of that number. When working on this unit, ensure pupils understand that all numbers can be considered decimals, but in whole numbers, all of the decimal digits are zero and so they, and the decimal point, are usually not included.

Learning pupils will have achieved at the end of the unit

- Pupils will be able to use the column method to divide a decimal number by a whole number (Q1, Q2, Q3, Q4)
- Pupils will be able to express dividends with several decimal places (by adding zeros) in order to complete a division calculation (Q1, Q2)
- Pupils will be able to construct number sentences to solve word problems (Q3, Q4)

Resources

mini whiteboards; **Resource 6.2.7a** Same value, different appearance; **Resource 6.2.7b** Extra zeros; **Resource 6.2.7c** Number and word sentences

Vocabulary

dividend, divisor, quotient, product

Questions 1 and 2

1 A 1.5-litre bottle of juice is shared equally between 5 people. How many litres of juice does each person get?

If it is shared equally between 4 people, how many litres does each get?

$1.5 \div 5 = \boxed{}$

$$5 \overline{)1 \,.\, 5}$$

$1.5 \div 4 = \boxed{}$

$$4 \overline{)1 \,.\, 5}$$

2 Choose the column method to calculate the following. (Check the answers to the questions marked with *.)

(a) $7.8 \div 4 =$

(b) *$26.1 \div 6 =$

(c) $5.1 \div 60 =$

(d) $0.9 \div 30 =$

(e) $5.98 \div 52 =$

(f) *$4.2 \div 24 =$

What learning will pupils have achieved at the conclusion of Questions 1 and 2?

- Pupils will be able to use the column method to divide a decimal number by a whole number.
- Pupils will be able to express dividends with several decimal places (by adding zeros) in order to complete a division calculation.

Activities for whole-class instruction

- Show pupils **Resource 6.2.7a** Same value, different appearance. Pupil pairs should connect the numbers that have the same value. Share ideas and agree that zeros can be added at the end of a decimal number without affecting its value.

Resource 6.2.7a

Same value, different appearance

Draw lines to match all of the numbers that have the same value, even though they may look different.

1.900 000   1.90

$\frac{19}{10}$

1.0900   1.9

1.09

10.9

$\frac{19}{100}$

0.19

10.90

1.900

Answers: 1.90, 1.900 000, 1.9, 1.900, $\frac{19}{10}$; 1.0900, 1.09; $\frac{19}{100}$, 0.19

- Display the following.

$1.9 \div 2 = \blacksquare$

$$2 \overline{)1 \,.\, 9}$$

$1.9 \div 5 = \blacksquare$

$$5 \overline{)1 \,.\, 9}$$

Together, fill in the gaps to complete the first calculation. Draw attention to the way in which an additional zero can be added to the end of the dividend without changing its value in order to allow the quotient to be found.

Pupil pairs should complete the second calculation.

- Pupils should complete Questions 1 and 2 in the Practice Book.

Same-day intervention

- Work with pupils on **Resource 6.2.7b** Extra zeros, which gives them more frames to complete by adding extra zeros.

Answers: **1.** 0.475; **2.** 0.55; **3.** 0.575; **4.** 0.625

Same-day enrichment

- Display the following.

  Try placing different digits in the gap.

  $$4\overline{)1.\blacksquare\,7}$$

  What happens if you use an even digit in the gap?
  What happens if you use an odd digit in the gap?
  Can you explain why?

- Pupils should notice that even digits always result in 75 as the final digits, while completing the gap with an odd digit gives 25.

Questions 3 and 4

3 Write the number sentences and then calculate the answers.

(a) The product of 7.2 and 18 is divided by 4. What is the quotient?

(b) The quotient of 1.04 divided by 26 is subtracted from the sum of eight hundred 0.0125s. What is the difference?

4 Solve these problems.

(a) A clothes shop has made 40 sets of clothes of the same size with 100 metres of cloth. How many metres of cloth were used for one set of clothes?

(b) A 0.24 m long wire is used to form a square. How long is the side of the square? What is the perimeter of the square?

(c) One box of Danish cookies weighs 500 g and costs £2.88, while one box of Continental cookies weighs 800 g and costs £3.88. Which type of cookie is the best value?

What learning will pupils have achieved at the conclusion of Questions 3 and 4?

- Pupils will be able to use the column method to divide a decimal number by a whole number.
- Pupils will be able to construct number sentences to solve word problems.

Activities for whole-class instruction

- Display the following.

  The sum of 1.4 and 3.2 is divided by 5. What is the quotient?

  The product of 1.4 and 3.2 is divided by 5. What is the quotient?

  Ask pupils to discuss, without calculating, which of these will give the largest quotient, and to explain why. Ensure that they use correct mathematical language for both the numbers and the operations involved.

- Change 1.4 to 0.4, display:

  The sum of 0.4 and 3.2 is divided by 5. What is the quotient?

  The product of 0.4 and 3.2 is divided by 5. What is the quotient?

Ask: *What has changed? Which of the quotients is larger? Why?*

Share ideas. Emphasise the need to read the question carefully and pause to consider the best route through the problem, before starting to calculate.

- Pupils should complete Questions 3 and 4 in the Practice Book.

Same-day intervention

- Use the matching cards on **Resource 6.2.7c** Number and word sentences, to work with pupils on interpreting word problems and writing them as number sentences.

Resource 6.2.7c

Number and word sentences

Match these cards first.		Then add these cards to the matched pairs.
Find the **product** of the **quotient** of 2.1 and 6 and the sum of 0.7 and 1.3.	Find the **quotient** of the sum of 2.1 and 6 and the sum of 0.7 and 1.3.	2.35
(2.1 ÷ 6) × (0.7 + 1.3)	(2.1 × 6) ÷ (0.7 + 1.3)	6.3
(2.1 ÷ 6) ÷ (0.7 + 1.3)	(2.1 + 6) ÷ (0.7 + 1.3)	0.7
Find the **quotient** of the **product** of 2.1 and 6 and the sum of 0.7 and 1.3.	Find the **sum** of the **quotient** of 2.1 and 6 and the sum of 0.7 and 1.3.	4.05

© HarperCollinsPublishers 2018

- Once pupils have completed the matching task, give them the extra cards with the results and ask them to first estimate, then calculate which of the cards solve which problem.

Same-day enrichment

- Display the following.

> **Quotient, product, difference, sum …**
> Look at the sentence.
> Find the __ of the __ of 6.73 and 5, and the __ of 3 and 1.
> Fill in the gaps with words from this list:
> quotient
> product
> difference
> sum

- Pupils should use each word only once. Their aim is to make the problem with the largest possible result.

- Following this, challenge them to use the same word in every gap. Ask them to predict first which word will give the largest result. Pupils should calculate to check their prediction.

Challenge and extension questions

Question 5

> 5 A supermarket is selling t-shirts in two different-sized packs: (a) a pack of 5 t-shirts is £19, and (b) a pack of 8 t-shirts is £28. What is the maximum number of t-shirts a customer can buy with £122?

Pupils should understand that the key to buying the most t-shirts is to find whether the 5 pack or the 8 pack of shirts is cheaper per t-shirt. Once they have established this, they can work on maximising the number of these (the 8 packs), filling in any gaps with the remaining size of pack.

As with Questions 3 and 4, encourage pupils to think carefully about which strategies are likely to be efficient before starting the problem.

Question 6

> 6 During the holidays, many supermarkets offer promotions. Ms Durrani bought four 2-litre bottles of olive oil at £5.45 per bottle. Ms Smith also bought four 2-litre bottles of the same olive oil at £6.12 per bottle, but with a promotion to 'buy three, get one free'. Who had a better deal? How many methods can you find to make the comparison?

Key to this problem is pupils' understanding of using either the 'price per bottle' or the 'volume per pound' (or equivalent units) as a way to compare. Pupils may be familiar with one of these but need prompting to consider the other methods of comparison.

Unit 2.8
Division of decimals by whole numbers (4)

Conceptual context

Pupils' knowledge about division with decimals is expanded in this unit, as they divide two whole numbers to give a decimal quotient. It is not necessarily obvious to pupils that, when calculating with integers, decimals can result.

Pupils will apply what they learned in the previous unit about adding zeros.

Learning pupils will have achieved at the end of the unit

- Pupils will be able to use known facts and their recent learning about adjustment and reverse-adjustment to solve problems without using a written method (Q1)
- Pupils will understand that dividing a whole number by a whole number can result in a decimal quotient (Q2, Q3)
- Pupils will be able to use the column method to calculate decimal quotients, adding extra zeros after the decimal point where necessary (Q2, Q3, Q4, Q5)
- Pupils will be able to construct number sentences to solve word problems (Q4, Q5)
- Pupils will understand that multiplication can be thought of as scaling a value (Q5)

Resources

place value sliders; piece of elastic at least 1 m long; mini whiteboards; **Resource 6.2.8a** Place value sliders – decimal division; **Resource 6.2.8b** Changing divisors; **Resource 6.2.8c** How many times more?

Vocabulary

whole number, quotient, dividend, divisor, multiplicand, multiplier, stretch

Question 1

> **1** Use the fact that **54 ÷ 24 = 2.25** to write the quotients of these division calculations.
>
> (a) 0.54 ÷ 24 = ☐   (b) 5400 ÷ 24 = ☐
>
> (c) 540 ÷ 24 = ☐   (d) 5.4 ÷ 24 = ☐
>
> (e) 0.0054 ÷ 24 = ☐   (f) 0.054 ÷ 24 = ☐

What learning will pupils have achieved at the conclusion of Question 1?

- Pupils will be able to use known facts and their recent learning about adjustment and reverse-adjustment to solve problems without using a written method.

Activities for whole-class instruction

- Display the following diagram on half of the board, leaving space for a second diagram.

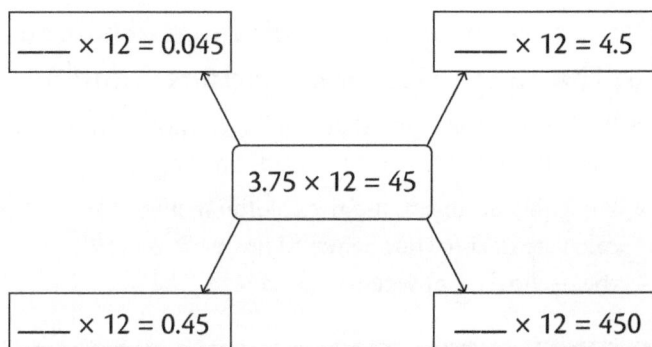

___ × 12 = 0.045   ___ × 12 = 4.5

3.75 × 12 = 45

___ × 12 = 0.45   ___ × 12 = 450

In pairs, pupils should find the missing numbers and explain how they found them.

Share ideas, emphasising the way that moving digits around the decimal point in only the multiplier, while keeping the multiplicand constant, affects the position of the digits in the product. (Ensure pupils understand that the digits move because the number has been multiplied or divided by 10, 100, 1000, …)

- Display the following on the board.

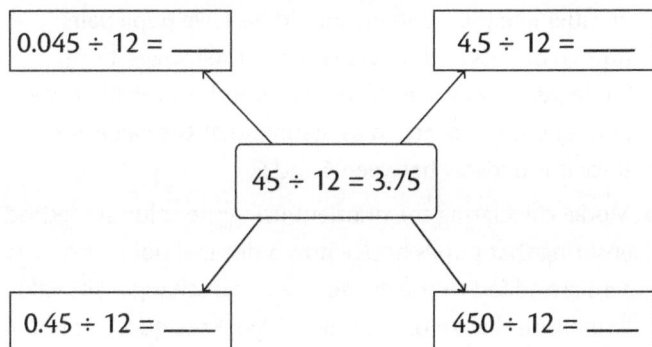

0.045 ÷ 12 = ___   4.5 ÷ 12 = ___

45 ÷ 12 = 3.75

0.45 ÷ 12 = ___   450 ÷ 12 = ___

Pupil pairs should fill in the gaps without using a written method, and explain their reasoning.

- Draw pupils' attention to the similarities with the multiplication diagram, then add extra sections to the division diagram, such as 0.0045 ÷ 12 = ___ and 4500 ÷ 12 = ___ .

Pupil pairs should write down the missing values.

- Draw pupils' attention to the way in which changing only the dividend, while keeping the divisor constant, affects the quotient.

All say … *Moving digits a number of places in relation to the decimal point in the dividend means that digits in the quotient move the same number of places.*

- Pupils should complete Question 1 in the Practice Book

Same-day intervention

- Use two place value sliders for this task.
- Set up a division calculation that pupils are comfortable with, using one of the sliders as the dividend and the other as the quotient. For example, show 56 ÷ 7 = 8 with 56 on one slider and 8 on the other.

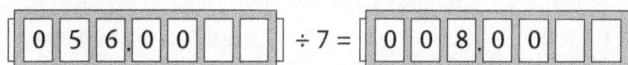

0 5 6.0 0 ÷ 7 = 0 0 8.0 0

- Now move the slider showing the dividend, and show that the quotient must also move by the same amount.

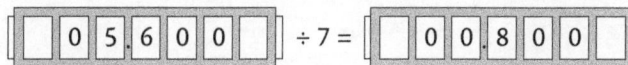

0 5.6 0 0 ÷ 7 = 0 0.8 0 0

- Remind pupils that digits move because the number has been multiplied or divided by 10, 100, 1000, …
- Provide pupils with **Resource 6.2.8a** Place value sliders – decimal division, for pupils to use to work out quotients.

Resource 6.2.8a

Place value sliders – decimal division

The top slider shows that 47 ÷ 5 = 9.4.
Use this to complete the other calculations.

| 4 | 7 | | | | | ÷ 5 = | | 9 | 4 | | | |

| 4 | 7 | 0 | | | | ÷ 5 = | | | | | | |

| | 0 | 4 | 7 | | | ÷ 5 = | | | | | | |

| | 0 | 0 | 4 | 7 | | ÷ 5 = | | | | | | |

The top slider shows that 29 ÷ 4 = 7.25.
Use this to complete the other calculations.

| 2 | 9 | | | | | ÷ 4 = | | 7 | 2 | 5 | | |

| | 2 | 9 | | | | ÷ 4 = | | | | | | |

| 2 | 9 | 0 | | | | ÷ 4 = | | | | | | |

| | 0 | 2 | 9 | | | ÷ 4 = | | | | | | |

© HarperCollinsPublishers 2018

Answers: 94, 0.094, 0.0094; 0.725, 72.5, 0.0725

Same-day enrichment

- Give pupils **Resource 6.2.8b** Changing divisors, in which the digits of the divisor are moved in relation to the decimal point and pupils are asked to explain the effect of this on the quotient.

Resource 6.2.8b

Changing divisors

Based on 54 ÷ 24 = 2.25, directly write the quotients of the divisions below.

54 ÷ 0.24 = _____   54 ÷ 2400 = _____   54 ÷ 240 = _____

54 ÷ 2.4 = _____   54 ÷ 0.0024 = _____   54 ÷ 0.024 = _____

Explain why these answers follow a different pattern to those in Question 1 in the Practice Book.

_____

© HarperCollinsPublishers 2018

Answers: 54 ÷ 0.24 = 225; 54 ÷ 2.4 = 22.5;
54 ÷ 2400 = 0.0225; 54 ÷ 0.0024 = 22 500;
54 ÷ 240 = 0.225; 54 ÷ 0.024 = 2250.

Questions 2 and 3

2 Complete the working.

(a)
```
        6
   4 ) 2 7
       2 4
       ____
         3 0
```

(b)
```
        0 .
   8 ) 6 . 0
```

3 Use the column method to calculate the answers.

(a) 36 ÷ 90 =

(b) 8 ÷ 32 =

(c) 10 ÷ 125 =

(d) 27 ÷ 72 =

(e) 1 ÷ 16 =

(f) 34 ÷ 8 =

What learning will pupils have achieved at the conclusion of Questions 2 and 3?

- Pupils will understand that dividing a whole number by a whole number can result in a decimal quotient.
- Pupils will be able to use the column method to calculate decimal quotients, adding extra zeros after the decimal point where necessary.

Activities for whole-class instruction

- Display a 0–10 number line on the board. Write 24 ÷ 4 = ____ and ask pupils where on the number line this quotient should be. Agree that it has the same value as 6 and mark it accordingly.

  Write on the board 24 ÷ 6 = ____ and ask pupils where on the number line this quotient should be. Agree that it has the same value as 4 and mark it accordingly.

  Now write 24 ÷ 5 = ____ and ask pupils where on the number line the quotient should be. Give pupil pairs time to discuss and record some of their suggestions. Some pupils may use informal methods to calculate the quotient as 4.8, others may assume that the value is 5 since it is midway between 4 and 6.

- Model calculating the quotient using the column method, ensuring that pupils notice how a decimal point and extra zero are added to the dividend without changing its value. Emphasise that zeros are only added if the quotient is not yet resolved.

- Draw pupils' attention to the fact that both the dividend and divisor are whole numbers, but the quotient is a decimal number.
- Ask pupil pairs to now calculate $34 \div 5$ and $54 \div 5$, using the same method. Share ideas and discuss challenges. Ensure that pupils have used place value correctly when working on $54.5 \div 5$.
- Pupils should complete Questions 2 and 3 in the Practice Book.

Same-day intervention

- Display the following calculations on the board.

$36 \div 8 =$

8) 3 6 . 0

$37 \div 8 =$

8) 3 7 . 0 0 0

$38 \div 8 =$

8) 3 8 . 0 0

$39 \div 8 =$

8) 3 9 . 0 0 0

- Together, find the quotients. Ask: *Without the added zeros, what would have happened?* Agree that adding the zeros makes it possible to complete the calculation without changing the value of the dividend.

Same-day enrichment

- Working in pairs, ask pupils to:
  - use the column method to calculate $2 \div 11$ (the value is 0.181 818…)
  - predict what the value for $3 \div 11$ might be
  - test their prediction
  - make and test a prediction about the decimal part of the quotient where the divisor is 11.

Questions 4 and 5

4 Write the number sentences and then calculate the answers.
(a) How many times 26 is 65?

(b) The product of 3 and 0.5 is divided by 12. What is the quotient?

5 Solve these problems.
(a) The weight of an elephant is 4.5 tonnes, which is 90 times as much as an ostrich. What is the weight of an ostrich?

(b) The height of the skyscraper at 30 St Mary Axe in London, also known as the Gherkin, is 180 m. The height of the Shard is 306 m. How many times the height of the Gherkin is that of the Shard?

(c) Ayesha bought 9 exercise books and Mary bought 5 exercise books, each at the same price. Mary spent £31.80 less than Ayesha. How much did each exercise book cost? How much did they spend in total?

What learning will pupils have achieved at the conclusion of Questions 4 and 5?

- Pupils will be able to construct number sentences to solve word problems.
- Pupils will understand that multiplication can be thought of as scaling a value.
- Pupils will be able to use the column method to calculate decimal quotients, adding extra zeros after the decimal point where necessary.

Activities for whole-class instruction

- Use a 1 m length of elastic and mark it, unstretched, in ten equal intervals. Hold it up to the board and label one end 0 and the other 10.

  Hold the '0' end firmly against the board. Ask a pupil to hold the '10' end and stretch the elastic until the mark that was on the 2 has moved to the 3.

- Working in pairs, ask pupils to discuss these questions.
  - *If the end of the elastic was previously on 10, where is it now?*

– *What number does the mark that was on the 4 now align with?*

– *What number does the mark that was on the 5 now align with?*

– *How many times longer is the elastic now than it was originally? How do you know?*

Share ideas, stress the language of 'how many times' (longer) and agree that the elastic is now 1.5 (or $1\frac{1}{2}$) times longer than the original.

- Return the elastic to its original length, then stretch it so that the mark that was originally on the 4 is now on the 5.

  Pupil pairs should discuss how many times longer the elastic is now than it was originally. Ask: *How do you know?*

  Share ideas. Agree that the elastic is now 1.25 (or $1\frac{1}{4}$) times longer than the original.

- Tell pupils that, when we say that an object is 1.25 times larger, longer or heavier than another object, then 1.25 is the multiplier. Agree that this can be found by dividing the new length by the original.

- Reflect on when the elastic was stretched so that 2 moved on to 3 and use the column method to show that $3 \div 2 = 1.5$. Repeat this for the situation where 4 moved on to 5 to show that $5 \div 4 = 1.25$.

- Tell pupils that you will stretch the elastic so that 5 moves on to 9 and ask pupil pairs to discuss:

  – *How many times longer will the elastic be?*

  – *What number will the end of the elastic be on?*

  Share ideas then test predictions.

- Pupils should complete Questions 4 and 5 in the Practice Book.

Same-day intervention

- Give pupils **Resource 6.2.8c** How many times more? and work with them to decide whether the quantities given are 2 times greater, 2.3 times greater or 2.5 times greater than the originals.

Same-day enrichment

- Display the following on the board.

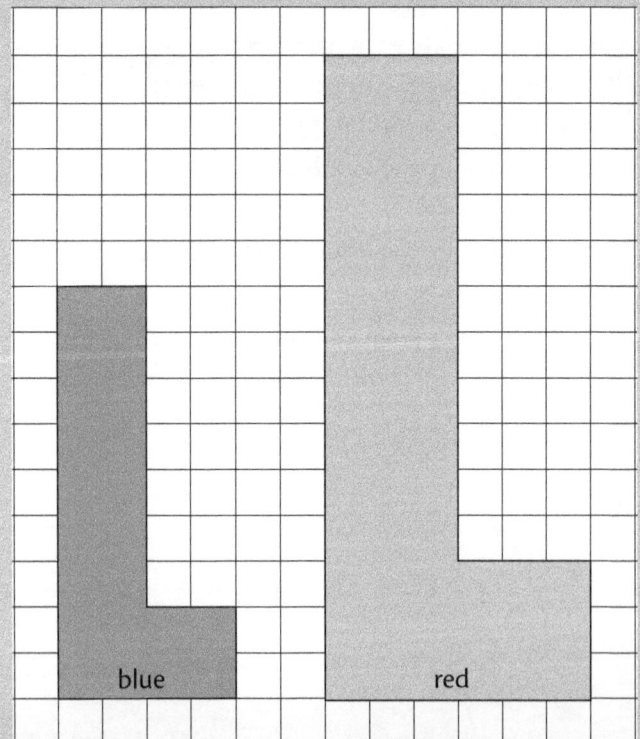

- Ask: *Is the red L shape an exact, but larger, copy of the blue L shape? How do you know?*

● Pupils should justify their reasoning. They should notice that the multiplier for the height is different to the multiplier for the width and so the red shape is not an exact, larger copy.

Challenge and extension questions

Question 6

> 6 A store had a promotion for a brand of soft drink, 'buy three 2-litre bottles and get two 650-millilitre bottles free'. Jamal bought six 2-litre bottles of the soft drink. How many millilitres of the soft drink in total should he get?

The main challenge in this question is in identifying the calculations necessary to solve it. Pupils should know that there are 1000 ml in 1 l, and so the two free 650 ml bottles per three large bottles give a total of 1.3 l free.

Question 7

> 7 150 pupils from Year 6 went on a school trip to a Science and Technology Centre. The admission ticket was £3 per person plus £0.25 for insurance per person. Three coaches were hired at the cost of £144 each. What was the cost of the visit for each pupil?

There are many different routes that pupils may take to reach an answer to this question.

An inefficient approach is to multiply the £3 entry and £0.25 insurance by 150, then add on the three buses at £144 each, before dividing by 150.

Look out for pupils who are able to simplify this problem, noticing that the cost of £144 per coach means that 2 coaches will take 100 pupils, giving a simple calculation of £288 for 100 pupils.

Adding this £2.88 cost per pupil to the £3 and £0.25 gives a more elegant route through the problem.

Unit 2.9
Calculation with calculators

Conceptual context

In this unit, pupils use calculators to calculate quotients and products.

A focus for the unit is that pupils use calculators to identify a pattern, then use this pattern to make predictions which may be checked using a calculator. It is important for pupils to realise that the calculator is a tool for them to use, but that they need to be aware and mindful of the results of the calculation. In this unit, the answer to an individual calculation is less relevant than the pattern that it reveals.

Learning pupils will have achieved at the end of the unit

- Pupils will be able to use a calculator efficiently (Q1)
- Pupils will be able to use a calculator efficiently and understand its limitations (Q2, Q3, Q4)
- Pupils will be able to multiply and divide decimal and whole numbers using the column method (Q1)
- Pupils will be able to identify patterns and make conjectures (Q2, Q3)
- Pupils will be able to construct number sentences to solve word problems (Q4)

Resources

calculators; mini whiteboards; **Resource 6.2.9a** Calculator maze; **Resource 6.2.9b** Dividing by 37; **Resource 6.2.9c** 9s and 9s and 9s ...

Vocabulary

divisor, dividend, quotient, multiplier, multiplicand, product, predict

Question 1

> **1** Use the column method to calculate the following, then check the answers
> with a calculator.
>
> (a) 4.38 × 65 =
>
> (b) 0.978 × 36 =
>
> (c) 96.32 × 16 =
>
> (d) 934.72 ÷ 25 =
>
> (e) 298.15 ÷ 67 =
>
> (f) 443.7 ÷ 15 =

What learning will pupils have achieved at the conclusion of Question 1?

- Pupils will be able to use a calculator efficiently.
- Pupils will be able to multiply and divide decimal and whole numbers using the column method.

Activities for whole-class instruction

- Give some pupils calculators. Tell pupils that you're going to do a short multiplication and division quiz and that those pupils with calculators **must** use them for every calculation.

  Ask pupils multiplication questions that are easier to carry out mentally than on a calculator, for example 3 × 5, 7 × 8, 70 ÷ 10, …

  Can pupils see that using a calculator is slower than those calculating mentally? Agree that calculators do not always make calculating faster.

- Tell pupils that, in Question 1, they will use the column method and then check answers with a calculator. Ask: *If the column method answer and the calculator answer do not agree, how can you check which is correct?* Agree that checking the calculator answer is likely to be quickest so they should do that first – they might have pressed the wrong buttons at the first attempt.

- Pupils should complete Question 1 in the Practice Book.

Same-day intervention

- Use **Resource 6.2.9a** Calculator maze, to work with pupils to identify the correct order to enter digits into the calculator and then evaluate each calculation.

Answers: **1.** 2.73; **2.** 1.18; **3.** 99; **4.** 60; **5.** 98.7; **6.** 1.4

Same-day enrichment

- Give pupils **Resource 6.2.9b** Dividing by 37, which provides practice with using a calculator to test a conjecture.

Questions 2, 3 and 4

2 Use a calculator to work out questions (b)–(d). Use reasoning to find the answers to questions (e) and (f).

(a) 6 × 6 = ☐

(b) 66 × 66 = ☐

(c) 666 × 666 = ☐

(d) 6666 × 6666 = ☐

(e) 66 666 × 66 666 = ☐

(f) 666 666 × 666 666 = ☐

3 Use a calculator to answer the first four questions below. Explore the pattern and then write the answers to the remaining questions. The first one has been done for you.

> Note: We use 0.1̇ to represent 0.11111 ..., in which 1 is repeated forever after the decimal point. A decimal number in which a digit or a sequence of digits in the decimal part repeats forever is called a **recurring decimal**.

(a) 1 ÷ 9 = 0.1̇   (b) 2 ÷ 9 = ☐

(c) 3 ÷ 9 = ☐   (d) 4 ÷ 9 = ☐

(e) 5 ÷ 9 = ☐   (f) 6 ÷ 9 = ☐

(g) 7 ÷ 9 = ☐   (h) 8 ÷ 9 = ☐

4 Solve these problems.

(a) A spaceship flew in a circular orbit. One round of the circular orbit is about 42 371 km long. It took the spaceship 90 minutes to fly once round the orbit. How many kilometres did the spaceship fly per second? (Use a calculator.)

(b) According to available statistics, an untightened tap leaks about 0.018 tonnes of water in a day.

(i) Based on the statistics, how much water is wasted in one year (take one year as 365 days) from an untightened tap?

(ii) If that amount of water is poured into drinking water tanks, each with a capacity of about 19 kg of water, about how many tanks can it fill up?

(iii) Suppose that every household uses 3 tanks of water each month. For how many months can the amount of water be used? About how many years is this equivalent to?

What learning will pupils have achieved at the conclusion of Questions 2, 3 and 4?

- Pupils will be able to use a calculator efficiently and understand its limitations.
- Pupils will be able to identify patterns and make conjectures.
- Pupils will be able to construct number sentences to solve word problems.

Activities for whole-class instruction

- Write these calculations on the board:

37 × 3 = 111

37 × 6 = 222

37 × 9 = 333

…?

Ask: *What calculation will come next in the pattern? What will the product be?*

Agree that the next calculation is 37 × 12 = 444. Draw pupils' attention to the way that the multiplicand is increasing by 3 each time.

- Display the following:

37 × 3 = 111
37 × 6 = 222
37 × 9 = 333
37 × 12 = 444
37 × 15 = 555
37 × 18 = 666
37 × 21 = 777
37 × 24 = 888
37 × 27 = …?
37 × 30 = …?
37 × 33 = …?
37 × 36 = …?

Working in pairs, pupils should complete the missing values, without calculating. Share ideas. Check with calculators.

Point out that the next two questions in the Practice Book are about using calculators to explore number patterns, and using the patterns to make predictions.

- Ask pupils to use calculators to calculate 21 ÷ 37.

Write on the board the result that their calculator shows and discuss whether this is an exact value for the quotient. Agree with pupils that the calculator only shows the first few digits, but that we can see how the pattern repeats.

- Ask pupils to use calculators to calculate 24 ÷ 37 and again, discuss the result and the way that it is presented.

Tell pupils that numbers in which the decimal part is repeated forever, are called 'recurring decimals'.

21 ÷ 37 = 0.5̇67̇ = 0.567 567 567…

24 ÷ 37 = 0.6̇48̇ = 0.648 648 648…

- Pupils should complete Questions 2, 3 and 4 in the Practice Book.

Same-day intervention

- Use **Resource 6.2.9c** 9s and 9s and 9s … to work with pupils as they use calculators to explore the number patterns.

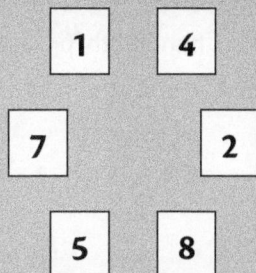

- Encourage pupils to make suggestions about what they think is a likely result, before testing their ideas using a calculator.

Same-day enrichment

- Display the following on the board:

1	4
7	2
5	8

- Ask pupils to calculate 1 ÷ 7, 2 ÷ 7, 3 ÷ 7, … and to pay attention to the digits in their answer.
- What do they notice? Can they predict the decimal part of 4 ÷ 7? 5 ÷ 7?
- Without calculating, can they predict the decimal part of 43 ÷ 7?

Challenge and extension question

Question 5

5 Use a calculator to find the answers to the first four questions below. Find the pattern and then write the answers to the remaining questions.

(a) 12 345 679 × 1 × 9 =
(b) 12 345 679 × 2 × 9 =
(c) 12 345 679 × 3 × 9 =
(d) 12 345 679 × 4 × 9 =
(e) 12 345 679 × 5 × 9 =
(f) 12 345 679 × 6 × 9 =
(g) 12 345 679 × 7 × 9 =
(h) 12 345 679 × 8 × 9 =
(i) 12 345 679 × 9 × 9 =

This question gives pupils an opportunity to explore a number pattern using a calculator. Pupils should use a calculator only to get an idea of the pattern, then they should make predictions and use a calculator to test them.

Ensure that pupils notice that the multiplier includes all of the digits from 1 to 9, apart from the digit 8.

Unit 2.10
Approximation of products and quotients

Conceptual context

In this unit, pupils will revisit rounding to tenths and hundredths, and deepen their understanding by incorporating knowledge of multiplication and division with decimal numbers.

As before, avoid using vocabulary such as 'round up' and 'round down' as pupils may interpret this as meaning that, for example, since 5.6 rounded up to the nearest whole number is 6 then 5.6 rounded down to the nearest whole number is 4.

Learning pupils will have achieved at the end of the unit

- Pupils will be able to round decimals to the nearest whole number, tenth and hundredth (Q1, Q2, Q3)
- Pupils will be able to calculate products and quotients using decimal numbers (Q2, Q3)

Resources

calculators; **Resource 6.2.10a** Rounding diagrams; **Resource 6.2.10b** Rounding results; **Resource 6.2.10c** Swapping digits

Vocabulary

round, nearest, tenths, hundredth, product, quotient

Question 1

1	Round each decimal number...		
	... to the nearest one	... to the nearest tenth	... to the nearest hundredth
3.409			
16.032			
5.697			
29.993			

What learning will pupils have achieved at the conclusion of Question 1?

- Pupils will be able to round decimals to the nearest whole number, tenth and hundredth.

Activities for whole-class instruction

- Display the following diagram on the board.

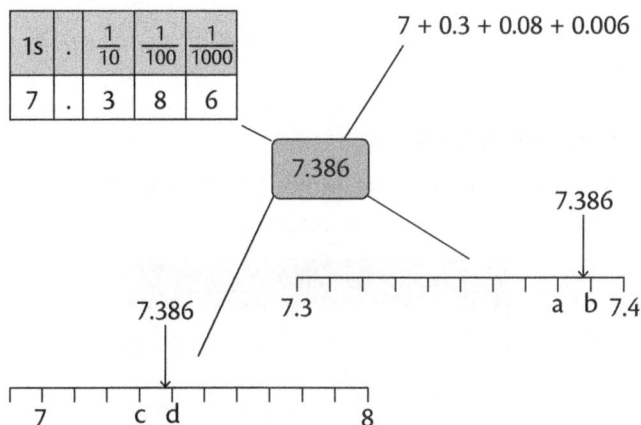

1s	.	$\frac{1}{10}$	$\frac{1}{100}$	$\frac{1}{1000}$
7	.	3	8	6

7 + 0.3 + 0.08 + 0.006

7.386

7.386

7.386   7.3   a b 7.4

7.386

7   c d   8

Discuss the different representations of the decimal numbers shown in the diagram.

- Ask pupil pairs: *What is the same and what is different about the two number line images?*

- Can pupils identify values at a, b, c and d? Agree 7.38 and 7.39, 7.3 and 7.4. Discuss whether the arrow in the first number line image is closer to 7.38 or 7.39, and agree that it is closer to 7.39.

  All say... *7.386 rounded to the nearest hundredth is 7.39.*

- Look at the place value table and the addition calculation and discuss how these could be used to identify that 7.386 is between 7.38 and 7.39, but is closer to 7.39.

  Repeat with the second number line image, considering whether 7.386 is nearer to 7.3 or 7.4.

  All say... *7.386 rounded to the nearest tenth is 3.4.*

- Ask: *Which whole number is 7.386 nearest to? How do you know?* Share ideas.

- Pupils should write 5.827 on their whiteboards and create a spider diagram. Ask pupils to round 5.827 to the nearest hundredth, tenth and whole number. Share ideas.

- Pupils should complete Question 1 in the Practice Book.

Same-day intervention

- Show pupils **Resource 6.2.10a** Rounding diagrams, which includes an extract from Unit 6.1.4.

- Work with pupils to complete the extract, connecting the instructions to the diagrams on the resource sheet.

Resource 6.2.10a

Rounding diagrams

Answers: **1.** less, 5.5, 1, 10.26 ; **2.** and **3.** Accept either diagram as long as pupils can explain their methodology. **4.** Question 3, Diagram B because 5.06 can be located on the number line.

Same-day enrichment

- Display the following.

5.99 rounded to the nearest whole number is 6.0.	5.99 rounded to the nearest whole number is 6.
Pedro	Nellie

- Pupils should decide who they agree with and write a paragraph explaining their reasoning.

Questions 2 and 3

2 Use the column method to calculate the answers.

(a) 7.54 × 48
(Round to the nearest one.)

(b) 0.345 × 81
(Round to the nearest hundredth.)

(c) 63.4 ÷ 25
(Round to the nearest tenth.)

(d) 25.11 ÷ 62
(Round to the nearest hundredth.)

3 Solve these problems.

(a) Mary wanted to buy some fruit for a canteen. The price of apples was £1.65 per kg. She bought 18.5 kg of apples. How much did she pay?

(b) The capacity of an oil bottle is 3 litres. There are 39.75 litres of oil. How many oil bottles are needed?

(c) The table shows the exchange rates on one day in March 2018. Use these exchange rates to solve the following questions. You may use a calculator to work out the calculation.

	GBP (£)
US $1	0.6289
Euro €1	0.8372
Chinese Yuan (CNY, ¥1)	0.0996

(i) On a day in March 2018, Anne's aunt sent her a book from the United States. The price of the book was US $12. What was the price in GBP £?

(ii) Anne's mother exchanged 980 Euros to GBP £. How many British pounds did she get?

(iii) How much would 9995 CNY be when exchanged for GBP £?

What learning will pupils have achieved at the conclusion of Questions 2 and 3?

- Pupils will be able to round decimals to the nearest whole number, tenth and hundredth.
- Pupils will be able to calculate products and quotients using decimals.

Activities for whole-class instruction

- Write these calculations on the board:

0.31 × 52

0.32 × 51

Draw attention to the way that the two digits in the tenths place have swapped in the two calculations.

Ask pupils to predict, without calculating:

- whether the answer to the two calculations will be the same or different when it is rounded to the nearest tenth

- whether it will be the same when rounded to the nearest whole number.

- Ask pupil pairs to carry out the calculations, using the column method to check their predictions. Share ideas.

- Repeat for 0.32 × 53 and 0.33 × 52.

- Pupils should complete Questions 2 and 3 in the Practice Book.

Same-day intervention

- Work with pupils on **Resource 6.2.10b** Rounding results, as they round the result of calculations.

Resource 6.2.10b

Rounding results

1. 0.37 × 38 = 14.06
   Round to the nearest tenth.
   Fill in the spaces with the answer.
   __ __ . __ | __ (Look at the digit after the line. How does that help you to round?)
   Write 14.06 to the nearest tenth here.
   __ __ . __

2. 2.34 × 1.07 = 2.5038
   Round to the nearest hundredth.
   Fill in the spaces with the answer.
   __ . __ __ | __ __
   Write 2.5038 to the nearest hundredth here.
   __ . __ __

3. 46.48 ÷ 35 = 1.328
   Round to the nearest hundredth.
   Fill in the spaces with the answer.
   __ . __ __ | __
   Write 1.328 to the nearest hundredth here.
   __ . __ __

4. 145.05 ÷ 25 = 5.802
   Round to the nearest hundredth.
   Fill in the spaces with the answer.
   __ . __ __ | __
   Write 5.802 to the nearest hundredth here.
   __ . __ __

5. 16.5 ÷ 6 = 2.75
   Round to the nearest tenth.
   Fill in the spaces with the answer.
   __ . __ | __
   Write 2.75 to the nearest tenth here.
   __ . __

© HarperCollinsPublishers 2018

Answers: **1.** 14.1; **2.** 2.50; **3.** 1.33; **4.** 5.80; **5.** 2.8

Same-day enrichment

- Draw pupils' attention to the way that the answers calculated with the whole class both differ by 0.2.
- Provide pupil pairs with **Resource 6.2.10c** Swapping digits, in which pupils are asked to explore this further.

Resource 6.2.10c

Swapping digits

You have already calculated:
$0.31 \times 52 = 16.12$
$0.32 \times 51 = 16.32$

and

$0.32 \times 53 = 16.96$
$0.33 \times 52 = 17.16$

In both pairs of calculations, swapping the two decimal parts of the calculation gives results that:
- are 0.2 apart
- give the same result when rounded to the nearest whole number.

Do you think that this will always happen?

Try with these pairs of calculations:

0.33×54 and 0.34×53

0.34×55 and 3.5×54

0.35×56 and 0.36×55

0.36×57 and 0.37×56

0.37×58 and 0.38×57

0.38×59 and 0.39×58

Was your prediction correct?

© HarperCollinsPublishers 2018

Challenge and extension questions

Question 4

4 Calculate the following.

$$0.\dot{1} + 0.0\dot{1} + 0.00\dot{1} + 0.000\dot{1} + 0.0000\dot{1} = \boxed{}$$

Pupils will need to understand the notation used to access the question.

$0.\dot{1}$ means $0.111\,111\,111\,111...$ It has an infinite number of 1s after the decimal point and, when said aloud, is: 'zero point one recurring'.

$0.0\dot{1}$ means $0.011\,111\,111\,111\,1...$ It has a zero followed by an infinite number of 1s after the decimal point and, when said aloud is: 'zero point zero one recurring'.

Pupils need to use these ideas to reason about what will happen when these infinite numbers are added together.

Question 5

5 In $4 \div 7$, the digit in the tenth position in the quotient after the decimal point is $\boxed{}$.

The sum of the first 100 digits in the quotient after the decimal point is $\boxed{}$.

This question relies on pupils noticing that the decimal part of the quotient repeats every six digits

$0.571\,428\,571\,428\,571\,428...$

This means that pupils don't need to calculate all 100 digits to be able to find the sum, but can use reasoning to identify how many of each digit there will be in the decimal number.

Unit 2.11
Practice and exercise (1)

Conceptual context

This unit consolidates concepts learned in this chapter.

Key understandings that pupils have learned to apply are related to using associative, commutative and distributive laws to calculate, and the use of place value to adjust calculations with decimals.

The use of column methods to multiply and divide with decimals has also been developed through the chapter.

Learning pupils will have achieved at the end of the unit

- Pupils will have built their understanding of the associative, commutative and distributive laws (Q1, Q2, Q3, Q4)
- Pupils will have built fluency in methods to multiply and divide decimal numbers (Q1, Q2, Q3, Q4, Q5, Q6, Q7)
- Pupils will be able to interpret and use the order of operations with decimal numbers (Q5, Q6, Q7)

Resources

Resource 6.2.11a More blanks; **Resource 6.2.11b** Tree stories

Vocabulary

decimal number, product, quotient, order of operations

Questions 1, 2, 3 and 4

1 Use the laws of operations to fill in boxes with a suitable number and the ◯ with an operation sign.

(a) [ ] × 0.84 = [ ] × 7

(b) [ ] × (3.28 × 8) = (12.5 × 8) × [ ]

(c) [ ] × (0.125 + 2.5) = [ ] × [ ] ◯ [ ] × 4

2 Use the column method to calculate the answers. Round to the nearest tenth. (Check the answer to the question marked with *.)

(a) 9 × 0.0247

(b) 13.6 ÷ 27

(c) *8.84 ÷ 17

3 Combine the two number sentences into one number sentence using the order of operations.

(a) 60.8 ÷ 16 = 3.8
13.5 − 3.8 = 9.7

(b) 4.25 + 5.8 = 10.05
14 × 10.05 = 140.7

4 Work these out step by step. (Calculate smartly if possible.)

(a) 9.18 − 9.18 ÷ 9 × 3

(b) 18.7 − 8.7 ÷ 25

(c) 19.5 × 5.8 + 5.2 × 19.5 − 19.5

(d) 7.8 ÷ (39 ÷ 5)

(e) 43.2 ÷ 8 × 25

(f) 87.25 − (7.25 + 4.83 + 5.17)

What learning will pupils have achieved at the conclusion of Questions 1, 2, 3 and 4?

- Pupils will have built their understanding of the associative, commutative and distributive laws.
- Pupils will have built fluency in methods to multiply and divide decimal numbers.

Activities for whole-class instruction

- Display the following on the board.

$3.7 \times \blacksquare = 5 \times 3.7$

$21 \times 3.4 + 21 \times 1.2 = \blacksquare \times 4.6$

$$
\begin{array}{r}
2\ 1 \\
\times\ \ \ 4\,.\,6 \\
\hline
\blacksquare\ \blacksquare\ \blacksquare \\
\blacksquare\ \blacksquare\ \blacksquare \\
\hline
9\ \ 6\,.\,6
\end{array}
$$

Given that $21 \times 4.6 = 96.6$
and $3.4 + 96.6 = 100$
then $3.4 + 21 \times \blacksquare = 100$

- Working in pairs, ask pupils to complete the blanks on their whiteboards.
- Ask: *Which were the easiest and which were the most challenging blanks to complete?*
- Discuss strategies and review key points.
- Pupils should complete Questions 1, 2, 3 and 4 in the Practice Book.

Same-day intervention

- Work with pupils on part of **Resource 6.2.11a** More blanks.

Answers: 2.3, 2.3, 5, 2.3, 2.3; 1, 0, 5, 1, 2; 8, 2, 6.

Same-day enrichment

- Display the following on the board.

1.2	1.4	1.6	2	10
		+ − × ÷		

- Ask pupils to use all of the numbers and all of the operations exactly once, using brackets where necessary to write a number sentence that gives the largest possible total.

Questions 5, 6 and 7

5 Write the number sentences and then calculate the answers.

(a) 27.9 is divided by the difference between 19.52 and 16.52. What is the result?

_____

(b) Number A is 3.6, which is 4.4 less than 4 times Number B. What is Number B?

_____

6 Solve these problems.

(a) 38 litres of orange juice needs to be poured into bottles, each with a capacity of 750 ml. How many bottles can be filled up? How many litres of orange juice will be left over?

(b) It took a bird half an hour to fly 6.5 km. At this speed, how much time would it take for the bird to fly 13.91 km?

(c) A beekeeper collected 73.8 kg of honey from 36 beehives. Assuming the amount of honey collected from each beehive is the same, how much honey can be collected from 56 beehives?

7 Fill in the spaces to make each statement correct.

(a) All of the digits in a number were moved three places to the right across the decimal point, then moved two places to the left across the decimal point. The resulting number was 4.4.

The original number was [ ] .

(b) Put 5.91, 5.9̇, 5.9, 5.912, and 5.912 912 in order, from the least to the greatest.

The second number is [ ] .

(c) Without calculating the answers, fill in the ( ) with >, < or =.

78×1.4 ◯ 78×0.4 $5.65 \div 5$ ◯ $565 \div 50$

$3.13 \div 91$ ◯ $3.13 \div 19$ 54 ◯ 54×0.72

97×1.5 ◯ $97 \div 1.5$ $2.67 \div 3$ ◯ 2.67

(d) When a number with three decimal places is rounded off, it is 4.90.

The least possible value of this number is [ ] and the greatest is [ ] .

What learning will pupils have achieved at the conclusion of Questions 5, 6 and 7?

- Pupils will have built fluency in methods to multiply and divide decimal numbers.
- Pupils will be able to interpret and use the order of operations with decimal numbers.

Activities for whole-class instruction

- Display the following diagram on the board.

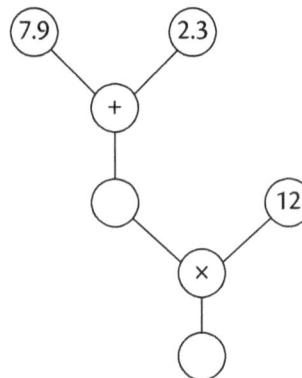

Find the product of 12 and the sum of 7.9 and 2.3.

$12 \times (7.9 + 2.3) =$

Tell pupils that these are three different ways to represent the same calculation; diagram, words and symbols.

Discuss with pupils which representation they find most useful and why.

- Ask pupils to create a tree diagram and number sentence to represent:

3.2 is divided by 5. How much larger is this quotient than 2.6?

Share ideas and include questions:

- *Did you use brackets in your number sentence? Are they necessary?*

- *Which operation did you put in the top row of the tree diagram? How did you know to put it there?*

- *In the tree diagram, the first calculation is the one at the top. How do you know the first calculation from your number sentence?*

- Pupils should complete Questions 5, 6 and 7 in the Practice Book.

Same-day intervention

- Provide pupils with **Resource 6.2.11b** Tree stories, and work with them relating word problems to tree diagrams.

- Focus particularly on the order in which the calculations are carried out.
- Work with pupils to then write the number sentences. Pay particular attention to the order of operations and the way in which it is communicated through the symbols.

Answers: £1.60, £2.89.

Same-day enrichment

- Display the following calculation on the board.

- Ask pupils to fill in the blanks so that the calculation is correct.
- Say to pupils that there are two possible solutions. (The solutions are 18.84 ÷ 3 and 18.84 ÷ 6.)

Challenge and extension question

Question 8

8 The sum of A and B is 6.55. The sum of A and C is 7.55, and the sum of B and C is 7.1. What are A, B, and C, respectively?

A =   B =   C =

This question offers a set of equations for pupils to solve. Pupils might see that the equations can be manipulated to reach a solution. An efficient strategy is to use the fact that $(A + B) + (A + C) - (B + C) = 6.55 + 7.55 - 7.1$ and simplify this to show that $2A = 7$ and so A must be 3.5, and use this to calculate the other values – but many pupils are likely to use a trial and inspection strategy.

Encourage pupils to work systematically and to pay attention to the impact of changing any value on outcomes.

Chapter 2 test (Practice Book 6A, pages 64–67)

Test question number	Relevant unit	Relevant questions within unit
1	Unit 2.2	Q3
	Unit 2.3	Q1, Q2
2	Unit 2.2	Q1, Q2
	Unit 2.5	Q2, Q3
3	Unit 2.4	Q1, Q2, Q3
4	Unit 2.5	Q4
	Unit 2.6	Q4
5	Unit 2.5	Q5
6	Unit 2.6	Q5
7	Unit 2.3	Q4
8	Unit 2.8	Q5
9	Unit 2.4	Q4
10	Unit 2.2	Q3
	Unit 2.8	Q1
11	Unit 2.1	Q3
	Unit 2.11	Q7
12	Unit 2.1	Q1
	Unit 2.11	Q7
13	Unit 2.10	Q1
14	Unit 2.9	Q3
	Unit 2.10	Q4
15	Unit 2.10	Q1
16	Unit 2.10	Q2
17	Unit 2.11	Q7

Chapter 3
Introduction to algebra

Area of mathematics	National Curriculum statutory requirements for Key Stage 2	Shanghai Maths Project reference
Number – multiplication and division	Year 5 Programme of study: Pupils should be taught to: ■ recognise and use square numbers and cube numbers, and the notation for squared (^{2}) and cubed (^{3}) ■ solve problems involving addition, subtraction, multiplication and division and a combination of these, including understanding the meaning of the equals sign.	Year 6, Units 3.1, 3.2, 3.4, 3.5 Year 6, Units 3.1, 3.5
Measurement	Year 5 Programme of study: Pupils should be taught to: ■ measure and calculate the perimeter of composite rectilinear shapes in centimetres and metres ■ calculate and compare the area of rectangles (including squares), and including using standard units, square centimetres (cm^2) and square metres (m^2) and estimate the area of irregular shapes.	Year 6, Units 3.1, 3.3, 3.4, 3.5, 3.8 Year 6, Units 3.1, 3.3, 3.4, 3.5. 3.8
Geometry – properties of shapes	Year 5 Programme of study: Pupils should be taught to: ■ use the properties of rectangles to deduce related facts and find missing lengths and angles.	Year 6, Units 3.1, 3.5
Geometry – properties of shapes	Year 6 Programme of study: Pupils should be taught to: ■ compare and classify geometric shapes based on their properties and sizes and find unknown angles in any triangles, quadrilaterals, and regular polygons.	Year 6, Units 3.1, 3.2, 3.3, 3.8

Algebra	Year 6 Programme of study:	
	Pupils should be taught to:	
	■ use simple formulae	Year 6, Units 3.1, 3.2, 3.3, 3.4
	■ generate and describe linear number sequences	Year 6, Units 3.1, 3.2, 3.4
	■ express missing number problems algebraically	Year 6, Units 3.1, 3.2, 3.3, 3.4, 3.5, 3.6, 3.7, 3.8. 3.9, 3.10
	■ find pairs of numbers that satisfy an equation with two unknowns	Year 6, Units 3.5, 3.6
	■ enumerate possibilities of combinations of two variables.	Year 6, Units 3.2, 3.3, 3.4, 3.5, 3.6

Pre-requisite knowledge

For pupils to be successful with the work in this chapter, they will need to have achieved mastery in their learning in previous relevant units. Teaching there will have introduced and developed concepts and skills that are necessary to work with the Year 6 content. A summary of pre-requisite knowledge is set out in the table below. If you believe that some pupils need to revisit particular areas, the units in which it was taught are also shown in the table so that you can locate appropriate guidance in Teacher's Guides and Practice Books. Guidance provided for Chapter 3 on the following pages will therefore focus on new learning.

Pre-requisite knowledge, understanding or skill	Where this was taught in The Shanghai Maths Project
Pupils can understand and create number sequences	Year 1A, Units 3.1, 3.3 Year 2A, Unit 1.2, 4.1 Year 3A, Units 2.4 (Challenge question), 3.3, 3.4 Year 3B, Units 6.4, 6.6 Year 4A, Unit 2.2 Year 6A, Unit 1.1
Pupils can understand and apply the laws of operation	Year 1A, Unit 3.6 Year 2A, Units 4.6, 5.4, 5.5 Year 4B, Units 10.11, 10.12, 10.13, 10.14 Year 6A, Unit 2.4
Pupils can understand and apply brackets appropriately	Year 4B, Units 10.3, 10.5, 10.6 Year 5A, Units 5.3, 5.4, 5.5, 5.6
Pupils can apply their understanding of angle properties of triangles	Year 5B, Unit 8.9
Pupils can apply their understanding of perimeter and area of triangles, squares and rectangles	Year 3B, Units 10.6, 10.7 Year 4B, Units 8.9, 8.10, 9.2, 9.3
Pupils can apply their understanding of volume of cubes and cuboids	Year 5B, Units 9.5, 9.6
Pupils can understand and apply ratio in context	Year 2A, Unit 5.16 Year 3B, Unit 9.20 Year 4B, Units 10.1, 10.2 Year 5A, Units 3.1, 3.2
Pupils can understand the concept of negative numbers	Year 5B, Units 7.1, 7.2, 7.3, 7.4

Unit 3.1
Using letters to represent numbers (1)

Conceptual context

This is the first of ten units introducing algebra and its application to solving problems. Pupils will have previously met algebra in contexts such as number problems and formulae. This unit introduces, develops and deepens understanding of letters representing numbers in equations and formulae. Understanding will be developed through linear number sequences, equations, algebraic notation and simple formulae.

Learning pupils will have achieved at the end of the unit

- Pupils will have developed their use of letters to represent numbers (Q1)
- Pupils will be able to generate linear number sequences and find missing numbers (Q1)
- Simple equations with one unknown will have been investigated and solved (Q1)
- Correct algebraic notation will have been introduced and consolidated (Q2)
- Understanding of the laws of operations will have been consolidated and developed through applying them to expressions that include letters (Q3)
- The term 'expanding the brackets' will be securely understood and used fluently (Q3)
- Pupils will have consolidated and extended their understanding of formulae (Q4, Q5)
- The use of algebraic expressions to describe the relations between quantities will have been introduced and applied (Q4, Q5)

Resources

0–100 number cards; lettered flashcards; blank cards; counters; **Resource 6.3.1a** Find the values; **Resource 6.3.1b** True or false?; **Resource 6.3.1c** Expressions matching; **Resource 6.3.1d** Laws matching

Vocabulary

linear, sequence, algebra, equation, solve, notation, brackets, expansion, formulae

Question 1

> **1** Write the number that each letter represents.
>
> (a) 3, 6, 9, A, 15   A = ☐
>
> (b) 2, 1, 2, 3, 2, 4, 5, 6, B, 7, 8, 9   B = ☐
>
> (c) 2 + 6 = 3 + M   M = ☐
>
> (d) 15 ÷ 3 = 10 − Y   Y = ☐
>
> (e) 1, 4, 9, 16, 25, 36, 49, C, 81   C = ☐
>
> (f) 1, 5, 2, 10, 3, 15, X, 20, 5, Y, 6   X = ☐ ; Y = ☐

What learning will pupils have achieved at the conclusion of Question 1?

- Pupils will have developed their use of letters to represent numbers.
- Pupils will be able to generate linear number sequences and find missing numbers.
- Simple equations with one unknown will have been investigated and solved.

Activities for whole-class instruction

- Together, generate linear number sequences, for example, 6, 12, 18, 24, … and 49, 42, 35, 28, … Discuss how each sequence is generated and the meaning of 'linear' (the amount added on or subtracted each time is the same).

  Discuss how any multiplication table is a linear number sequence, for example, the 8 times table is a linear number sequence. It is generated by adding 8 to each number.

- In mixed attainment groups of four, ask pupils to generate their own linear number sequences and describe how they are generated.

- Show pupils a linear number sequence, for example: 2, 5, 8, … Ask: *What is the next number in the sequence?* Ask pupils to work in pairs to find the answer. They should see that:
  - the first term of the linear number sequence is 2
  - it is generated by adding 3 to each number to obtain the next number
  - the next number in the sequence Is 11.

- Write on the board: 4, 7, 10, Z, …

  Ask: *What number does the letter represent?* Suggest pupils discuss the answer in pairs. Do they notice that:
  - the first term of the linear number sequence is 4
  - the sequence is generated by adding 3 to each number to obtain the next number
  - the letter Z represents the number 13?

All say… *The letter 'Z' represents the number 13.*

- Write on the board: 2, E, 8, 11, F, … Ask: *What numbers do the letters represent?* Pupils work in pairs. They should notice that:
  - the first term of the linear number sequence is 2
  - the sequence is generated by adding 3 to each number to obtain the next number
  - E represents the number 5, F represents the number 14.

- Tell pupils that the word 'algebra' is used to describe letters representing numbers.

- Now show pupils these sequences:

24, A, 16, B, 8, C	[A = 20, B = 12, C = 4]
3, E, 11, 15, F, 23, G	[E = 7, F = 19, G = 27]
3, 2, H, 4, 3, 2, L, 4	[H = 1, L = 5]

- Ask: *What is different about the third sequence?* Agree that it is not linear. Ask pupils to work in pairs to discuss what the letters represent.

- Give mixed attainment groups of four two sets of number cards and lettered flashcards. Working in pairs, pupils generate number sequences, using letters to replace numbers. Each pair then finds the missing numbers for the other pair. They should explain their reasoning.

- Write on the board: 23 + 17 = a. Tell pupils that this is an example of an equation. Ask: *What do you think 'equation' means?* Gather answers and explain that the word 'equation' is linked to the word 'equal'.

All say… *An equation has values on both sides of an equals sign.*

- Ask: *What does the letter* a *represent in the equation?* Agree a = 40. Together, draw a bar model to represent both sides of the equation.

a	
23	17

- Ask pupils, working in pairs, to draw a bar model representing 35 − 24 = D. They should draw the bar model below.

35	
24	D

- Now ask pupils, in pairs, to draw bar models and work out what each letter represents in the following:

  8 + 6 = D + 2

  S + 3 = 4 + 9

$3 \times 8 = 4 + E$

- Together, discuss the solutions:

8 + 6	
D	2

- So, $D = 14 - 2$. $D = 12$.

4 + 9	
S	3

- So, $S = 13 - 3$. $S = 10$.

3 × 8	
E	4

- So, $E = 24 - 4$. $E = 20$.

- Working in pairs, ask pupil pairs to draw a bar model like those above and fill it in to represent an equation of their own. They can then swap with another pair to solve and discuss their reasoning.

- Pupils should complete Question 1 in the Practice Book.

Same-day intervention

- Together, generate a linear number sequence using the six times table (6, 12, 18, 24, 30, …). Explain that each number in the sequence is 6 more than the term before.

- Show the first three terms of a linear number sequence using counters, for example, 3, 5, 8, … Ask: *What is the next number in the sequence?*

  Repeat, generating different linear number sequences, sometimes leaving gaps and asking pupils about the missing numbers or the next number.

- Instead of leaving gaps to show unknown numbers, replace the missing number with a letter. Ask: *What number does the letter represent?*

- Pupils can generate their own linear number sequences using counters and replace different sets of counters with lettered flashcards. Ask them to describe what numbers the letters represent.

Same-day enrichment

- Give pupils **Resource 6.3.1a** Find the values, to complete.

Resource 6.3.1a

Find the values

1. Find the values of the letters in these sequences.
   a) 0, 1, 1, 2, 3, 5, A, 13, 21, 34, C, D
      A = ☐   C = ☐   D = ☐
   b) 1, 4, 9, E, 25, 36, F, 64, 81, G
      E = ☐   F = ☐   G = ☐
   c) 1, 2, 4, 8, H, 32, J, K, 256
      H = ☐   J = ☐   K = ☐
   d) L, M, 125, N, 27, R, 1
      L = ☐   M = ☐   N = ☐
   e) 27, P, 16, 10.5, R, –0.5, S
      P = ☐   R = ☐   S = ☐

2. Solve these equations. (Hint: Find the value of each letter.)
   a) A + 7.5 = 25 – 10.5

   b) X – 2.25 = 3.5 × 7

   c) 3 × C + 4 = 100 – 7.5 + 3

   d) 4 + E + 25.5 = 3 × 4 + 15.5

   e) 2 × 3 + 32 = 3 × S – 10.45

Answers: **1.** a) A = 8, C = 55, D = 89; b) E = 16, F = 49, G = 100; c) H = 16, J = 64, K = 128; d) L = 343, M = 216, N = 64; e) P = 21.5, R = 5, S = –6
2. a) 7; b) 26.75; c) 30.5; d) 2; e) 16.15

Question 2

> 2 Complete each statement.
> (a) $m \times 8$ can be simply written as
> _____
> (b) $x \times 3 \times y$ can be simply written as
> _____
> (c) $(9 + a) \times 6$ can be simply written as
> _____
> (d) $n \times 1 + a \div 2$ can be simply written as
> _____
> (e) $a \times a \times a$ can be simply written as
> _____
> (f) $b + b + b + b \times b$ can be simply written as
> _____

What learning will pupils have achieved at the conclusion of Question 2?

- Correct algebraic notation will have been introduced and consolidated:
  - one unknown, for example, $a + a + a = 3a$
  - two unknowns, for example, $8 \times c \times d = 8cd$
  - brackets, for example, $5 \times (8 + a) = 5(8 + a)$
  - unknowns in longer expressions, for example, $3 \times a + b \div 2 = 3a + 0.5b$
  - powers, for example, $a \times a \times a = a^3$.

Activities for whole-class instruction

- Show pupils 11 identical letters. For example, $n, n, n \dots n$. Ask: *How many n's can you see? How could the number of n's be represented without writing them all down?* Pupils should suggest writing $11 \times n$ or $n \times 11$.

- On the board, write $11n$. Explain that $11n$ means 11 multiplied by n and that there is no multiplication sign between the 11 and the n.

All say … $11n$ means 11 multiplied by n.

- Write on the board: r, r, r, r, r. Ask: *How could this be represented?* Agree $5r$.
  Ask: *What addition does 5r represent?* Agree $5r = r + r + r + r + r$.

- Now show pupils these expressions:

> $3x$
> $6y$
> $2a + 2b$
> $4a + 3b$

- Ask pupils to work in pairs to discuss what each expression represents.

- Show a number and two unknowns, for example, $8 \times c \times d$. Ask: *How would this expression be represented?* Agree $8cd$.

All say … $8cd$ means 8 multiplied by c multiplied by d.

- Now show pupils these expressions:

> $5 \times d$
> $7 \times P \times Q$
> $4 \times r \times s$
> $11 \times t$

- Working in pairs, ask pupils to discuss how each expression is represented. Pupil pairs can then complete section A on **Resource 6.3.1b** True or false?

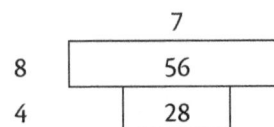

Answers. a) False; b) True; c) True; d) False; e) True; f) False

- Write on the board: $7 \times (8 + 4)$. Ask: *What is this? What does it represent?* Ask pupils to discuss in pairs. They should see that:

$7 \times (8 + 4) = 7 \times 8 + 7 \times 4$

Together, draw an array and set out the calculation:

$7 \times (8 + 4) = 7 \times 8 + 7 \times 4$
$7 \times (8 + 4) = 56 + 28$
$7 \times (8 + 4) = 84$

- Now ask pupils, working in pairs, to draw an array and set out the calculation for $12 \times (13 + 23)$. They should draw:

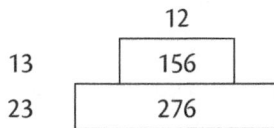

```
          12
   13 | 156 |
   23 | 276 |
```

$12 \times (13 + 23) = 12 \times 13 + 12 \times 23$

$12 \times (13 + 23) = 156 + 276$

$12 \times (13 + 23) = 432$

- Write on the board: $17 \times (28 - 14)$. Ask: *What does this represent?* Ask pupils to discuss in pairs. They should see that:

$17 \times (28 - 14) = 17 \times 28 - 17 \times 14$

Ask pupils to set out the calculation. They should write:

$17 \times (28 - 14) = 17 \times 28 - 17 \times 14$

$17 \times (28 - 14) = 476 - 238$

$17 \times (28 - 14) = 238$

- On the board, write: $7 \times (a + b)$. Ask: *What is this? What does it represent?* Pupils should discuss their responses in pairs. Agree $7 \times a + 7 \times b$.

Explain that the multiplication sign is not shown between the number and the first bracket. Together, draw the array and set out the expression:

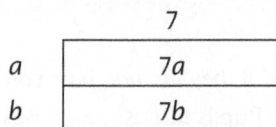

```
          7
   a | 7a |
   b | 7b |
```

$7 (a + b) = 7 \times a + 7 \times b$

$7 (a + b) = 7a + 7b$

- Display these expressions on the board:

$4 \times (s + t)$

$6 \times (x + y)$

$10 \times (a + b)$

$7 \times (r + s)$

- Working in pairs, ask pupils to draw an array and set out the expression for each.

- Write $M \times M$ on the board. Ask: *How would this expression be represented?* Do pupils see that this is M^2?

- Write $M \times M \times M$. Ask: *How would this expression be represented?* Do pupils see that this is M^3?

- Write on the board:

$b \times b \times b$

$b \times b \times b \times c \times c \times c$

$r \times s \times r \times s \times s$

Pupils discuss, in pairs, how each expression is represented.

- Now write $x \div 2$. Ask: *How would this expression be represented?* Agree $\frac{1}{2}x$. Point out that this is the same as $\frac{x}{2}$ and $0.5x$.

- Provide pupil pairs with **Resource 6.3.1b** True or false? and ask them to complete section B.

  Answers: a) False; b) False; c) True; d) False; e) True; f) True

- Pupils should complete Question 2 in the Practice Book.

Same-day intervention

- Generate some statements involving expressions, excluding brackets and powers, using number cards and lettered flashcards (include blank cards for equal signs, and so on). For some of the statements, do not include letters, numbers or symbols at certain points so that the pupils can explain what they should be. For example: $11 \times \_\_ = 11d$, $a + \_\_ + a = 3a$ and $r \_\_ s = rs$. Ask pupils to explain what the expressions mean.

- Repeat as above, but include brackets and powers. For example: $4 \_\_ (s + t) = 4 (s + t)$, $c \times \_\_ + b \times b \times b = c^2 + b\_\_$ and $5 (d \_\_ e) + e \div \_\_ = 5 \times (d + e) + 0.5e$. Ask pupils to explain what the expressions mean.

Same-day enrichment

- Ask pupils to complete section C of **Resource 6.3.1b** True or false?

  Answers: a) True; b) False; c) False; d) True; e) $7(c^2 + d) + d^3 \div 8$; f) $0.01(x^2 - ef)$; g) $0.125d^3 + 0.125e^2$

Question 3

> **3** Complete each statement. The first one has been done for you
>
> (a) $(a + b) + c = a + (b + c)$
>
> (b) $a (b + c) = ab + \boxed{}$
>
> (c) $a \div b = (a \div c) \div (b \div \boxed{})$ $(b \neq 0, c \neq 0)$
>
> (d) $a - b - c = a - (b \bigcirc c)$

What learning will pupils have achieved at the conclusion of Question 3?

- Understanding of the laws of operations will have been consolidated and developed through applying them to expressions that include letters.

- The term 'expanding the brackets' will be securely understood and used fluently.

Activities for whole-class instruction

- Give mixed attainment groups of four a set of cards from **Resource 6.3.1c** Expressions matching.

Resource 6.3.1c

- Ask pupils to match the cards and work together sharing solutions.

(i) Pupils have previously used the laws of operations to calculate efficiently. This question consolidates their understanding by applying the laws to algebra.

- Give mixed attainment groups of four a set of cards from **Resource 6.3.1d** Laws matching.

Resource 6.3.1d

- For each law, ask pupils: *What does this law mean?* Ask pupils to discuss answers and definitions in pairs. Pupils then match and complete the cards.

- Write $F \times (G + H) = F \times G + F \times H = FG + FH$ on the board to introduce pupils to the term 'expanding the brackets'.

- Display the following lists.

Expression	Expanded expressions
$p(d + f)$	$ab - 2a + dc + 2d$
$g(h + y)$	$pd + pf$
$f(g - h)$	$bc - bd + gh + gj$
$b(c - d) + g(h + j)$	$gh + gy$
$a(b - 2) + d(c + 2)$	$fg - fh$

- Working in pairs, ask pupils to match the expressions with the expanded versions. Share ideas.

$p(d + f)$	$pd + pf$
$g(h + y)$	$gh + gy$
$f(g - h)$	$fg - fh$
$b(c - d) + g(h + j)$	$bc - bd + gh + gj$
$a(b - 2) + d(c + 2)$	$ab - 2a + dc + 2d$

- Show pupils:

  $14 - 7 - 3 = 14 - 7 + 3$

  $20 \div 10 = 20 \div 2 \div 10 \div 2$

- Ask: *Are these equations true? If they are not, how can they be corrected so that they are?* Pupils discuss responses in pairs. They should suggest:

  – first question

    add 6 to the left-hand side, or

    add 2 to the left-hand side and subtract 4 from the right-hand side

  – second question

    divide the left-hand side by 20, or

    divide the left-hand side by 2 and multiply the right-hand side by 10.

- Discuss pupils' examples, especially where brackets are used, for example, $14 - 7 - 3 = 14 - (7 + 3)$ and $20 \div 10 = (20 \div 2) \div (10 \div 2)$. Discuss the importance of the brackets in both examples and what happens if they are not there. Explore whether they are all necessary to keep the equation true.

(Look out for) Misconceptions about the use of brackets are often evident when pupils solve equations and rearrange formulae.

- Display the following and ask pupils to work out whether the equations are true or false.

$14 - 6 - 2 = 14 - (6 + 2)$	[True]
$40 \div 4 = 40 \div (2 \div 4) \div 2$	[False]
$15 + (4 - 1) = 15 - (4 + 1)$	[False]
$c \div d = (c \div e) \div (d \div e)$	[True]
$11 - 6 + 5 = 11 - (6 - 5)$	[True]
$20 \div 2 = 20 \div (4 \div 2) \div 4$	[False]
$c - (d + e) = c - d - e$	[True]

- Give pupils **Resource 6.3.1e** Pairing expressions and ask them to work in pairs to complete it.

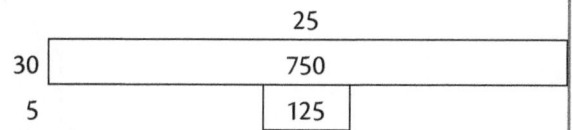

Answers:

$n^2 - 2f$	$n \times n - 2 \times f$	
$c - (d + e)$	$c - e - d$	
$x \div 6y$	$(x \div 2) \div (6y \div 2)$	[blank – an example]
$5r + 5s - y^2 \div 2$	$5(r + s) - 0.5g^2$	[blank]
$14 - 6 - 2$	$14 - (6 + 2)$	[blank]
$(e^3 \div h) \div (f^3 \div h)$	$[(e^3 \div h) \div (f^2 \div h)]$ $e^3 \div f^2$ $[e^3 \div f^3]$	
$gf + gh$	$g(f + h)$	
$(20 \div 4) \div (2 \div 4)$	$20 \div 2$	
$wy - y^2 - 2xy$	$w \times y - (-2xy + y \times y)$ $[w \times y - (2xy + y \times y)]$	
$s^2r^2 + 2s^3$ $[s^2r + 2s^3]$ $s \times r \times s + 2 \times s^2 \times s$	$[s \times s \times r \times r + 2 \times s^2 \times s]$	
$b - (c + d)$	$b - c - d$	

- Pupils should complete Question 3 in the Practice Book.

Same-day intervention

- Give pupils some calculations that they can simplify using the distributive law, including brackets. For example, 25×35. Together, agree how the calculation could be set out:

$$25 \times 35 = 25 \times 30 + 25 \times 5$$
$$= 750 + 125$$
$$= 875$$

- Show that $25 \times 35 = 25 \times (30 + 5) = 25 \times 30 + 25 \times 5$.

  You could also show each calculation as an array to support pupils' understanding:

	25
30	750
5	125

- Repeat the above using letters and numbers, then just letters. For example, $a \times 35$.

$$a \times 35 = (a \times 30) + (a \times 5)$$
$$= 30a + 5a$$
$$= 35a$$

- Show pupils that:

  $a \times 35 = a \times (30 + 5) = (a \times 30) + (a \times 5)$.

  $a \times (b + c) = (a \times b) + (a \times c)$
  $$= ab + ac$$

Same-day enrichment

- Ask pupils to complete **Resource 6.3.1f** Spot the equation errors.

Resource 6.3.1f

Spot the equation errors

Answers: **A.** Example answer: The w has been written as a cube. It should be $3w$. The z needs to be written as $3z$. The rest stays the same. The corrected equation should be: $3w + 3z + y + x^2$; **B.** Example answer: The calculation replaces dividing by 4 with dividing by the quotient of 2 divided by 4 (which equals 0.5) and then dividing by 3. This is not the same as dividing by 4. The 3 needs to be replaced with a 2 for the calculation to make sense. The corrected equation should be: $y^2 \div (2 \div 4) \div 2$.

Questions 4 and 5

4 Complete each statement using expressions with letters to show the relations between quantities.

(a) In a triangle, if $\angle 1 = a°$ and $\angle 2 = b°$, then $\angle 3 =$ _____.

(b) In an isosceles triangle, if the base angle is $a°$, the size of the vertex angle is _____.

(c) If the perimeter of a square is C, then the side length of the square is _____.

(d) If A represents the unit price, that is, price per item, X represents the quantity, that is, number of items, and C represents the total price of all the items, then $X =$ _____.

(e) If the area of a rectangle is S and the length is a, then the width is _____.

(f) One frog has 1 mouth, 2 eyes and 4 legs. Two frogs have 2 mouths, 4 eyes and 8 legs.

Three frogs have ☐ mouths, ☐ eyes and ☐ legs.

n frogs have ☐ mouths, ☐ eyes and ☐ legs.

5 Complete the table. Use expressions with letters to show the relations between the three quantities.

Speed (m/minute)	Time	Distance
65	t	
v		210
	6	s

Number of sets made per day	Number of working days	Total number of sets made
x		480
	25	x
30	x	

Unit price	Quantity	Total price
8.5	b	
	y	x
a		z

What learning will pupils have achieved at the conclusion of Questions 4 and 5?

- Pupils will have consolidated and extended their understanding of formulae.
- The use of algebraic expressions to describe the relations between quantities will have been introduced and applied.

Activities for whole-class instruction

- Working in pairs, ask pupils to decide whether the right-hand side of each equation below is correct and, if not, describe what should happen to make the equation true. Display:

$15 - (4 - 1) = 15 - 4 - 1$	[false: $15 - (4 - 1) = 15 - 4 + 1$]
$2(x^2 + y^2) - x^3 + y^2 = 2x^2 - x^3 + 3y^2$	[true: $2y^2 + y^2 = 3y^2$]
$x^3 \div y = x^3 \div (2 \div y) \div 3$	[false: $x^3 \div y = (x^3 \div 2) \div (y \div 2)$]

- Display the following on the board:

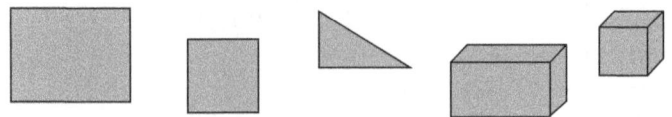

- Ask pupils to work in pairs and discuss what they know about the shapes.

- Ask: *How are perimeters, areas and volumes calculated? How do we use algebra to describe rules?* Pupils should suggest $l \times w =$ area and $2l + 2w =$ perimeter.

Agree that the rule or formula for calculating perimeter is also described as $P = 2(l + w)$.

- During or after the discussion, ask pupils to copy and complete this table.

Shape	Area	Perimeter	Volume
triangle		$P = a + b + c$	
rectangle	$A = l \times w = lw$	$P = 2(l + w)$	
square	$A = l \times l = l^2$	$P = 4l$	
cuboid			$V = l \times w \times h$ $= lwh$
cube			$V = l \times l \times l$ $= l^3$

- Ask pupils to rewrite some of the formulae so that the first letter changes. For example, for the rectangle's area formula, make l the first letter $l = A \div w$. They should rewrite at least five of the formulae.

- Pupils should complete Questions 4 and 5 in the Practice Book.

Same-day intervention

- Give pupils some equations that focus on the relationships between the four operations. For example, $A \times 5 = 20$, $s + 2 + 4 = 20$ and $45 \div T = 15$. Ask them to find the values of the letters, explaining verbally the mathematical steps they are carrying out. Use manipulatives, bar modelling and so on, to support understanding.

- Provide further equations, replacing numbers with letters.

Same-day enrichment

- Display these formulae on the board:

$v = u + at$	(an equation of motion)
$F = 1.8°C + 32$	(Fahrenheit and Centigrade)
mile = 1.6 km	(miles and kilometres)

- Ask pupils to write each formula as a sentence (in words). Next, they should rewrite these formulae, changing the order in which items are presented and then rewrite their word sentences to reflect the changed order.

Challenge and extension questions

Question 6

> 6 When the sum of three consecutive even numbers is a, then the number in the middle is _____, the least number is _____ and the greatest number is _____.

This question encourages pupils to use algebra to represent the relationship between three consecutive even numbers. There are different approaches. For example:

- using trial and error, with numbers, to find the relationship and then using letters

- starting with letters, creating the equation $x = (a - 6) \div 3$ where x is the first of the three numbers, which is then solved

- considering the middle number as being the average (mean), recognising that its value is $a \div 3$.

Question 7

> 7 In the following column calculations, the same letter represents the same number and different letters represent different numbers. What numbers do A, B, C and D represent respectively to make the column expression true? Fill in the boxes below.
>
> ```
>        A   B              A   B
>    +   C   D          -   C   D
>    ───────────        ───────────
>        9   4              5   8
> ```
>
> A = _____ B = _____ C = _____ D = _____

This question encourages pupils to use algebra to represent numbers in relationships. One approach is to consider the difference between 94 and 58 and where the number AB is within this range. Once established, CD can be found from $(94 - 58) \div 2$ and then AB can be found.

Unit 3.2
Using letters to represent numbers (2)

Conceptual context

This unit continues to develop and deepen understanding of letters representing numbers in equations and formulae. Understanding will be developed through relationships and given conditions expressed algebraically, sequences and the nth term, and problem solving.

Learning pupils will have achieved at the end of the unit

- Pupils will have consolidated their use of letters to represent numbers (Q1)
- Understanding of algebraic notation will have been consolidated (Q1)
- Relations between algebraic quantities will have been explored (Q1)
- Pupils will have revised words related to operations, order of operations and brackets (Q2)
  Pupils will be able to construct algebraic expressions to describe the relations between quantities (Q2)
- Pupils will be able to construct algebraic expressions describing given conditions (Q3, Q4)
- Pupils will have deepened their understanding of sequences (Q5)
- The term-to-term rule and nth term will have been introduced and applied (Q5)
- Pupils will have applied algebra in order to solve word problems (Q6)

Resources

mini whiteboards; counters; 0–100 number cards; letter flashcards; blank cards; **Resource 6.3.2a** Matching terms and sequences; **Resource 6.3.2b** Word problems

Vocabulary

linear, sequence, equation, term, term-to-term rule, position-to-term rule, nth term, algebra, solve, notation, brackets, expansion, formulae

Question 1

1 Multiple choice questions. (For each question, choose the correct answer and write the letter in the box.)

(a) a^2 is equal to ☐ .

    A. $a \times 2$ B. $a + 2$ C. $a \times a$

(b) $2x - x^2$ is ☐ .

    A. greater than 0   B. less than 0

    C. equal to 0   D. not sure

(c) Laila is younger than Helen. Laila is a years old and Helen is b years old. After two years, Laila is ☐ years younger than Helen.

    A. 2   B. $b - a$ C. $a - b$ D. $b - a + 2$

(d) Number A is a, which is b less than 4 times Number B. Number B is ☐ .

    A. $a \div 4 - b$ B. $(a - b) \div 4$ C. $(a + b) \div 4$

What learning will pupils have achieved at the conclusion of Question 1?

- Pupils will have consolidated their use of letters to represent numbers.
- Understanding of algebraic notation will have been consolidated.
- Relations between algebraic quantities will have been explored.

Activities for whole-class instruction

- Check pupils' understanding of algebraic notation by asking:
  - *Show me what 8m means.*
  - *Show me an example of a number multiplied by x squared.*
  - *Change the right-hand side of $5(a + b) = 5a - b$ so that it is correct.*
  - *Identify what is wrong with $20 \div 2 = 20 \div (3 \div 2) \div 4$.*
- Display the following and ask pupils to discuss, in pairs, whether the comparisons are true or false.

10^3 is greater than 999	[True]
0.125 is less than $\frac{1}{9}$	[False]
$25 \times 35 > 870$	[True]
$6500 \div 50 \geq 130$	[False]
$\frac{1}{11} < \frac{4}{13} < \frac{3}{7}$	[True]

- Share ideas. Repeat with:

$x + 2$ is greater than x	[True]
$5x$ is less than x	[Sometimes]
$z^2 > z$	[Sometimes]
$x^2 + 2 \geq 2$	[True]
$5(a + b) + 3 < a + b$	[False]

- Ask: *Can you give a value for x that makes the first comparison true?* Agree that any value works.

  Ask: *Can you give a value for x that makes the first comparison false?* Agree that there are no values. Agree, therefore, that the comparison is true.

  Ask: *Is there a value for x that makes the second comparison true?* Ask pupils to discuss the question in pairs. Tell them to try integers first. Can they see that, for example, if x was −1 then $5x$ would be less than x?

  Ask: *Can you give a value for x that makes the second comparison false?* Ask pupils to discuss their ideas pairs. Can they see that, for example, 5×0 is not less than 0?

  Agree that the comparison is, therefore, sometimes true.

- Now show pupils:

$x + 2 > x$
$1 + 2 > 1$
$0 + 2 > 0$
$-1 + 2 > -1$
$0.5 + 2 > 0.5$

Working in pairs, pupils should discuss the comparisons to decide whether each is true or false. Share ideas, discussing reasons.

Ask: *What general statement can you make?* Pupils should explain that when something is added to a value, the result will always be greater than the original value. Can they go further and see that this is only true if the second number added is a positive number?

- Show pupils this problem:

Sanjit is A years old. He is 5 years older than Pierre. How old is Pierre?

Together, draw a bar model to represent the problem and work out a solution.

A	
P	5

So, $P = A - 5$ and $A = P + 5$.

Ask pupils to draw a bar model to show the question: How old will Sanjit and Pierre will be next year? Use a bar model to agree:

A + 1	
P + 1	5

So, $P + 1 = A + 1 - 5$.

$P = A - 5$ and $A = P + 5$ (same as before).

- Show pupils this problem:

> One bean plant is R cm tall and the other is S cm tall.
> $R < S$.
> In three months, both bean plants grow 5 cm.
> What is the difference between the heights at
> three months?

Ask pupils, working in pairs, to draw a bar model to represent the problem and work out a solution. They should draw:

$S + 5$	
$R + 5$	?

So, $? = S + 5 - (R + 5)$. $? = S - R$.

- Show pupils this problem:

> Angle B is $t°$ and it is 5° more than 3 times angle C.
> What is the size of angle C?

Working in pairs, ask pupils to draw a bar model to represent the problem and work out a solution. They should draw:

t			
C	C	C	5

So, $t = 3C + 5$. $C = (t - 5) ÷ 3$.

- In groups of four, ask pairs of pupils to create three similar problems. Each pair then solves the problems for the other pair.

- Pupils should complete Question 1 in the Practice Book.

Same-day intervention

- Together, use counters to represent a comparison, then replace one of the elements with a letter. Manipulate the counters and record the number sentence to show how to reveal the value of the number. For example:

$12 + 15 = 27$

$12 + m = 27$

$27 - 12 = m$ (correct because m is 15 as we see at the start)

$5 × 20 = 100$

$s × 20 = 100$

$100 ÷ 20 = s$ (correct because $s = 5$ as we see at the start)

- Tell pupils that Ahmed is younger than Sam by 3 years.

Together, draw a bar model to represent the problem:

Sam's age (S)	
Ahmed's age (A)	3

Ask: *How can we show the relationship between Sam's age and Ahmed's age using letters and symbols?*

Work with pupils to agree: $S = A + 3$ and $A = S - 3$.

Now ask: *What can we draw or write that describes what their ages will be in 3 years' time?*

Agree:

Sam's age (S)		3
Ahmed's age (A)	3	3

In 3 years: $S + 3 = A + 3 + 3$.

And, $A = S + 3 - 6$.

Same-day enrichment

- Ask pupils to represent these problems algebraically and then solve them:

> Alison has twin brothers. The sum of all the ages of the children is found to be 41.
> After 5 years, the twins are 21 years old.
> How old is Alison after 5 years?

Answer: $a + 2b = 41$; $b + 5 = 21$; $b = 16$; $a + 2 × 16 = 41$; $a = 9$; Alison's age after 5 years = 14 years old

> Amanda has twin sisters. The sum of all the ages of the children is found to be B.
> After 3 years, the twins will be C years old.
> How old is Amanda after 3 years?

Answer: $p + 2q = B$; $q + 3 = C$; $q = C - 3$; $p + 2(C - 3) = B$; $p = B - 2(C - 3)$; Amanda's age after 3 years $= B - 2(C - 3) + 3$

Question 2

> **2** Use expressions with letters to represent the relations between quantities. The first one has been done for you.
>
> (a) 100 minus the sum of a and b. $100 - (a + b)$
>
> (b) The quotient of 5 divided by x plus n.   _____
>
> (c) 6 times s minus 2.   _____
>
> (d) Subtract 12 times m from 320.   _____
>
> (e) The sum of 80 and b is multiplied by 5.   _____
>
> (f) 6 times the sum of b and 90.   _____

What learning will pupils have achieved at the conclusion of Question 2?

- Pupils will have revised words related to operations, order of operations and brackets.
- Pupils will be able to construct algebraic expressions to describe the relations between quantities.

Activities for whole-class instruction

- Write on the board: $12 - 6 \times 4$. Ask: *What is the correct order of operations for this calculation? How could we show it using brackets?* Agree: $12 - (6 \times 4)$.
- Remind pupils that the calculation within the brackets is done first.
- Show pupils these expressions:

  $a - 50 + b$
  $r - 12 \times 5$
  $13 \times 3 - a$
  $14 \div a + b$
  $b + c \times 3$

- Ask: *How would you describe the relationship between quantities in the first expression, in words?* Ask pupils to discuss responses in pairs. They should suggest:

  – *a* subtract the sum of 50 and *b* or 50 plus *b* subtracted from *a*.

- Repeat for the other expressions on the list.
- In groups of four, ask pairs of pupils to create five relations between quantities using words. Each pair then writes the expressions for the other pair.
- Pupils should complete Question 2 in the Practice Book.

Same-day intervention

- Write on the board: $14 - 4 \times 3 = ?$

  Agree that the calculation would be carried out in two steps: 4×3, then subtract the answer from 14.

  Together, draw a bar model to represent the calculation.

14				
?	3	3	3	3

  Agree ? = 2.

- Write on the board: $(14 - 4) \times 3 = ?$

  Agree that the $14 - 4$ is calculated first. Together, draw a bar model to represent the calculation.

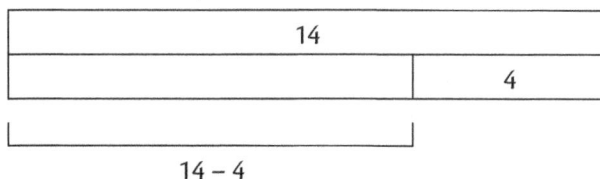

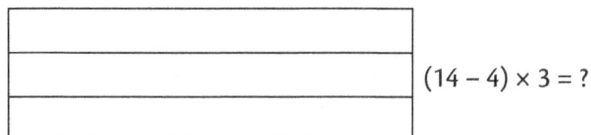

14	
	4

14 – 4

	$(14 - 4) \times 3 = ?$

  Agree $14 - 4 = 10$ then $3 \times 10 = 30$.

- Repeat for $4 \times 7 + 2$, $4 + 6 \div 2$, $12 - 4 + 2$, and so on.
- Write $a - 40 + b$ on the board.

  Discuss with pupils that the expression is in three parts that are added or subtracted: a, -40 and $+b$.

  Ask: *How would you say this expression in words?* Agree, for example, '*a* minus forty plus *b*.'

- Repeat for $r - 4 \times 5$, $14 \div a + b$, and so on.

Same-day enrichment

- Display these calculations on the board.

$4 \div 2 \times 3 + 1 =$	$[4 \div 2 \times 3 + 1 = 7; 4 \div (2 \times 3) + 1 = 1\frac{2}{3}; 4 \div 2 \times (3 + 1) = 8]$
$5 - 4 + 3 \times 2 =$	$[5 - 4 + 3 \times 2 = 7; 5 - (4 + 3) \times 2 = -9]$
$3 \times 7 - 6 \div 4 =$	$[3 \times 7 - 6 \div 4 = 19.5; 3 \times (7 - 6) \div 4 = 0.75]$
$7 + 2 \div 6 - 7 =$	$[7 + 2 \div 6 - 7 = \frac{1}{3}; (7 + 2) \div 6 - 7 = -5.5; 7 + 2 \div (6 - 7) = 5]$

- Pupils should find the different values the statements can have, using no brackets and using one pair of brackets in different parts of the calculation. Ask: *What do you notice?* Pupils should assert that the presence and position of brackets affects the answer, often significantly.

Questions 3 and 4

---

3 Write the expressions based on the given conditions.

A toy robot costs 50 pounds, a toy aeroplane costs *m* pounds, and a toy car costs *n* pounds.

(a) To buy a toy robot and a toy car costs _____ pounds in total.

(b) To buy a toy aeroplane and 2 toy cars costs _____ pounds in total.

(c) To buy a toy robot, a toy aeroplane and a toy car costs _____ pounds in total.

(d) To buy 2 toy aeroplanes and 3 toy cars costs _____ pounds in total.

(e) A toy aeroplane costs _____ pounds more than a toy car.

4 Use expressions with letters to represent these quantities.

(a) A car has travelled *t* hours at a speed of 85 km per hour. It has travelled _____ km in total.

(b) Jack spent 6 days reading *m* pages of a book. He read _____ pages of the book every day on average.

(c) There are 24 basketballs and *n* footballs. The footballs are _____ fewer than the basketballs.

(d) A shirt costs *a* pounds, and a pair of trousers costs *b* pounds. The total cost of buying 3 sets of these clothes is _____ pounds.

What learning will pupils have achieved at the conclusion of Questions 3 and 4?

- Pupils will be able to construct algebraic expressions describing given conditions.

Activities for whole-class instruction

- In pairs, ask pupils to find the values of the following calculations using the target number and brackets, and write expressions to represent the statements.

$15 - 4 \times 3$	target = 3	$[15 - (4 \times 3)]$
$4 \times 6 + 2$	target = 32	$[4 \times (6 + 2)]$
$4.5 + 6 \div 2$	target = 7.5	$[4.5 + (6 \div 2)]$
$12 - 4.5 \div 2 - 0.5$	target = 9	$[12 - 4.5 + (2 - 0.5)]$
25 minus the sum of *a* and *b*		$[25 - (a + b)]$
The quotient of 6 divided by *y* plus *p*		$[6 \div (y + p)]$
The difference of 7 multiplied by *a* subtracted by 3 multiplied by *p*		$[7a - 3p]$
The sum of *f* and 5, times by x^2		$[x^2(f + 5)]$

- Work through the first one together and then ask pupils to work in pairs to discuss and record their answers. Share ideas.

- Show pupils this problem:

> The same car costs £14 500 at Tahir's garage, £S at Sam's garage and £P at Pat's garage.
> What is the total cost if one car is bought from each of the garages?

Together, draw a bar model to represent the problem:

?		
14 500	S	P

So, ? = 14 500 + S + P.

- Ask: *What is the total cost of two cars from Sam's garage and one from Tahir's garage?* Ask pupils to work in pairs to draw a bar model representing the problem.

?		
14 500	S	S

So, ? = 2S + 14 500.

- Ask: *What is the price of the car at Sam's garage if it is three quarters the price it is at Pat's garage?*

In pairs, pupils should draw a bar model to represent the problem.

P			

S

So, S = 0.75P and S = 3 × (P ÷ 4).

- Working in pairs, ask pupils to create similar problems, for another pair to answer. Encourage the use of two unknowns, different operations, and answers to questions needing, for example, brackets: P = 2(a + 5).

(i) At this point in their learning, pupils should not deal with more than two unknowns.

- Show pupils this problem:

> Sam walked 12 km on Thursday and *R* km on Friday.
> He spent 15 hours walking in total.
> On average, how many kilometres did Sam walk per hour?

Together, draw a bar model to represent the problem.

15	
12	R

So, (12 + R) ÷ 15

- Show pupils this problem:

> Freda buys three salads from the deli counter. They cost £1.50, £R and £S.
> Describe the total cost if she bought two of each.

Pupil pairs should draw a bar model to represent the problem.

?					
1.50	1.50	R	R	S	S

So, ? = 1.50 + 1.50 + R + R + S + S.

? = 2 × 1.50 + 2R + 2S

? = 3.00 + 2(R + S)

- In groups of four, ask pupils to create two similar problems, for another group to answer. Encourage the use of two unknowns, different operations, and, for example, brackets: P = 2(a + 5).

- Pupils should complete Questions 3 and 4 in the Practice Book.

Same-day intervention

- Show pupils this problem:

  A book costs £x, a card costs £y and a pen costs £z.

- Ask: *What different combinations of books, cards and pens can we have? How much will they cost?*

- Create, with pupils, the costs for different combinations of books, cards and pens, using bar models to represent the expressions that would be created.

Same-day enrichment

- Display these expressions:

  R – S

  (8 + t) ÷ 4

  3(p + q)

- Ask pupils to create problems and questions that have these expressions as answers.

Question 5

5 Look at each number sequence carefully and complete its 5th, 6th and nth terms. The first one has been done for you.

(a) 2, 4, 6, 8, __10__ , __12__ , … , __2n__

(b) 0, 5, 10, 15, _____ , _____ , … ,

(c) 0, 1, 2, 3, _____ , _____ , … ,

(d) 4, 5, 6, 7, _____ , _____ , … ,

(e) 13, 23, 33, 43, _____ , _____ , … , _____

What learning will pupils have achieved at the conclusion of Question 5?

- Pupils will have deepened their understanding of sequences.

- The term-to-term rule and *n*th term will have been introduced and applied.

Activities for whole-class instruction

- Together, generate linear number sequences, for example: 4, 7, 10, A, 16, B, … and 50, 43, C, 29, 22, D, …

Explain that we use 'term' to refer to each value, describing where it is in the sequence. For example in the first sequence, the first term is 4, the second term is 7, the third term is 10 and so on.

Ask: *What is the 8th term in the sequence? What is the 10th term?* Agree, 25 and 31.

Ask: *What is changing between one term and the next each time?* Pupils should explain:

- in the first sequence, each term is 3 more than the term before

- in the second sequence, each term is 7 less than the term before.

Tell pupils that we can say the term-to-term rule is:

- add 3 in the first sequence

- subtract 7 in the second sequence.

- Ask pupils, working in pairs, to generate linear number sequences using multiplication tables. For each, they should describe the term-to-term rule and identify the 4th, 7th and 11th term.

- Display the following table (leave the last two columns blank):

Term	1st	2nd	3rd	4th	5th	6th	7th	17th	nth
Value	4	8	12	16	20	24	28	[68]	[4n]

- Ask: *What is the relationship between the position of the term and its value?* Agree value = term × 4.

All say … *The number of the term multiplied by 4 gives the value of the term.*

- Show pupils these linear number sequences: (Add, as necessary, more sequences; leave the last two columns blank.)

Term	1st	2nd	3rd	4th	5th	17th	nth
Value	3	6	9	12	15	[51]	[3n]

Term	1st	2nd	3rd	4th	5th	17th	nth
Value	5	10	15	20	25	[85]	[5n]

Term	1st	2nd	3rd	4th	5th	17th	nth
Value	7	14	21	28	35	[119]	[7n]

- Ask: *What is the relationship between the position of the term and its value?*

- Can pupils see that:
  - in the first sequence, the value is 3× the term number
  - in the second sequence, the value is 5× the term number
  - in the third sequence, the value is 7× the term number.
- Fill in the top row of the penultimate column with position 17.
- Ask: *What is the 17th term for each sequence? How is it obtained?* Pupils discuss responses in pairs.
- Ask: *How would you work out what the 25th term will be? The 100th term?* Can pupils see that, since the relationship is ×3, ×5 and ×7, they should multiply the term number by those multipliers to find the value each time?
- Complete the table. Add the heading of the last column n. Tell pupils that n can stand for any number.
- Ask: *What will be the value of the nth term?* Agree that it will be $3n$, $5n$ and $7n$ respectively.
- Display the following, omitting the numbers in the square brackets:

Term	1st	2nd	3rd	4th	5th	7th	17th	nth
Value	3	[4]	5	6	[7]	9	[19]	$[n + 2]$

- Ask: *What are the missing numbers, the term-to-term rule and the nth term for this sequence?* Pupils discuss their responses in pairs.
- They should see that:
  - the missing numbers are 4, 7 and 19
  - the term-to-term rule is + 1
  - the nth term is $n + 2$.
- Display the following, omitting the numbers in the square brackets:

Term	1st	2nd	3rd	4th	5th	7th	17th	nth
Value	[8]	12	16	[20]	24	[32]	72	$[4n + 4]$

- Ask: *What are the missing numbers, the term-to-term rule and the nth term for this sequence?* Pupils discuss their responses in pairs.
- They should see that:
  - the missing numbers are 8, 20 and 32
  - the term-to-term rule is + 4
  - the nth term is $4n + 4$.
- Give pairs of pupils **Resource 6.3.2a** Matching terms and sequences to complete.

Resource 6.3.2a

Matching terms and sequences

Answers: (2, 5, 10, 17, 26, 37, 50, 65), $(n^2 + 1)$; (0, 0.5, 1, 1.5, 2, 2.5, 3, 3.5), $(0.5n - 0.5)$; (1, 6, 11, 16, 21, 26, 31, 36), $(5n - 4)$; (1, 3, 5, 7, 9, 11, 13, 15), $(2n - 1)$; (5, 8, 11, 14, 17, 20, 23, 26), $(3n + 2)$

- Pupils should complete Question 5 In the Practice Book.

Same-day intervention

- Together, generate linear number sequences using multiplication tables. Represent the numbers using counters and describe them as 'terms' in the sequence. For each sequence, ask: *How is each number sequence generated?* Discuss this as the term-to-term rule. Discuss the position of the numbers in the sequence. Use number cards above the numbers to show their position.
- Representing each value in turn in a sequence with base 10 blocks will help pupils to perceive the term-to-term rule if they have difficulty with only abstract representation.
- Discuss the nth term for each generated sequence.

Same-day enrichment

- Display the following. Ask pupils to find the nth terms for these sequences and explain how the sequences are generated.

0, 6, 12, 18, …	$[6(n - 1)]$
−1, 1, 3, 5, …	$[2n - 3]$
−1.5, −1, −0.5, 0, …	$[0.5n - 2]$
8, 5, 2, −1, …	$[11 - 3n]$

Question 6

> **6** Solve these problems.
>
> (a) On a public holiday, a particular model of mobile phone was selling well in a phone shop. 75 of these mobile phones were sold in the morning and 100 in the afternoon. Given that each costs a pounds, what is the total value of the sales in the whole day? How much less was the sales value in the morning than in the afternoon?
>
> _____
>
> (b) A highway construction team was tasked to build an x metre long highway. It planned to build m metres of highway every day. However, in practice, on each day, the team built 2.5 more metres of highway than planned. In how many days was the task completed?
>
> _____ days

What learning will pupils have achieved at the conclusion of Question 6?

- Pupils will have applied algebra in order to solve word problems.

Activities for whole-class instruction

- Show pupils the following and ask them to fill in the blanks.

9 , __, __, 18, 21 = 3__ + 6
$5n$ + __ = __, 14, __, 24, 29
$6n$ − __ = 0, 6, 12, __, 24, __
$1.5n$ __ 1 = 0.5, 2, __, __, 6.5

Share ideas.

- Now show pupils this problem:

> Tim spent £3 on lunch each day for A days and £4.50 on dinner each day for B days.
> How much did he spend on lunch and dinner altogether?

Discuss the problem with pupils. Ask questions such as:

- _What is the question asking?_
- _What is the problem that needs to be solved?_
- _What do we need to find out/work out?_
- _Is the problem about a whole and its parts?_
- _Is it a problem about something being a number of times bigger or smaller than something else? Is it about something else? How do we know?_
- _What operations are going to be used?_
- _What is the calculation that needs to be done? If there is more than one step, in what order should the steps be carried out?_

Together, draw a bar model to represent the problem:

?	
3A	4.5B

So, ? = 3A + 4.5B.

- Show pupils this problem:

> Sandra bought 24 cupcakes on Monday and 38 cupcakes on Tuesday. The price of each is £s.
> How much did she spend on cupcakes over the 2 days?

Ask pupils, working in pairs, to draw bar models to represent the problem:

?	
24s	38s

So, ? = 24s + 38s.

Say: _Draw a bar model to show how much more Sandra spent on Tuesday than on Monday._

38s	
24s	?

So, ? = 38s − 24s. ? = 14s.

- Provide pupils with **Resource 6.3.2b** and ask them to work in pairs to complete task A.

Answers: **1.** a) 25 + t, b) 75; **2.** m (n + 2)

Same-day intervention

- Show pupils this problem:

> Last week, Andrew spent £3 per day on fruit and £2 per day on salad. He did this for 3 days.
> How much money did he spend altogether?

Together, represent the problem using counters and draw a bar model.

?					
3	3	3	2	2	2

Agree 3 × 3 + 3 × 2 = 15 or 3 (3 + 2) = 15

● Show pupils this problem:

> This week, Andrew spent £3 per day on fruit and £T per day on salad. He did this for 4 days.
> How much money did he spend altogether?

Together, draw a bar model for the problem.

?							
3	3	3	3	T	T	T	T

Agree $4 \times 3 + 4 \times T = 12 + 4T$ or $4(3 + T)$

● Repeat for similar problems, using one unknown, then two.

Same-day enrichment

● Give pupils **Resource 6.3.2b** Word problems and ask them to solve task B.

Answers: **1.** A complete answer needs both $7g + 8h$ and $8g + 7h$; **2.** The reasoning should include 'four times the amount of time is needed'.

Challenge and extension question

Question 7

7　The figures below show three identical squares, each containing a different number of circles of the same radius. Look at them carefully and then fill in the table.

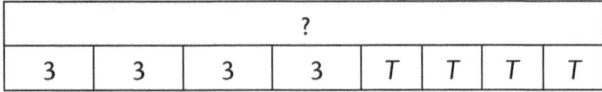

(1)　　　(2)　　　(3)

Figure number	(1)	(2)	(3)	(4)	(5)	(6)	...
Number of circles							

The number of circles in the nth square is _____.

Based on the pattern you identified, there are _____ circles in the 2018th figure.

This question allows for sequences and the nth term to be applied in a practical context. The approach is to consider the pattern created by the figures, complete the table and find the nth term.

Unit 3.3
Simplification and evaluation (1)

Conceptual context

This unit develops understanding of simplification and evaluation, equations and formulae. Pupils' knowledge will become more secure and fluent as they construct or simplify expressions both in and out of context. They will need to apply their knowledge about simplification when solving word problems.

(i) An **expression** is a combination of numbers, symbols, and operations arranged to show the value of something.

An **equation** is a mathematical statement containing an equals sign.

Simplify means to bring terms of the same type together.

Evaluate means to find the value of a mathematical statement.

Learning pupils will have achieved at the end of the unit

- Pupils' understanding of algebra will have been deepened through simplifying and evaluating algebraic expressions (Q1, Q2)
- Pupils will have used algebra, including simplification, to solve word problems (Q3, Q4)

Resources

A1/flip chart paper; marker pens; blank card; **Resource 6.3.3a** Expressions spiders; **Resource 6.3.3b** Expressions matching; **Resource 6.3.3c** Problem diagrams (1); **Resource 6.3.3d** Problem diagrams (2)

Vocabulary

expression, sequence, *n*th term, equation, algebra, brackets, expansion, formulae, equivalent

Questions 1 and 2

> **1** True or false? Put a ✓ or ✗ in each box.
>
> (a) $6 + a = 6a$ ☐
>
> (b) $n + n - m + m = 2n - 2m$ ☐
>
> (c) $5x + 4 + x = 10x$ ☐
>
> (d) $3x + 4y = 7xy$ ☐
>
> **2** Simplify the following expressions. The first three have been done for you.
>
> (a) $5x + 4x = 9x$
>
> (b) $5b + 4b - 9a = 9b - 9a$
>
> (c) $7x + 7 + 6x = 13x + 7$
>
> (d) $5b + 4b - 9b = \underline{\hspace{3cm}}$
>
> (e) $36s - 15t - 24s + 35t = \underline{\hspace{3cm}}$
>
> (f) $48x + 75y - 18x - 6x = \underline{\hspace{3cm}}$
>
> (g) $5 \times 12a = \underline{\hspace{3cm}}$
>
> (h) $36k \div 9 = \underline{\hspace{3cm}}$
>
> (i) $6 \times 3x \div 2 = \underline{\hspace{3cm}}$
>
> (j) $4y \div 2 \times 10 = \underline{\hspace{3cm}}$
>
> (k) $75x \div 15 + 6 \times 9x = \underline{\hspace{3cm}}$
>
> (l) $4n \times 7 - 63n \div 9 - 3n = \underline{\hspace{3cm}}$

What learning will pupils have achieved at the conclusion of Questions 1 and 2?

- Pupils' understanding of algebra will have been deepened through simplifying and evaluating algebraic expressions.

Activities for whole-class instruction

- Show pupils these statements:

2.5, 4.5, 6.5, 8.5 … nth term is $2n + 1$	[False]
$N \times 3 \div p \times 3$ is $N \div p$	[False]
d = distance, s = speed, t = time so $d = s \div t$	[False]
$5(c - d) + 2 < c - d$	[Sometimes]
The sum of g and 6, times by x^2 is $x^2(g + 6)$	[True]

- Ask pupils, working in pairs, to decide if the statements are true or false. Share decisions.

- Write $5a$ in the middle of the board. (You will gradually build up the following spider diagram.)

- Draw one line and write $a + a + a + a + a$.

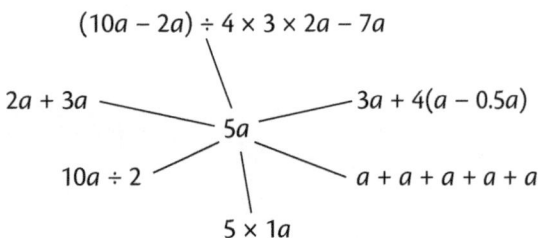

$$(10a - 2a) \div 4 \times 3 \times 2a - 7a$$

$2a + 3a$ — $5a$ — $3a + 4(a - 0.5a)$

$10a \div 2$ — $a + a + a + a + a$

$5 \times 1a$

- Ask: *Does 5a equal a + a + a + a + a?* Agree, yes.

> **Look out for** … pupils not recognising $5a = 5 \times a = a + a + a + a + a$. Use this bar model to explain why:

5a				
a	a	a	a	a

'Merge' some cells on the bottom bar and label $2a + 3a$.

5a	
2a	3a

Ask: *Does 5a equal 2a + 3a?* Agree, yes with pupils.

Ask: *Does 5a equal 2a − a + a − a + 4a?* Ask pupils to discuss responses in pairs. They should see that:

$2a - a = a$

$a - a = 0$

$a + 4a = 5a$

> **Look out for** … pupils not recognising $a - a = 0$. Substitute values for a in this equation to prove that its value is zero.

Ask: *Does 5a equal 5 × 1a?* Agree, yes.

Ask: *Does 5a equal 10a ÷ 2?* Pupils discuss responses in pairs. They should see that $10 \div 2 = 5$.

> **Look out for** … pupils not recognising that $10a$ can be divided into two parts. Draw a bar model twice as wide as $5a$ to show that $10a = 2 \times 5a$. Agree that $5a$ does equal $10a \div 2$.

Working in pairs, ask pupils to find three more expressions that equal $5a$. Share ideas.

- Write $7g$ in the middle of the board, with 8 lines radiating from it. Ask: *Can you find eight expressions that equal 7g?*

- In groups of four, pupils add $7g$ to A1/flip chart paper and find eight expressions that equal $7g$. Show the following Hint card to support discussion:

> **Hint**
> You could use:
> (,), +, −, ×, ÷, zero, integers, decimals, fractions

Share ideas and add them to the board.

- Write $8b$ on the board with space around it. Can pupils add expressions that equal $8b$?

> **Look out for** … pupils who think that the following expressions (or something similar) are correct.

$$8(b + 1)$$

$$(32 \div 2) \div 2 + b$$

$$16b \div 2b$$

$$2 \times 5b - (4b - 2) \longrightarrow 8b \longrightarrow 8b - 2 + 2b$$

$$10b - 2$$

$$6b + 2$$

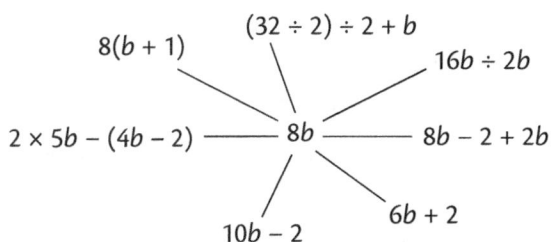

In each case, one or more of the references to b is being used incorrectly. Discuss such errors where they arise, using bar models to decide how the expression should be corrected.

- Write $9d$ on the board with space around it. Ask: *Can you find eight expressions that DO NOT equal $9d$?*

  In groups of four, ask pupils to add $9d$ to A1/flip chart paper and write eight expressions that do not equal $9d$. Encourage them to create just minor errors. Provide the Hint card as shown previously. Share ideas.

- Write $5a + 4b$ with eight lines radiating from it. At the end of one line write: $2a - 3b + 3a + 7b$. Ask pupils to check that this expression equals $5a + 4b$. Can they see that $2a + 3a = 5a$ and $-3b + 7b = 4b$?

  Ask: *Can you find eight more expressions that equal $5a + 4b$?*

  In groups of four, ask pupils to add $5a + 4b$ to A1/flip chart paper and find eight expressions that equal $5a + 4b$. Provide the Hint card as shown previously. Share ideas.

- **Look out for** ... pupils who think that $x + x - y + y = 2x - 2y$. Substitute values for x and y in this equation to prove that it's not true.

  ... pupils who think that $2x + 3y = 5xy$. Use this bar model to explain why it is not:

2x		3y		
x	x	y	y	y

- Write $10x - 3y$ with eight lines radiating from it.

  At the end of one line, write $12x + 2y - 2x - 5y$. Ask pupils to check that this expression equals $10x - 3y$.

  Ask: *Can you find eight more expressions that equal $10x - 3y$?*

  In groups of four, ask pupils to add $10x - 3y$ to A1/flip chart paper and find eight expressions that equal $10x - 3y$. Provide the Hint card as shown previously. Share ideas.

- Working in pairs, ask pupils to complete section A of **Resource 6.3.3a** Expressions spiders.

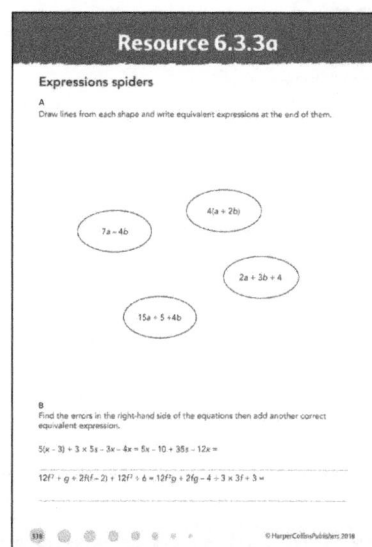

Resource 6.3.3a — Expressions spiders

- Pupils should complete Questions 1 and 2 in the Practice Book.

Same-day intervention

- Show pupils these calculations:

$3 \times 4 + 12$
$6 \times 7 - 5 \times 3$
$15 \div 5 + 4 - 3$

  Ask pupils to find calculations that are equivalent to those in the list. Share ideas.

- Show pupils these expressions:

$3a$
$5a - 2b$
$4a \div 2 + 4$

  Together find expressions that are equivalent to those in the list.

- Use bar models to support pupil understanding.

Same-day enrichment

- Give pupils **Resource 6.3.3a** and ask them to complete section B.

  Answers: Corrected right-hand sides:
  $5x - 15 + 15s - 7x$; $12f^2 + g + 2f^2 - 4f + 12f^2 \div 6$

Question 3

> **3** Complete each statement.
>
> (a) In an equilateral triangle, each side is a metres. Its perimeter
>
> is _____ metres.
>
> (b) Joe has x pencils. Roy has 3 more pencils than Joe. They have
>
> _____ pencils altogether.
>
> (c) Each pack of flour weighs 10 kg. Each pack of rice weighs x kg. y packs
>
> of flour and 5 packs of rice weigh _____ kg in total.
>
> (d) A school bought x boxes of red pens and 10 times as many white pens
> as red pens.
>
> The school bought _____ boxes of pens altogether.
>
> (e) Don, Evans and Frank each bought 4 pens at a pounds each.
>
> They paid _____ pounds in total for the pens. They also each
> bought b exercise books. Each book costs 2 pounds.
>
> They paid _____ pounds in total for the books.

What learning will pupils have achieved at the conclusion of Question 3?

- Pupils will have used algebra, including simplification, to solve word problems.

Activities for whole-class instruction

- Give mixed attainment groups of four a set of cards from **Resource 6.3.3b** Expressions matching. Ask pupils to match cards, then share solutions.

Resource 6.3.3b

Expressions matching

Answers: $3n + n - 2n + 4p = (6 \div 1.5) p + 1.5n \div 0.5 - n$; $d(7a - 4) + 45a \div 3 = 15a - ad - 2d - 2d + 8ad$; $3(4x + 25y - 18y) = 42 \div 2 \times 3y \div 9) \times 3 + 4 \times 3x$; $4a \div 2 \times 11 = 6 \times 4a \div 8 + 19a$; $7(e + f) - 2f^2 = 7f + 0 \times 3e + 7e - 4f^2 \div 2$; $65x + 76x = 10[7.6x + (0.5 + 6)x]$

- Show pupils this diagram:

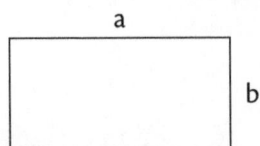

Say: *Use the names of the sides to describe the perimeter of the rectangle.* Pupil pairs should suggest:

Perimeter $= a + a + b + b = 2a + 2b = 2(a + b)$

Say: *Use the names of the sides to describe the area of the rectangle.* Pupil pairs should suggest:

Area $= ab$

- Show pupils this problem:

> Rectangle A has length p and width q. Rectangle B is double the length but the same width.
> What is the length of the perimeter of rectangle B?
> What is the area of rectangle B?

- Discuss the problem with pupils, asking questions such as:
  - *What is the question asking?*
  - *What is the problem that needs to be solved?*
  - *What do we need to find out/work out?*
  - *Could we draw a diagram?*
  - *Is it a problem about something being a number of times bigger or smaller than something else? Is it about something else? How do we know?*
  - *What operations are going to be used?*
  - *What is the calculation that needs to be done? If there is more than one step, in what order should the steps be carried out?*

Together, draw a diagram that represents the problem:

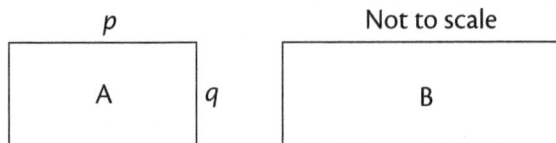

With help from pupils, draw these bar models to represent the problem and work out a solution:

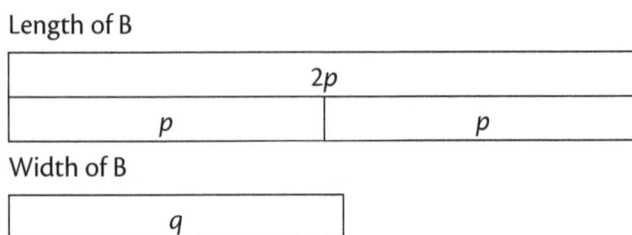

Length of B

Width of B

Perimeter of B

$2p + 2p + q + q = 4p + 2q = 2(2p + q)$

Area of B

$2p \times q = 2pq$

Show pupils this problem:

> On Monday morning Peter ran b km and Andrew walked 5 km more.
> On Monday afternoon Andrew ran 12 km and Peter walked c km less.
> How many km did they walk and run in total?

Discuss the problem, asking pupils questions as previously.

Together, draw these bar models to represent the problem and work out a solution.

Monday morning

A	
b	5

Monday afternoon

12	
P	c

Total distance

$b + A + 12 + P = b + b + 5 + 12 + 12 − c = 2b − c + 29$

- Show pupils this problem:

> Last week in the supermarket Ann, Mohammed and Peter each stacked 5 shelves with A boxes on each.
> This week they each stacked B shelves with 7 boxes on each.
> How many boxes have they stacked altogether?

Discuss the problem, asking pupils questions as previously.

Together, draw these bar models to represent the problem and work out a solution:

Last week

Ann	Mohammed	Peter
5A	5A	5A

This week

Ann	Mohammed	Peter
7B	7B	7B

Total number of boxes

$3 × 5A + 3 × 7B = 15A + 21B = 3(5A + 7B)$

- Give pupils **Resource 6.3.3c** Problem diagrams (1) and ask them to complete section A in pairs.

Answers: **1.** a) 11g, b) $3g^2$, c) $4g^2$; **2.** 12s + 16g

- Pupils should complete Question 3 in the Practice Book.

Same-day intervention

- Show pupils this problem:

> On Monday morning Ann ran 8 km and Peter walked c km more.
> How many km did Peter walk?
> How many km did they walk altogether?

Discuss the problem, asking pupils questions as previously.

Together, draw a bar model to represent the problem and work out a solution:

P	
8	c

Peter

$P = 8 + c$

Peter and Ann

$8 + 8 + c$

- Repeat with a second day. For example:

  On Tuesday afternoon Peter ran 12 km and Ann walked d km less.

Same-day enrichment

- Ask pupils to complete section B of **Resource 6.3.3c** Problem diagrams (1).

Answer: Last week = 12(s + 2) = 12s + 24
This week = 20(g − 3) = 20g − 60
Total distance = 12s + 20g − 36

Question 4

4 Solve these problems.

(a) £10 can buy 3*a* kg of pineapples. Fiona bought 9.6*a*kg of pineapples with £50. How much change did she get?

(b) It took Jade *m* hours to make 21 paper flowers. It took Mariam 2 hours to make *n* paper flowers.

   (i) How many paper flowers did each of them make on average?

   (ii) How many paper flowers did both of them make every hour, on average?

(c) The dividend is 6 times the divisor. If the divisor is *x*, what is the sum of the dividend, divisor and quotient?

(d) Rob is 4 years older than his younger brother Mike.

   (i) Let *x* represent Mike's age and *y* represent Rob's age. Express *y* in terms of *x*, and we can get *y* = _____ .

   (ii) Complete the table to show how old Rob is when Mike is at a certain age.

Mike's age: x	1	2	3	4	...	n	...
Rob's age: y							

What learning will pupils have achieved at the conclusion of Question 4?

- Pupils will have used algebra, including simplification, to solve word problems.

Activities for whole-class instruction

- Show pupils these equations. Working in pairs, ask pupils to decide if the equations are true or false.

$7a + 8 = 15a$	[False]
$3x + 7y = 21xy$	[False]
$35s - 16t + 16t = 35s$	[True]
$4n \times 8 - 75n \div 15 + 4 = 32n + 9n$	[False]
$48x - 15t + 48x - 15t = 0$	[False]

Share ideas.

- Show pupils this problem:

£12 can buy 2*b* kg of sausages.
Peter buys 5*b* kg of sausages for his catering firm.
How much does Peter pay for the sausages?

Discuss the problem, asking pupils questions as previously.

Together, draw these bar models to represent the problem and work out a solution:

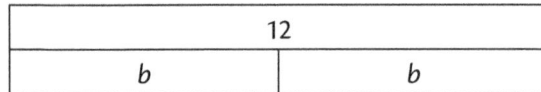

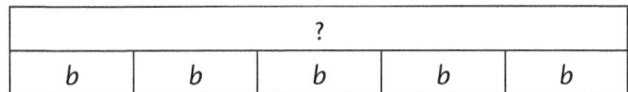

12	
b	b

?				
b	b	b	b	b

$2b = 12$

$5b = 2b + 2b + b$

$5b = 12 + 12 + 6 = 30$

$5b \div 2b = 2.5$ times more

$2.5 \times 12 = 30$

- Show pupils this problem:

Sanjit repaired 35 clocks in *g* hours.
On average, how many clocks does Sanjit repair per hour?

Ask pupils to discuss the problem in pairs. They should see that the average is $35 \div g$.

Ask: *How is g ÷ 35 different to the answer we found?* Pupils should see that $g \div 35$ is the number of hours per clock.

- Show pupils this problem:

Chi is *d* years old and Dave is *f* years old. Chi is 5 years younger than Dave.

Ask pupils, working in pairs, to draw a bar model to represent the comparison and write it in algebra.

They should draw:

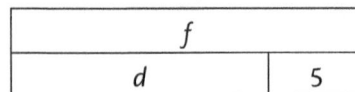

f	
d	5

$d = f - 5$

Point out that $d = f - 5$ is *d* expressed in terms of *f*.

Point out that $f = d + 5$ is *f* expressed in terms of *d*.

Ask: *When Chi is 24 how old will Dave be?* Pupils discuss responses in pairs. They should see that Dave is always 5 years older, so he is 29.

Ask: *How old will Dave be when Chi is* n *years old?* Pupils discuss responses in pairs. They should see that: $f = n + 5$.

● In pairs, ask pupils to complete section A of **Resource 6.3.3d** Problem diagrams (2).

Answers: **1.** £1.12 or £1.125 or 112.5p or £1.13; **2.** £2.85; **3.** £5.022 or £5.02; **4.** Terry: 5 ÷ n, Mustafa: g ÷ 5; **5.** Terry: $n \div 5$, Mustafa: $5 \div g$; **6.** a) $Y = 5 + X$; b) $X = Y - 5$; c) $5 + n$; d) $2n - 5$

● Pupils should complete Question 4 in the Practice Book.

Same-day intervention

● Show pupils this problem:

> £15 can buy 3 kg of grapes.
> How much is 1 kg?
> Peter buys 12 kg of grapes for his catering firm.
> How much does Peter pay for the grapes?

Discuss responses with pupils and ask questions as previously.

Together, draw these bar models to represent the problem and work out a solution:

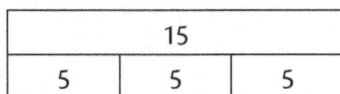

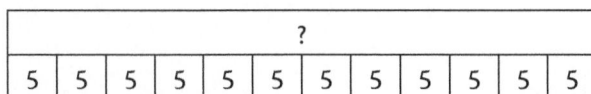

15		
5	5	5

?											
5	5	5	5	5	5	5	5	5	5	5	5

3 kg = 15

12 kg = 15 + 15 + 15 + 15

12 kg = 4 × 15 = 60

● Repeat, using algebra.

Same-day enrichment

● Ask pupils to complete section B of **Resource 6.3.3d** Problem diagrams (2).

Answers: $n + 3.5$; $2n - 4.5$

Challenge and extension questions

Question 5

5 Three small rectangles, each with length 5 cm and width *a* cm, form a large rectangle. What is the area of the large rectangle? What is the perimeter?

This question requires deeper understanding of area and perimeter of rectangles. The approach needs pupils to know that the rectangle is made up of smaller rectangles and to be able to simplify expressions.

Question 6

6 The length and width of a rectangle are *a* cm and *b* cm respectively, and *a* > *b*. The side length of a square equals the difference between the two sides of the rectangle. What is the sum of their perimeters?

This question takes a deeper look at perimeter of rectangles and squares. The approach needs an understanding of the relationship between the side length of the square and the length and width of the rectangle.

Unit 3.4
Simplification and evaluation (2)

Conceptual context

This unit continues to develop understanding of simplification and evaluation, and solving algebraic problems. Understanding will be developed through creating, simplifying and evaluating algebraic expressions, including the *n*th term. Pupils will appreciate the value of being able to think algebraically when they use their new algebraic knowledge to solve word problems.

Learning pupils will have achieved at the end of the unit

- Pupils' understanding of the *n*th term will have been extended (Q1, Q2)
- Pupils will be able to construct and evaluate algebraic expressions in order to solve word problems (Q1, Q2, Q3, Q4)
- Simplifying and evaluating of algebraic expressions will have been practised using given expressions (Q5)
- Pupils will have applied algebra to solving problems (Q6)

Resources

Resource 6.3.4a Sequences and *n*th terms; **Resource 6.3.4b** Word problems – applying algebra (1); **Resource 6.3.4c** Word problems – applying algebra (2)

Vocabulary

expression, sequence, *n*th term, evaluation, equation, algebra, formula

Questions 1 and 2

1 Using the formula for the nth term for each number sequence below, write its first 5 terms. The first one has been done for you.

nth term	First 5 terms
n	1 , 2 , 3 , 4 , 5
$4n$	____ , ____ , ____ , ____ , ____
$5n - 3$	____ , ____ , ____ , ____ , ____
$7 + 7n$	____ , ____ , ____ , ____ , ____
$\frac{2n}{3} + 2$	____ , ____ , ____ , ____ , ____

2 Complete the table.

Adam wants to buy a number of books priced at £7 each. The relation between the total price he pays, b, and the number of books he buys, a, can be represented as $7a = b$. When $a = 1, 3, 5, 7, 9, ...$, what values does b represent, respectively?

a	1	3	5	7	9
b					

What learning will pupils have achieved at the conclusion of Questions 1 and 2?

- Pupils' understanding of the nth term will have been extended.
- Pupils will be able to construct and evaluate algebraic expressions in order to solve word problems.

Activities for whole-class instruction

(i) The **nth term**: 'n' stands for the **term** number (or position). The **nth term** is a formula containing 'n'. Using the nth term enables any **term** of a sequence to be known without having to list all terms. For example, to find the 50th **term** we would just substitute 50 in the formula in place of 'n'. In this unit, pupils are introduced to the idea of the nth term being a formula that can generate a sequence. For example, the nth term $3n$ generates 3, 6, 9, ... because the value in position 1 will be 3×1, the value in position 2 will be 3×2, the value in position 3 will be 3×3, and so on.

- Show pupils these two lists.

Sequence	nth term
0, 3, 6, 9, 12, ...	$n - 1$
3, 7, 11, 15, 19, ...	$9n + 14$
0, 1, 2, 3, 4, ...	$3n - 3$
1, 1.5, 2, 2.5, 3, ...	$4n - 1$
23, 32, 41, 50, 59, ...	$0.5(n + 1)$

Working in pairs, pupils should copy the lists and match corresponding sequences with the nth term.

Answers:

Sequence	nth term
0, 3, 6, 9, 12, ...	$n - 1$
3, 7, 11, 15, 19, ...	$9n + 14$
0, 1, 2, 3, 4, ...	$3n - 3$
1, 1.5, 2, 2.5, 3, ...	$4n - 1$
23, 32, 41, 50, 59, ...	$0.5(n + 1)$

- Write on the board: $n + 1$.

  Tell pupils that this is a formula for an nth term for a number sequence. Tell them it means that the value in position 1 will be $1 + 1$, the value in position 2 will be $2 + 1$, the value in position 3 will be $3 + 1$, and so on.

  Ask: *What is the sequence? How can we find it?* Pupils discuss responses in pairs. They should tell you that:

  - n means the position in the sequence – that is, position 1 or 2 or 3 or 345

  - in each position in the sequence, the number will be the position number + 1. So, the number that appears in position 4 will be 5 because it is $4 + 1$; and the number in position 345 will be 346 because it is $345 + 1$

  - the sequence, therefore, starts with 2 and continues 3, 4, 5, ...

- Write on the board: $2n - 1$.

  Ask: *What is the sequence? How can we find it?* Pupils discuss responses in pairs. They should see that:

  - in each position in the sequence, the number will be double the position number minus 1. So the number that appears in position 4 will be 7 because it is double 4, then subtract 1; and the number in position 345 will be 689 because it is double 345 then subtract 1

  - the sequence, therefore, starts with 1 and continues 3, 5, 7, 9, 11, 13, ...

- Write on the board: $3n + 2$.

  Ask: *What are the first five terms of the sequence using this formula for an nth term?* Agree 5, 8, 11, 14, 17.

- Write on the board: $0.5n + 1$.

  Ask: *What are the first five terms of the sequence using this formula for an nth term?* Agree 1.5, 2, 2.5, 3, 3.5.

- Now show pupils this table:

Formula for *n*th term	Terms						
	1	2	3	4	5	10	15
$n + 2$							
$2n - 2$							
$3n + 3$							
$0.5n + 1$							

- Tell pupils to use the formulae of the *n*th terms to find the terms in each sequence, then ask them to work in pairs to complete the table.

Answers:

Formula for *n*th term	Terms						
	1	2	3	4	5	10	15
$n + 2$	[3]	[4]	[5]	[6]	[7]	[12]	[17]
$2n - 2$	[0]	[2]	[4]	[6]	[8]	[18]	[28]
$3n + 3$	[6]	[9]	[12]	[15]	[18]	[33]	[48]
$0.5n + 1$	[1.5]	[2]	[2.5]	[3]	[3.5]	[6]	[8.5]

- Write on the board: $\frac{1}{3}n$ and $\frac{n}{3}$.

  Ask pupils: *What are these two expressions the same as?* Agree $n \div 3$.

- Write $\frac{2}{7}n$ and $\frac{2n}{7}$.

  Ask: *What are these two expressions the same as?* Agree $2n \div 7$.

- Ask: *In what ways could the expression $3n \div 7 + 4$ be written?* Pupils discuss responses in pairs. They should notice that:

  $3n \div 7 + 4 = \frac{3n}{7} + 4$

  $3n \div 7 + 4 = \frac{3}{7}n + 4$

  Share ideas.

- Ask: *In what ways could the expression $8n \div 7 - 3$ be written?* Pupils discuss responses in pairs. They should notice that:

  $8n \div 7 - 3 = \frac{8n}{7} - 3$

  $8n \div 7 - 3 = \frac{8}{7}n - 3$

- Share ideas.

- Write on the board: $\frac{n}{3} + 1$.

- Ask: *What are the first five terms of the sequence using this formula for an nth term?* Pupils discuss responses in pairs. They should see that the first five terms are $1\frac{1}{3}$, $1\frac{2}{3}$, 2, $2\frac{1}{3}$, $2\frac{2}{3}$.

- Write on the board $\frac{4n}{3} + 1$.

  Ask: *What are the first five terms of the sequence using this formula for an nth term?* Pupils discuss responses in pairs. They should see that the first five terms are $2\frac{1}{3}$, $3\frac{2}{3}$, 5, $6\frac{1}{3}$, $7\frac{2}{3}$.

- Show pupils this table:

Formula for *n*th term	Terms						
	1	2	3	4	5	10	15
$\frac{n}{3} + 2$							
$\frac{4n}{3} + 2$							
$\frac{2n}{7} + 1$							

Ask pupils to use the *n*th term formulae to find the terms in each sequence. Pupils work in pairs to complete the table.

Answers:

Formula for *n*th term	Terms						
	1	2	3	4	5	10	15
$\frac{n}{3} + 2$	$[2\frac{1}{3}]$	$[2\frac{2}{3}]$	[3]	$[3\frac{1}{3}]$	$[3\frac{2}{3}]$	$[5\frac{1}{3}]$	[7]
$\frac{4n}{3} + 2$	$[3\frac{1}{3}]$	$[4\frac{2}{3}]$	[6]	$[7\frac{1}{3}]$	$[8\frac{2}{3}]$	$[15\frac{1}{3}]$	[22]
$\frac{2n}{7} + 1$	$[1\frac{2}{7}]$	$[1\frac{4}{7}]$	$[1\frac{6}{7}]$	$[2\frac{1}{7}]$	$[2\frac{3}{7}]$	$[3\frac{6}{7}]$	$[5\frac{2}{7}]$

- Now show pupils this problem:

> James wants to read 7 pages of his book each day. He will read the book for 2 weeks.
> He writes this formula $P = 7d$.
> *d* represents the number of days he reads the book.
> *P* represents the total number of pages he reads.
> How many pages has he read after 5 days?
> How many pages has he read after 11 days?

Ask pupils to discuss, in pairs, solutions to the questions. They should see that:

$P = 7 \times 5$, so $P = 35$.

$P = 7 \times 11$, so $P = 77$.

- In pairs, ask pupils to complete sections A and B of **Resource 6.3.4a** Sequences and *n*th terms.

Resource 6.3.4a

Sequences and nth terms

Answers: Section A: $(2n + 4)$, $(6, 8, 10, 12, 14, 16)$; $(3n - 1)$, $(2, 5, 8, 11, 14, 17)$; $(5n + 3)$, $(8, 13, 18, 23, 28, 33)$; $(\frac{2}{3}n + 3)$, $(3\frac{2}{3}, 4\frac{1}{3}, 5, 5\frac{2}{3}, 6\frac{1}{3}, 7)$.

Section B: **1.** $t = 1$, $s = 3$; $t = 4$ $s = 12$; $t = 11$, $s = 33$; **2.** $q = 2$, $P = 30$; $q = 6$, $P = 90$; $q = 10$, $P = 150$

- Pupils should complete Questions 1 and 2 in the Practice Book.

Same-day intervention

- Show pupils this table:

	Terms						
Formula for nth term	1	2	3	4	5	10	15
$n + 1$							

Together, find each term in the sequence.

Answers:

	Terms						
Formula for nth term	1	2	3	4	5	10	15
$n + 1$	[2]	[3]	[4]	[5]	[6]	[11]	[16]

- Show pupils these calculations:

$\frac{1}{3} + 2$

$\frac{5}{3} + 3$

$\frac{2}{7} + 2$

$\frac{8}{7} + 6$

where $n = 2$

Answers: $2\frac{1}{3}$; $4\frac{2}{3}$; $2\frac{2}{7}$; $7\frac{1}{7}$

- Working in pairs, pupils should find the answers and give them as mixed numbers. Support pupils with bar models and other diagrams as necessary.

Same-day enrichment

- Ask pupils to complete section C of **Resource 6.3.4a** Sequences and nth terms.

Answers: **1.** −5, 0, 5, 10, 15; **2.** −1, 2, 5, 8, 11; **3.** 7.6, 9.2, 10.8, 12.4, 14; **4.** 3, −1, −5, −9, −13

Questions 3 and 4

3 To repair a section of a road, a team repaired c metres of the road every day for the first 6 days, leaving s metres of road still needing repair.

(a) Use an expression to express the length of the road section: _____.

(b) When $c = 50$ and $s = 200$, the length is _____.

4 The side length of a square is a m. Its perimeter is _____ m and its area is _____ m². When $a = 5$ m, the perimeter is _____ m and the area is _____ m².

What learning will pupils have achieved at the conclusion of Questions 3 and 4?

- Pupils will be able to construct and evaluate algebraic expressions in order to solve word problems.

Activities for whole-class instruction

- Show pupils these statements:

If $x = 2$, $y = 4$, then $2x + 2y = 12$.
If $m = 2$, $n = 1$, then $13m + 2n = 24$.
If $r = 3$, $s = 4$, then $3r - 5s = 34$.
If $r = 0$, $t = 3$, then $12 + 4r - 3t = 3$.
If $x = 2$, $r = 4$, then $4x + 4r \div 2 = 15$.
If $t = 2$, $r = 0$, then $36t \div 9 + 4r = 84$.

Answers: True; False; False; True; False; False

Ask: *Is the first statement true or false? How do we know?* Agree that $2 \times 2 = 4$ and $2 \times 4 = 8$, so $4 + 8 = 12$. So, the statement is true.

Ask: *Is the second statement true or false? How do we know?* Agree that $13 \times 2 = 26$ and $2 \times 1 = 2$, so $26 + 2 = 28$, not 24. So, the statement is false.

Working in pairs, pupils decide if the other statements are true or false. Share conclusions.

- Show pupils this problem:

Every day, for two weeks, Ann ran d km and Peter ran f km.
What expression can represent the total number of kilometres, T, they both ran?

Together, draw this bar model to represent the problem and find a solution:

T	
$14d$	$14f$

Total number of kilometres: $T = 14d + 14f$.

Ask: *If $d = 5$ and $f = 4$, what does T equal? How do we know?* Pupils should discuss responses in pairs. They should see that:

$14 \times 5 = 70$

$14 \times 4 = 56$

$T = 70 + 56 = 126$ km

● Show pupils this problem:

> Sanjit takes the bus to town every day for 10 days. The bus drives r km to get to town.
>
> Peter cycles to town every day for 8 days. He cycles f km to get town.
>
> If $r = 5$ and $f = 6$, what is the total distance travelled by Sanjit and Peter?

Working in pairs, pupils should draw a bar model to represent the problem and find a solution.

They should draw:

?	
10r	8f

Total distance

$? = 10r + 8f$

$? = 10 \times 5 + 6 \times 8 = 50 + 48 = 98$ km

● Show pupils this problem:

> A rectangle has length $2a$ and width $3b$.
> What is the length of the perimeter? What is the area?

Pupils should see that:

- Perimeter $= 2a + 2a + 3b + 3b = 2 \times 2a + 2 \times 3b$
  $= 4a + 6b$

- Area $= 2a \times 3b = 6ab$

Ask: *If $a = 3$ and $b = 4$, what is the perimeter and area of the rectangle?* Pupils discuss responses in pairs. They should see that:

- Perimeter $= 4 \times 3 + 6 \times 4 = 36$

- Area $= 6 \times 3 \times 4 = 72$

● Give pupils **Resource 6.3.4b** Word problems – applying algebra (1), and ask them to complete section A.

Resource 6.3.4b 1 of 2

Answers: **1.** a) $3d + 30$; b) 255 loaves; **2.** 274 minutes; **3.** 34.6 cm

● Pupils should complete Questions 3 and 4 in the Practice Book.

Same-day intervention

● Show pupils this problem:

> In the local swimming pool, d swimmers are taking part in a competition. They have to swim 30 lengths of the pool each.
> a) Use an expression to express the number of lengths swum altogether.
> b) Another e swimmers have to swim 25 lengths of the pool each.
> Use an expression to express the number of lengths swum altogether.
> c) If $d = 10$ and $e = 15$, how many lengths were swum altogether by both groups of swimmers?
> Together, write the expressions and draw the bar model to represent the problem. Then work out a solution.

Answers: a) 30d; b) 25e; c)

?	
30d	25e

Total number of lengths: 30d + 25e

$30 \times 10 + 25 \times 15 = 300 + 375 = 675$ lengths

Same-day enrichment

● Ask pupils to complete section B of **Resource 6.3.4b** Word problems – applying algebra (1)

Resource 6.3.4b 2 of 2

Answers: **1.** 1650 kg; **2.** 14 cm; **3.** 14 700 mm²

Question 5

> **5** Simplify first and then evaluate. The first one has been done for you.
> (a) When x = 2.5, find the value of 18x − 8x + 6x.
>
>   18x − 8x + 6x = (18 − 8 + 6)x = 16x = 16 × 2.5 = 40
> (b) When y = 2, find the value of 12y + 72y ÷ 6.
>
> (c) When m = 4 and n = 1.8, find the value of 15m + 5m − 18n − 12n.
>
> (d) When a = 0.5 and b = 0.6, find the value of
>   3.5a × 8 + 75b ÷ 15 + a − 4b.

What learning will pupils have achieved at the conclusion of Question 5?

- Simplifying and evaluating of algebraic expressions will have been practised using given expressions.

Activities for whole-class instruction

- Show pupils these two lists:

Expression	Simplification
x + 2y − 7x + 4y	9 − 4.5s
14f − 15g + 2 × 12f − 12.5g	7f − 5g
2x + 3x − 3y − 4x + 2x + 3y	6(y − x)
45s ÷ 15 + 24r ÷ 2r − 3(2.5s + 1)	3x
3.5f − 2.5g + 3.5f − 2.5g	38f − 27.5g

- Working in pairs, ask pupils to match expressions with the corresponding simplification. Share ideas.

  Answers:

Expression	Simplification
x + 2y − 7x + 4y	6(y − x)
14f − 15g + 2 × 12f − 12.5g	38f − 27.5g
2x + 3x − 3y − 4x + 2x + 3y	3x
45s ÷ 15 + 24r ÷ 2r − 3(2.5s + 1)	9 − 4.5s
3.5f − 2.5g + 3.5f − 2.5g	7f − 5g

- On the board, write 3x + 2y − 5x + 3y.

  Ask: *How is the value of the expression found when x = 3 and y = 4?* Agree the expression can be simplified to 5y − 2x so the solution is 14.

  Ask: *What is the value of the expression when x = 2.5 and y = 3.5?* Agree 12.5.

- Write on the board: 45d ÷ 5 − 32e ÷ 4 + d + e.

  Ask: *How is the value of the expression found when d = 4.5 and e = 3.5?* Agree the expression can be simplified to 10d − 7e so the solution is 20.5.

- Tell the pupils that when the value of an expression is being found it is called 'evaluation'.

> (All say...) *Evaluation means finding the value of an expression.*

- Working in pairs, ask pupils to create ten expressions using two unknowns that need simplifying and evaluating. They should swap with another pair who must simplify and evaluate, using decimal numbers.

- Pupils should complete Question 5 in the Practice Book.

Same-day intervention

- Show pupils these expressions:

  > 2x + 2y − 7x + 4y
  > 2 × 12f − 3 × 3f
  > 4y + 3z − 3y − 4z + 2y + 4z
  > 2.5f − 2.5g + 2.5f − 2.5g

  Together, evaluate the expressions using numbers chosen by the pupils. Tell them to begin with whole numbers, then choose decimals.

Same-day enrichment

- Write these numbers on the board:

  3.5

  6.5

  0.6

  2.3

- Ask pupils to create expressions using two unknowns that need simplifying, and evaluate to these four numbers.

Question 6

6 Answer these questions using the information given.

(a) A farm has cultivated sycamores and cedars. They are each in x rows. Sycamores are in rows of 12 and cedars are in rows of 14.

(i) How many sycamores and cedars has the farm cultivated in total?

(ii) When $x = 20$, how many sycamores and cedars are there on the farm?

(b) A car travelled at a speed of a km per hour. It travelled 4 hours in the morning and b km in the afternoon.

(i) Use an expression with letters to represent the distance that the car travelled.

(ii) When $a = 80$ and $b = 200$, what is the distance the car travelled?

What learning will pupils have achieved at the conclusion of Question 6?

- Pupils will have applied algebra to solve word problems.

Activities for whole-class instruction

- Show pupils this problem:

> The length of one edge of the cube is $3a$ cm.
> What is the total length of all the edges?

Pupils discuss the question in pairs. They should see that:

there are 12 edges

$12 \times 3a = 36a$.

Ask: *What is the total length of all the edges if $a = 8$?*
Agree that $36 \times 8 = 288$ cm.

Ask: *What is total area of all the faces?* Pupils discuss in pairs. They should see that:

there are 6 faces

the area of 1 face is $9a^2$

the total area is $6 \times 9a^2 = 54a^2$.

Ask: *What is the total area of all the faces if $a = 5$?*
Agree that $54 \times 25 = 1350$ cm^2.

- Show pupils this problem:

> A boatyard has 4 yachts per row, in g rows and 5 motor boats per row, in h rows.
> When $g = 7$ and $h = 6$, how many yachts and motor boats are there altogether?

Together, draw this bar model and work out a solution.

Total yachts and motor boats	
$4g$	$5h$

$? = 4g + 5h$

$? = 4 \times 7 + 5 \times 6 = 28 + 30 = 58$

Ask: *If both yachts and motor boats were in j rows, how many yachts and motor boats would there be altogether if $j = 8$?*

Pupils discuss response in pairs. They should see that:

$? = 4j + 5j = 9j$

$? = 9 \times 8 = 72$

- Show pupils this problem:

> A van travelled at b km per hour. It travelled 6 hours in the morning and c km in the afternoon.
> How far did it travel if $b = 90$ and $c = 100$?

Ask pupil pairs to a draw bar model to represent the problem and work out a solution. They should draw:

?	
$6b$	c

Total distance travelled:

$? = 6b + c$

$? = 6 \times 90 + 100 = 540 + 100 = 640$ km

- Pupils should create three similar problems where expressions will need simplifying and evaluating, and swap with a partner to solve, explaining their reasoning to each other.

- Pupils should complete Question 6 in the Practice Book.

Same-day intervention

● Show pupils this problem:

A car park has 5 cars per row, in *s* rows, and 4 lorries per row, in *t* rows.

Together, draw a diagram of the car park:

Ask: *How many cars altogether?* Agree 5*s*.

Ask: *How many lorries altogether?* Agree 4*t*.

Ask: *How many cars and lorries altogether?*

car	car	car	car	car

s rows

t rows

lorry	lorry	lorry	lorry

Together, draw this bar model to explore the question:

Total number of cars and lorries	
5*s*	4*t*

Total number of cars and lorries = 5*s* + 4*t*.

Ask: *If s = 5 and t = 6, how many cars and lorries are there altogether?*

Agree 5 × 5 + 4 × 6 = 25 + 24 = 49

● Now ask pupils to change the numbers and letters in the problem and answer it again, using bar modelling.

Same-day enrichment

● Give pupils **Resource 6.3.4c** Word problems – applying algebra (2) to complete.

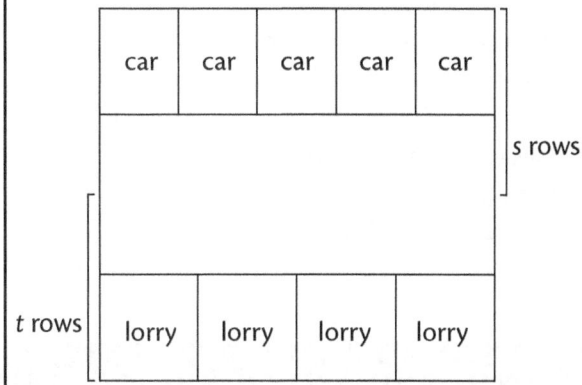

Answers: **1.** a) 869; b) 41(*r* + *s*), 3075; **2.** 570 km, 9.5 hours, 71.25 km per hour

Challenge and extension question

Question 7

7 There are *a* pupils in a school's athletics team. The number of pupils in the hockey team is 4 fewer than twice the number in the athletics team.

(a) Use an expression with letters to represent the total number of pupils in the two teams. _____

(b) When *a* = 24, how many pupils are there in the two teams?

_____

This question allows for a deeper look at simplification and evaluation through problem solving. The approach needs an understanding of the relation between quantities before the expression can be written and solved.

Unit 3.5
Simple equations (1)

Conceptual context

This unit begins with clarification of the vocabulary associated with algebra so that pupils are able to secure their conceptual understanding by securing their understanding of the relationships between aspects of their new knowledge.

This is the first in a series of three units in which pupils will solve equations with one unknown. Questions and problems are presented in many different representations so that pupils develop a sense of when and how different aspects of their algebraic knowledge are relevant and likely to be useful.

Learning pupils will have achieved at the end of the unit

- Pupils' understanding of the vocabulary of algebra will have been clarified and secured as they articulate the relationship between expressions, variables, unknowns, equations and solutions (Q1, Q2)
- An understanding of how to establish equations from given information will have been developed (Q3, Q4)
- Pupils will have found values that satisfy an equation of the form $x + y = z$ (Q5)

Resources

0–100 number cards; lettered flashcards; blank cards; counters; **Resource 6.3.5** Establish equations

Vocabulary

expression, satisfy, unknown, variable, equation, inequality, algebra, solve/solution

Questions 1 and 2

1 True or false? (Put a ✓ for true and a ✗ for false in each box.)

(a) An expression with variables is an equation. ☐

(b) A variable in an equation is also called an unknown. ☐

(c) $9 - 3x$ is not an equation. ☐

(d) $4x - 20 = y$ is not an equation. ☐

(e) $6x \div 2 = 2x + 8$ is an equation. ☐

2 Multiple choice questions. (For each question, choose the correct answer and write the letter in the box.)

(a) In the following, ☐ is not an equation.

    A. $18x + 5x = 23x$ B. $5(a + b) = 5a + 5b$

    C. $6x - x - 2x$ D. $6y - 8 = 40$

(b) In the following, ☐ is an equation.

    A. $2(a + b)$ B. $18 - 2m < 5$

    C. $9 \times 0.9 > 8$ D. $x \div 6 = 0$

(c) Given that ▲ + ▲ + ⬤ = 19 and ▲ + ⬤ = 12, then ☐.

    A. ▲ = 9 and ⬤ = 3   B. ▲ = 8 and ⬤ = 4

    C. ▲ = 7 and ⬤ = 5   D. ▲ = 5 and ⬤ = 7

(d) Given that ⬤ = ▲ + ▲ + ▲ and ⬤ × ▲ = 108, then ⬤ + ▲ = ☐.

    A. 18   B. 24   C. 54   D. 72

What learning will pupils have achieved at the conclusion of Questions 1 and 2?

- Pupils' understanding of the vocabulary of algebra will have been clarified and secured as they articulate the relationship between expressions, variables, unknowns, equations and solutions.

Activities for whole-class instruction

- Show pupils the following:

$2x + y$
$12 + 18$
$4x - 7 = 12 + t$
$0.5(a + 1)$
$12 \leq 3 + 4z$

Ask: *What is the same and what is different about the items in the list?* Can pupils see that:

– all the items involve numbers, or letters and numbers

– there is only one item that has an equals sign

– there is one inequality?

- Write on the board: $4x - 8 = 12$.

Ask: *What does the equals sign tell us?* Discuss with pupils and agree that both sides have the same value. Tell pupils this means it is called an 'equation'.

All say ... *An equation is a statement that shows things that have equal value.*

- Show pupils this list:

$3 \times 5 - 5$
$3e + 4 = 5$
$D > E$
$4r - e = 5 - 2r$

Ask: *Which of these are equations?* Share ideas. Point out that, sometimes, more than one different letter is used.

Ask: *What do letters represent when they appear in expressions and equations?* Pupils should know that a letter represents a value, but we don't know what the value is.

- Show pupils the list below. Ask: *What letter is the variable in each of these?* (Pupils do not need to solve the equation, they just need to identify the letter used to represent the value.)

$6e + 5 = 23$
$42 - 8a = 2$
$100y = 50$
$z \div 3 = 61$

All say ... *Letters used to represent values that are unknown are called variables.*

- On the board, write $3e + 4 = 5$.

Agree with pupils that this is an equation. Ask: *What do we know about the letter e?* Ask pupils to discuss the question in pairs. They should see that e:

– is an 'unknown'

– is a variable

– is multiplied by 3

– has a value that can be found.

- Circle the letter e and write 'unknown' or 'variable' next to it, as shown:

$3ⓔ + 4 = 5$

unknown or variable

Emphasise that the unknown can be any letter or other symbol and that an equation can have more than one unknown.

- In pairs, pupils should write five equations for their partner who must then circle the unknowns.

Look out for ... pupils writing down expressions that don't have an equals sign. Re-emphasise the importance of the equals sign in equations.

- Show pupils these questions. Pupils must decide, in pairs, which total is correct:

$s = v + v + v + v + v$ and $s \times v = 80$ What does $s + v$ equal?	a) 16 b) 24 c) 28
$p = 3q + q$ and $q \times p = 144$ What does $p + q$ equal?	a) 30 b) 28 c) 36
$s = 2w + 3w$ and $s \times w = 45$ What does $s - w$ equal?	a) 16 b) 18 c) 12
☺ + ☺ + ☺ = ㋕ and ☺ × ㋕ × ㋕ = 72 What does ㋕ + ☺ equal?	a) 6 b) 8 c) 12

Answers: 24, 30, 12, 8

- Share ideas.

- Pupils should complete Questions 1 and 2 in the Practice Book.

Same-day intervention

- On the board, write: $3 = 3$. Ask: *Is this statement true?* Agree that it is.

- Now write:

  $4 + 5 = 5 + 4$

  $3 \times 5 = 5 \times 3$

  Ask: *Are these statements true?* Agree that they are.

  Ask: *Looking at the three statements, what does the equals sign tell us?* Discuss and agree that it means that the left-hand side has the same value as the right-hand side.

- Write on the board: $x + 2 = 7$. Also, represent it with counters:

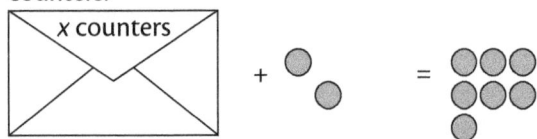

  Ask: *What does the equals sign tell us?* Agree that it means that $x + 2$ has the same value as 7. Ask: *How many counters must be in the envelope? How do you know?*

- Repeat with two further similar examples.

- Ask pupils to create their own equations using counters and cards.

Same-day enrichment

- Ask pupils to write five of their own equations in the style of the examples used previously:

$6e + 5 = 23$
$42 - 8a = 2$
$100y = 50$
$z \div 3 = 61$

Questions 3 and 4

> **3** Establish an equation with the information given in each diagram below. The first one has been done for you.
>
> | m | n |
> |---|---|
> | 3m | |
>
> | y | y | y | y |
> |---|---|---|---|
> | 30 | | | |
>
> | x | 8 |
> |---|---|
> | y | |
>
> $m + n = 3m$ _____ = _____   _____ = _____
>
> **4** Establish equations based on the relation between equal quantities. The first one has been done for you.
>
> (a) 2 times x equals 36. Answer: $2x = 36$
>
> (b) The difference between 45 and x is 15. _____
>
> (c) 12 more than 3 times x is 72. _____
>
> (d) 48 is 2 times the sum of x and 3. _____
>
> (e) Half of y is 25. _____
>
> (f) 20 divided by 10 and then plus x is 8. _____
>
> (g) 2 times x is 1 more than 3 times 5. _____
>
> (h) 15 multiplied by 9 is 5 less than 4 times y. _____

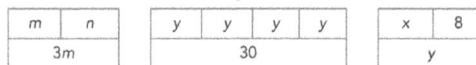

What learning will pupils have achieved at the conclusion of Questions 3 and 4?

- An understanding of how to establish equations from given information will have been developed.

Activities for whole-class instruction

(i) In this unit, pupils practise establishing equations with one or two unknowns, but they are only expected to solve equations with one unknown.

- Check pupils' understanding of equations by asking:

  - *Show me an equation.*

  - *Show me an inequality.*

  - *Show me an expression.*

  - *From this list (on the board) choose the equation.*

- Display this bar model on the board.

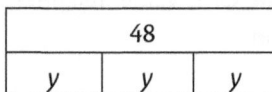

48		
y	y	y

Ask pupils: *What equation is being represented?* Pupils discuss responses in pairs. They should see that $3y = 48$.

● Display this bar model on the board.

$3x + 5$		
x	x	15

Ask: *What equation is being represented?* Pupils discuss responses in pairs. They should see that $2x + 15 = 3x + 5$.

● Display this bar model on the board.

$3y - 2$				
z	z	z	z	25

Ask: *What equation is being modelled?* Pupils discuss responses in pairs. They should see that $4z + 25 = 3y - 2$.

● Write on the board: 2 times x equals 36.

Ask pupils, working in pairs, to draw a bar model to represent the information. They should draw:

36	
x	x

Ask: *What equation would you establish?* Agree $2x = 36$.

● On the board, write: The difference between 35 and y is 12.

Ask pupils, working in pairs, to draw a bar model to represent the information. They should draw:

35	
y	12

Ask: *What equation needs to be established?* Agree $35 - y = 12$.

● On the board, write: 10 more than $4x$ is 55.

Ask pupils, working in pairs, to draw a bar model to represent the information. They should draw:

55				
x	x	x	x	10

Ask: *What equation needs to be established?* Agree $4x + 10 = 55$.

● Now show pupils these statements:

25 is 3 times the sum of d and 4.
Half of g is 34.
24 multiplied by x is 3 times $x - 2$.
3 times f is 4 less than $55f$ divided by 7.

Answers: $3(d + 4) = 25$; $g \div 2 = 34$; $24x = 3(x - 2)$; $3f = 55f \div 7 - 4$

Pupils must establish the correct equations from the statements, drawing bar models if necessary. Share ideas.

Working in pairs, ask pupils to create five similar statements and swap with another pair to establish equations. Share ideas.

● Pupils should complete Questions 3 and 4 in the Practice Book.

Same-day intervention

● Write on the board: The sum of y and 10 has the same value as $3x$.

Together, draw a bar model representing the statement:

$3x$	
y	10

Ask pupils: *What other information is shown by the bar model?* Agree, for example: The difference of $3x$ and y is 10.

Together, establish equations from the bar model: $3x = y + 10$ or $3x - y = 10$ or $3x - 10 = y$.

● Repeat for statements that give $5x - 4y = 10$, $T \div 7 = 3T - 8$, and so on.

Same-day enrichment

● Show pupils these equations:

$25(w + 3x) = x + 4$
$g \div 2 = 33 \div (x + 2)$
$24 \times a - 45 \times b + 19 = 3$
$3 \times g = 75 \times f \div 15 - 4$

● Ask pupils to express the relations in words.

Question 5

5 The sum of Tim's age and his sister Jane's age is 10. Let x be Tim's age and y be Jane's age.

(a) Establish an equation with x and y. _____

(b) Complete the table below to list all the possible combinations of x and y that satisfy the equation. (Note: x and y must both be positive integers.)

x	1	2	3	4	5	6	7	8	9
y									

(c) If Tim is 6 years older than Jane, how old are they?

Tim = _____ Jane = _____

What learning will pupils have achieved at the conclusion of Question 5?

● Pupils will have found values that satisfy an equation of the form $x + y = z$.

Activities for whole-class instruction

- Show pupils these statements, ask: *Are these statements true or false?*

> The difference between 35y and 45 is 5. The equation is 45 − 35y = 5.
>
> 5 is 8 more than 3 less than 4 times r. The equation is 4r − 3 + 8 = 5.
>
> S divided by 5 is 9 less than 3 multiplied by S. The equation is 5 ÷ S = 9 − 3s.
>
> 6 divided by the difference of 7 and R is 35. The equation is 6(7 ÷ R) = 35.
>
> 15 multiplied by 9 is 5 less than 4 times y. The equation is 15 × 9 = 4y − 5.

Answers: False, True, False, False, True

Share ideas.

- Write on the board: $d + f = 12$.

  Ask: *How many different pairs of positive integers are there?* Agree 11.

  Ask: *How many different pairs of integers are there for d and f?* Agree that there are an infinite number of different pairs of integers.

- Write these equations on the board:

  $g + j = 12$

  $e + f = 15$

  In pairs, ask pupils to find all the pairs of positive integers that satisfy the equations.

- Now write on the board: The sum of Fred's and Dave's ages is 12. Fred's age is x and Dave's age is y. Ask: *What equation can we establish for x and y?* Agree $x + y = 12$.

  Ask: *If Fred is 2, what age is Dave?* Agree 10. Ask: *If Dave is 11, what age is Fred?* Agree 1.

- Write on the board: The sum of two angles is 120°. Ask: *What equation can be established for the two angles?* Agree $x + y = 120°$ (or other letters).

  Ask pupils to write down five pairs of angles, all positive integers, that satisfy the equation. Share ideas.

- Write on the board: The sum of two lengths is 145 mm. Ask: *What equation can be established for the two lengths?* Agree $x + y = 145$ mm (or other letters).

  Ask pupils to write down five pairs of lengths that satisfy the equation.

- Pupils, working in pairs, should now complete section A on **Resource 6.3.5** Establish equations.

Answers: **1.** a) $a + b = 13$; b)

a	1	2	3	4	5	6	7	8	9	10	11	12
b	[12]	[11]	[10]	[9]	[8]	[7]	[6]	[5]	[4]	[3]	[2]	[1]

2. a) $g + h = 33$; b)

g	22	24	26	28	30	32
h	[11]	[9]	[7]	[5]	[3]	[1]

- Pupils should complete Question 5 in the Practice Book.

Same-day intervention

- Write on the board: $d + g = 12$.

  Set up the equation with an envelope and counters as in the previous activity and ask pupils to replace d and g with counters to make the equation true.

  Ask: *In how many different ways can d and g be replaced?* Pupils should explore the problem and record their responses. Agree that there are 11 different ways.

  Repeat the activity with another similar equation.

- Write on the board: $f + h = 15$.

  Ask: *In how many different ways can f and h be replaced to make the equation true?*

  Pupils should explore and record their responses.

  Repeat with another similar equation, but use the words 'positive integers' instead.

Same-day enrichment

- Ask pupils to work in pairs to complete section B of **Resource 6.3.5** Establish equations.

  Answers: **1.** min: 1.2 m, max: 1.3 m; **2.** 16, 4; 15, 3; 14, 2; 13, 1; **3.** 3.5 m

Challenge and extension question

Question 6

6 Look at the figure. The side length of the larger squares are a cm, and the side length of the smaller squares are b cm. Use letter expressions to represent the relation between a and b. What is the perimeter and the area of the whole figure? If a is 6 cm, find the length of b, the perimeter and the area of the whole figure.

This question provokes a deeper look at establishing equations through problem solving. The approach needs an understanding of the relation between the variables and the perimeter and area of squares.

Unit 3.6
Simple equations (2)

Conceptual context

This unit continues to consolidate pupils' understanding of equations by introducing and developing a method for solving equations, and by providing opportunities to establish and solve them.

Learning pupils will have achieved at the end of the unit

- Pupils' understanding of the vocabulary of algebra will be strengthened as they focus on the relationship between equations and solutions (Q1)
- Pupils' ability to think flexibly will have been developed by solving equations and evaluating procedures for finding solutions (Q2, Q3)
- A method for establishing an equation and then solving it will have continued to be practised (Q4)
- An understanding of how values can satisfy an equation will have continued to be developed (Q5)

Resources

0–100 number cards; lettered flashcards; blank cards; counters; money; **Resource 6.3.6a** Solve equations (1); **Resource 6.3.6b** Solve equations (2); **Resource 6.3.6c** Equations match; **Resource 6.3.6d** Equation problems

Vocabulary

expression, satisfy, unknown, variable, equation, algebra, solve, solution

Question 1

1 Complete each statement.

(a) A _____ to an equation is a value we can put in place of the unknown that makes the equation true.

(b) The process to find the _____ to an equation is called 'solving the equation'.

(c) The solution to the equation $2y = 30$ is _____.

(d) The solution to the equation $x + 1.2 + 2.4 = 5$ is _____.

What learning will pupils have achieved at the conclusion of Question 1?

● Pupils' understanding of the vocabulary of algebra will be strengthened as they focus on the relationship between equations and solutions.

Activities for whole-class instruction

● Show pupils these equations:

$x + 6 = 11$
$y - 7 = 18$
$4e = 18$
$25 = 3e + 6$
$10d ÷ 5 = 4$
$12 = 4r - 4$
$4(c + 2) = 45d ÷ 15$

Ask pupils to copy the equations and circle the unknowns.

● Write on the board: $x + 6 = 11$ and ask pupils to draw a bar model of the equation.

They should draw:

11	
x	6

Ask: *How would the working be set out?* Discuss, then agree:

$x = 11 - 6$

$x = 5$

Agree that 5 satisfies the equation. Tell pupils that this is called 'solving the equation' and so the solution is 5. Write 'solution' next to the 5.

(All say...) *Solving an equation means finding the solution.*

● Show pupils these equations:

$r + 7 = 15$
$3.3 = e + 2.4$
$3.2 + 3.5 + r = 9$

Ask pupils, working in pairs, to draw bar models and solve the equations. They should draw:

$r + 7 = 15$

15	
r	7

$r = 15 - 7$

$r = 8$

$3.3 = e + 2.4$

3.3	
e	2.4

$e = 3.3 - 2.4$

$e = 0.9$

$3.2 + 3.5 + r = 9$

9		
3.2	3.5	r

$r = 9 - 3.2 - 3.5$

$r = 2.3$

● Now write on the board: $3y = 36$.

Ask pupils to draw a bar model for the equation. They should draw:

36		
y	y	y

Ask: *How would the working be set out?* Agree:

$y = 36 ÷ 3$

$y = 12$

● Show pupils these equations:

$7h = 21$
$25.5 = 5x$
$2.5W = 10$

Ask pupils, working in pairs, to draw bar models and solve the equations. They should draw:

$7h = 21$

21						
h	h	h	h	h	h	h

$h = 21 ÷ 7$

$h = 3$

$25.5 = 5x$

25.5				
x	x	x	x	x

$x = 25.5 \div 5$

$x = 5.1$

$2.5W = 10$

10		
W	W	$0.5W$

$W = 10 \div 2.5$

$W = 4$

- Show pupils these equations:

$H + 4 = 19$
$g + 4.5 = 20$
$7 = 3.8 + b$
$x + 4.2 + 4.8 = 25$
$5r = 20$
$27 = 3e$
$3.5h = 10.5$

Answers: 15; 15.5; 3.2; 16; 4; 9; 3

Working in pairs, pupils solve the equations.

- Pupils should complete Question 1 in the Practice Book.

Same-day intervention

- Write on the board: $y + 4 = 11$.

  Represent the equation using counters and an envelope. Out of sight of pupils, put seven counters in the envelope.

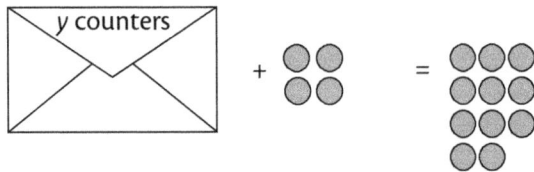

  Together, draw a bar model of the equation:

11	
y	4

  Now, set out the working, moving/removing counters.

$y = 11 - 4$

$y = 7$

All say... Solving an equation means finding the solution. The solution is 7.

- Repeat the task with other equations, for example, $13 = d + 12$, $6g = 18$, and so on.

Same-day enrichment

- Show pupils these solutions to equations:

4.7
1.2
5.7
1.5

- Ask pupils to create equations and their bar models for these solutions.

Question 2

2 Multiple choice questions. (For each question, choose the correct answer and write the letter in the box.)

(a) $x = 7$ is the solution to equation ☐.

  A. $x + 5 = 10$ B. $5 - x = 2$

  C. $3 + y = 10$ D. $37 - x = 30$

(b) The pairs of numbers for x and y that satisfy the equation $3x + y = 4$ are ☐. (Choose all the correct answers.)

  A. $x = 1, y = 1$ B. $x = 2, y = 0$

  C. $x = 1.33, y = 0$ D. $x = 0, y = 4$

(c) In solving the equation $50 \div x = 0.5$, the correct working shown below is ☐.

  A. $50 \div x = 0.5$ B. $50 \div x = 0.5$
      Solution: $x = 0.5 \div 50$ Solution: $= 50 \div 0.5$
      $x = 0.01$ $= 100$

  C. $50 \div x = 0.5$ D. $50 \div x = 0.5$
      Solution: $x = 50 \div 0.5$ Solution: $x = 0.5 \times 50$
      $x = 100$ $x = 25$

What learning will pupils have achieved at the conclusion of Question 2?

- Pupils' ability to think flexibly will have been developed by solving equations and evaluating procedures for finding solutions.

Activities for whole-class instruction

- Show pupils these equations and solutions:

$h + 7 = 12.5$	$h = 19$
$21 = e + 12.4$	$e = 8.6$
$12d = 50$	$d = 6$
$x + 3.3 + 4.7 = 25$	$x = 17$
$24.6 = 6s$	$s = 4.1$

Answers: False, True, False, True, True

Working in pairs, pupils should decide if the solutions are true or false.

- Write on the board: $y - 7 = 18$. Ask pupils to draw a bar model for the equation. They should draw:

y	
18	7

Ask: *How would the working be set out?* Agree:

$y = 18 + 7$

$y = 25$

● Show pupils these equations:

$y - 3 = 18$
$4.5 = g - 2.3$
$3.8 = y - 1.2$

Working in pairs, pupils should draw bar models and work out the solutions. They should draw:

$y - 3 = 18$

y	
18	3

$y = 18 + 3$

$y = 21$

$4.5 = g - 2.3$

g	
4.5	2.3

$g = 4.5 + 2.3$

$g = 6.8$

$3.8 = y - 1.2$

y	
3.8	1.2

$y = 3.8 + 1.2$

$y = 5$

● Discuss solutions with pupils.

Write on the board: $17 - x = 12$. Ask: *What bar model would represent this equation?* Agree:

17	
12	x

Ask: *How would the working be set out?* Agree:

$x = 17 - 12$

$x = 5$

● Display these equations on the board:

$17 - x = 4$
$2.4 = 6.6 - y$
$2.3 - x = 0.5$

Working in pairs, pupils should draw bar models and solve the equations. Agree:

$17 - x = 4$

17	
4	x

$x = 17 - 4$

$x = 13$

$2.4 = 6.6 - y$

6.6	
2.4	y

$y = 6.6 - 2.4$

$y = 4.2$

$2.3 - x = 0.5$

2.3	
0.5	x

$x = 2.3 - 0.5$

$x = 1.8$

● Write on the board: $x \div 3 = 5$. Ask pupils to draw a bar model for the equation.

x		
5	5	5

Ask: *How would the working be set out?* Agree:

$x = 3 \times 5$

$x = 15$

● Display these equations on the board:

$B \div 4 = 13$
$4.5 = j \div 3$
$2.8 = r \div 5$

Ask pupil pairs to draw bar models and solve the equations. They should draw:

$B \div 4 = 13$

B			
13	13	13	13

$B = 4 \times 13$

$B = 52$

$4.5 = j \div 3$

j		
4.5	4.5	4.5

$j = 3 \times 4.5$

$j = 13.5$

$2.8 = r \div 5$

r				
2.8	2.8	2.8	2.8	2.8

$r = 5 \times 2.8$

$r = 14$

- Now write on the board: $36 \div x = 4$.

  Ask pupils: *What is the question asking?* Can pupils see that 36 is divided into a number of equal parts? The number of parts is unknown, but the equation does tell us that there are 4 in each part. The question is asking: 'How many parts (or groups) is 36 divided into if there are 4 in each part?'

  Ask: *How will you work this out? Is there a diagram or bar model that will help?*

  Pupils should tell you that they need to find how many times 4 'goes into' 36; how many 4s are in 36. Agree, $36 \div 4$ is 9 – there are nine 4s in 36.

  $x = 36 \div 4$

  $x = 9$

- Repeat for:

  $12 \div c = 6$

  $9 \div f = 6$

  $12 = g \div 2$

- Provide pupil pairs with **Resource 6.3.6a** Solve equations (1), and ask them to complete section A.

Answers: **1.** 22; **2.** 10.4; **3.** 3; **4.** 6.8; **5.** 44; **6.** 12.5; **7.** 5; **8.** 3.5

- Write on the board: $3x + y = 10$.

  Ask: *Using positive integers, how many different values for x and y are there?* Pupils discuss responses in pairs. They should see that three pairs are possible: 1, 7; 2, 4; 3, 1.

- Write on the board: $x + 2y = 14$.

- Ask: *Using positive integers, how many different values for x and y are there?* Pupils discuss responses in pairs. They should see that six pairs are possible: 12, 1; 10, 2; 8, 3; 6, 4; 4, 5; 2, 6.

- Working in pairs, pupils should complete section B of **Resource 6.3.6a** Solve equations (1).

Answers: **1.** $x = 1$, $y = 8$; $x = 2$, $y = 6$; $x = 3$, $y = 4$; $x = 4$, $y = 2$; **2.** $x = 2$, $y = 4$; $x = 6$, $y = 3$; $x = 10$, $y = 2$; $x = 14$, $y = 1$; **3.** Possible answers include: $x = 6$, $y = 3$; $x = 7$, $y = 6$; $x = 8$, $y = 9$; $x = 9$, $y = 12$; $x = 10$, $y = 15$

- Pupils should complete Question 2 in the Practice Book.

Same-day intervention

- Write on the board: $y - 4 = 11$.

  Represent the equation using counters and an envelope as previously. Together, draw a bar model of the equation:

y	
11	4

  Then, set out the working, moving/removing counters:

  $y = 11 + 4$

  $y = 15$

- Repeat for: $13 = d - 5$, $g \div 4 = 18$, and so on.

Same-day enrichment

- Show pupils these solutions to equations:

3.7
2.2

  Ask pupils to create equations for these solutions.

• Pupils should now complete section C of **Resource 6.3.6a** Solve equations (1).

Answers: **1.** Possible answers include: $x = 0$, $y = -4$; $x = 6$, $y = 0$; $x = 15$, $y = 6$; $x = 24$, $y = 12$;

2. Possible answers include: $x = -12$, $y = -6$; $x = 0$, $y = -3$; $x = 12$, $y = 0$; $x = 20$, $y = 2$; $x = 24$, $y = 3$

Question 3

> **3** Solve the equations and then check your answers. The first one has been done for you.
>
> (a) $x + 8.25 = 11.39$
> Solution: $x = 11.39 - 8.25$
> $= 3.14$
>
> Check: $3.14 + 8.25 = 11.39$
>
> (b) $72.6 - x = 36.8$
>
> (c) $x - 2.4 = 2.4$
>
> (d) $0.25x = 0.4$
>
> (e) $x \div 3.6 = 0$
>
> (f) $x \div 2.6 = 2.6$

What learning will pupils have achieved at the conclusion of Question 3?

• Pupils' ability to think flexibly will have been developed by solving equations and evaluating procedures for finding solutions.

Activities for whole-class instruction

• Show pupils these equations:

> $g + 12.5 = 19.5$
> $h - 7.2 = 3.4$
> $13 - x = 4.8$
> $13.5 = 4.5f$
> $S \div 3.5 = 10$
> $8 \div x = 0.5$

Answers: 7, 10.6, 8.2, 3, 35, 16

Ask pupils to work in pairs to find the solutions. Suggest to pupils that it is helpful to keep the equals signs in line when showing their working.

Tell pupils that it is useful to check that the solution is correct.

Show an example:

$g + 12.5 = 19.5$
$\quad g = 19.5 - 12.5$
$\quad\quad = 7$

Check: $7 + 12.5 = 19.5$.
It checks.

• Write on the board: $14 - x = 5.3$. Ask: *How would the working and check be set out?*

Tell pupils that x is usually kept on the left-hand side of the equals sign. Agree:

$14 - x = 5.3$
$\quad x = 14 - 5.3$
$\quad\quad = 8.7$

Check: $14 - 8.7 = 5.3$.
It checks.

• Write on the board: $15.5 = 5f$. Ask: *How would the working and check be set out?* Agree:

$15. 5 = 5f$
$\quad f = 15.5 \div 5$
$\quad\quad = 3.1$

Check: $15.5 = 5 \times 3.1$.
It checks.

• Give pupils **Resource 6.3.6b** Solve equations (2), and ask them to complete sections A and B.

Answers: **A 2.** 2.4; **3.** 41.4; **4.** 12.8; **B 1.** 4.1; **2.** 8; **3.** 17; **4.** 0.5; **5.** 0

• Pupils should complete Question 3 in the Practice Book.

Same-day intervention

● Write on the board: $v + 2.5 = 6$.

Together, draw a bar model of the equation:

6	
v	2.5

Now set out the working and the check. Ask pupils to explain the steps as they are carried out.

$v + 2.5 = 6$

$v = 6 - 2.5$

$= 3.5$

Check: $3.5 + 2.5 = 6$.

It checks.

● Repeat for: $13 = d - 5$, $g \div 4 = 18$, and so on.

Same-day enrichment

● Ask pupils to complete section C of **Resource 6.3.6b** Solve equations (2).

Answers: 1. 5.1; 2. 0.25; 3. 0.8

Question 4

4 Write an equation for each picture. Find the solution.

(a) Luke is x years old. Dad is 40. *I am 28 years older than you.*

(b) 152 cm y cm *I am 5 cm shorter than you.*

(c) *I ran 2.8 km this week.* If Eve ran the same distance every day, she ran s m every day.

(d) a sweets. Shared equally between 25 children, 3 sweets each.

(a) _____ Solution: _____
(b) _____ Solution: _____
(c) _____ Solution: _____
(d) _____ Solution: _____

What learning will pupils have achieved at the conclusion of Question 4?

● A method for establishing an equation and then solving it will have continued to be practised.

Activities for whole-class instruction

● Give groups of four a set of cards from **Resource 6.3.6c** Equations match. Ask pupils to match the cards and share solutions.

Resource 6.3.6c — Equations match

$x \div 0.7 = 5$	3.5	$30.23 = 10.81 + f$
19.42	$11.6 = c + 6.8$	4.8
$w + 12.5 = 19.5$	7	$12.44 - g = 5.6$
6.84	$8.5 \div r = 17$	0.5

Answers: $x = 3.5$; $f = 19.42$; $c = 4.8$; $w = 7$; $g = 6.84$; $r = 0.5$

● Show pupils the following problem:

Patrick the tortoise is 37 years older than his brother Brendan. Brendan is d years old and Patrick is 70. Establish an equation and find the solution.

Ask: *What bar model would represent this?* Agree:

70	
d	37

Ask: *What equation should be established?* Agree: $d + 37 = 70$ or $70 - d = 37$. Now ask: *Using $d + 37 = 70$, how is the working and check set out?* Agree:

$d + 37 = 70$

$d = 70 - 37$

$= 33$

Check: $33 + 37 = 70$.

It checks.

Brendan is 33 years old.

● Show pupils this problem:

A ferry is 59 m shorter than a small oil tanker. The tanker is 226 m long and the ferry is y m. Establish an equation and find the solution.

Ask: *What bar model would represent this?* Agree:

226	
y	59

Ask pupils: *What equation should be established?* Agree
y + 59 = 226 or 226 − *y* = 59. Now ask: *Using y + 59 = 226,
how is the working and check set out?* Agree:

y + 59 = 226

$\quad$ *y* = 226 − 59

$\qquad$ = 167

Check: 167 + 59 = 226.

It checks.

The ferry is 167 m long.

- Ask pupils: *What can be said about the equations that were established?* Pupils should discuss responses in pairs. Can they see that more than one equation could be established for a problem?

- Show pupils this problem:

> Pete walked 35.7 km last week. He walked *J* km every day.
> Write an equation and find the solution.

Ask: *What bar model would represent this?* Agree:

35.7						
J	*J*	*J*	*J*	*J*	*J*	*J*

Ask: *What equation should be established?* Agree 7*J* = 35.7.
Ask: *How is the working and check set out?* Agree:

7*J* = 35.7

$\quad$ *J* = 35.7 ÷ 7

$\qquad$ = 5.1

Check: 7 × 5.1 = 35.7.

It checks.

Pete walked 5.1 km every day.

- Show pupils this problem:

> There are *x* biscuits and 35 students. They had 4 biscuits each.
> Establish an equation and find and check the solution.

x ÷ 35 = 4

$\quad$ *x* = 35 × 4

$\qquad$ = 140

Check: 140 ÷ 35 = 4.

It checks.

There 140 biscuits.

- Ask: *What can be said about the equations that were established?* Pupils discuss in pairs. Can they see that there was just one equation to establish? Discuss conclusions.

- Give pupils **Resource 6.3.6d** Equation problems and ask them to complete section A.

Answers: 1. *y* = 55 − 15.5, *y* = 39.5 years old; **2.** *v* = 350 − 85, *v* = 265 cm; **3.** *t* = 16.8 ÷ 7, *t* = 2.4 km; **4.** *S* = 45 × 3, *S* = 135 carrots

- Pupils should complete Question 4 in the Practice Book.

Same-day intervention

- Show pupils this problem:

> A classroom is 35 m shorter than the school hall. The school hall is 45 m long and the classroom is *k* m long.
> Write an equation and find the solution.

Together, draw a diagram of the problem:

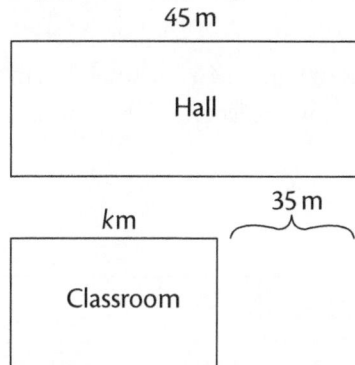

Draw a bar model for the problem:

45	
k	35

Together, establish the equation and set out the working. Ask pupils to explain the steps as they are carried out:

k + 35 = 45 or 45 − *k* = 35

- Using $k + 35 = 45$:

$$k + 35 = 45$$
$$k = 45 - 35$$
$$= 10$$

Check: 10 + 35 = 45.
It checks.
The classroom is 10 m long.

- Create other similar problems for multiplication and division.

Same-day enrichment

- Ask pupils to complete section B of **Resource 6.3.6d** Equation problems.

Resource 6.3.6d 2 of 2

B

1. Look again at Question 3 from section A. Ahmed made a mistake. He actually walked 22.4 km on the treadmill last week. He also drove a total of 31.5 km to get to the gym. Can you help him find how many km he drove and walked each day?

2. Look again at Question 4 from section A. D pieces of fruit and R drinks were also used by the students. In total, 270 carrots, pieces of fruit and drinks were used by the students. Can you suggest what each student had? Explain your reasoning.

© HarperCollinsPublishers 2018

Answers: **1.** walked: 3.2 km, drove: 4.5 km, total: 7.7 km
2. Possible answer: 3 carrots, 2 pieces of fruit, 1 drink

Question 5

5 Emily was given £30 in £2 coins and £5 notes. Let x be the number of £2 coins and y be the number of £5 notes.

(a) Establish an equation with x and y.

(b) List all the possible combinations of x and y that satisfy the equation. (Note: x and y must be positive integers.)

What learning will pupils have achieved at the conclusion of Question 5?

- An understanding of how values can satisfy an equation will have continued to be developed.

Activities for whole-class instruction

- Show pupils this problem:

Peter has £15 in £5 notes and £2 coins.
x is the number of £5 notes and y the number of £2 coins.
Establish the equation.

Ask pupils to work in pairs to write the equation. Agree: $5x + 2y = 15$.

Ask pupils to make a table to record all the possible values of x and y. They should work systematically and test possible combinations. Agree:

Number of £5 notes	Value of £5 notes	Number of £2 coins	Value of £2 coins	Total value £
1	£5	5	£10	£15
2	£10	Not possible to make £5 with £2 coins		
3	£15	0	£0	£15

- Can pupils see that two pairs are possible?
- Show pupils this problem:

A shop has 60 kg of clothes in boxes of 5 kg and 4 kg.
G is the number of 5 kg boxes and H is the number of 4 kg boxes.

Working in pairs, pupils should establish the equation. Agree: $5G + 4H = 60$.

- Ask pupils to make a table to record all the possible values of G and H. They should work systematically and test possible combinations. Agree:

Number of 5 kg boxes	Clothes in 5 kg boxes	Number of 4 kg boxes	Clothes in 4 kg boxes	Total kg
1	5 kg	Not possible to make 55 with 4 kg boxes		
2	10 kg	Not possible to make 50 with 4 kg boxes		
3	15 kg	Not possible to make 45 with 4 kg boxes		
4	20 kg	10	40 kg	60 kg
5	25 kg	Not possible to make 35 with 4 kg boxes		

6	30 kg	Not possible to make 30 with 4 kg boxes		
7	35 kg	Not possible to make 25 with 4 kg boxes		
8	40 kg	5	20 kg	60 kg
9	45 kg	Not possible to make 15 with 4 kg boxes		
10	50 kg	Not possible to make 10 with 4 kg boxes		
11	55 kg	Not possible to make 5 with 4 kg boxes		
12	60 kg	0	0 kg	60 kg

Can they see that three combinations are possible?

8 × 5 kg boxes + 5 × 4 kg boxes

4 × 5 kg boxes + 10 × 4 kg boxes

12 × 5 kg boxes

- Repeat the task above for the following problem.

> A café has 200 loaves of bread in bags of 22 and 18 slices.

Ask: *If you use positive integers, how many of each type bag can the café have?* Pupils discuss in pairs. They should see that:

1 pair is possible

5 × 22 slices + 5 × 18 slices.

- Pupils should complete Question 5 in the Practice Book.

Same-day intervention

- Show pupils this problem:

> Peter has £23 in £2 coins and £5 notes.
> x is the number of £2 coins and y the number of £5 notes.

Using money or counters, together explore combinations that total £23. Then draw a bar model for the problem:

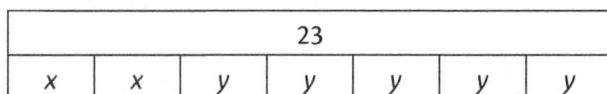

23						
x	x	y	y	y	y	y

Together, establish the equation and test possible values. Work systematically and record in a table.

Possible combinations are: 4, 3; 9, 1.

- Create other similar problems for pupils.

Same-day enrichment

- Ask pupils to work in pairs to establish the equations for the following problems and draw appropriate bar models:

> 1. Jack, Keri and Peter together have 50 marbles. Keri has twice as many marbles as Jack, and Peter has 12. How many marbles does Jack have?
> 2. Jack and Keri together have 37 marbles, and Keri has 15. How many does Jack have?
> 3. The number of hours that were left in the day was one-third of the number of hours already passed. How many hours were left in the day?

Answers:

1. Relationship: Jack's marbles + Keri's marbles + Peter's marbles = total marbles
Equation: $n + 2n + 12 = 50$;

2. Relationship: Jack's marbles + Keri's marbles = total marbles Equation ___ + 15 = 37;

3. Relationship: hours already passed + hours left = total hours
Equation: $p + \frac{1}{3}p = 24$

Challenge and extension question

Question 6

6 A department store received 324 pairs of sports shoes packed in boxes with the same number in each. If 2 boxes contain 72 pairs of the shoes, how many boxes did the store receive?

This question allows for a deeper look at establishing equations through problem solving. It is a two-step problem, using an equation as a first step.

Unit 3.7
Simple equations (3)

Conceptual context

This unit continues to consolidate pupils' understanding of equations by developing the method for solving equations through more complex examples, and by providing opportunities to establish and solve them.

Learning pupils will have achieved at the end of the unit

- Following further practice, pupils will be able to solve equations more fluently (Q1, Q2)
- Pupils will be able to construct increasingly complex equations from mathematical situations presented in words (Q3, Q4)
- Pupils will understand how to establish an equation and solve it from given information (Q4)

Resources

0–100 number cards; lettered flashcards; blank cards; counters; A1/flip chart paper; marker pens; **Resource 6.3.7a** Connect equations and solutions; **Resource 6.3.7b** Solve the equations; **Resource 6.3.7c** Find the solutions (1); **Resource 6.3.7d** Equations and solutions

Vocabulary

satisfy, unknown, variable, equation, algebra, solve, solution

Questions 1 and 2

1 Fill in the answers.

(a) $16 + x = 44$, solution: _____

(b) $12 \div x = 3$, solution: _____

(c) $6x = 108$, solution: _____

(d) $2x = 3 - x$, solution: _____

(e) $7x + 9x - 15x =$ _____

(f) $16x \div 4 \times 3 - 5x =$ _____

2 Solve the equations. (Check the answers to the questions marked with *.)

(a) $*4x + 2.4 = 16.4$
Solution: $4x = 16.4 - 2.4$
$4x = 14$
$x = 14 \div 4$
$= 3.5$
Check: $3.5 \times 4 + 2.4 = 16.4$

(b) $*7.8 - x \div 3 = 2.2$

(c) $7.2 - 0.3x = 1.8 + 0.3x$

(d) $*(6.8 + 1.2) \div x = 0.8$

(e) $18(3 + x) = 144$

(f) $*(x + 8) \div 0.5 = 20$

What learning will pupils have achieved at the conclusion of Questions 1 and 2?

- Following further practice, pupils will be able to solve equations more fluently.

Activities for whole-class instruction

- Give pupils **Resource 6.3.7a** Connect equations and solutions to complete. Discuss the answers.

Resource 6.3.7a

Answers: **A:** $H + 5.5 = 17.8$ [12.3]; $J - 7.8 = 3.42$ [11.22]; $15 - x = 4.82$ [10.18]; $x + 4.2 + 3.8 = 38.25$ [30.25]; $3.3h = 1.65$ [0.5]; $9 \div x = 6$ [1.5]; **B: 1.** $4x$; **2.** $3c$; **3.** $3v$; **4.** $7j$; **5.** $6n$; **6.** $22f + 1.5$

- Give groups of four a set of cards from **Resource 6.3.7b** Solve the equations. Using A1/flip chart paper and marker pens, pupils should explore how the equations can be solved.

Resource 6.3.7b

Solve the equations

| $4r + 2 = 6$ | $2v - 2 = 4$ | $2q \div 3 = 6$ |
| $s \div 2 = 6 - s$ | $3x = 4 + x$ | $t - 6 = 3 - t$ |

Answers: $r = 1$; $v = 3$; $q = 9$; $s = 4$; $x = 2$; $t = 4.5$

- Pupils work in small groups. Display the following equations (without the answers). Ask each group to solve and check one of the equations. (They might also include bar models.)

$4r + 2 = 6$ $\quad 4r = 6 - 2$ $\quad 4r = 4$ $\quad r = 4 \div 4$ $\quad = 1$ Check: $4 \times 1 + 2 = 6$. It checks.	$2v - 2 = 4$ $\quad 2v = 4 + 2$ $\quad 2v = 6$ $\quad v = 6 \div 2$ $\quad = 3$ Check: $2 \times 3 - 2 = 4$. It checks.
$2q \div 3 = 6$ $\quad 2q = 6 \times 3$ $\quad q = 18 \div 2$ $\quad = 9$ Check: $2 \times 9 \div 3 = 6$. It checks.	$s \div 2 = 6 - s$ $s \div 2 + s = 6$ $\quad 1.5s = 6$ $\quad s = 6 \div 1.5$ $\quad = 4$ Check: $4 \div 2 = 6 - 4$. It checks.

$3x = 4 + x$
$3x - x = 4$
$2x = 4$
$x = 4 \div 2$
$= 2$
Check: $3 \times 2 = 4 + 2$.
It checks.

$t - 6 = 3 - t$
$t - 6 + t = 3$
$2t - 6 = 3$
$2t = 3 + 6$
$2t = 9$
$t = 9 \div 2$
$= 4.5$
Check: $4.5 - 6 = 3 - 4.5$.
It checks.

Each group should present the solving of one of the equations to the rest of the class. Discuss conclusions.

Look out for … pupils who misunderstand simplification. Use extra examples for practice.

- Tell pupils that it is useful if the unknown is on the left-hand side of the equals sign.

- Write on the board: $5 - 2x = 3 + 2x$.

  Ask: *How can the equation be solved?* Agree:

  $5 - 2x = 3 + 2x$
  $3 + 2x + 2x = 5$
  $3 + 4x = 5$
  $4x = 5 - 3$
  $4x = 2$
  $x = 2 \div 4$
  $= 0.5$

  Check: $5 - 2 \times 0.5 = 3 + 2 \times 0.5$.
  It checks.

- Tell pupils that, at the first step, all the unknowns are on the left-hand side of the equals sign.

- Write on the board: $(j - 8) \div 0.5 = 4$. Ask: *How can the equation be solved?* Work through it together, pausing frequently to ask what can be done to both sides of the equation so that it stays true but becomes easier to work out. For example, agree:

  $(j - 8) \div 0.5 = 4$ (Ask: *What can be done to both sides of the equation so that it stays true but becomes easier to work out?* Agree, multiply by 0.5 on both sides because this eliminates the 0.5 on the left.)

  So, we now have
  $(j - 8) = 2$ (Ask: *What can be done to both sides of the equation so that it stays true but becomes easier to work out?* Agree, add 8 to both sides because this eliminates −8 on the left.)

  So, we now have $j = 10$

  Check: $(10 - 8) \div 0.5 = 4$.
  It checks.

- Write on the board: $6 = (y - 6) \div 1.5$. Ask: *How can the equation be solved?* Work through it together, as with the previous example, pause frequently to ask what can be done to both sides of the equation so that it stays true but becomes easier to work out.

  $6 = (y - 6) \div 1.5$
  $(y - 6) = 6 \times 1.5$
  $y - 6 = 9$
  $y = 9 + 6$
  $= 15$

  Check: $6 = (15 - 6) \div 1.5$.
  It checks.

- Write on the board: $(11.2 + 0.8) \div a = 4$. Ask: *How can the equation be solved?* Pupils discuss in pairs. Go through it as previously, pausing frequently to ask what can be done to both sides of the equation so that it stays true but becomes easier to work out.

  $(11.2 + 0.8) \div a = 4$
  $12 \div a = 4$
  $a = 12 \div 4$
  $= 3$

  Check: $(11.2 + 0.8) \div 3 = 4$.
  It checks.

- Write on the board: $4 = (21 - 12.6) \div t$. Ask: *How can the equation be solved?* Pupils discuss in pairs. Go through it as previously, pausing frequently to ask what can be done to both sides of the equation so that it stays true but becomes easier to work out.

  $4 = (21 - 12.6) \div t$
  $8.4 \div t = 4$
  $t = 8.4 \div 4$
  $= 2.1$

  Check: $4 = (21 - 12.6) \div 2.1$.
  It checks.

- Write on the board: $44 = 5(6 + t)$. Ask: *How can the equation be solved?* Agree with pupils that the brackets could be expanded:

  $44 = 5(6 + t)$
  $30 + 5t = 44$
  $5t = 44 - 30$
  $5t = 14$
  $t = 14 \div 5$
  $= 2.8$

  Check: $44 = 5(6 + 2.8)$.
  It checks.

Look out for … pupils misunderstanding expansion of brackets. Use extra examples for practice.

- Ask pupils: *Is there another way to solve 44 = 5(6 + t)?* Agree 44 ÷ 5 as a first step:

    44 = 5 (6 + t)

    6 + t = 44 ÷ 5

    6 + t = 8.8

        t = 8.8 − 6

          = 2.8

  Check: 44 = 5(6 + 2.8).

  It checks.

  Ask: *Which method seemed smarter? Why?* Ask pupils to discuss in pairs. Share ideas.

- Write on the board: 14.4 = 4(3.2 + t). Ask: *How can the equation be solved?* Pupils discuss in pairs. They could show:

    14.4 = 4(3.2 + t)

    12.8 + 4t = 14.4

        4t = 14.4 − 12.8

        4t = 1.6

         t = 1.6 ÷ 4

          = 0.4

  Check: 14.4 = 4(3.2 + 0.4).

  Or

    14.4 = 4(3.2 + t)

    3.2 + t = 14.4 ÷ 4

    3.2 + t = 3.6

        t = 3.6 − 3.2

          = 0.4

  Check: 14.4 = 4(3.2 + 0.4).

  It checks.

  Ask: *Which method seemed smarter? Why?* Pupils discuss in pairs. Share ideas.

- In pairs, ask pupils to complete section A of **Resource 6.3.7c** Find the solutions (1).

Resource 6.3.7c 1 of 2

Resource 6.3.7c 2 of 2

Answers: **1.** H = 6.1; **2.** b = 3.3; **3.** x = 8; **4.** e = 14.4; **5.** x = 2; **6.** y = 10; **7.** f = 1.6; **8.** k = 6; **9.** h = 4; **10.** s = 3.5; **11.** c = 9; **12.** s = 155.5

- Pupils should complete Question 2 in the Practice Book.

Same-day intervention

- Write on the board: 2y + 4 = 14. Represent the equation using counters and cards.

  Together, draw a bar model representing the equation:

14		
y	y	4

  Then set out the working, removing counters to show the step, as each line is written:

    2y + 4 = 14

        2y = 14 − 4

        2y = 10

         y = 10 ÷ 2

          = 5

  Check: 2 × 5 + 4 = 14.

  It checks.

- Repeat for 2q ÷ 3 = 6, s ÷ 2 = 6 − s, and so on.

Same-day enrichment

- Ask pupils to complete section B of **Resource 6.3.7c** Find the solutions (1).

  Answers: Various answers are possible.

Question 3

3 Write the equation and then find the solution.

  (a) The sum of 4 times x and 3.2 is 9.8. Find x.

  (b) 5 times the difference of 12 and x is 40. Find x.

  (c) 102 less than 3 times x is 78. Find x.

What learning will pupils have achieved at the conclusion of Question 3?

- Pupils will be able to construct increasingly complex equations from mathematical situations presented in words.

Activities for whole-class instruction

- Show pupils these statements:

> 2 times x equals 36.
> The difference between 35 and y is 12.
> 10 more than $4x$ is 54.
> 6 times the sum of 7 and R is 54.
> 8 times the difference between d and 4 is 56.

In pairs, ask pupils to draw bar models and establish the equations. They should draw:

36	
x	x

2 times x equals 36. Therefore x equals half of 36, which is 18. $2x = 36$.

35	
y	12

The difference between 35 and y is 12. Therefore y equals 23. $35 - y = 12$.

54				
x	x	x	x	10

10 more than $4x$ is 54. Therefore $4x$ equals 44. So, x is 11. $4x + 10 = 54$.

54					
$7 + R$	$7 + R$	$7 + R$	$7 + R$	$7 + R$	$7 + R$

6 times the sum of 7 and R is 54. Therefore $7 + R$ equals 9. So, $R = 2$. $6(7 + R) = 54$.

56							
$d - 4$	$d - 4$	$d - 4$	$d - 4$	$d - 4$	$d - 4$	$d - 4$	$d - 4$

56 is 8 times the difference of d and 4. Therefore $d - 4$ equals 7. So, $d = 11$. $8(d - 4) = 56$.

- Discuss responses. Ask: *How would you set out the working and check?* Pupils discuss in pairs. They should show:

$2x = 36$
$x = 36 \div 2$
$\quad = 18$

Check: $2 \times 18 = 36$.
It checks.

$35 - y = 12$
$\quad y = 35 - 12$
$\qquad = 23$

Check: $35 - 23 = 12$.
It checks.

$4x + 10 = 54$
$\quad 4x = 54 - 10$
$\quad 4x = 44$
$\quad\ x = 44 \div 4$
$\qquad = 11$

Check: $4 \times 11 + 10 = 54$.
It checks.

$6(7 + R) = 54$
$42 + 6R = 54$
$\quad\ 6R = 54 - 42$
$\quad\ 6R = 12$
$\quad\ R = 12 \div 6$
$\qquad = 2$

Check: $6(7 + 2) = 54$.
It checks.

- Or

$6(7 + R) = 54$
$\quad 7 + R = 54 \div 6$
$\quad 7 + R = 9$
$\qquad R = 9 - 7$
$\qquad\ = 2$

Check: $6(7 + 2) = 54$.
It checks.

$8(d - 4) = 56$
$8d - 32 = 56$
$\quad\ 8d = 56 + 32$
$\quad\ 8d = 88$
$\quad\ d = 88 \div 8$
$\qquad = 11$

Check: $8(11 - 4) = 56$.
It checks.

- Or

$8(d - 4) = 56$
$\quad d - 4 = 56 \div 8$
$\quad d - 4 = 7$
$\qquad d = 7 + 4$
$\qquad\ = 11$

Check: $8(11 - 4) = 56$.
It checks.

- Discuss conclusions. Include which methods are smarter and why.
- Working in pairs, ask pupils to create eight statements and solve their equations. Suggest that, at first, they draw bar models to represent how one unknown (represented by a letter) relates to known values. These can then be

written as statements in words and finally as symbols only. Pupils can then share their statements with another pair to solve the equations.

- Pupils should complete Question 3 in the Practice Book.

Same-day intervention

- Show pupils these statements:

> The sum of 25 times x and 45 is 95.
> 5 is 4 less than 3 times r.
> 6 times the sum of 7 and R is 66.
> 5 times the difference between d and 5 is 30.

Together, focus on the meanings of the words and use bar modelling to represent the statements. Then establish the equations, using counters and cards. Solve the equations.

Answers: $25x + 45 = 95$, $x = 2$; $3r - 4 = 5$, $r = 3$; $6(7 + R) = 66$, $R = 4$; $5(d - 5) = 30$, $d = 11$

Same-day enrichment

- Show pupils these solutions to equations:

5
1.5
3.8
2.4

- Ask pupils to create statements and equations with these solutions.

Question 4

> **4** Write the equations based on the information given below and then find the solutions.
>
> (a) Leila bought x books from a shop with £50. Each book cost £8. She had £2 left. Find x.
>
> (b) A canteen bought 3 baskets of carrots with x kg in each basket. 40 kg of carrots was used, which left 38 kg of carrots. Find x.
>
> (c) Mr Singh bought 3 e-readers at x pounds each. He paid £200 and got £8 change back. Find x.

What learning will pupils have achieved at the conclusion of Question 4?

- Pupils will be able to construct increasingly complex equations from mathematical situations presented in words.

- Pupils will understand how to establish an equation and solve it from given information.

Activities for whole-class instruction

- Read aloud these six statements to pupils:

> The sum of 4 times x and 3.3 is 9.7.
> 10.3 is the difference between 3 times y and 16.
> 15 multiplied by the difference between 5 and n is 24.2.
> 45.2 is the difference between 5 and $6y$, multiplied by 5.5.
> 99 is 44.6 less than the product of t and 65.
> 10.3 less than 4 times the sum of g and 6 is 45.6.

In pairs, pupils write the equations that represent the statements and explain their reasoning.

- Read aloud this problem to pupils:

> Cabbages are sold for £3 each. I use a £20 note to buy d cabbages. My change is £2. How many cabbages did I buy?

Working in pairs, pupils draw a bar model to represent the statement and then establish its equation. Pupils should show:

20	
$3d$	2

$3d + 2 = 20$ or $20 - 3d = 2$

$3d + 2 = 20$

$\quad 3d = 20 - 2$

$\quad 3d = 18$

$\quad\ d = 18 \div 3$

$\qquad = 6$

Check: $3 \times 6 + 2 = 20$.

It checks.

- Now read aloud this problem to pupils:

> DVDs are £3.50 each. I bought x DVDs and paid with a £50 note. My change was £29. How many DVDs did I buy?

Working in pairs, ask pupils to draw a bar model to represent the statement and then establish its equation. They should show:

50	
$3.5x$	29

$3.5x + 29 = 50$ or $50 - 3.5x = 29$

$3.5x + 29 = 50$

$\quad 3.5x = 50 - 29$

$\quad 3.5x = 21$

$\quad\quad x = 21 \div 3.5$

$\quad\quad\quad = 6$

Check: $3.5 \times 6 + 29 = 50$.

It checks.

● Read aloud this problem to pupils:

> Peter runs 5 km for g days. He ran 25 km and then had 30 km left to run. For how many days was Peter running?

In pairs, pupils should draw a bar model to represent the statement and then establish its equation. They should show:

5g	
25	30

$5g - 25 = 30$ or $5g - 30 = 25$

$5g - 25 = 30$

$\quad 5g = 30 + 25$

$\quad 5g = 55$

$\quad\, g = 55 \div 5$

$\quad\quad = 11$

Check: $5 \times 11 - 25 = 30$.

It checks.

● Working in pairs, pupils should write three similar statements, drawing bar models and solving the equations. Ask them to share their statements with another pair who then solve the equations.

● Give pairs of pupils **Resource 6.3.7d** Equations and solutions, and ask them to complete section A.

Answers: **1.** $50 - 3d = 8$, $d = 14$; **2.** $30 - 2.5s = 10$, $s = 8$; **3.** $8x - 60 = 28$, $x = 11$ kg; **4.** $4g - 14 = 18$, $g = 8$; **5.** $200 - 5r = 14$, $r = £37.20$; **6.** $50 - 1.5e = 23$, $e = 18$; **7.** $12x - 70 = 38$, $x = 9$ kg; **8.** $50 - 3.5s = 18.5$, $s = 9$

● Pupils should complete Question 4 in the Practice Book.

Same-day intervention

● Read aloud this problem to pupils:

> Books are sold for £4 each. I use a £20 note to buy x books. My change is £8. Find x.

Together, draw a bar model to represent the statement and then establish its equation:

20	
4x	8

$4x + 8 = 20$ or $20 - 4x = 8$

Represent the equation using counters and cards.

Then, together, solve the equation. Ask pupils to explain the different steps, for example:

$4x + 8 = 20$

$\quad 4x = 20 - 8$

$\quad 4x = 12$

$\quad\, x = 12 \div 4$

$\quad\quad = 3$

Check: $4 \times 3 + 8 = 20$.

It checks.

● Repeat with other similar problems.

Same-day enrichment

● Ask pupils to complete section B of **Resource 6.3.7d** Equations and solutions.

Answers: Possible answers: $d = 2$, $e = 45$; $d = 6$, $e = 30$; $d = 10$, $e = 15$; $d = 14$, $e = 0$

Challenge and extension question

Question 5

> **5** Write an equation based on the diagram and use reasoning to find x and y.
>
> | x | x | x | x |
> |---|---|---|---|
> | y | | y | y |
> | x | | 4.5 | |
>
> Equation: _____ $x =$ _____
>
> Equation: _____ $y =$ _____

This question allows for a deeper look at establishing equations through problem solving. It is a two-step problem, the solution to one equation being substituted into another.

Unit 3.8
Using equations to solve problems (1)

Conceptual context

This is the first of three units in which pupils will apply what they have learned about algebra to solve problems set in real-life contexts. They will also review generic relationships between quantities that they already know and consider these as algebraic expressions, providing them with experience of algebra in real-world contexts.

Learning pupils will have achieved at the end of the unit

- Pupils will have strengthened their knowledge through further experience of solving equations (Q1)
- Pupils will know that algebra is relevant to real-life contexts and situations (Q2)
- Pupils will have solved real-world problems by considering them algebraically (Q3)

Resources

0–100 number cards; lettered flashcards; blank cards; counters; mini whiteboards; **Resource 6.3.8a** Find the solutions (2); **Resource 6.3.8b** Real-life problems (1)

Vocabulary

unknown, equation, algebra, solve, solution

Question 1

> **1** Solve the equations.
> (a) $x \div 5 - 3 = 8$
> (b) $6x + 1.5 = 4.5$
>
> (c) $3x + 4.7 - x = 7.4$
> (d) $2(x - 1.5) + x = 12$

What learning will pupils have achieved at the conclusion of Question 1?

- Pupils will have strengthened their knowledge through further experience of solving equations.

Activities for whole-class instruction

- Check pupils' understanding of equations by asking quickfire questions for them to answer using their whiteboards. Say to pupils: *Show me three unknowns; Show me an expression for the product of g and 15; How can you change 3x + 2 so that it is three times bigger? If 3 is the solution what is the equation? What is wrong with 3(x − 2) = 3x + 4? What is the next line in the working?* (with a section of working shown)

- Write on the board: $2x \div 4 - 5 = 9$. In pairs, pupils should discuss how the equation is solved. They should show:

$$2x \div 4 - 5 = 9$$
$$2x \div 4 = 9 + 5$$
$$2x \div 4 = 14$$
$$2x = 14 \times 4$$
$$2x = 56$$
$$x = 56 \div 2$$
$$= 28$$

Check: $2 \times 28 \div 4 - 5 = 9$.
It checks.

Or

$$2x \div 4 - 5 = 9$$
$$0.5x - 5 = 9$$
$$0.5x = 9 + 5$$
$$0.5x = 14$$
$$x = 14 \div 0.5$$
$$= 28$$

Check: $2 \times 28 \div 4 - 5 = 9$.
It checks.

Discuss conclusions, including which method is smarter and why.

- Write on the board: $6x + 2.5 - x = 11.2$. In pairs, pupils should discuss how the equation is solved. They should show:

$$6x + 2.5 - x = 11.2$$
$$5x + 2.5 = 11.2$$
$$5x = 11.2 - 2.5$$
$$5x = 8.7$$
$$x = 8.7 \div 5$$
$$= 1.74$$

Check: $6 \times 1.74 + 2.5 - 1.74 = 11.2$.
It checks.

Or

$$6x + 2.5 - x = 11.2$$
$$6x - x = 11.2 - 2.5$$
$$6x - x = 8.7$$
$$5x = 8.7$$
$$x = 8.7 \div 5$$
$$= 1.74$$

Check: $6 \times 1.74 + 2.5 - 1.74 = 11.2$.
It checks.

Discuss conclusions, including which method is smarter and why.

- Write on the board: $4(x - 2.5) + x = 23$. In pairs, pupils should discuss how the equation is solved. They should show:

$$4(x - 2.5) + x = 23$$
$$4x - 10 + x = 23$$
$$5x - 10 = 23$$
$$5x = 23 + 10$$
$$5x = 33$$
$$= 6.6$$

Check: $4(6.6 - 2.5) + 6.6 = 23$.
It checks.

Or

$$4(x - 2.5) + x = 23$$
$$4x - 10 + x = 23$$
$$4x + x = 23 + 10$$
$$4x + x = 33$$
$$5x = 33$$
$$= 6.6$$

Check: $4(6.6 - 2.5) + 6.6 = 23$.
It checks.

Discuss conclusions, including which method is smarter and why.

- Give pupil pairs **Resource 6.3.8a** Find the solutions (2) and ask them to complete section A.

Answers: **1.** $c = 16$; **2.** $v = 4$; **3.** $b = 7.84$; **4.** $x = 0.14$; **5.** $x = 3.1$; **6.** $d = 0.75$; **7.** $x = 2.5$; **8.** $x = 1.8$; **9.** $y = 0.18$

- Pupils should complete Question 1 in the Practice Book.

Same-day intervention

- Write on the board: $x \div 4 - 3 = 6$. Represent the equation using counters and cards.

  Together, solve the equation, choosing pupils to explain the different steps. For example:

  $$x \div 4 - 3 = 6$$
  $$x \div 4 = 6 + 3$$
  $$x \div 4 = 9$$
  $$x = 9 \times 4$$
  $$= 36$$

  Check: $36 \div 4 - 3 = 6$.
  It checks.

- Repeat for further equations: $6x + 2.5 - x = 11.5$; $4(x - 1.5) + x = 14$, and so on.

Same-day enrichment

- Ask pupils to complete section B of **Resource 6.3.8a** Find the solutions (2).

  Answers: Various answers are possible.

Question 2

2 Complete the equations on the relations between quantities.

   (a) Unit price of pencils × _____ = Total price of pencils

   (b) _____ – Number of pear trees = Number of peach trees more than that of pear trees

   (c) Amount of work ÷ _____ = Work efficiency

   (d) Number of pupils in Class A + _____ = Total number of pupils in Class A and Class B

What learning will pupils have achieved at the conclusion of Question 2?

- Pupils will know that algebra is relevant to real-life contexts and situations.

Activities for whole-class instruction

- Write on the board: What is an equation?

  Ask pupils to write down their own definition. They should see that:

  - an equation represents a relationship
  - both sides of the equals sign have the same value
  - equations can be used to solve problems.

- Now draw a rectangle on the board.

  Ask pupils to copy the rectangle and label the length and width. Ask: *What do you know about the length and width of this rectangle?* Agree that the length is longer than the width.

  Ask: *What is the relationship between the area of the rectangle and its length and width? Can the relationship be written as an equation?* Pupils should discuss responses in pairs. Can they see that:

  - Area = length × width
  - $A = l \times w$?

  Discuss conclusions with the pupils.

- Draw a triangle on the board.

  Ask pupils to copy the triangle and label the three angles using letters. Ask: *What do you know about the size of each interior angle?* Agree that each angle is less than 90°.

  Ask: *What is the relationship between 180 degrees and the three angles? Can the relationship be written as an equation?* Pupils discuss their responses in pairs. They should point out that:

  - the sum of the three angles is 180°
  - $a + b + c = 180°$ (a, b and c being the angles).

  Discuss conclusions with the pupils.

- Display the following:

  A group of people are divided into two groups – some people are in Group A and some are in Group B.

Ask pupils: *What bar model would represent this statement?* Together, draw the bar chart:

t	
A	B

Ask: *Are there relationships between these three parts? Can any relationships be written as equations?* Pupils discuss their responses in pairs. They should see that:

- total number of people = people in Group A + people in Group B

  $t = A + B$

- people in Group A = total number of people − people in Group B

  $A = t − B$

- people in Group B = total number of people − people in Group A

  $B = t − A$

Discuss conclusions.

Look out for … pupils who are unable to choose letters for the unknowns. Suggest letters from within the problem, for example, the first letter of a word.

- Display the following on the board:

  A number of chairs are set out in equal rows.

Ask: *What equation would represent this statement?* Agree with pupils:

Total number of chairs (T) = number of rows (R) × number of chairs in each row (C)

Ask: Are there other ways this could be expressed? Pupils might suggest:

- $T = R × C$

- number of rows = total number of chairs ÷ number of chairs in each row or $R = T ÷ C$

- number of chairs in each row = total number of chairs ÷ number of rows or $C = T ÷ R$.

- Repeat the discussion with a new example:

  In the car park, all the cars are either green or blue.

- Working in pairs, ask pupils to construct equations that describe relationships between:

  total distance covered, number of lengths, length of swimming pool

  bees in hive R, bees in hive S

  speed, distance, time

  people on ferry 1, people on ferry 2, total number of people

  unit price, total price, quantity

  work time, work efficiency, amount of work

Look out for … pupils who might need reminding of the meaning of terms, for example, work efficiency; unit price, and so on.

- Pupils should complete Question 2 in the Practice Book.

Same-day intervention

- Display on the board:

  - total number of people

  - number of coaches

  - number of people on each coach

  Together, focus on the meanings of the words and use arrays and other diagrams, counters, and so on, to represent the relationship. Establish the equations.

- Now display on the board:

  - cars in the red car park

  - cars in the pink car park

  - total number of cars

  Together, focus on the meanings of the words and use bar models and other diagrams, counters, and so on, to represent the relationship. Establish the equations.

Same-day enrichment

- Show these equations to pupils:

  $v = u + at$

  $F = 1.8C + 32$

- Ask pupils to create relations between quantities based on these equations.

Question 3

> **3** Write equations and then solve the application problems. The first one has been done for you.
>
> (a) There were 105 cars parked in a car park. After some cars were driven away, there were 34 cars left. How many cars were driven away?
>
> > If x is the number of cars that were driven away
> > then, $x + 34 = 105$
> > $x = 105 - 34 = 71$
> > therefore, 71 cars were driven away.
>
> (b) Tom has read 98 pages of a book in two days. He read 55 pages on the first day. How many pages did he read on the second day?
>
> (c) A school bought 480 ropes. They were shared equally among 32 classes. How many ropes did each class receive?
>
> (d) A school choir has 64 pupils, which is twice the number of pupils in the dancing group. How many pupils are there in the dancing group?
>
> (e) Amy can type 86 words in one minute, which is 8 words more than Ayesha can type in one minute. How many words can Ayesha type in one minute?
>
> (f) The area of a rectangle is 36 cm². The length is 8 cm. What is the width of the rectangle?
>
> (g) Mr Brown bought 1 football and 6 volleyballs for £112 in total. The volleyballs were priced at £15 each. How much did the football cost?

What learning will pupils have achieved at the conclusion of Question 3?

- Pupils will have solved real-world problems by considering them algebraically.

Activities for whole-class instruction

- On the board, display this list:

> addition
> subtraction
> multiplication
> division

Ask pupils to write down as many words and phrases that have same meaning as the operations, then share ideas.

- Show pupils this problem:

> There were 143 cows in a field. At milking time there were 56 cows left in the field.
> How many cows went for milking?

Discuss the problem. Ask questions such as:

What is the question asking?

What is the problem that needs to be solved?

What do we need to find out/work out?

Is the problem about a whole and its parts?

Is it a problem about something being a number of times bigger or smaller than something else? Is it about something else? How do we know?

What operations are going to be used?

What is the calculation that needs to be done? If there is more than one step, in what order should the steps be carried out?

Together, draw a bar model to represent the problem:

143	
56	x

Ask: *What equation should be established?*
Agree: $56 + x = 143$ or $143 - x = 56$.

Ask: *Using $56 + x = 143$, how is the working and check set out?* Agree:

$56 + x = 143$
$x = 143 - 56$
$= 87$

Check: $56 + 87 = 143$.
It checks.

- Now show pupils this problem:

> A café sold 87 pies over two days. They sold 34 pies on the first day.
> How many pies did the café sell on the second day?

Ask: *What bar model would represent the problem? What equation should be established? How is the working and check set out?*

Pupils discuss in pairs and should show:

87	
34	x

$34 + x = 87$ or $87 - x = 34$.

- If using $34 + x = 87$:

$34 + x = 87$
$x = 87 - 34$
$= 53$

Check: $34 + 53 = 87$.
It checks.

● Show pupils this problem:

> A bank buys 578 security devices. The devices are
> shared equally between 17 branches.
> How many security devices did each bank receive?

Together, draw a bar model to represent the problem:

578																
d	d	d	d	d	d	d	d	d	d	d	d	d	d	d	d	d

Ask: *What equation should be established?*

Agree: $17d = 578$ or $d = 578 \div 17$.

Ask: *How is the working and check set out?* Agree:

$17d = 578$

$\quad d = 578 \div 17$

$\quad\quad = 34$

Check: $17 \times 34 = 578$.

It checks.

● Repeat with further problems, for example:

  – A hedge is 675 m long. It is divided into 15 m lengths.
    How many lengths of hedge are there?

  – Peter bought 1 pair of sandals and 7 pairs of shoes. The
    total cost was £134. The shoes were priced at £17 each.
    How much did the pair of sandals cost?

  – May bought 2 pairs of boots and 9 pairs of shoes. The
    total cost was £186. The shoes were priced at £18 each.
    How much did a pair of boots cost?

● Give pupil pairs **Resource 6.3.8b** Real-life problems (1)
and ask them to complete section A.

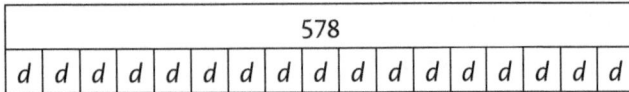

Answers: **1.** 78 people; **2.** 58 km; **3.** 37 kg; **4.** 37 labradors;
5. 85 press ups; **6.** 8 km; **7.** £388

● Pupils should complete Question 3 in the Practice Book.

Same-day intervention

● Show pupils this problem:

> There were 112 sheep in a field. At lambing time,
> there were 88 sheep left in the field.
> How many sheep went for lambing?

Together, draw a bar model to represent the problem
and establish its equation:

112	
88	x

Agree: $88 + x = 112$ or $112 - x = 88$.

Represent the equation using counters and cards.

Together, solve the equation, choosing pupils to explain
the different steps. For example:

$88 + x = 112$

$\quad x = 112 - 88$

$\quad\quad = 24$

Check: $88 + 24 = 112$.

It checks.

● Repeat with other similar problems.

Same-day enrichment

● Ask pupils to complete section B of **Resource 6.3.8b**
Real-life problems (1).

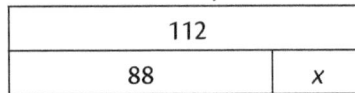

Answers: **1.** 234 programmes; **2.** $x + 7 + 11 = 90$ (where
x = the amount of time spent lifting weights), 72
minutes

Challenge and extension questions

Question 4

> 4 Jamelia bought 1 bath towel and 4 hand towels for £20. Given that the price of the bath towel was £6, how much did each hand towel cost?

This question allows for a deeper look at establishing and solving equations through application problems. One equation has to be established then solved.

Question 5

> 5 There are two pieces of purple ribbon. The first piece is 4.5 m long. If the second piece has 3.5 m cut from it, the length of the remaining part is 1.2 times the length of the first piece. How long is the second piece?

This question allows for a deeper look at establishing and solving application problems. More than one step is needed to establish the equation.

Unit 3.9
Using equations to solve problems (2)

Conceptual context

This unit continues to consolidate an understanding of algebra. Pupils solve more real-life problems presented in words by establishing and solving appropriate equations.

Learning pupils will have achieved at the end of the unit

- Pupils will have strengthened their knowledge through further experience of solving equations (Q1)
- Pupils will have applied their deepening understanding to solve real-world problems by considering them algebraically (Q2)

Resources

counters; **Resource 6.3.9a** Complete the working; **Resource 6.3.9b** Real-life problems (2)

Vocabulary

equation, algebra, solve, solution

Question 1

1 Solve these equations.
(a) $7x - 3.5 = 9.1$ (b) $6x = 180 \div 4$

(c) $3(x + 2.3) = 9.6$ (d) $10x \div 2 - x = 6.4$

What learning will pupils have achieved at the conclusion of Question 1?

- Pupils will have strengthened their knowledge through further experience of solving equations.

Activities for whole-class instruction

- Display on the board:

$7x - \underline{\ \ } = 8.4$
$7x = \underline{\ \ } + 10.5$
$7x = 18.9$
$x = 18.9 \div \underline{\ \ }$
$= 2.7$

Ask: *What should the missing values be?* Pupil pairs discuss. Can they see 10.5, 8.4 and 7?

- Display on the board:

$8x = 216 \div 5$
$\underline{\ \ }x = 43.2$
$x = \underline{\ \ } \div 8$
$= 5.4$

Ask: *What should the missing values be?* Pupils pairs discuss. Can they see 8 and 43.2?

- Display on the board:

$\underline{\ \ }(x + 2.7) = 20$
$4x + 10.8 = \underline{\ \ }$
$4x = 20 - \underline{\ \ }$
$4x = \underline{\ \ }$
$x = 9.2 \div 4$
$= 2.3$

Ask: *What should the missing values be?* Pupil pairs discuss. Can they see 4, 20, 10.8 and 9.2?

- Ask: *Could $4(x + 2.7) = 20$ be solved in any other way?* Pupil pairs discuss. They should show:

$4(x + 27) = 20$
$x + 2.7 = 20 \div 4$
$x + 2.7 = 5$
$x = 5 - 2.7$
$= 2.3$

- Discuss conclusions.
- Remaining in pairs, ask pupils to create five similar problems, with no more than four values missing. Pupils then swap with another pair and solve each other's problems.
- Give pupils **Resource 6.3.9a** Complete the working and ask them to complete section A in pairs.

Answers: **1.** 2.1

2. $18.4 = 5g + 6.9$
$5g = 18.4 - 6.9$
$5g = 11.5$
$g = 11.5 \div 5$
$= 2.3$

Check: $18.4 = 5 \times 2.3 + 6.9$.
It checks.

3. 8.5

4. $7x = 157.5 \div 3$
$7x = 52.5$
$x = 52.5 \div 7$
$= 7.5$

Check: $7 \times 7.5 = 157.5 \div 3$.
It checks.

5. 0.9

6. 0.8

7. $12e \div 4 - e = 2.4$
$3e - e = 2.4$
$2e = 2.4$
$e = 2.4 \div 2$
$= 1.2$

Check: 12 × 1.2 ÷ 4 − 1.2 = 2.4.

It checks.

8. 0.65

● Pupils should complete Question 1 in the Practice Book.

Same-day intervention

● Display on the board:

$$5x = 10$$
$$x = 10 \div 5$$
$$\_\_ \times \_\_ = \_\_$$
Check: __ × __ = __
It checks.

Together, draw a bar model representing 2 = 10 ÷ 5.

10				
2	2	2	2	2

Ask: *What other equations does the bar model represent?* Agree 5 × 2 = 10.

Ask: *What is missing from __x = 10?* Agree 5.

● Together, complete the working:

$$5x + 5 = 15$$
$$5x = 10$$
$$x = 10 \div 5$$
$$= 2$$

Check: 5 × 2 = 10.
It checks.

● Show pupils the bar model:

10				
P + 1	P + 1	P + 1	P + 1	P + 1

Agree that this shows 5(P + 1) = 10. Solve the equation together.

Now add to the bar model:

23					
P + 1	P + 1	P + 1	P + 1	P + 1	3

Agree that this shows 5(P + 1) + 3 = 23. Solve the equation together.

● Repeat with other bar models as starting points to construct (establish) equations and solve to find the unknown value.

Same-day enrichment

● Ask pupils to complete section B of **Resource 6.3.9a** Complete the working.

Question 2

2 Write equations and then solve the problems.

(a) In a primary school, the number of pupils in the chess team multiplied by 4 and then added to 12 is equal to the number of the pupils in the tennis team. There are 80 pupils in the tennis team. How many pupils are there in the chess team?

(b) A box of apples weighs 18 kg, which is 3 kg less than 1.5 times the mass of a box of oranges. What is the mass of a box of oranges?

(c) A pen costs £0.30 more than 3 ballpoint pens. The pen is £1.50. What is the price of a ballpoint pen?

(d) The length of the River Severn is 354 km, which is 338 km shorter than twice the length of the River Thames. How long is the River Thames?

(e) A pair of trainers is priced at £78, which is £14 more than twice the price of a pair of sandals. What is the price of a pair of sandals?

(f) There are some people in a sports field doing physical exercise. 28 people are playing football. If 8 more people join the footballers, the number of people playing football will be 3 times the number of people running. How many people are running?

(g) A new mobile phone shop sold 375 mobile phones in the first month, which was 25 more than half of all the mobile phones in stock. How many mobile phones did the shop have in stock?

What learning will pupils have achieved at the conclusion of Question 2?

● Pupils will have applied their deepening understanding to solve real-world problems by considering them algebraically.

Activities for whole-class instruction

● Show pupils these equations.

45 = 0.5x	[90]
1.5x = 9	[6]
0.15 ÷ y = 0.2	[0.75]

Ask: *In what different ways could these equations be solved? Are any of them smarter? Pupils discuss in pairs.* They should see:

$45 \div 0.5$

45×2

$9 \div 1.5$

$90 \div 15$

$0.15 \div 0.2$

$15 \div 20$

Discuss conclusions.

- Show pupils this problem:

> A box of toys weighs 14 kg. This is 2 kg more than 1.5 times the weight of a box of books.
> What is the weight of the box of books?

Discuss the problem with pupils, asking questions such as:

- *What is the question asking?*
- *What is the problem that needs to be solved?*
- *What do we need to find out/work out?*
- *Is the problem about a whole and its parts?*
- *Is it a problem about something being a number of times bigger or smaller than something else? Is it about something else? How do we know?*
- *What operations are going to be used?*
- *What is the calculation that needs to be done? If there is more than one step, in what order should the steps be carried out?*

Together, draw a bar model to represent the problem:

14		
b	$0.5b$	2

Ask: *What equation should be established?* Agree
$1.5b + 2 = 14$ or $14 - 2 = 1.5b$.

Ask: *Using $1.5b + 2 = 14$, how is the working and check set out?* Agree:

$1.5b + 2 = 14$

$\quad 1.5b = 14 - 2$

$\quad 1.5b = 12$

$\quad\quad b = 12 \div 1.5$

$\quad\quad\quad = 8$

Check: $1.5 \times 8 + 2 = 14$.
It checks.

- Read this problem aloud:

> A large ball costs £0.40 more than 4 tennis balls. The large ball is £1.60. What is the cost of a tennis ball?

Ask: *What bar model would represent the problem? What equation should be established? How is the working and check set out?* Pupils discuss in pairs. They should show:

1.60				
t	t	t	t	0.40

$4t + 0.40 = 1.60$ or $1.60 - 4t = 0.40$

If using $4t + 0.40 = 1.60$:

$4t + 0.40 = 1.60$

$\quad\quad 4t = 1.60 - 0.40$

$\quad\quad 4t = 1.20$

$\quad\quad\ t = 1.20 \div 4$

$\quad\quad\quad = 0.30$

Check: $4 \times 0.30 + 0.40 = 1.60$.
It checks.

- Display this problem:

> There are some people in a town. 32 are shopping. If 12 more people also start shopping, the number of people shopping will be 4 times the number of people eating. How many people are eating?

Ask: *What bar model would represent the problem? What equation should be established? How is the working and check set out?* Pupils discuss in pairs. They should show:

32 + 12			
e	e	e	e

$4e = 32 + 12$

$4e = 32 + 12$

$4e = 44$

$\ e = 44 \div 4$

$\quad = 11$

Check: $4 \times 11 = 32 + 12$.
It checks.

- Ask pupils to work in pairs to complete section A of **Resource 6.3.9b** Real-life problems (2).

Answers: **1.** 14 people; **2.** 17 kg; **3.** £0.10; **4.** 550 m;
5. £16.75; **6.** 12 people; **7.** 970 cars

● Pupils should complete Question 2 in the Practice Book.

Same-day intervention

● Display this problem on the board:

> Company A employs 12 people. Company B employs double the number at Company A
> How many people are at company B?

Together, use counters to represent Company A. Ask: *How do we find the number of people employed by Company B?*

With pupils, draw a bar model to represent the problem and establish its equation:

B	
A	A

Agree $0.5B = 12$ (note that $B = 2A$ or $B = 2 \times 12$ are also correct).

Together, discuss different ways the equation could be solved.

Set out the working: Ask: *What can we do to both sides of the equation to keep it true and make the equation simpler?* Agree to multiply both sides by 2 to eliminate the 0.5 on the left.

Return to the problem.

Check: $0.5 \times 24 = 12$.
It checks.

● Together, represent and solve $1.5y = 12$ and $0.15 \div y = 0.25$.

Same-day enrichment

● Ask pupils to complete section B of **Resource 6.3.9b** Real-life problems (2).

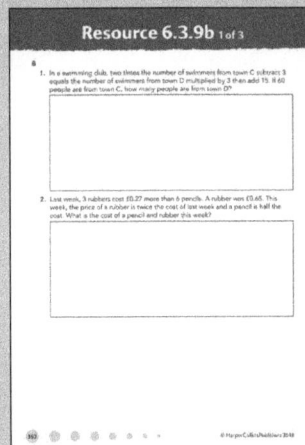

Resource 6.3.9b 1 of 3

Answers: **1.** 34 people; **2.** rubber = £1.30, pencil = 14p

Challenge and extension question

Question 3

3 There are 9 boxes of eggs, each with the same mass. If 15 kg of eggs are taken from each box, the mass of the remaining eggs in the 9 boxes is equal to the original mass of 4 boxes. What was the original mass of each box of eggs?

This question allows for a deeper look at establishing and solving equations through application problems. The equation that is formed uses brackets and the expansion of brackets can be a first step for solving it.

Unit 3.10
Using equations to solve problems (3)

Conceptual context

This is the final unit in the series of units about using equations to solve problems. Pupils' knowledge and algebraic reasoning will continue to develop and they will solve problems fluently.

Learning pupils will have achieved at the end of the unit

- Pupils will have strengthened their knowledge through further experience of solving equations (Q1)
- Pupils will have further strengthened their understanding through solving real-world problems by considering them algebraically (Q2)

Resources

0–100 number cards; lettered flashcards; blank cards; counters; **Resource 6.3.10a** Match equations and solutions; **Resource 6.3.10b** Create expressions; **Resource 6.3.10c** Real-life problems (3)

Vocabulary

equation, algebra, solve, solution

Question 1

> **1** Solve these equations.
>
> (a) $90 - 5x = 35$
>
> (b) $1.8x + 1.5x + 3.4 = 10$
>
> (c) $(9x + 27) \div 2 = 81$
>
> (d) $3x - 2(x + 1) = 8$

What learning will pupils have achieved at the conclusion of Question 1?

- Pupils will have strengthened their knowledge through further experience of solving equations.

Activities for whole-class instruction

- Discuss these calculations and expressions. Pupils should decide if the statements are true or false.

> $14 - 6 - 2 = 14 - (6 + 2)$
> $15 + (4 - 1) = (15 + 4) - 1$
> $11 - 6 + 5 = 11 - (6 - 5)$
> $c - (d + e) = c - d - e$
> $e - (f - g) = e - f - g$

Answers: True, True, True, True, False

Discuss responses.

- Show these equations to pupils and ask: *In what different ways could the equations be solved? Which are smarter?* Pupil pairs should discuss.

> $80 - 5a = 45$ $[a = 7]$
> $1.6x + 1.8x + 5.2 = 12$
> $(8b + 24) \div 3 = 72$ $[b = 24]$
> $4x - 3(x + 2) = 9$

Pupils should see:

$1.6x + 1.8x + 5.2 = 12$
$\qquad 3.4x + 5.2 = 12$
$\qquad\qquad 3.4x = 12 - 5.2$
$\qquad\qquad 3.4x = 6.8$
$\qquad\qquad\quad x = 6.8 \div 3.4$
$\qquad\qquad\qquad = 2$

Check: $1.6 \times 2 + 1.8 \times 2 + 5.2 = 12$.
It checks.

Or

$1.6x + 1.8x + 5.2 = 12$
$\qquad 1.6x + 1.8x = 12 - 5.2$
$\qquad 1.6x + 1.8x = 6.8$
$\qquad\qquad 3.4x = 6.8$
$\qquad\qquad\quad x = 6.8 \div 3.4$
$\qquad\qquad\qquad = 2$

Check: $1.6 \times 2 + 1.8 \times 2 + 5.2 = 12$.
It checks.

$4x - 3(x + 2) = 9$
$\qquad 4x - 9 = 3(x + 2)$
$\qquad 4x - 9 = 3x + 6$
$\quad 4x - 3x - 9 = 6$
$\qquad\qquad x = 9 + 6$
$\qquad\qquad\quad = 15$

Check: $4 \times 15 - 3(15 + 2) = 9$.
It checks.

Or

$4x - 3(x + 2) = 9$
$\quad 4x - 3x - 6 = 9$
$\qquad\quad x - 6 = 9$
$\qquad\qquad x = 9 + 6$
$\qquad\qquad\quad = 15$

Check: $4 \times 15 - 3(15 + 2) = 9$.
It checks.

Discuss conclusions.

- Ask pupils, working in pairs, to cut out cards from **Resource 6.3.10a** Match equations and solutions, and to go through the equations, matching them to their solutions.

Resource 6.3.10a

Answers: $x = 7.84$; $y = 10$; $r = 2$; $z = 20$; $e = 35.8$; $f = 3.45$; $c = 0.2$; $t = 18$

Share ideas.

● Pupils should complete Question 1 in the Practice Book.

Same-day intervention

● On the board, write: $5x + 7x + 6 = 30$. Represent the equation using bar model, counters and cards.

Together, solve the equation, choosing pupils to explain the different steps. Investigate alternative methods:

$$5x + 7x + 6 = 30$$
$$12x + 6 = 30$$
$$12x = 30 - 6$$
$$12x = 24$$
$$x = 24 \div 12$$
$$= 2$$

Check: $5 \times 2 + 7 \times 2 + 6 = 30$.
It checks.

Or

$$5x + 7x + 6 = 30$$
$$5x + 7x = 30 - 6$$
$$5x + 7x = 24$$
$$12x = 24$$
$$x = 24 \div 12$$
$$= 2$$

Check: $5 \times 2 + 7 \times 2 + 6 = 30$.
It checks.

● Repeat for $2(x + 3) = 12$, using two methods.

Same-day enrichment

● Give pupils **Resource 6.3.10b** Create expressions and ask pupils to make a set of matching cards by writing their own expressions and solutions. Provide **Resource 6.3.10a** Match expressions and solutions for examples.

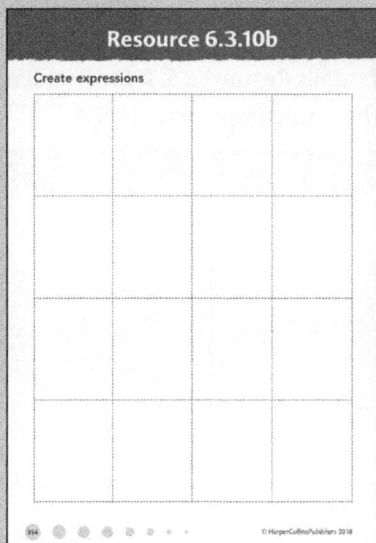

Resource 6.3.10b

Create expressions

Question 2

2 Write equations and then solve the problems.

(a) A canteen received a delivery of 150 kg of rice, which was 30 kg less than 3 times the flour it received at the same time. What was the mass of the flour the canteen received?

(b) Warehouse A stored 56 tonnes of food. The amount was 8 tonnes more than twice the food stored in Warehouse B. How many tonnes of food did Warehouse B store?

(c) Jack's mum is 35 years old. This is 2 years more than 3 times Jack's age. How old is Jack?

(d) 36 white rabbits and some grey rabbits are on the grass. There are 3 times as many white rabbits as grey rabbits. How many grey rabbits are on the grass?

(e) The volume of a big bottle is 2.5 litres, which is 250 ml less than 5 times the volume of a small bottle. What is the volume of the small bottle?

(f) Dad's age is 4 times the age of his son. Dad is 48 years older than his son. How old are the son and dad?

(g) A tailor bought 72 m of cloth, which was exactly enough to make 20 sets of adult clothes and 16 sets of children's clothes. 2.4 m of cloth is needed for each set of adult clothes. What is the length of cloth needed for each set of children's clothes?

(h) Three years ago, a mum's age was 6 times the age of her daughter. The mum is 33 years old this year. How old is her daughter this year?

What learning will pupils have achieved at the conclusion of Question 2?

● Pupils will have further strengthened their understanding through solving real-world problems by considering them algebraically.

Activities for whole-class instruction

- Working in pairs, ask pupils to find the values of the unknowns in the following equations.

> $5s - 50 = 130$
> $0.5x = 15$
> $12p + 8f = 30$, where $p = 1.5$
> $12 \div y = 48$
> $16g = (5 + 3) \div j$, where $g = 2.5$

Answers: $s = 36$; $x = 30$; $f = 1.5$; $y = 0.25$; $j = 0.2$

Discuss pupils' responses.

- Show pupils this problem:

> A hotel received 250 guests in November. This was 20 people fewer than 3 times the number of people who visited in October.
> How many guests visited in October?

Discuss the problem, asking questions such as:

What is the question asking?

What is the problem that needs to be solved?

What do we need to find out/work out?

Is the problem about a whole and its parts?

Is it a problem about something being a number of times bigger or smaller than something else? Is it about something else? How do we know?

What operations are going to be used?

What is the calculation that needs to be done? If there is more than one step, in what order should the steps be carried out?

Together, draw a bar model to represent the problem:

October	x	x	x	
	250 (November)			20

Ask: *What equation should be established?* Agree $3x - 20 = 250$ or $3x - 250 = 20$.

Ask: *Using $3x - 20 = 250$, how is the working and check set out?* Agree:

$3x - 20 = 250$
$\qquad 3x = 250 + 20$
$\qquad 3x = 270$
$\qquad\quad x = 270 \div 3$
$\qquad\quad\ \ = 90$

Check: $3 \times 90 - 20 = 250$.
It checks.

- Show pupils this problem:

> There are 64 sparrows and some pigeons in the trees.
> There are 8 times as many sparrows as pigeons.
> How many sparrows and pigeons are there altogether?

Ask: *What bar model would represent the problem? What equation should be established? How is the working and check set out?*

Pupils discuss in pairs. They should show:

Sparrows	a	a	a	a	a	a	a	a

Total sparrows = 64

Pigeons	a

Total sparrows and pigeons = $9a$.

Agree $8a = 64$.

So, $a = 8$.

Therefore, sparrows and pigeons together = $8a + 1a$.

$9a = 9 \times 8 = 72$

Discuss responses.

- Show pupils this problem:

> The volume of container A is 1.5 litres. This is 125 ml less than 5 times the volume of container B.
> What is the volume of the small container?

Ask: *What bar model would represent the problem? What equation should be established? How is the working and check set out?* Pupils should discuss responses in pairs.
They should show:

Container B	x	x	x	x	x
	1.5 (Container A)				0.125

$5x - 0.125 = 1.5$ or $5x - 1.5 = 0.125$

Using $5x - 0.125 = 1.5$

$5x - 0.125 = 1.5$
$\qquad\quad 5x = 1.5 + 0.125$
$\qquad\quad 5x = 1.625$
$\qquad\quad\ \ x = 1.625 \div 5$
$\qquad\qquad\ = 0.325$

Check: $5 \times 0.325 - 0.125 = 1.5$.
It checks.

Discuss responses.

- Give pairs of pupils **Resource 6.3.10c** Real-life problems (3) and ask them to complete section A.

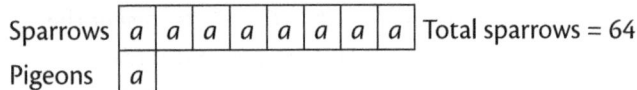

Answers: **1.** 20 kg; **2.** 27 km; **3.** 11; **4.** 6; **5.** 250 ml or 0.25 l; **6.** 56 years; **7.** 3 m; **8.** 56 years

● Pupils should complete Question 2 in the Practice Book.

Same-day intervention

● Display on the board:

> Rhian is 5 times the age of Paul.

Ask: *If Paul is 5, how old is Rhian?* Use counters to agree 25.

● Display on the board:

> Amanda is 15. This is 5 years less than age of Owen.

Ask: *How old is Owen?* Use counters to agree 15 + 5 = 20.

● Display:

> Moyra is 15. This is 5 years less than 4 times the age of Priti.

Ask: *How old is Priti?* Use counters to agree 15 + 5 = 20 and 20 ÷ 4 = 5.

Together, draw a bar model to represent the problem and establish its equation:

P	P	P	P
15			5

Agree $4P - 5 = 15$ or $4P - 15 = 5$.

Together, solve the equation, pupils explaining the different steps:

$$4P - 5 = 15$$
$$4P = 15 + 5$$
$$4P = 20$$
$$P = 20 \div 4$$
$$= 5$$

Check: $4 \times 5 - 5 = 15$.
It checks.

● Repeat with a problem that creates $5P + 4 = 29$.

Same-day enrichment

● Ask pupils to complete section B of **Resource 6.3.10c** Real-life problems (3).

Resource 6.3.10c 3 of 3

Answers: **1.** 135 kg; **2.** 8 km

Challenge and extension question

Question 3

> 3 A farm had the same number of goats and sheep. After the farmer sold 200 goats and bought 300 sheep, there were 6 times as many sheep as goats. How many goats and sheep were there on the farm at first?

This question allows for a deeper look at establishing and solving equations through application problems. The equation is formed after the addition and subtraction of values.

Chapter 3 test (Practice Book 6A, pages 102–107)

Test question number	Relevant unit	Relevant questions within unit
1	Unit 3.3	Q1, Q2
	Unit 3.4	Q5
	Unit 3.6	Q2, Q3
	Unit 3.7	Q1, Q2
	Unit 3.8	Q1
2	Unit 3.1	Q2, Q3
	Unit 3.3	Q1, Q2, Q3, Q4
	Unit 3.4	Q1, Q2, Q3, Q4, Q5, Q6
	Unit 3.5	Q2, Q5
	Unit 3.6	Q2, Q5
	Unit 3.7	Q2
	Unit 3.8	Q1
	Unit 3.9	Q1
	Unit 3.10	Q1
3	Unit 3.1	Q2, Q3
	Unit 3.2	Q1, Q2, Q3
	Unit 3.3	Q3
	Unit 3.5	Q4
	Unit 3.6	Q1, Q3, Q4
	Unit 3.7	Q1, Q2, Q3, Q4
	Unit 3.8	Q1, Q3
	Unit 3.9	Q1, Q2
	Unit 3.10	Q1, Q2
4	Unit 3.2	Q1, Q2, Q3
	Unit 3.3	Q3
	Unit 3.5	Q4
	Unit 3.6	Q1, Q3, Q4
	Unit 3.7	Q1, Q2, Q3, Q4
	Unit 3.8	Q1, Q3
	Unit 3.9	Q1, Q2
	Unit 3.10	Q1, Q2
5	Unit 3.2	Q1, Q2, Q3
	Unit 3.3	Q3
	Unit 3.5	Q4
	Unit 3.6	Q1, Q3, Q4
	Unit 3.7	Q1, Q2, Q3, Q4
	Unit 3.8	Q1, Q3
	Unit 3.9	Q1, Q2
	Unit 3.10	Q1, Q2
6	Unit 3.2	Q1, Q2, Q3
	Unit 3.3	Q3
	Unit 3.5	Q4
	Unit 3.6	Q1, Q3, Q4
	Unit 3.7	Q1, Q2, Q3, Q4
	Unit 3.8	Q1, Q3
	Unit 3.9	Q1, Q2
	Unit 3.10	Q1, Q2
7	Unit 3.2	Q1, Q2, Q3
	Unit 3.3	Q3
	Unit 3.5	Q4
	Unit 3.6	Q1, Q3, Q4
	Unit 3.7	Q1, Q2, Q3, Q4
	Unit 3.8	Q1, Q3
	Unit 3.9	Q1, Q2
	Unit 3.10	Q1, Q2
8	Unit 3.1	Q2
	Unit 3.2	Q1, Q2, Q3
	Unit 3.3	Q1, Q2, Q3, Q4
	Unit 3.4	Q2, Q3, Q4, Q5, Q6
	Unit 3.5	Q2, Q4, Q5
	Unit 3.6	Q1, Q2, Q3, Q4, Q5
	Unit 3.7	Q1, Q2, Q3, Q4
	Unit 3.8	Q1, Q3
	Unit 3.9	Q1, Q2
	Unit 3.10	Q1, Q2

9	Unit 3.1	Q2
	Unit 3.2	Q1, Q2, Q3
	Unit 3.3	Q1, Q2, Q3, Q4
	Unit 3.4	Q2, Q3, Q4, Q5, Q6
	Unit 3.5	Q2, Q4, Q5
	Unit 3.6	Q1, Q2, Q3, Q4, Q5
	Unit 3.7	Q1, Q2, Q3, Q4
	Unit 3.8	Q1, Q3
	Unit 3.9	Q1, Q2
	Unit 3.10	Q1, Q2
10	Unit 3.1	Q5
	Unit 3.2	Q4
	Unit 3.3	Q4
11	Unit 3.2	Q4
	Unit 3.3	Q3
12	Unit 3.2	Q4
	Unit 3.3	Q3
13	Unit 3.2	Q1, Q2, Q3
	Unit 3.3	Q3
14	Unit 3.1	Q2
	Unit 3.2	Q3, Q4
	Unit 3.3	Q1, Q2, Q3
	Unit 3.4	Q5
15	Unit 3.1	Q2
	Unit 3.2	Q1, Q2, Q3
	Unit 3.3	Q1, Q2, Q3, Q4
	Unit 3.4	Q2, Q3, Q4, Q5, Q6
	Unit 3.5	Q2, Q4, Q5
16	Unit 3.1	Q2, Q4
	Unit 3.2	Q1
	Unit 3.4	Q4
17	Unit 3.2	Q4
	Unit 3.3	Q3
18	Unit 3.1	Q2
	Unit 3.2	Q1
19	Unit 3.5	Q1, Q2
20	Unit 3.1	Q2
	Unit 3.3	Q1, Q2, Q3
	Unit 3.4	Q5
20	Unit 3.6	Q1, Q2

22	Unit 3.1	Q2
	Unit 3.2	Q1, Q2, Q3
	Unit 3.3	Q1, Q2, Q3, Q4
	Unit 3.4	Q5
	Unit 3.5	Q4
	Unit 3.6	Q1, Q3, Q4
	Unit 3.7	Q1, Q2, Q3, Q4
	Unit 3.8	Q1, Q3
	Unit 3.9	Q1, Q2
	Unit 3.10	Q1, Q2
23	Unit 3.5	Q1, Q2
24	Unit 3.3	Q4
	Unit 3.4	Q2, Q3, Q4, Q5, Q6
	Unit 3.5	Q2, Q5
	Unit 3.6	Q2, Q5
25	Unit 3.3	Q4
	Unit 3.4	Q2, Q3, Q4, Q5, Q6
	Unit 3.5	Q2, Q5
	Unit 3.6	Q2, Q5
26	Unit 3.1	Q2
	Unit 3.3	Q1, Q2, Q3
	Unit 3.4	Q5
	Unit 3.5	Q6
27	Unit 3.2	Q1, Q2, Q3
	Unit 3.5	Q4
	Unit 3.6	Q1, Q3, Q4
	Unit 3.7	Q1, Q2, Q3, Q4
	Unit 3.8	Q1, Q3
	Unit 3.9	Q1, Q2
	Unit 3.10	Q1, Q2
28	Unit 3.1	Q2, Q3
	Unit 3.6	Q1, Q3, Q4
	Unit 3.7	Q1, Q2, Q3, Q4
	Unit 3.8	Q1, Q3
	Unit 3.9	Q1, Q2
	Unit 3.10	Q1, Q2

Chapter 4
Geometry and measurement (1)

Chapter overview

Area of mathematics	National Curriculum statutory requirements for Key Stage 2	Shanghai Maths Project reference
Geometry – properties of shapes	Year 3 Programme of study: Pupils should be taught to: ■ identify horizontal and vertical lines and pairs of perpendicular and parallel lines.	Year 6, Units 4.1, 4.2, 4.8
Geometry – properties of shapes	Year 4 Programme of study: Pupils should be taught to: ■ compare and classify geometric shapes, including quadrilaterals and triangles, based on their properties and sizes.	Year 6, Units 4.3, 4.4, 4.8
Geometry – properties of shapes	Year 5 Programme of study: Pupils should be taught to: ■ use the properties of rectangles to deduce related facts and find missing lengths and angles.	Year 6, Units 4.3, 4.4, 4.8
Measurement	Year 6 Programme of study: Pupils should be taught to: ■ calculate the area of parallelograms and triangles.	Year 6, Units 4.5, 4.6, 4.7, 4.8

Pre-requisite knowledge

For pupils to be successful with the work in this chapter, they will need to have achieved mastery in their learning in previous relevant units. Teaching there will have introduced and developed concepts and skills that are necessary to work with the content in this chapter. A summary of prerequisite knowledge is set out in the table below. If you believe that some pupils need to revisit particular areas, the units in which those areas were taught are also shown in the table, so that you can locate appropriate guidance in Teacher's Guides and Practice Books. Guidance provided for Chapter 4 on the following pages will therefore focus on new learning.

Pre-requisite knowledge, understanding or skill	Where this was taught in The Shanghai Maths Project
Pupils are able to identify an angle in terms of its vertex and sides, use the angle symbol ∠, and name an angle by the three letters on the shape that define the angle, with the middle letter being where the angle actually is.	Year 5, Unit 8.4
Pupils are secure in their understanding of angle size knowing that a right angle is an angle that is exactly 90 degrees; an acute angle is an angle less than 90 degrees (one right angle); and an obtuse angle is an angle greater than 90 degrees but less than 180 degrees (two right angles).	Year 4, Unit 8.1 Year 5, Unit 8.5
Pupils are able to identify the properties of common 2-D shapes including the number of angles and sides, and draw examples of such shapes. They know that when a triangle has two equal sides and two equal angles it is an isosceles triangle, and when all three sides and angles are equal it is also an equilateral triangle. They also know that a quadrilateral with four congruent sides and four congruent angles is a square.	Year 4, Units 8.2, 8.3. 8.4, 8.5, 8.7 Year 5, Unit 8.9
Pupils are able to multiply and divide whole numbers up to four digits by a one- or two-digit whole number using mental and written strategies based on place value and the properties of operations. They are able to fluently multiply and divide numbers using the standard algorithm for each operation.	Year 4, Units 3.4, 3.5, 3.6, 5.1, 5.4
When multiplying by decimals, pupils are able to apply their knowledge of the base 10 number system and use the same algorithms for calculating with whole numbers.	Year 5, Units 6.1, 6.2
Pupils are able to use the inverse relationship of addition and subtraction, and the inverse relationship of multiplication and division, as a strategy to solve problems.	Year 5, Units 1.1, 3.3, 3.4, 3.5

Pupils are fluent with the basic operations (addition, subtraction, multiplication, division), use of properties (commutative, associative, distributive) and the knowledge of how to apply these to multi-step problem solving, for example solving simple equations using inverse operations.	Year 4, Units 5.2, 5.3, 10.5, 10.6, 10.11, 10.12, 10.13, 10.14, 10.15, 10.16, 10.17, 10.18 Year 5, Units 5.3, 5.4, 5.5
Pupils are able to use the four operations to solve multi-step word problems composed of whole numbers. They are able to analyse word problems for key clue words, write the representative expression and solve the problem using more than one strategy.	Year 4, Units 10.9, 10.10, 10.15
Pupils will have connected the concepts of counting each square unit and multiplying the side lengths to compute the area of a rectangle. They will have extended this knowledge by calculating a side length, when given only the area and the other side length. They understand that when a unit of measurement is multiplied, an exponent is used to show that two of the same units of measurement have been multiplied together, for example square metres (m^2). Pupils understand that perimeter is a measurement of the distance around a shape and is the sum of the lengths of the sides of a polygon.	Year 4, Units 8.8, 8.9, 8.10, 8.11, 9.2, 9.3

Unit 4.1
Perpendicular lines

Conceptual context

Pupils have previously learned, in depth, about angles and their properties and have some knowledge of the interior angles of polygons. Now they will focus on perpendicular lines, learning definitions and notations for lines that intersect at a right angle.

Learning pupils will have achieved at the end of the unit

- Pupils will be able to identify perpendicular lines as lines that intersect at a right angle (Q1, Q2, Q3)
- Pupils will be able to read and use the symbol indicating a right angle to imply and infer where lines are perpendicular on a geometric diagram (Q1, Q2)
- Pupils will have learned to use the $\perp$ symbol to identify perpendicular lines in writing (Q1, Q2)
- Pupils will have learned that the shortest distance from a point to a line is along the connecting line that intersects at the perpendicular foot (Q1, Q2, Q3)

Resources

mini whiteboards; analogue clocks; red, green and blue pencils; set square; 'My geometry notebook' (from Year 5); string; weight; long strips of paper; marker; metre rules; **Resource 6.4.1a** Perpendicular pairs; **Resource 6.4.1b** Paths of shortest distance

Vocabulary

perpendicular, perpendicular lines, perpendicular foot, right angle, adjacent sides, line segment

Question 1

1 Complete each statement. (For questions (a) and (b), choose from
'perpendicular', 'perpendicular foot', 'angles' and 'right angles'.)

(a) When two straight lines intersect at a right angle, these two lines

are _____ to each other, and one of the lines is

called a _____ line to the other line. The point

where the two lines intersect is called the _____ .

(b) When two lines intersect they form four _____ .
If one of the angles is a right angle, then the other three angles are

also _____ , and the two lines are

_____ to each other.

(c) In the figure on the right, AB and CD are
_____ to each other, denoted as

AB ⊥ _____ or

CD ⊥ _____ .

They are read as AB

is _____ to CD

or CD is _____ to AB.

(d) The two adjacent sides of a rectangle are _____ to
each other.

(e) At _____ o'clock, the hour hand and the minute
hand on a clock face are perpendicular to each other.

(f) When two lines are perpendicular to each other, all the angles they

form are _____ .

What learning will pupils have achieved at the conclusion of Question 1?

- Pupils will be able to identify perpendicular lines as lines that intersect at a right angle.
- Pupils will be able to read and use the symbol indicating a right angle to imply and infer where lines are perpendicular on a geometric diagram.
- Pupils will have learned to use the ⊥ symbol to identify perpendicular lines in writing.
- Pupils will have learned that the shortest distance from a point to a line is along the connecting line that intersects at the perpendicular foot.

Activities for whole-class instruction

- Display the following diagram on the board:

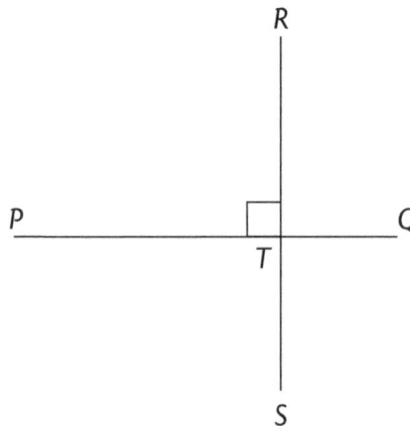

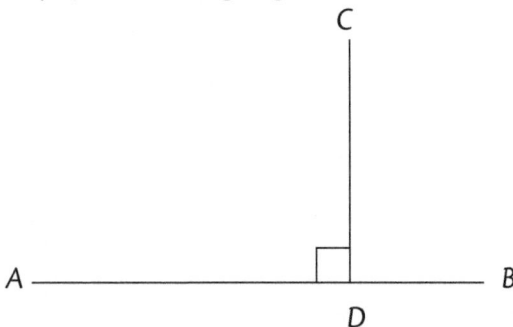

- Ask: *What do we know about angle ADC?* (It is a right angle.) *How do you know?* Agree that the small box is the symbol for a right angle. Ask: *If angle ADC is a right angle what can we say about angle CDB?* (It is also a right angle.)

Explain that when lines intersect at a right angle we say that the lines are perpendicular to each other. We refer to the lines as perpendicular lines. Write the term 'perpendicular lines' beside the diagram. Explain that in the diagram, line AD is perpendicular to line CD, and CD is perpendicular to line AD.

Ask pupils if they can identify other perpendicular lines in the diagram. Agree that lines CD and BD are perpendicular to each other.

Point to the intersection of lines AB and CD and tell pupils that the point where the two lines intersect is called the 'perpendicular foot', meaning the foot of the perpendicular. Annotate and label the point of intersection with 'perpendicular foot'.

- Introduce the sign for perpendicular lines, ⊥. On the board, write AB ⊥ CD. Explain that we use the symbol to denote perpendicular lines, writing the symbol between the lines that are perpendicular to each other.

Provide whiteboards and ask pupils to copy the diagram from the board. Ask them to write a statement that uses the perpendicular symbol to show a different pair of perpendicular lines. Invite them to hold up their boards and confirm that pupils have written CD ⊥ BD (or BD ⊥ CD).

- Display the following diagram on the board:

- Ask pupils to describe the diagram to a partner. Ask: *Can you identify the four angles at point T as right angles?* Agree if one of the angles is a right angle, then the other three angles are also right angles.

Ask: *What can we say about lines PQ and RS?* (They are perpendicular.) *Why?* (Perpendicular lines intersect at a right angle.)

- Draw a rectangle on the board:

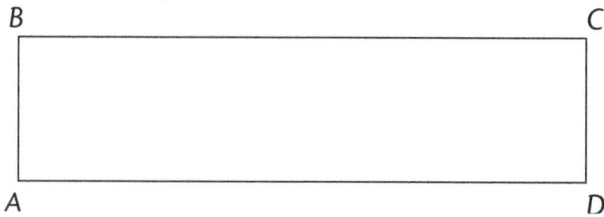

Ask: *What do we know about the interior angles of a rectangle?* Invite a pupil to the board to mark the right angles with the small square symbol.

Explain that the two sides that meet at a vertex of a polygon are called adjacent sides. Ask pupils to name a pair of adjacent sides. Expect: *AB/BC, BC/CD, CD/AD or AD/AB*. Ask: *What is special about the adjacent sides of a rectangle?* Prompt pupils by reminding them the angles of a rectangle are right. Elicit that pairs of adjacent sides of a rectangle are perpendicular to each other.

- Ask pupils to work in pairs. Provide analogue clocks if available. If not, distribute whiteboards and ask pupils to draw the hands of a clock so that the hour hand and the minute hand are perpendicular to each other. Invite pupils to share their clocks and confirm that the hands are perpendicular.

- Pupils should complete Question 1 in the Practice Book.

Same-day intervention

- Draw a square and a rectangle on the board labelled *ABCD* and *EFGH* respectively. Ask pupils to copy the shapes in their 'My geometry notebook' (begun in Year 5; if not, provide notebooks that will used throughout this unit) and mark the angles with a right-angle symbol. Highlight a pair of adjacent sides in both shapes and ask pupils to mark and label the sides on their drawing. Direct pupils to underline perpendicular lines in both shapes with a red pencil and label the sides as 'perpendicular sides'. On the board, write: 'Adjacent sides of a square/rectangle are perpendicular.'

All say ... *Adjacent sides of a square/rectangle are perpendicular.*

- Repeat for a drawing that shows lines intersecting at a perpendicular foot and lines that cross at right angles.

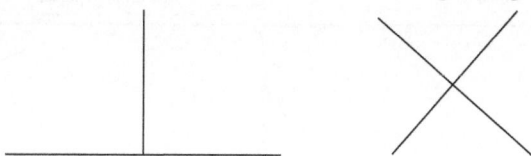

- Label the lines and mark the right angles. Write a definition below for pupils to copy: 'Lines that intersect at right angles are perpendicular to each other.'

Question 2

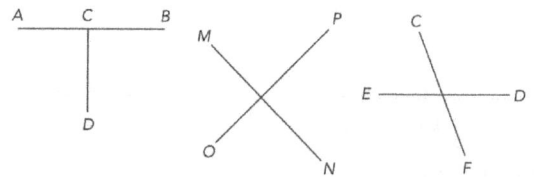

2 Use a set square to measure and then find whether each pair of lines are perpendicular to each other. If they are perpendicular, mark them in the figure with the right angle sign and denote them with letters and the perpendicular sign '⊥' in the boxes below.

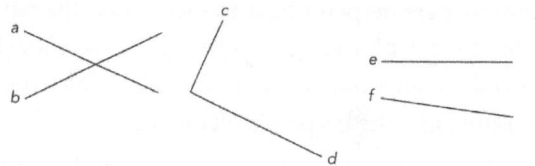

What learning will pupils have achieved at the conclusion of Question 2?

- Pupils will be able to identify perpendicular lines as lines that intersect at a right angle.

- Pupils will be able to read and use the symbol indicating a right angle to imply and infer where lines are perpendicular on a geometric diagram.

- Pupils will have learned to use the ⊥ symbol to identify perpendicular lines in writing.

- Pupils will have learned that the shortest distance from a point to a line is along the connecting line that intersects at the perpendicular foot.

Activities for whole-class instruction

- Provide each pupil with a set square and a copy of **Resource 6.4.1a** Perpendicular pairs. Discuss how perpendicular lines don't need to be horizontal and vertical lines. They can be in different orientations.

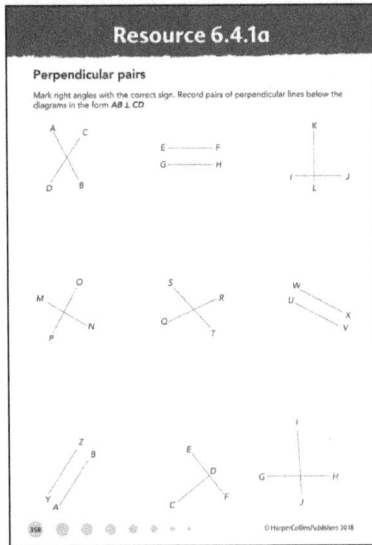

Answers: KL ⊥ IJ, MN ⊥ OP, CD ⊥ EF; right angles marked correctly

- Pupils should measure and identify pairs of intersecting lines that are perpendicular to each other. They should mark them with the right-angle sign. Below, they should record the lines that are perpendicular using letter notation and the perpendicular sign, ⊥.

- Pupil pairs swap sheets for marking. They check that right angles are marked with the correct sign and that the pairs of perpendicular lines have been recorded using the correct notation.

- Pupils should complete Question 2 in the Practice Book.

Same-day intervention

- Hold up a set square and remind pupils that the tool can be used to find or draw right angles.

- Distribute set squares and ask pupils to point to the vertex or 'corner' that is a right angle.

- Draw pairs of intersecting lines on the board and use a large set square to demonstrate how to determine an angle is right. For lines that are perpendicular to each other (*AB*, *CD*), ask: *This angle is a right angle. What does this tell us about the pair of lines AB and CD?*

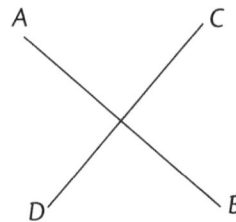

Same-day enrichment

- Ask pupils to practise drawing lines perpendicular to a fixed line using a set square. The perpendicular lines should be made at intervals along the fixed line. Remind pupils that the resulting lines should be parallel with each other.

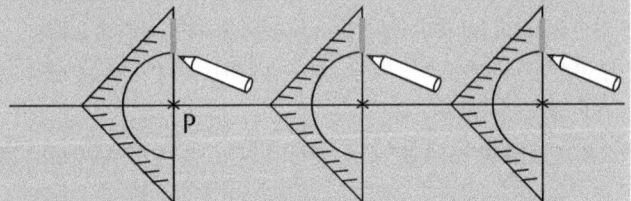

- Pupils then devise a worksheet for a partner to answer that includes drawings of pairs of intersecting lines – some perpendicular and some not perpendicular. Pupils swap sheets with a partner to identify right angles on each other's diagrams and record which lines are perpendicular to each other using the ⊥ symbol. Swap back for marking.

Question 3

3 Measure and complete each statement.

The figure on the right shows four line segments *PA*, *PQ*, *PB* and *PC*. A, Q, B and C are all on the line *l* and *P* is a point outside the line *l*. The shortest line segment is [   ], and it is the _____ from point *P* to the line *l*.

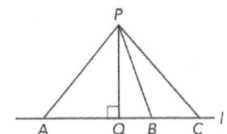

A **line segment** (or simply a segment) is part of a line with two endpoints.

What learning will pupils have achieved at the conclusion of Question 3?

- Pupils will be able to identify perpendicular lines as lines that intersect at a right angle.
- Pupils will have learned that the shortest distance from a point to a line is along the connecting line that intersects at the perpendicular foot.

Activities for whole-class instruction

- Draw a point on the board. Label the point A. Mark a point B at a distance from point A and use a ruler to join A and B. Say: *When two points are connected with a straight line, we get a line segment. We call this line segment AB.*

Alongside the line segment AB draw a line as shown below:

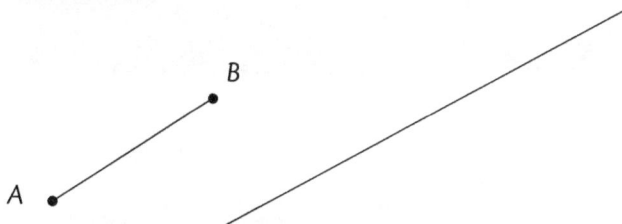

Ask: *What are the differences between the two diagrams? Is the diagram on the right a line segment? If not, why?* Explain that the diagram on the right is a line and not a line segment. Say: *The line has no beginning point or end point.* Explain that we imagine that the line continues indefinitely in both directions.

Draw and name a line 'l' on the board. Mark a point P directly above the line. Ask: *What will be the shortest distance between point P, a point not on the line, and line l?* Accept comments but do not confirm whether pupils are right or wrong at this stage.

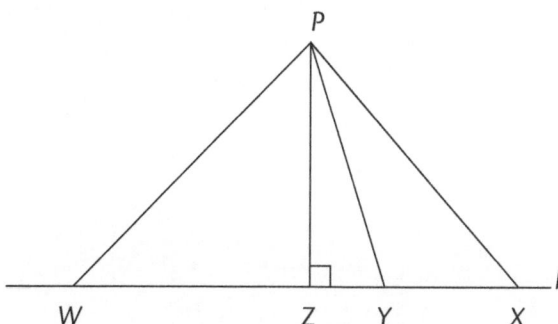

Mark a point W on the line towards the left and then draw a line segment PW. Provide a ruler and invite a pupil to the board to measure the line. Record the length PW.

Mark another point X on the line towards the right then draw a line segment PX. Again, ask a pupil to measure and record the length of the line.

Mark a third point Y on the line closer towards to the perpendicular distance from point P then draw a line segment PY. Again, ask a pupil to measure and record the length of the line.

Ask: *Have you changed your mind about the shortest distance from P to the line? If so, what do you think it is now?* Accept comments. Demonstrate that the shortest line segment joining point P to the line 'l' is the one that meets the line at a right angle. Label the intersection as point Z. Measure and record the length of line segment PZ and agree that line l and line segment PZ are perpendicular to each other (PZ ⊥ line 'l').

On the board, write: 'The shortest distance from a point to a line is the connecting line segment that is perpendicular to the line.'

The shortest distance from a point to a line is the connecting line segment that is perpendicular to the line.

- Provide whiteboards and rulers. Ask pupils to draw a diagram similar to that above and place points at various locations on the line. They should measure the line segments to a point P above the line and confirm that the perpendicular distance is the shortest.
- Pupils should complete Question 3 in the Practice Book.

Same-day intervention

- Ask pupils to work in pairs. Provide each pair with a string, a weight, a long strip of paper and a metre rule. Ask pupils to use the ruler to draw a vertical line down the middle of the paper. They then attach the weight to one end of the string and the other end is held directly above the line so that the string rests over the line marked on the paper.

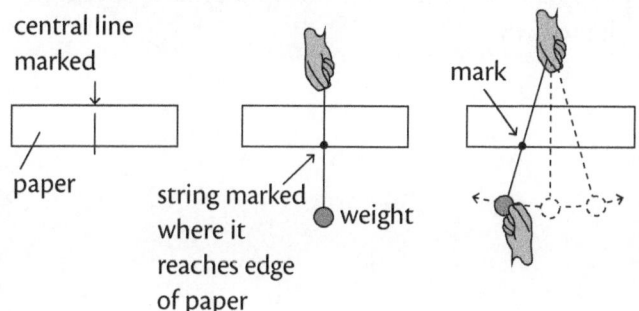

central line marked

paper

string marked where it reaches edge of paper

weight

mark

- Holding the string taut at the weight end, the string forms a perpendicular line with the paper. Using a marker pen, one pupil marks the point where the string reaches the edge of the paper. They move the weight along the line backwards and forward across the midpoint keeping the string taut but allowing it to move freely. Ask pupils to observe what happens to the mark on the line.

- Can pupils say what this demonstrates about the length of the string at various points on its journey along the line? Ask: *At which points is the string the shortest?* Agree that it is at a point directly below the line and establish that this is the perpendicular distance.

Same-day enrichment

- Ask pupils to work in pairs and provide each group with a copy of **Resource 6.4.1b** Paths of shortest distance. Pupils need to recognise that the shortest line is the perpendicular distance from the line to the point.

Resource 6.4.1b

Paths of shortest distance

Mark a point P on a piece of paper. Draw three lines, AB, CD and EF at different distances from point P (see diagram below).

Draw a dotted line from each of the lines AB, CD and EF to P so that, in each case, the dotted line is the shortest possible distance between the line and the point.
Next, on the back of the sheet, draw another point and three lines for your partner, who must add the dotted lines to show the shortest distance between each line and the point.

© HarperCollinsPublishers 2018

Answers: dotted lines should be perpendicular to each line drawn.

Challenge and extension question

Question 4

4 Hands-on activity.
The figure below shows an isosceles triangle. Can you fold it to form a right angle? Is it possible to fold it to form two right angles? How many right angles can you fold at the most? Try it yourself. Draw in lines to show your results.

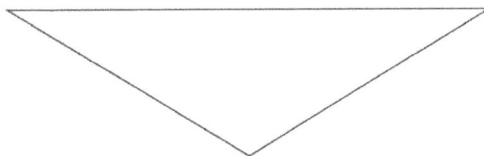

Pupils are asked to fold an isosceles triangle to create one or more right angles. They should recognise that if they fold the triangle exactly in half, the fold line will be the perpendicular distance from the folded vertex to the base of the triangle. The fold line will form two right angles at the perpendicular foot.

Unit 4.2
Parallel lines

Conceptual context

In this unit, pupils will focus on parallel lines. They will learn that parallel lines never share a common point (never join or cross); they are always the same distance apart.

Pupils' geometrical knowledge is expanding, having learned about perpendicular and parallel lines, and they will relate this to their existing knowledge about shapes, enabling them to define polygons more formally and explore the relationships among them.

Learning pupils will have achieved at the end of the unit

- Pupils will be able to identify parallel lines and describe them as two lines that are always the same distance apart and never touch (Q1, Q2, Q3, Q4)
- Pupils will be able to describe, sketch and draw parallel lines using conventional terms and notation, and use this knowledge to describe polygons and other simple geometric constructions (Q2, Q3, Q4)
- Using a set square and a ruler, pupils will be able to identify parallel sides in polygons (Q3)

Resources

large piece of squared paper; dotted paper; rulers; set squares; 2-D shapes; red highlighter pen; tracing paper; 'My geometry notebook'; long ropes or skipping ropes; different coloured pens; **Resource 6.4.1a** Perpendicular pairs, **Resource 6.4.2a** Shapes; **Resource 6.4.2b** Parallel pairs; **Resource 6.4.2c** Flags

Vocabulary

parallel, parallel lines, perpendicular lines, intersection

Question 1

> **1** Look at the figures. Which two lines are parallel? Circle the letter(s) to show your answer.
>
> A   B   C   D

What learning will pupils have achieved at the conclusion of Question 1?

- Pupils will be able to identify parallel lines and describe them as two lines that are always the same distance apart and never touch.

Activities for whole-class instruction

- On the board, attach a large piece of squared paper. Use a ruler and the gridlines to draw pairs of parallel lines.

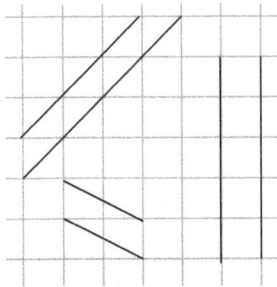

Ask: *Does anyone know the mathematical term for the pairs of lines shown on this squared paper?* Tell pupils that these are pairs of 'parallel lines'. In each pair, the lines are the same perpendicular distance apart at any point along their length. Establish that since lines go on forever, it follows that the lines will never cross no matter how long they are. Lines that never intersect are said to be parallel.

Ask: *Who can give me a real-life example of parallel lines?* Accept suggestions and record them on the board, for example: train tracks, guitar strings, suspension cables of a bridge, writing lines on a piece of lined paper, the rungs of a ladder.

Ask pupils to consider railway tracks: *What would happen if they pointed together or apart? Would they still be parallel? Why not?* (No, the tracks would cross over at some point.) Demonstrate this by drawing a pair of parallel lines and then another pair where one of the lines of the pair has shifted. Extend the line so that it crosses over the other.

- Provide each pupil with a copy of **Resource 6.4.1a** Perpendicular pairs (from previous unit). Ask them to identify and circle the pairs of lines that are parallel.

- Pupils should complete Question 1 in the Practice Book.

Same-day intervention

- Give pupils a variety of practical investigations to reinforce the concept of parallel lines as lines that are always the same distance apart.

  - Provide each pupil with a sheet of paper. Ask them to fold it (accurately) in half, then in half again in the same direction. They unfold the paper and comment on the fold lines formed. Ask: *What kind of lines are these?* (parallel lines) *How would you make more parallel lines?* (Continue to fold the paper in the same direction.)

  - Provide sheets of dotted paper and rulers. Ask pupils to draw sets of parallel lines using a ruler with the dots for guidance. Encourage them to draw examples of parallel lines in different orientations with varying separation distances.

  - Once pupils are secure with the concept of parallel lines, ask them to draw a set of parallel lines and make accompanying notes in their 'My geometry notebook'.

  - Give pupils an *aide memoire* for parallel lines: the world 'parallel'. The pair of lower case l's are themselves parallel. They may wish to include this in their 'My geometry notebook' notes.

Same-day enrichment

- Ask pupils to work in pairs. Provide each pair with a tray of paper shapes that have been laminated (use **Resource 6.4.2a** Shapes). Give them the opportunity to investigate the shapes and comment on those that have one or more pairs of parallel sides.

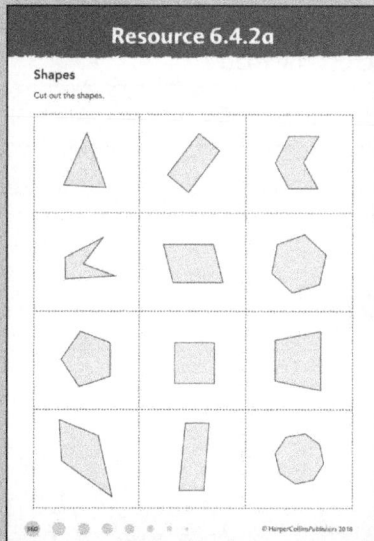

- Provide large pieces of paper and ask pupils to draw a two-set Venn diagram. They label the sets 'Parallel sides' and 'Perpendicular sides' and sort the shapes into each set. Shapes that have both parallel and perpendicular sides should be sorted in the intersection.

- Pupils play a game of 'Guess the shape'. They take turns to describe a shape tile taken from a bag or box, commenting on properties, such as opposite parallel, and adjacent perpendicular sides. Their partner must try to guess the shape from the description provided.

Question 2

2 True or false? (Put a ✓ for true and a ✗ for false in each box.)

(a) Two parallel lines never intersect. ☐

(b) Two lines are either parallel or perpendicular. ☐

(c) If two lines a and b are parallel, we write $a // b$. ☐

(d) A rectangle has two pairs of parallel lines and four pairs of perpendicular lines. ☐

(e) In the figure below, line b and line c are parallel. ☐

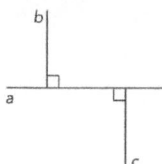

What learning will pupils have achieved at the conclusion of Question 2?

- Pupils will be able to identify parallel lines and describe them as two lines that are always the same distance apart and never touch.

- Pupils will be able to describe, sketch and draw parallel lines using conventional terms and notation, and use this knowledge to describe polygons and other simple geometric constructions.

Activities for whole-class instruction

- Pupils should work in pairs. Provide each pair with squared or dotted paper. On the board, draw a pair of parallel lines and a pair of perpendicular lines. Ask: *Is it true that all pairs of lines are either parallel or perpendicular?* Give pupils time to discuss the question. Tell pupils that if the answer to the question is 'No' then they should draw an example of lines that are neither parallel nor perpendicular. Invite groups to share their diagrams and establish that lines can be drawn that are not perpendicular but do intersect and are therefore not parallel.

- Provide each group with a tray of paper shapes that have been laminated (use **Resource 6.4.2a** Shapes). Ask them to find examples of shapes with parallel sides. Establish that squares and rectangles have pairs of parallel sides, as do some other quadrilaterals: parallelogram, rhombus and trapezium.

- Attach a large piece of squared paper to the board and draw a rectangle *ABCD* and a square *PQRS*. Provide a red highlighter pen and ask pupils to come to the board to highlight examples of parallel sides. Confirm that sides *AB* and *CD* of the rectangle are parallel and write: *AB // CD*. Explain that the symbol // is used to denote parallel lines and the convention for recording is writing the symbol between the lines that are parallel.

Ask: *Who can come to the board and use the parallel lines sign to record two other sides that are parallel?* Expect: *BC // AD, PQ // RS or QR // SP.*

Point to the rectangle and ask: *How many pairs of parallel sides does a rectangle have?* (2) *How many pairs does a square have?* (2) Return to the rectangle and ask: *How many pairs of perpendicular sides does a rectangle have?* Remind pupils that perpendicular sides or lines will be at right angles to each other. If pupils say two then demonstrate by using a highlighter than there are four pairs of perpendicular sides: a pair of adjacent perpendicular sides at each vertex.

- On the board, draw a pair of vertical parallel lines. Draw a point on one line and ask: *What is the shortest distance between this point and the other line?* Expect pupils to identify that it is the perpendicular distance. Using a large protractor draw a line segment between the point and the line that intersects with both lines at right angles. Mark each angle with the right-angle sign. Establish that as the angles are right at each intersection, and are therefore equal, then the lines are parallel.

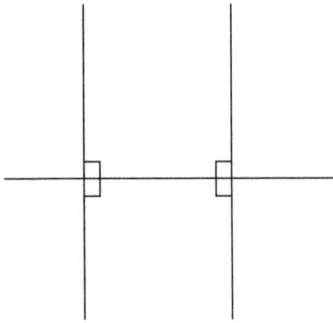

- Pupils should complete Question 2 in the Practice Book.

Same-day intervention

- Tell pupils they are going to draw a plan of the roads in a town centre. Ask pupils to work in pairs and provide each pair with squared paper. Begin by asking them to draw a road down the middle of the paper with sides that are parallel. Move around the groups and confirm that they are able to draw parallel lines. Ask: *If the road were to extend beyond the paper, would the sides of the road ever come together?*

Ask pupils to draw a road that is at right angles to the first and to describe the relationship between the two roads. (They are perpendicular to each other.)

Ask: *Draw a road with sides that start to come together and then meet. Are the sides perpendicular, parallel or neither?* (neither) Confirm that the sides intersect but are neither parallel nor perpendicular.

Ask pupils to draw a rectangular park on the plan and say how many pairs of parallel sides and perpendicular sides the shape has.

Give pupils time to continue to develop the town plan and include other features constructed using parallel and perpendicular lines. Invite pairs to share their work with the group.

Same-day enrichment

- Display the following problem for pupils to solve:

A street has parallel sides. Two points on one side of the street, A and B, are the positions of two traffic lights. Two points on the other side of the street, C and D, are the positions of two more traffic lights. Draw parallel lines with these labels to create a crossing across the road

Ask pupils to expand the drawing into a map of a town that features other streets that have parallel sides, and streets that are parallel or perpendicular to each other.

Question 3

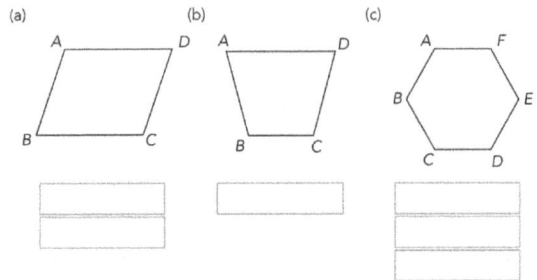

What learning will pupils have achieved at the conclusion of Question 3?

- Pupils will be able to identify parallel lines and describe them as two lines that are always the same distance apart and never touch.
- Pupils will be able to describe, sketch and draw parallel lines using conventional terms and notations, and use this knowledge to describe polygons and other simple geometric constructions.
- Using a set square and a ruler, pupils will be able to identify parallel sides in polygons.

Activities for whole-class instruction

- Distribute a set square, a ruler and a copy of **Resource 6.4.2b** Parallel pairs, to each pupil.

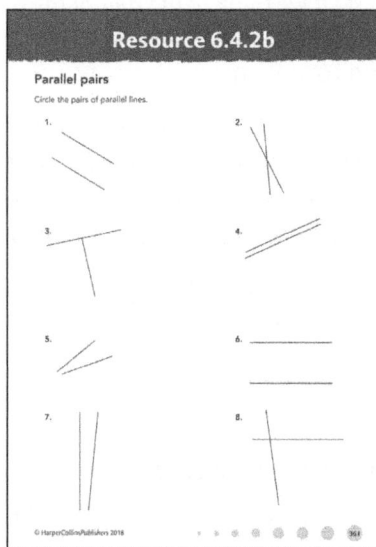

Answers: 1, 4, 6.

● Display a large copy of the resource sheet on a projector or attach a large copy to the board. Demonstrate a method of checking for parallel lines by taking pupils through the following steps using the square at the top of the sheet:

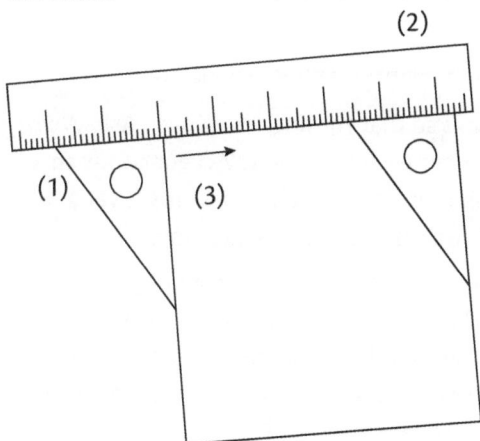

- Step 1: Align the set square with one side of the shape; the side that is one of a pair of possible parallel sides.

- Step 2: Place a ruler on the base of the set square, as shown.

- Step 3: Slide the set square along the ruler until the perpendicular side of the set square is aligned with the other side of the shape. The alignment indicates the two sides are parallel.

Ask pupils to use this method to identify parallel sides in other shapes on the resource sheet. They should record pairs of parallel lines using the sign //.

● Pupils should complete Question 3 in the Practice Book.

Same-day intervention

● For pupils who have difficulty using a set square, provide tracing paper and rulers, and ask them to trace the shapes from **Resource 6.4.2a** Shapes. Provide squared paper and ask pupils to place the traced shapes on top of the paper to check for parallel sides. They align one side of the shape with a gridline and check for a second side that aligns with a parallel gridline.

Remind pupils of the convention for recording parallel lines; writing the sign // between the sides that are parallel.

Same-day enrichment

● Ask pupils to draw each of the following shapes. They mark each pair of parallel sides with a different colour pen.

  - A pentagon with one pair of parallel sides.

  - A hexagon with three pairs of parallel sides.

  - A heptagon with two pairs of parallel sides.

  - An octagon with four pairs of parallel sides.

● Display the following problem for pupils to solve:

A quadrilateral with side AB has a parallel side that passes through a point P. Draw the side AB and mark a point 5 to 10 cm to the right or left of the side. Use a ruler and set square to draw the other parallel side then complete the shape.

Answer:

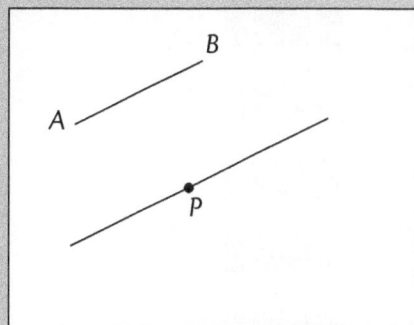

Question 4

> 4 Look at the image of the ladder. Think carefully and then choose from the following terms to complete the statements:
>
> vertical   horizontal   parallel   perpendicular
> $a /\!/ b$ $a \perp b$ $c /\!/ d /\!/ e$
> a is parallel to b   a is perpendicular to b   equal
>
> (a) In the ladder shown on the right, the two sides a
>   and b are both _____ .
> a is _____ to b. It can be
>   denoted as _____ and read as
>   _____ .
>
> (b) The steps c, d and e are all
>   _____ and they
>   are _____ to each other.
>   It can be denoted as _____ .
>   The lengths of them are
>   all _____ .

What learning will pupils have achieved at the conclusion of Question 4?

- Pupils will be able to identify parallel lines and describe them as two lines that are always the same distance apart and never touch.
- Pupils will be able to describe, sketch and draw parallel lines using conventional terms and notations, and use this knowledge to describe polygons and other simple geometric constructions.

Activities for whole-class instruction

- Display this image.

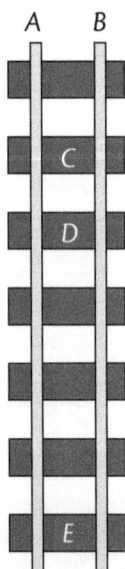

- Explain that this is a view of a train track from above with track rails named A and B and wooden sleepers named

C, D and E. Ask: *If we think of the rails of the track in a vertical direction, how would we describe the direction of the sleepers?* (horizontal)

- Ask: *How would you describe the rails A and B?* (parallel lines) *Which other objects or lines are parallel?* (C, D and E.) *What is the relationship between the line of rail A (or B) and the line of sleeper C (or D or E)?* (perpendicular)

- On the board write: A __ B, A __ C, E __ D, C __ D __ E. Ask pupils to copy and complete the statements with the signs for parallel and perpendicular lines.

- Pupils should complete Question 4 in the Practice Book.

Same-day intervention

- Ask four pupils to come up to the front of the class and demonstrate different types of lines. Provide two long ropes or skipping ropes and give each pupil one end to hold. Position pupils so the ropes form a pair of parallel lines. Ask: *Which type of lines have we formed?* (parallel) Remind pupils that parallel lines are lines that extend forever and never touch.

- Position pupils so that the lines cross over. Ask: *Which type of lines have we formed now?* Accept comments and establish that since the two lines cross over at a single point, we call the lines intersecting.

- Position pupils so that the ropes cross at right angles. Ask: *Which type of lines have we formed now?* (perpendicular) Reinforce that perpendicular lines are a special form of intersecting lines because the lines intersect at 90 degrees.

- Provide skipping ropes and invite the remaining pupils to model the three types of lines.

Same-day enrichment

● Provide copies of **Resource 6.4.2c** Flags. Ask pupils to identify and mark parallel and perpendicular lines on the 10 flags given. For an extra challenge, ask pupils to design their own flag that features parallel and perpendicular lines.

Resource 6.4.2c

Flags

Use a highlighter pen to mark parallel and perpendicular lines.

Central African Republic

St. Kitts & Nevis

Syria

Sao Tome & Principe

Georgia

Togo

Greece

Norway

Seychelles

Panama

© HarperCollins*Publishers* 2015

Challenge and extension question

Question 5

5 How many pairs of parallel sides are there in a square, in a regular hexagon, and in a regular octagon? Can you also tell how many pairs of parallel sides are in a regular *n*-gon, that is, a regular polygon with *n* sides, when *n* is an even number? Fill in the table.

Figure	square	regular hexagon	regular octagon	regular *n*-gon
Number of pairs of parallel sides				

Pupils find the number of pairs of parallel sides in a square, a regular hexagon and a regular octagon and use this to make a conjecture for the number of sides of a regular *n*-gon – a regular polygon with an even number of sides.

Unit 4.3
Parallelograms (1)

Conceptual context

This is the first of three units about parallelograms. In this unit, pupils will apply their new knowledge about conventions for recording parallel lines, together with what they know about angles and quadrilaterals to explore and describe the geometric properties of parallelograms using mathematical language.

Pupils are then able to formalise a definition of a parallelogram.

(i) A parallelogram is a quadrilateral with two pairs of opposite, equal and parallel sides. A rectangle is a special example of a parallelogram with all four interior angles fixed at right angles. A square is a special example of a rectangle in that it has sides of all the same length. It therefore follows that a square is also a parallelogram.

Learning pupils will have achieved at the end of the unit

- Using the definition of a parallelogram, (a four-sided 2-dimensional shape whose opposite sides are both equal and parallel, and opposite angles are equal), pupils will be able to apply this to prove that certain quadrilaterals are parallelograms (Q1, Q2)

- Pupils will be able to describe the properties of a parallelogram using appropriate geometrical terminology and symbols, including 'parallel' (//) and 'parallelogram' ▱ (Q1, Q2)

- Pupils will be able to demonstrate that any parallelogram can be deconstructed and reconstructed into a rectangle, and cutting a parallelogram along a diagonal gives two congruent triangles (Q1, Q2, Q4)

- Using squared paper, pupils will be able to draw examples of parallelograms in line with the definition 'a four-sided 2-dimensional shape whose opposite sides are both equal and parallel, and opposite angles are equal' (Q3)

- Working with practical resources, and applying new knowledge about properties of parallelograms, pupils will be able to deconstruct and reconstruct parallelograms and will have developed a deep understanding of the relationship between parallelograms and their component triangles (Q4)

Resources

'My geometry notebook'; squared paper; rulers; 2-D shape tiles: squares (or paper shapes); mini whiteboards; protractors; **Resource 6.4.3a** Parallelograms (1); **Resource 6.4.3b** Missing angles

Vocabulary

parallelogram, opposite sides, adjacent sides, parallel, perpendicular, diagonal, line of symmetry, deconstruct, reconstruct

Questions 1 and 2

1 Complete each statement.

(a) In the figure on the right,

_____ // _____

and _____ // _____ .

A quadrilateral like this in which two pairs of opposite sides

are _____ is called a _____ denoted as

▱ ABCD. AC and BD are called _____ of ▱ ABCD.

(b) The opposite sides of a parallelogram are parallel to each other, and

their lengths are _____ . The opposite angles are

also _____ .

(c) A parallelogram with one angle that is a right angle is

a _____ .

(d) A rectangle with all four sides of equal length is a _____ .

(e) Both _____ and _____ are special

parallelograms.

(f) In the following figures, the parallelogram(s)

is/are _____ .

2 True or false? (Put a ✓ for true and a ✗ for false in each box.)

(a) Any parallelogram can be cut into two identical triangles along its

diagonal. ☐

(b) Any two sides of a parallelogram are parallel to each other. ☐

(c) The opposite angles of a parallelogram are equal, and they are

right angles. ☐

(d) A quadrilateral with all four sides of equal length is called a square. ☐

(e) The total length of the four sides of a parallelogram is its perimeter. ☐

(f) A parallelogram is a symmetrical figure over a symmetry line. ☐

What learning will pupils have achieved at the conclusion of Questions 1 and 2?

- Using the definition of a parallelogram, (a four-sided 2-dimensional shape whose opposite sides are both equal and parallel, and opposite angles are equal), pupils will be able to apply this to prove that certain quadrilaterals are parallelograms.

- Pupils will be able to describe the properties of a parallelogram using appropriate geometrical terminology and symbols, including 'parallel' (//) and 'parallelogram' ▱.

- Pupils will be able to demonstrate that any parallelogram can be deconstructed and reconstructed into a rectangle, and cutting a parallelogram along a diagonal gives two congruent triangles.

Activities for whole-class instruction

- Ask pupils to come to the board to draw and name any quadrilateral. Continue until all the shapes that the class know are listed.

Write 'parallelogram' on the board. Ask: *Do you know what a parallelogram is?*

Attach a large piece of squared paper to the board and use a ruler to draw three non-rectangular parallelograms.

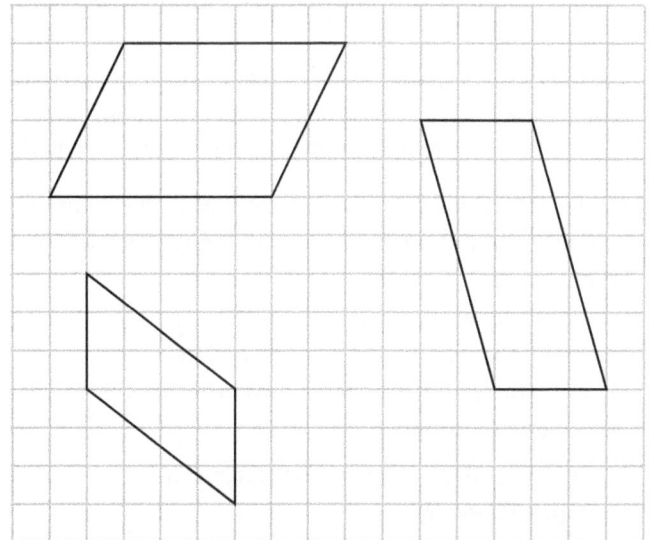

Point to the shapes and say that these are examples of parallelograms. Ask pupils to get into pairs and explain the parallelograms to their partner. Prompt them to use geometrical terms they have become familiar with, for example 'parallel', 'opposite sides'.

Share ideas. Highlight the sides of each parallelogram. Ask: *How many sides does a parallelogram have?* (4) So, *to what family of shapes does a parallelogram belong?* (quadrilaterals)

- On the board, begin a list of properties of a parallelogram:
  - A four-sided shape (quadrilateral)

Select one of the drawn parallelograms and use a ruler to measure the sides. Ask: *What does this tell us about a parallelogram?* Accept comments and establish that opposite sides are equal. Add this to the list of properties.

- Provide pupils with rulers and squared paper. Ask them to draw a parallelogram and then highlight a pair of opposite sides. Ask: *Do the lines meet?* Now do the same for the second pair of opposite sides. Ask: *Do these lines meet? So, what can we say about the opposite sides of a parallelogram?* (opposite sides are parallel) Add this to the list of properties of a parallelogram.

Ask: *What can you say about the angles in a parallelogram?* Pupils should measure with a protractor. Agree that opposite angles are equal.

Tell pupils that these properties are used to define a parallelogram. Write the definition on the board: 'A parallelogram is a four-sided 2-dimensional shape whose opposite sides are both equal and parallel, and opposite angles are equal.' Emphasise that 'parallelogram' is a term that describes a family of shapes that all have these properties, and that some of the 2-D shapes pupils already know are in this family.

All say ... *A parallelogram is a four-sided 2-dimensional shape whose opposite sides are both equal and parallel, and opposite angles are equal.*

- Draw a rectangle on squared paper. Ask: *Is this shape a parallelogram?* Give pupils time to discuss the question then accept comments. Ask: *What could we use to confirm whether any shape is a parallelogram or not?* Establish that we use the properties checklist on the board. With pupils assisting, rewrite the list of properties as a set of questions:
  - Does the shape have four sides? (or, Is it a quadrilateral?)
  - Does the shape have two pairs of parallel opposite sides?
  - Does the shape have two pairs of equal opposite sides?
  - Does the shape have two pairs of equal opposite angles?

  Point to the first question and ask: *Does the shape have four sides?* (yes) *Does the shape have two pairs of parallel opposite sides?* (yes) *Does the shape have two pairs of equal opposite sides?* (yes) Explain that the answers confirm a rectangle is a parallelogram.

  Ask: *What makes a rectangle different from the other parallelograms on the board?* Accept comments and establish that a rectangle is a special example of a parallelogram; one that has internal right angles and adjacent sides that are perpendicular.

- Draw a square on the paper. Ask: *Is this shape a parallelogram?* Give pupils time to discuss the question then accept comments. Go through the properties checklist together.

  Point to the first question and ask: *Does the shape have four sides?* (yes) *Does the shape have two pairs of parallel opposite sides?* (yes) *Does the shape have two pairs of equal opposite sides?* (yes) Explain that the answers confirm that a square is also a parallelogram.

  Ask: *What makes a square different from the other parallelograms?* Accept comments and establish that whereas a rectangle is a special example of a parallelogram, a square is a special example of a rectangle; one with four congruent sides.

- Draw a parallelogram *ABCD* on the board. Next to the shape, write: *AB* ___ *CD*. Pupils should copy and complete on their whiteboards. Do they recognise that *AB // CD*? Repeat for AD ___ *BC*.

Write ▱ *ABCD*. Explain that we use the sign ▱ to denote a parallelogram. Draw the diagonals *AC* and *BD* and explain that the diagonals of a parallelogram are the lines that connect the opposite vertices to each other.
Ask pupils to draw and label a different parallelogram and label it *PQRS*. They should list statements that describe the relationships between the sides of the shape and then draw and record the names of the diagonals.

Next to the parallelogram *ABCD* on the board, write: $\angle A = \angle C$, $\angle B = \angle D$. Ask: *What does this mean?* Agree it shows that opposite angles are equal.

- Ask: *Does a parallelogram have any lines of symmetry?* Draw a square and a rectangle on the board and invite pupils to come to the board to mark lines of symmetry. Agree that a square has four lines of symmetry and a rectangle has only two.

  Draw a non-rectangular parallelogram. Ask: *How many lines of symmetry does a non-rectangular parallelogram have?* Accept comments but do not confirm whether pupils are right or wrong at this stage.
  Pupils should draw and cut out a parallelogram and then fold it to find lines of symmetry. Discuss what they discover. Accept comments and confirm that a non-rectangular parallelogram has no lines of symmetry.

All say ... *A non-rectangular parallelogram has no lines of symmetry.*

- Ask: *What shapes do you get when you fold a parallelogram along a diagonal?* Discuss what pupils notice about the two triangles. If pupils mention that the two triangles are congruent then ask: *Why is a parallelogram not symmetrical along its diagonal?* Establish that a shape is symmetrical if the two folded parts sit on top of each other and align perfectly. Agree that this is not the case for the triangles of the folded diagonal.

Ask pupils to cut along the fold and compare the triangles. Ask: *Do they align in any orientation?* Agree that rotating one triangle means that both align. This means that both triangles are congruent.

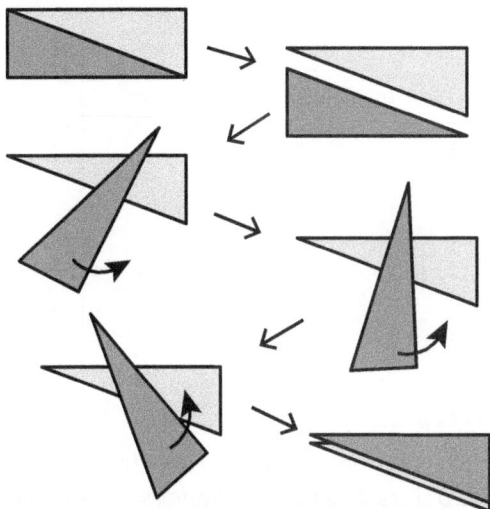

Establish that any parallelogram can be cut into two congruent triangles along its diagonal.

- Pupils should complete Questions 1 and 2 in the Practice Book.

Same-day intervention

- Take pupils through the following properties of a parallelogram and ask them to make notes and diagrams in their 'My geometry notebook'.

  Explain that a parallelogram has several important characteristics, but we only need to concentrate on three of them. If we use these clues, we will know if we are looking at a parallelogram.

  List and discuss these features with each sentence beginning, 'For a shape to be a parallelogram, it must have …

  … four sides.'

  … two opposite parallel sides.'

  … two opposite equal sides.'

  Establish that the most recognisable parallelograms are the square and the rectangle, and explain the special properties of each shape:

  - A square is a parallelogram that has four sides of equal length. The opposite sides are parallel and all the corners of a square are right angles.

  - A rectangle is a parallelogram that has four opposite, parallel, sides. The corners of a rectangle are all right angles. The only difference between a rectangle and a square is that the rectangle's sides are not all equal.

Same-day enrichment

- Display this statement:

  > All squares are parallelograms, but not all parallelograms are squares.

  Ask pupils to write a clear explanation of why this statement is true. They should accompany the explanation with diagrams.

Question 3

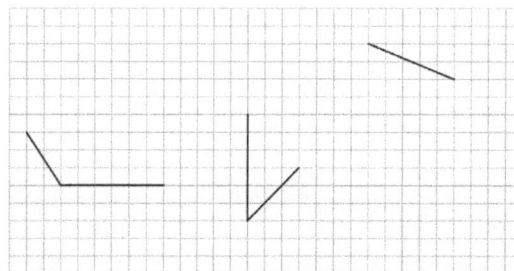

3 The figure below shows part of each of three parallelograms on a square grid. Draw lines to complete the parallelograms.

What learning will pupils have achieved at the conclusion of Question 3?

- Using squared paper, pupils will be able to draw examples of parallelograms in line with the definition: a four-sided 2-dimensional shape whose opposite sides are both equal and parallel, and opposite angles are equal.

Activities for whole-class instruction

- Tell pupils that they are going to practise drawing parallelograms. Attach a large piece of squared paper to the board. Explain a method for drawing a parallelogram that involves counting up and across the squares. Use a ruler to draw a 10-unit line along the bottom of the paper. From one end, count up six units and then four units to the right, and mark the point. Repeat this at the other end of the line and join up the points. Now join up the ends of the two 10-unit lines you have drawn to complete a parallelogram.

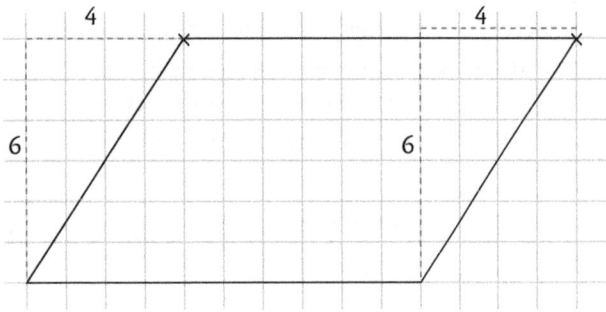

- Povide pupils with squared paper and ask them to use this technique to draw several parallelograms. They should vary the length of the parallelogram and the number of units along and across for the other parallel sides.

- On the board, draw two adjacent sides of a parallelogram.

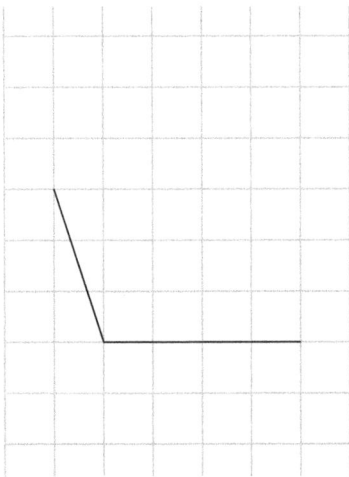

- Ask: *How would you complete the parallelogram?* Share ideas and establish that a good method is to examine the second 'diagonal' side of the parallelogram and work out how many units up and across the end of the side is from the adjacent horizontal or vertical side. Then, from the other end of the adjacent side count the same number of units up and across, mark a point and join up the sides. Invite a pupil to the board to the complete the parallelogram.

- Ask pupils to complete two sides of a parallelogram and then swap with a partner to complete the shape.

- Pupils should complete Question 3 in the Practice Book.

Same-day intervention

- Distribute copies of **Resource 6.4.3a** Parallelograms (1).

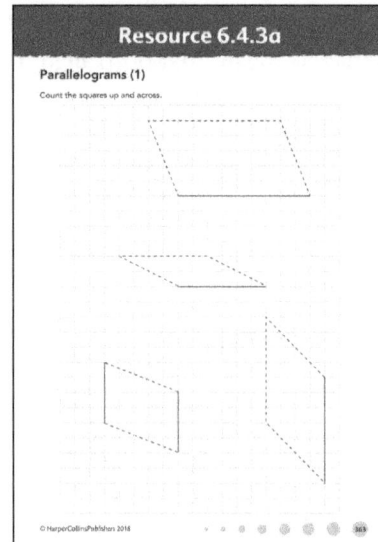

Demonstrate how to construct a parallelogram from one or two sides. Use the top shape as an example. Ask pupils to state the length of the side drawn in bold and the number of units and up and across for the 'slanted' sides. Explain how knowing the unit dimensions for one of the 'slanted' sides gives the dimensions of the opposite parallel side.

Ask pupils to use a ruler to complete the sides of each shape. They count the units up and across for each 'slanted' side and confirm that the opposite sides have the same dimensions.

Ask them to practise drawing a parallelogram given one side only, and then from two adjacent sides.

Same-day enrichment

- Provide pupils with rulers, set squares and paper. Display the following drawing challenges:

Draw non-rectangular parallelograms with:
- A base 5 cm in length and adjacent sides 7 cm in length.
- A base 8 cm in length and adjacent sides 3 cm in length.
- A perimeter of 20 cm.

Question 4

> **4** Multiple choice questions. (For each question, choose the correct answer and write the letter in the box.)
>
> (a) Cut a parallelogram into two pieces and then put them together.
> It is definitely possible for the new figure formed to be a ☐.
> (Choose all the correct answers.)
>
> A. rectangle B. square
> C. triangle D. parallelogram
>
> (b) Cut a parallelogram along its two diagonals to get four triangles. It is impossible that they are ☐.
>
> A. four acute-angled triangles
> B. four obtuse-angled triangles
> C. two right-angled triangles and two obtuse-angled triangles
> D. two acute-angled triangles and two obtuse-angled triangles

What learning will pupils have achieved at the conclusion of Question 4?

- Pupils will be able to demonstrate that any parallelogram can be deconstructed and reconstructed into a rectangle, and that cutting a parallelogram along a diagonal gives two congruent triangles.
- Working with practical resources, and applying new knowledge about properties of parallelograms, pupils will be able to deconstruct and reconstruct parallelograms and will have developed a deep understanding of the relationship between parallelograms and their component triangles.

Activities for whole-class instruction

- Distribute trays of paper squares, each with squares of different sizes – a few of each size. Ask pupils to take two squares and place them next to each other with the vertices aligned. Ask: *What shape have you got?* (a rectangle) *Which family of shapes do rectangles belong to?* (quadrilaterals; parallelograms) Explain that in this example, the squares have been put together to construct a rectangle. Introduce pupils to the idea of constructing shapes using other shapes. Allow them to explore the shapes, constructing new ones. Share ideas.

  Demonstrate an example of shape construction, for instance making a rectangle from two congruent right-angled triangles or making a square from two congruent right-angled isosceles triangles. Remind pupils that both squares and rectangles are also parallelograms.

- Explain that shapes can also be deconstructed or taken apart. Ask pupils to draw and cut out a rectangle from paper, fold it in half, and cut it along the fold. Ask: *What shapes have you got?* Agree that the two shapes are

rectangles, or two parallelograms. Ask: *What happens if we make a perpendicular fold anywhere and cut the rectangle into two parts?* Agree that we still get two rectangles.

Ask: *What happens if we cut one of the rectangles along its diagonal, from corner to corner?* Agree that this makes two triangles. Get pupils to try deconstructing rectangles of different sizes. Ask: *What is the result?* Establish that if you take any parallelogram and cut it from one opposite corner to the other, you will always get two triangles. Ask: *What happens when we put the triangles back together?* Agree that the rectangle is reconstructed.

- Display the following:

> If a parallelogram is cut along its diagonals to give four triangles, the triangles can neither be all obtuse nor all acute. They will either be all right-angled triangles, or a pair of obtuse and a pair of acute triangles.

Ask pupils to investigate the statement to confirm whether it is true or not by drawing and cutting out the shapes that they need. Some pupils should start with non-rectangular parallelograms and others with rectangles or squares.

Ask: *Did anyone get four triangles that are all obtuse? All acute? Why not?* Discuss ideas and establish that the combined angle at the intersection of the diagonals cannot be greater than 360 degrees and therefore could not be composed of four obtuse angles, nor four acute angles.

Ask: *What angle sizes are possible?* Agree that a pair of obtuse and a pair of acute angles would work. Ask: *Are there any other angles possible?* Elicit that four right angles would also be possible.

- Pupils should complete Question 4 in the Practice Book.

Same-day intervention

- Provide pupils with a summary of the definitions of construction and deconstruction and ask them to make notes in their 'My geometry notebook'. Concentrate on making the language as clear and as simple as possible.
  Explain that you can compose, or create, a parallelogram using two shapes, such as squares or triangles. You can decompose, or take apart, a parallelogram by cutting it down the middle or dividing it from opposite corners, either vertically or horizontally. This might give two parallelograms or maybe even two triangles.

- Provide a tray of paper triangles. Ask pupils to compose a shape from four congruent right-angled triangles with the right angles placed around a central point. Ask: *What shape do you get?* (rectangle) Ask them to do the same with four congruent right-angled isosceles triangles. Ask: *What shape do you get?* (square)

- Ask: *Can you make a parallelogram by putting four congruent obtuse-angled triangles together? What about four congruent acute-angled triangles?* Agree that neither work.

- Ask: *What about two obtuse angled-triangles and two acute-angled triangles?* Ask pupils to position two congruent obtuse-angled triangles with their obtuse angles touching and opposite. Ask: *What type of triangles would fit in the gaps?* Agree that a pair of acute-angled triangles would complete the parallelogram.

Same-day enrichment

- Provide pupils with copies of **Resource 6.4.3b** Missing angles, and ask them to solve the missing angle problems.

Resource 6.4.3b

Missing angles

Work out the missing angles in each problem.

1. A parallelogram is cut along its diagonals to give two acute-angled triangles and two obtuse-angled triangles. If the acute angle of one of the triangles ($\angle AXD$) is 63°, what size are the other three angles $\angle AXB$, $\angle BXC$ and $\angle CXD$?

   $\angle AXB =$ ___ °

   $\angle BXC =$ ___ °

   $\angle CXD =$ ___ °

2. Find the missing angles *a* to *g*.

   $\angle a =$ ___ ° $\angle b =$ ___ °

   $\angle c =$ ___ ° $\angle d =$ ___ °

   $\angle e =$ ___ ° $\angle f =$ ___ °

   $\angle g =$ ___ °

Answers: **1.** 117°, 63°, 117°; **2.** *a* = 35°, *b* = 122°, *c* = 58°, *d* = 32°, *e* = 122°, *f* = 23°, *g* = 32°

Challenge and extension questions

Question 5

5 How many parallelograms are there in this figure?

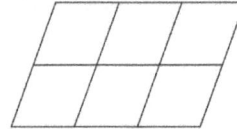

Pupils are presented with a parallelogram that is divided internally by three lines and asked to find the total number of parallelograms contained within the figure. They will need to use their knowledge of the properties of parallelograms and an awareness that congruent parallelograms combine to make larger parallelograms.

Question 6

6 There are six small sticks. Their lengths are 1 cm, 2 cm, 3 cm, 5 cm, 6 cm and 7 cm, respectively. To use these six small sticks to form a parallelogram, the opposite sides of the parallelogram will be _____

and _____ , or _____ and _____ .

Pupils are asked to combine six small sticks to form a parallelogram. To answer the question, pupils will need to remember that opposite sides of a parallelogram are equal.

Unit 4.4
Parallelograms (2)

Conceptual context

Having learned about general properties of parallelograms and that there is a relationship between parallelograms and triangles in the previous unit, pupils will now learn to recognise the height of a parallelogram in relation to any base. Knowing how to identify the base and height of a parallelogram is important preparation for later work involving the calculation of area.

Learning pupils will have achieved at the end of the unit

- Having reviewed the properties of parallelograms, pupils will be able to define and apply their knowledge of the shape (Q1)
- Pupils will be able to identify the height of a parallelogram given any base (Q1, Q2)
- Given the base and height, pupils will be able to construct a parallelogram (Q3)

Resources

2-D parallelogram shapes; squared paper; rulers; 'My geometry notebook'; geoboards and bands; geostrips; **Resource 6.4.4a** Parallelograms (2); **Resource 6.4.4b** Height of parallelograms; **Resource 6.4.4c** Parallelograms (3)

Vocabulary

height, base, parallel, perpendicular

Questions 1 and 2

1 Complete each statement.

(a) In the figure, *MN* is the _____ of parallelogram *ABCD*, and side *BC* is

called the _____ of the parallelogram.

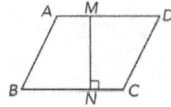

(b) Draw a perpendicular line from a point on one side of a parallelogram. The line segment between this point and the perpendicular foot is called the

_____ on the base of the parallelogram.

(c) The figure shows a parallelogram *ABCD*. If the base is *AB*, then the height

is _____. If the height is *AE*,

then the base is _____

or _____.

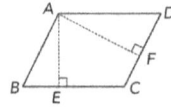

(d) The lengths of all the heights on the same base of a parallelogram

are _____.

(e) The figure on the right shows a parallelogram. Its height shown in

the figure should be _____

or _____.

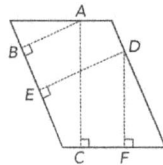

(f) Passing through a point on the base of a parallelogram, at

most _____ height(s) can be drawn.

(g) If two pairs of opposite sides of a quadrilateral are parallel to each other, and one of the angles is a right angle, then the

quadrilateral is called a _____; it is also called a

special _____.

2 Multiple choice questions. (For each question, choose the correct answer and write the letter in the box.)

(a) The base of parallelogram *ABCD* is *AB*,

and its height is ☐.

   A. *CD*   B. *AE*

   C. *DF*   D. *BC*

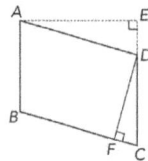

(b) The figure shows a parallelogram *ABCD*.

For ☐, the side is not the base for the height.

   A. *AB* and *CE*   B. *BC* and *MN*

   C. *AD* and *CD*   D. *CD* and *CE*

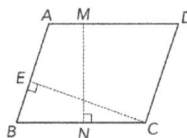

(c) On one side of a parallelogram, you can draw ☐ heights.

   A. 1   B. 2

   C. 4   D. infinitely many

What learning will pupils have achieved at the conclusion of Questions 1 and 2?

- Having reviewed the properties of parallelograms, pupils will be able to define and apply their knowledge of the shape.
- Pupils will be able to identify the height of a parallelogram given any base.

Activities for whole-class instruction

- Provide each pupil with a copy of **Resource 6.4.4a** Parallelograms (2). They should cut out a set of paper parallelograms.

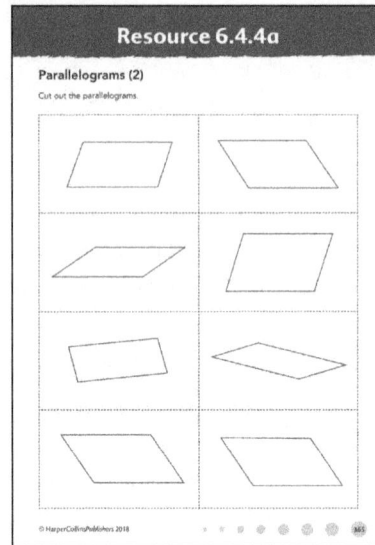

Ask pupils to explain how they know each shape is a parallelogram. Pupils should refer to the properties checklist used in the previous unit.

Ask pupils to choose one parallelogram, place it on the table in front of them and point to the base of the shape. Ask: *What is meant by the word 'base'?* Pairs should discuss. Share ideas.

Explain that any side of a parallelogram can be its base. It is simply the side on which the parallelogram 'sits'. Explain the dual meaning of the term in describing a particular side of the shape and its length.

Ask pupils to turn their parallelograms around to explore the four possible bases of the shape.

- Draw a parallelogram *ABCD* on the board and label the side *CD* as the base.

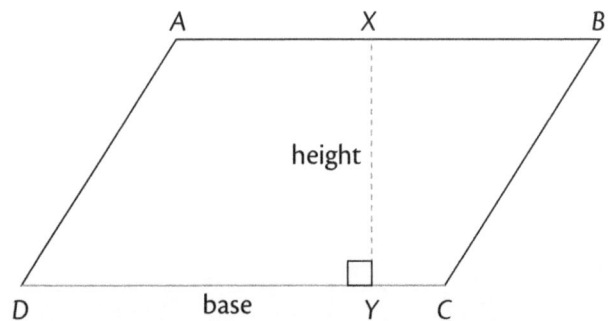

Agree that, when 'sitting on' any base, the height of the parallelogram must be perpendicular to the base.

Use a large protractor or set square to mark the height *XY* with a dashed line. Explain that the shortest distance

Chapter 4 Geometry and measurement (I)

between the base and the side opposite the base is called the height of the parallelogram. Label the dashed line to show the height. Ask: *Why do you think we use a dashed line and not a solid line to mark the height?* Establish that a dashed line is used to avoid confusion with the sides of the shape. Include a right-angle symbol to show that the height *XY* is perpendicular to the base *CD*.

Ask pupils how they know that the height (line *XY*) is the shortest distance between the base and the side opposite. In their responses, pupils should recall that the shortest distance between two parallel sides is always the length of a line drawn perpendicular to one of the lines – in this case, the base.

Ask: *If the height is the perpendicular distance from the base to the opposite side, is there just the one height for the base CD – one place that the dotted 'height line can be drawn?* Accept comments and establish that there are infinite number of heights that can be drawn since the dashed line can be drawn anywhere between the two sides as long as it forms a right angle with the base. Agree that all of the dashed lines will have the same measurement.

- Provide squared paper and ask pupils to draw a parallelogram. They should name the vertices, label the base and mark and label the height using a dashed line. Invite pupils to share their parallelograms and ensure that they are labelled correctly. Ask them to mark and label two more heights for their corresponding base using a dashed line.

- Display the following diagram:

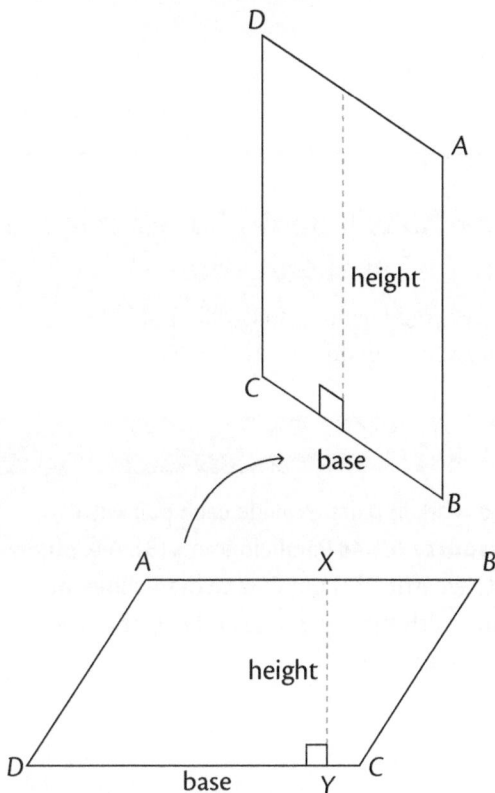

Ask pupils to imagine that the parallelogram has been turned clockwise around its vertex C so that the side CB is now the base. Establish that the parallelogram now not only has a new base, but it also has a new height. Use a protractor or set square to mark and label the new height. Explain that the choice of base determines the height of the parallelogram.

- Display the following diagram:

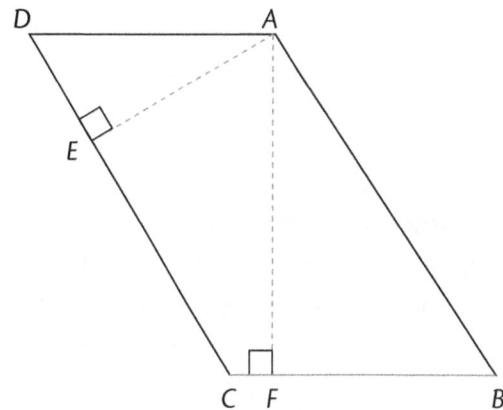

Ask: *If AB is the base of the parallelogram, what is the height?* Pupils should discuss. Share ideas. Establish that the height must be the perpendicular distance from side *AB* to the opposite side *CD* and so is *AE*.

Ask: *If AF is the height of the parallelogram, what must the base be?* Pupils should discuss. Share ideas.

- Ask pupils to draw and name a rectangle on squared paper. Remind them that a rectangle is a special form of a parallelogram whose sides form right angles. Ask: *How do you identify the base and height of a rectangle?* Invite a pupil to explain their answer. Establish that any side of a rectangle can be a base and the height is the length of an adjacent side.

- Pupils should complete Questions 1 and 2 in the Practice Book.

Same-day intervention

Look out for … any pupils who think that base and height are the adjacent sides of a parallelogram. This is true for rectangles (and squares) but not for parallelograms. Use geostrips to explore the relationship between parallelograms and rectangles. Have pupils construct a parallelogram and pull the shape to and fro to change the interior angles. Ask pupils to say how the height of the parallelogram changes as the interior angles increase and decrease. Establish that only when the angles are right angles and the shape is a rectangle is the height equal to the length of the lateral sides. For a non-rectangular parallelogram, the height will always be shorter than the length of the lateral sides.

- Take pupils through the definitions of base and height for a parallelogram and ask them to make notes and diagrams in their 'My geometry notebook'. Remind them that any side of a parallelogram can be called a base. The height of a parallelogram is the perpendicular distance between any two parallel bases.

- Ask pupils to draw a non-rectangular parallelogram on squared paper. Provide rulers and ask them to measure and record the base and height. To measure the dimensions, the zero mark of the ruler must be lined up with one vertex and the scale read at the other vertex.

- Provide geostrips and ask pupils to construct a parallelogram. Have them move the strips so that the shape leans to and fro, transforming from a rectangle to a non-rectangular parallelogram. Ask: *When you change the interior angles of the parallelogram, which measurement does not change, base or height?* Take comments and establish that the length of the base (and opposite side) remain the same. Ask: *What happens to the height of the parallelogram?* Confirm that the more a parallelogram leans, the less the height. Ask: *Is this the same measurement as the length of the sides?* Take comments and establish that the length of a lateral side of the parallelogram is a fixed dimension and not the same as the height except when the parallelogram is also a rectangle. Reinforce that in a non-rectangular parallelogram the height will always be less than the length.

Same-day enrichment

- Provide pupils with copies of **Resource 6.4.4b** Height of parallelograms. Pupils should first cut out the parallelograms from the sheet. Explain that the base of each parallelogram is drawn in grey. Pupils must work out where to mark and label the height.

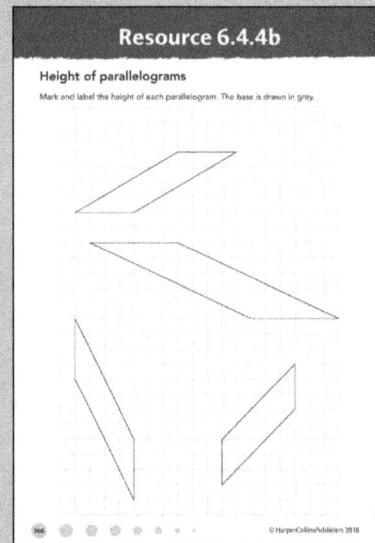

Resource 6.4.4b

Height of parallelograms

Mark and label the height of each parallelogram. The base is drawn in grey.

© HarperCollinsPublishers 2018

Question 3

3 Draw three different parallelograms in the 1 cm square grid below, each with a base of 3 cm and a height of 2 cm.

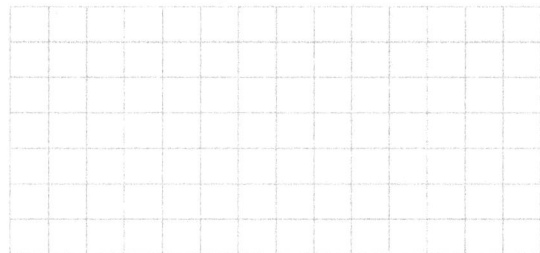

What learning will pupils have achieved at the conclusion of Question 3?

- Given the base and height, pupils will be able to construct a parallelogram.

Activities for whole-class instruction

- Ask pupils to work in pairs. Provide each pair with copies of **Resource 6.4.4c** Parallelograms (3). Ask pupils to investigate whether it is possible to draw different parallelograms with the same base and height as the parallelogram illustrated.

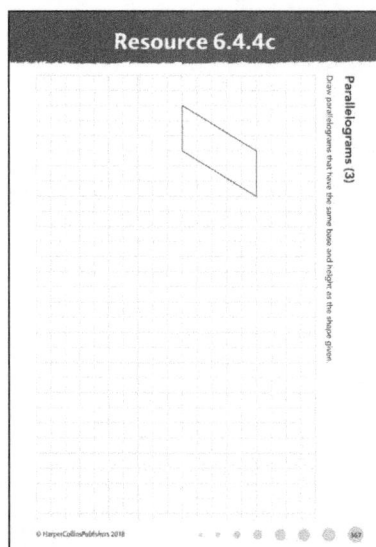

Give pupils time to construct parallelograms then invite groups to share their diagrams and discuss what they have discovered. Establish that different parallelograms are possible for the same base and height; they simply differ by the angle at which they 'lean' and the dimension of one pair of opposite sides. Ensure pupils understand that the base can be in any orientation – not only horizontal.

- Provide 1 cm squared paper and ask pupils to draw a parallelogram with a base of 5 cm and a height of 3 cm. Invite them to share their diagrams and explain how they constructed the figure.

Ask pupils to gather around a table as you demonstrate how to construct the parallelogram. Use a ruler to mark a line 5 cm long (5 squares long) on the squared paper. Then find the grid line that is 3 cm (3 squares) above this line. Mark a line 5 cm long anywhere along the gridline. Explain that this ensures the opposite side to the base is parallel and equal in length, something necessary for a parallelogram. Then join the sides to complete the parallelogram. Invite pupils to draw an example of a parallelogram with the same base and height but with a different 'leaning' angle.

- Pupils should complete Question 3 in the Practice Book.

Same-day intervention

- Some pupils may find it difficult to construct parallelograms on squared paper. For these pupils, provide a geoboard and ask them to construct figures using bands. Once constructed, they should find it straightforward to unhook the band that forms the opposite side to the base and hook it elsewhere at the same height while maintaining parallel sides.

Have pupils construct a parallelogram on a geoboard. Ask them to investigate whether it is possible to construct different parallelograms with the same base and height. Suggest that they place several geoboards alongside one another in a row to provide more space for other shapes. Remind pupils that when they construct the parallelograms they need to make sure that the length of the base and the perpendicular height is exactly the same as the first parallelogram. They should use the number of pegs across and up as a guide.

Give pupils time to construct parallelograms, then invite groups to share and discuss what they discover. Establish that different parallelograms are possible for the same base and height; they simply differ by the angle at which they 'lean' and the dimension of one pair of opposite sides.

- Ask pupils to gather around a table as you use a geoboard to construct a parallelogram. Explain that you are going to arrange the bands to form a parallelogram with a base measuring five pegs and a height measuring seven pegs. Attach a band horizontally across five pegs to form the base. Ask: *How will I make sure that the height measures seven pegs?* Invite a pupil to demonstrate. Establish that counting up seven pegs from anywhere along the base and attaching a band on the seventh peg is a good technique.

- Ask pupils to construct the following parallelograms on their geoboards:
  - A base six pegs in length and three pegs in height.
  - A base five pegs in length and nine pegs in height.

Same-day enrichment

- Ask pupils to construct a parallelogram with the following dimensions:

  - A parallelogram with a perimeter of 40 cm.

  - A parallelogram where the height is three times the base.

  - A parallelogram ABCD with sides AB = 6 cm and AD = 4 cm and angle A = 50°.

Challenge and extension questions

Question 4

> **4** In parallelogram ABCD shown on the right, AB is 6 cm and BC is 8 cm.
>
> The height AE can be ☐ cm.
>
> A. 5   B. 6   C. 7

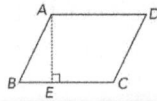

Pupils are presented with a parallelogram and given the base and the length of an adjacent side. They have a choice of three answers for the height of the parallelogram and to choose correctly they must recognise that the height of the parallelogram cannot be greater than the length of the side.

Question 5

> **5** The perimeter of parallelogram ABCD is 50 cm, AB is 15 cm, and then BC is ☐ cm.

Pupils are given the perimeter of a parallelogram and one dimension. To work out the other dimension they need to recall that perimeter is twice the sum of the two dimensions: $p = 2 (ab + bc)$.

Question 6

> **6** How many parallelograms are there in the figure on the right?

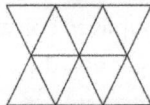

Pupils are asked to identify all the parallelograms contained within a geometrical construction. They need to recall the properties of the shape in order to spot them. (There are 20.)

Unit 4.5
Area of a parallelogram

Conceptual context

This unit builds on the work covered in the previous unit where pupils learned to identify the base and height of a parallelogram. Here, pupils will use the area formula for rectangles to discover the area formula for parallelograms given the base and height.

Pupils are introduced to the idea of transforming a figure into one for which they already know the area formula. Visuospatial skills will be utilised and developed as pupils need to visualise and mentally dissect and manipulate parts of parallelograms to transform them into rectangles.

Learning pupils will have achieved at the end of the unit

- Pupils will have found the area formula for a parallelogram by dissecting it and rearranging the parts to make a rectangle (Q1, Q2)
- Pupils will be able to use the formula they have derived to calculate the area of a parallelogram (given the base and the height) (Q1, Q2, Q3, Q4)
- Pupils will be able to apply the formula and concepts to complete simple problems represented as geometrical diagrams and word problems (Q2, Q3, Q4)

Resources

rulers; scissors; mini whiteboards; squared paper; **Resource 6.4.5a** Parallelograms (4); **Resource 6.4.5b** Parallelograms (5)

Vocabulary

height, base, parallel, perpendicular

Question 1

1 Complete the table.

Parallelogram	Base	3.2 m	24 cm	18 mm	3 cm
	Height	15 m	70 cm		
	Area			90 mm²	7.5 cm²

What learning will pupils have achieved at the conclusion of Question 1?

- Pupils will find the area formula for a parallelogram by dissecting it and rearranging the parts to make a rectangle.
- Pupils will be able to use the formula they have derived to calculate the area of a parallelogram (given the base and the height).

Activities for whole-class instruction

- Ask pupils to work in pairs. Provide each pair with squared paper, scissors and a ruler. Ask them to draw a parallelogram on the paper with its base aligned with a horizontal gridline.

Ask: *How do you turn a parallelogram into a rectangle?* Give pupils time to think. Suggest that they cut or fold the parallelogram. Share ideas.

Establish that a rectangle can be formed by cutting off a triangle from one side of the parallelogram and adding it to the opposite side.

1. Cut along the dotted line.

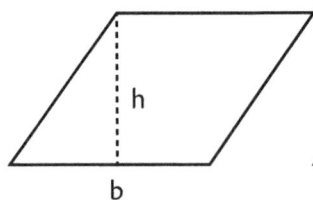

2. Remove triangular section.

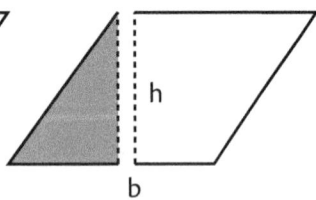

3. Place triangular section on opposite side.

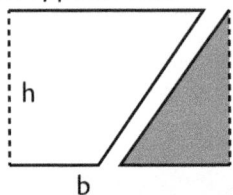

4. Position the triangular section so it forms a rectangle.

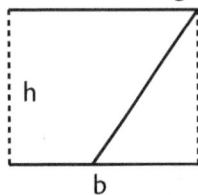

Ask: *What does this tell you about the area of a parallelogram?* Give pupils time to discuss. Share ideas. Agree that because the parallelogram can be transformed into a rectangle without adding or removing any paper,

just by rearranging it, the parallelogram must have the same area as the rectangle.

Point out that both the parallelogram and rectangle have exactly the same base length (solid horizontal line) and exactly the same height (vertical dotted line). Remind pupils that the height is measured perpendicular to the base, and the base can be any side.

- Ask: *How do we find the area of a rectangle?* Confirm base times height. Explain that because base × height gives the area of the rectangle, we can use the same measurements on the parallelogram to calculate its area: base × height. On the board, write: $A = b \times h$.

- Display the following table on the board:

	Base	7 cm	4.5 m	17 mm	6 cm
Parallelogram	Height	9 cm	12 m		
	Area			68 mm²	13.8 cm²

Ask pupil pairs to find the missing numbers in the table. Remind them to use the formula for the area of a parallelogram ($A = b \times h$) and strategies for multiplication and division including decimals, for example multiplying 4.5 by 12 as 45 by 12 and reintroducing the decimal point in the answer.

- Ask: *How would you find the height of a parallelogram given the base and area?* Give pupils time to discuss the problem then share ideas.

Write base: 16 cm, area: 96 cm². Together, talk through:
$A = b \times h$
$96 = 16 \times h$

Ask: *How do we find the height?* (divide the area by the base)
$h = \frac{96}{16} = 6$

Refocus pupils on the original question: If the base = 16 cm and the area = 96 cm², what is the height of the parallelogram? Ask: *What is the answer?* (The height of the parallelogram is 6 cm.)

- Pupils should complete Question 1 in the Practice Book.

Same-day intervention

● Show the following parallelogram:

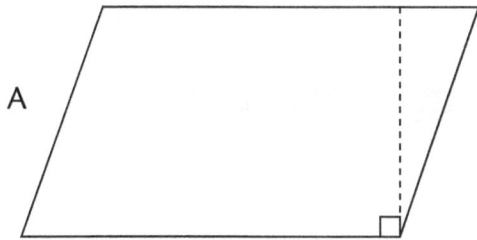

A

Write: base: 15 cm, height: 5 cm, length: 7 cm. Ask pupils to identify and label the base, height and length of the parallelogram. Emphasise that the height must be perpendicular to the base.

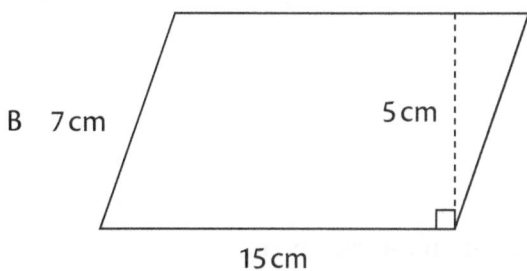

B   7 cm   5 cm

15 cm

Show pupils how to transform the parallelogram into a rectangle and reinforce that both shapes must have the same area.

Ask pupils to calculate the area of the parallelogram. Use the following questions to elicit thinking:

- *How did you decide which values to use when calculating the area?*

- *What is the value of the base/height? What type of angle must the base and the height of a parallelogram make?*

- *How did you calculate the area of the parallelogram?*

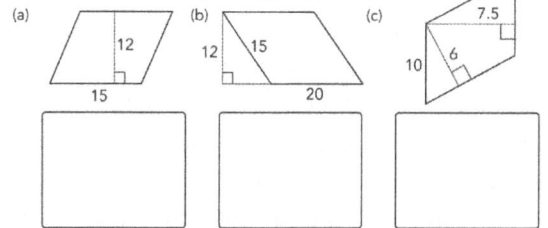

- *Which formula did you use? Can you tell me what each variable is?*

- *What calculation did you perform? Which strategy did you use to multiply the numbers? Why?*

Same-day enrichment

● Display the following three rows of figures:

7	60.8	8	9.2	6
6.8	9	52.8	4.4	50.4
7.6	8.4	12	61.2	64.4

Explain that the numbers are sets of base, height and area measurements for five parallelograms that been mixed up. Ask pupils to sort the sets into base, height and area for each parallelogram.

Question 2

2 Calculate the area of each parallelogram. (Unit: cm)
(a)   12   15   (b) 12 15 (c) 7.5 10 6
15   20

What learning will pupils have achieved at the conclusion of Question 2?

● Pupils will have found the area formula for a parallelogram by dissecting it and rearranging the parts to make a rectangle.

● Pupils will be able to use the formula they have derived to calculate the area of a parallelogram (given the base and the height).

● Pupils will be able to apply the formula and concepts to complete simple problems represented as geometrical diagrams and word problems.

Activities for whole-class instruction

● Display the following diagrams:

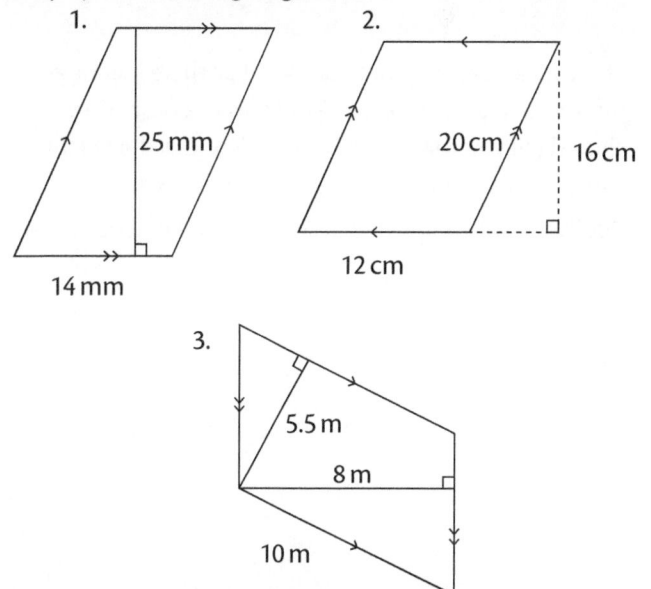

1.   25 mm   14 mm

2.   20 cm   16 cm   12 cm

3.   5.5 m   8 m   10 m

Ask: *How would you find the area of the first parallelogram?* Give pupils time to discuss. Share ideas. Agree that since both base and height are given, the problem is a straightforward application of the area formula: A = b × h. Individual pupils should come to the board to write the formula and substitute the known

199

values: A = 14 × 25. Provide whiteboards and ask pupils to solve the calculation. (350) Ask: *Which unit will the answer be in?* (square millimetres, mm²)

- Ask: *How would you find the area of the second parallelogram?* Give pupils time to discuss. Share ideas. Ask: *If the base is 12 cm, what is the height?* Confirm that the height, in this case, is shown by the dotted line drawn outside the shape. The line is perpendicular to the base and extends to the opposite side of the shape. Remind pupils that the height is not the same as the length of a side. Individual pupils should come to the board to write the area formula and substitute the known values: A = 12 × 16. Ask pupils to solve the calculation. (192) Ask: *Which unit will the answer be in?* (square centimetres, cm²)

- Ask: *How would you find the area of the third parallelogram?* Label the vertices A, B, C, D. Give pupils time to discuss.

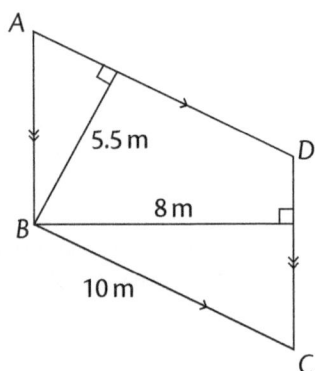

Share ideas. Ensure pupils can see that there is enough information given to use *AD* or *BC* as the base. They should tell you that, if the base is *AB* or *CD*, the height is 8 m; if the base is *AD* or *BC*, the height is 5.5 m.

- Pupils should complete Question 2 in the Practice Book.

Same-day intervention

- Provide each pupil with a copy of **Resource 6.4.5a** Parallelograms (4). If necessary, allow them to cut out the shapes so they can be folded.

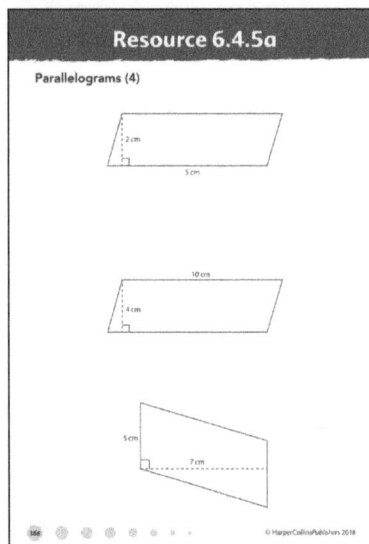

Answers: 10 cm², 40 cm², 35 cm²

- Solve the problems as guided examples. For pupils who make conceptual errors when calculating the area of a parallelogram, use questioning to develop thinking, for example ask:

  - *How did you decide which values to use when calculating the area of each shape?*

  - *Can you show me the base and height of the figure?*

  - *What is the area formula for a parallelogram? What does each variable represent?*

  - *Can you show me how to substitute these values in the formula?*

Same-day enrichment

- Display the following diagram. Explain that it is a plan for the building of a new playground. Ask pupils to calculate the area of the playground (84.5 m²).

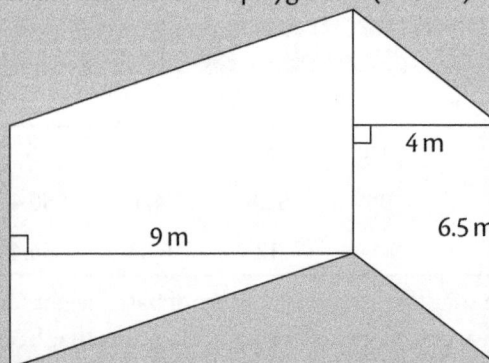

- Next, pupils should draw a similar plan, entering different measurements for a partner to find the area.

Question 3

> 3 Multiple choice questions. (For each question, choose the correct answer and write the letter in the box.)
>
> (a) Look at the figure. To find the area of the parallelogram, the correct calculation is ☐. (Unit: cm)
>
> A. 5×6 B. 8×4
>
> C. 8×5 D. 4×5
>
> (b) Look at the figure. To find the length of CD, the correct calculation is ☐. (Unit: cm)
>
> A. $5 \times 4 \div 3$ B. $3 \times 4 \div 5$
>
> C. $5 \times 3 \div 4$ D. $5 \times 3 \times 4$

What learning will pupils have achieved at the conclusion of Question 3?

- Pupils will be able to use the formula they have derived to calculate the area of a parallelogram (given the base and the height).

- Pupils will be able to apply the formula and concepts to complete simple problems represented as geometrical diagrams and word problems.

Activities for whole-class instruction

- Display the following diagrams:

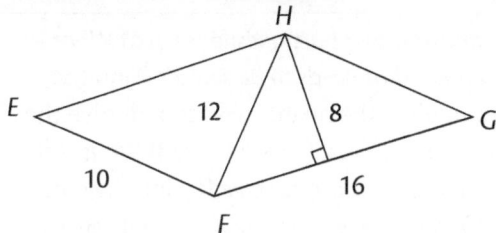

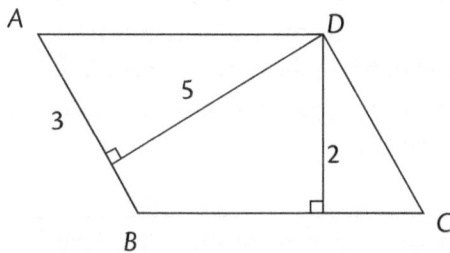

On the board write:

a) 10×12 b) 10×8 c) 16×8 d) 8×12

Ask: *Which of the calculations a, b, c or d will give the area of the first parallelogram (EFGH)? Why?* Agree that *FH* is a diagonal and not a height. Also, that the perpendicular (shown by the symbol ⊥) from *FG* = 8. So, *FG* is the base (16) and the height is 8. The correct calculation is therefore c) 16×8 (*b* × *h*).

Ask: *For the parallelogram, ABCD, how would you calculate the length BC?* Give pupils time to discuss. Share ideas.

Remind pupils that there are two possible values for height, depending on which side is chosen to be the base.

- Pupils should complete Question 3 in the Practice Book.

Same-day intervention

- Some pupils may benefit from using concrete manipulatives. Provide each pupil with a copy of **Resource 6.4.5b** Parallelograms (5). If necessary, allow them to cut out the diagram so it can be folded.

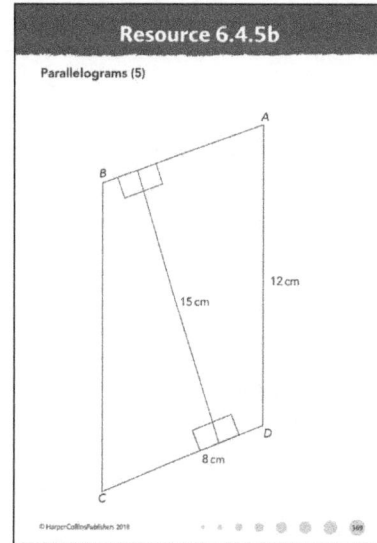

- On the board, write: a) 8×12 b) 8×15

  Ask: *Which values do we need to calculate the area of a parallelogram?* Agree that base and height are required. Point to the calculations on the board. Ask: *Which of the calculations a or b will give the area of the parallelogram ABCD?* Share ideas. Ask: *Why is it not calculation a?* Agree that *AD* is a dimension of the parallelogram and not the height.

  Invite a pupil to the board to write and solve the calculation for the area: $8 \times 15 = 120\,\text{cm}^2$.

Same-day enrichment

- Provide pupil pairs with squared paper. Ask them to draw and label two parallelograms. On the first, they provide four measurements for: both dimensions, a height and the length of one diagonal. On the other, they provide three measurements for: one side and two heights.

  They swap papers with their partner and ask them to find the area of the first parallelogram and the missing dimension of the second parallelogram. Once calculated, pupils return their papers for marking.

Question 4

> 4 Solve these problems.
>
> (a) The area of a parallelogram is 10.8 m² and its height is 24 m. Find the length of the base corresponding to the height.
>
> (b) The base of a parallelogram is 45 cm, which is 1.3 cm more than its height. Find the area.
>
> (c) A piece of land is in the shape of parallelogram with a base of 28 m and a height of 15 m. The owner plans to cover the land with turf, which costs £4.50 per m². What is the total cost to cover the whole area?
>
> (d) The figure shows a parallelogram with a perimeter of 36 cm. AB is 7.8 cm and AE is 5 cm. Find the area of the parallelogram.

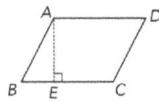

What learning will pupils have achieved at the conclusion of Question 4?

- Pupils will be able to use the formula they have derived to calculate the area of a parallelogram (given the base and height).
- Pupils will be able to apply the formula and concepts to complete simple problems represented as geometrical diagrams and word problems.

Activities for whole-class instruction

- Show Problem 1:

> A roof is shaped like a parallelogram. The height of the parallelogram is 5.5 metres and its area is 22 square metres. What is the length of the base corresponding to this height?

Ask: *How would you find the length of the base?* Invite a pupil to the board to write the area formula and substitute the known values: 22 = b × 5.5. Provide whiteboards and ask pupils to solve the calculation. (4) Remind pupils of the compact method for division and a

strategy for dividing by a decimal. Ask: *Which unit will the answer be in?* (square metres, m²)

- Show Problem 2:

> A dress designer uses a piece of fabric in the shape of a parallelogram. The height of the parallelogram is 52 cm, which is 4.6 cm less than its base. What is the area of the fabric?

Ask: *How would you find the area of the fabric?* Agree that the base must be 4.6 cm longer than the height. Invite a pupil to the board to write the area formula and substitute the known values:
$A = b × h = (52 + 4.6) × 52$.
Provide whiteboards and ask pupils to solve the calculation. (2943.2) Remind pupils of the compact method for multiplication and a strategy for multiplying a decimal. Ask: *Which unit will the answer be in?* (square centimetres, cm²)

- Show Problem 3:

> The plan drawing of a school hall shows that the floor is shaped like a parallelogram. The height of the parallelogram is 17 metres and the corresponding base is 14 metres. If the hall floor is to be replaced with new wooden timbers at £3.50 per m², what is the cost for the whole area?

Ask: *Is this a one or a two-part question?* (two) *What is the first calculation that needs to be solved?* (Find the area.) Invite a pupil to the board to write and solve the calculation to give the area. (17 × 14 = 238) *What is the second calculation that must be solved?* (Find the cost of the new floor.) *How do we calculate this?* (Multiply the area by the cost per square metre.) Invite a pupil to the board to write and solve the calculation to give the cost. (238 × 3.5) Remind pupils of the compact method for multiplication and a strategy for multiplying by a decimal. Confirm the answer: £833.

- Show Problem 4:

> A parallelogram has a perimeter of 50 cm. If its length is 16.6 cm and height is 12 cm, what is the area of the parallelogram?

Ask: *What do we know about the perimeter of a parallelogram?* (The perimeter is twice the sum of two adjacent sides.) Invite a pupil to the board to write the perimeter formula and substitute the known values.
$P = 2a + 2b$; 50 = (2 × 16.6) + 2b. Solve 2 × 16.6, with the pupil assisting: 50 = 33.2 + 2b. Ask: *What is 2b?* 50 – 33.2 = 16.8 = 2b. *What is the length of the base?* (8.4) Ask: *Now we know the base, how do we calculate the area?*

Invite a pupil to the board to write the area formula and substitute the known values:

A = b × h; 100.8 cm^2 = 8.4 × 12.

- Pupils should complete Question 4 in the Practice Book.

Same-day intervention

- Show the following problem:

> Cards for a game are shaped like parallelograms. The height of each parallelogram is 8.2 centimetres and the area is 41 square centimetres. What is the length of the base?

Agree that the formula for the area of a parallelogram should be used. Write: A = b × h. Ask: *Which values have we been given?* (area and height)

Ask: *Am I right in thinking that the formula gives us the area but not the base?* Share ideas. Establish that we can substitute known values in the formula then use an inverse operation to give the base. Invite a pupil to the board to substitute the values in the formula:

41 = b × 8.2.

Ask: *Which inverse operation would we use to find the base?* Agree that since height times the base gives the area, the base can be found by dividing the area by the height. Write the calculation for the base: b = 41 ÷ 8.2 and solve as a group. (5 cm)

Same-day enrichment

- Using Questions 4a and 4b in the Practice Book as templates, ask pupils to write four new questions for their partner to solve. They should substitute new values into the question and answer each one themselves. Pupils swap papers, solve the problems, then return them for marking.

Challenge and extension questions

Question 5

> **5** The figure shows the shaded parts of two parallelograms with one common base. The relationship between the areas of the shaded parts, A and B, is ☐ .
>
> A. A > B   B. A = B   C. A < B   D. not comparable

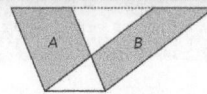

Pupils are presented with a diagram that features a pair of parallelograms with a shared base. Pupils must recognise that the parallelograms also have the same height and therefore are equal in area.

Question 6

> **6** In the figure, *EF // AD*, *BE // CG*, *BF // AG* and *CE // DF*. Write the parallelograms that have the same areas. (Use letters to represent the parallelograms.)

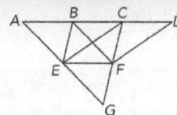

Pupils are presented with a diagram constructed from overlapping parallelograms. They need to determine which shapes share the same base and have equal height, and therefore are equal in area.

Unit 4.6
Area of a triangle (1)

Conceptual context

This is the sixth in a series of seven units about lines and shapes. In this unit pupils find a formula for calculating the area of a triangle by considering it as half of a rectangle. In calculating the area of triangles, pupils practise their preferred multiplication and division strategies.

Learning pupils will have achieved at the end of the unit

- By dissecting a parallelogram into two congruent triangles, pupils will be able to recognise the area of a triangle as half the area of a related rectangle (Q1, Q5)
- Pupils will be able to find the area of a triangle, given the base and height (Q1, Q4)
- Pupils will know that the height of a triangle is given by the perpendicular distance from the base to the opposite vertex and will be able to determine and mark the height on any triangle, given the base, using a set square (Q2, Q3)
- Pupils will be able to solve simple word problems that involve finding the area of a triangle (Q5, Q6)

Resources

set square; paper triangles; squared paper; scissors; rulers; **Resource 6.4.6** Heights of triangles

Vocabulary

height, base, parallel, perpendicular, congruent

Question 1

1 Complete the table					
	Base	15 m	27 cm	4.4 m	1.25 cm
Triangle	Height	12 m	8 cm	15 m	36 cm
	Area				

What learning will pupils have achieved at the conclusion of Question 1?

- By dissecting a parallelogram into two congruent triangles, pupils will be able to recognise the area of a triangle as half the area of a related rectangle.
- Pupils will be able to find the area of a triangle, given the base and height.

Activities for whole-class instruction

- Provide pupil pairs with squared paper, scissors and a ruler. Ask them to draw a parallelogram on the paper with its base aligned with a horizontal gridline.

  Ask: *How do you turn a parallelogram into two congruent triangles?* Explain that 'congruent triangles' means two triangles that have the same size and shape. Ask pupils to cut out the parallelogram then cut or fold it. Share ideas. Establish that this can be done by folding or cutting along one of the diagonals of the parallelogram.

  Ask: *What does this tell you about the area of each triangle?* (It is half the area of the related parallelogram.)

  Ask: *What do we know about the base and height of each triangle compared to its related parallelogram?* Give pupils time to investigate the relationship then share ideas. Can pupils explain that the base and height of each triangle is the same as its 'parent' parallelogram?

- Display the following image:

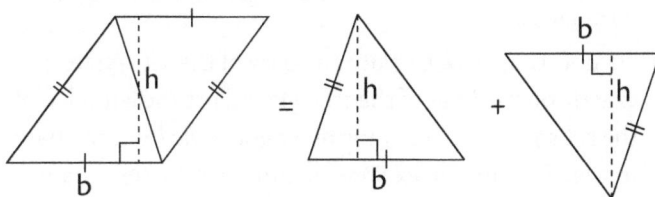

  Use the image to explain that as each congruent triangle shares the same base and height as the parent parallelogram, the area of each triangle can be found by halving the area of the parallelogram, that is half of base times height. Ask: *How do we describe the height of a triangle?* Agree that the height is the perpendicular distance from the base to the opposite vertex.

- On the board, write: $A = \frac{1}{2}bh$

Draw the following triangle:

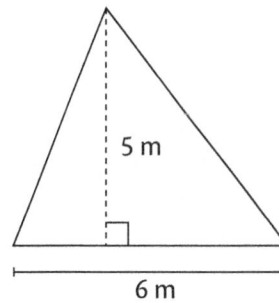

Ask: *What is the length of the base of the triangle? What is the height? How do you know?* Pupils should know that it is the perpendicular distance from the base to the opposite vertex as marked by the dotted line. Refer to the area formula for a triangle and ask pupils to calculate the area of the triangle. ($\frac{1}{2}$ of $6 \times 5 = 15 \, \text{m}^2$)

- Display the following triangle:

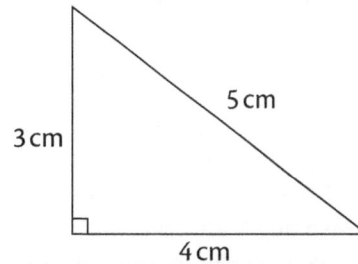

Agree that this is a right-angled triangle. Ask: *How would you find the area of this triangle?* Establish that the same area formula applies to a right-angled triangle since two congruent right-angled triangles would combine to form a rectangle. Pupils should check by cutting out two copies of a right-angled triangle and putting them together to make a rectangle. Ask: *What is the length of the base of the triangle in the image? What is the height? Why is it not 5 cm?* (5 cm is the length of the diagonal and not the perpendicular height.)

Ask pupils to use the formula to calculate the area of the right-angled triangle. ($\frac{1}{2}$ of $3 \times 4 = 6 \, \text{cm}^2$)

- Show this table:

	Base	25 m	33 cm	6.6 m	5.25 cm
Triangle	Height	14 m	6 cm	15 m	44 cm
	Area				

Pupils should work in pairs to find the missing values. Remind them to use the formula for the area of a triangle: $A = \frac{1}{2}bh$.

- Pupils should complete Question 1 in the Practice Book.

Same-day intervention

- Pupils usually have little difficulty with the formula for a parallelogram but may experience problems when dealing with triangles.

- Ask pupils to draw any triangle on a piece of squared paper, then draw the surrounding rectangle.

Next, ask them to cut the diagram into three triangles and place the two smaller triangles so that they fit on the shaded triangle. Repeat with different triangles and share among the group. Pupils should see that the unshaded parts have the same area as the shaded triangle. Agree that this shows the area of the triangle is half of the area of the rectangle that encloses it. Therefore, multiplying base × height of the triangle gives double the area of the triangle.

- Write the formula on the board in the form: A = (base × height) ÷ 2 to reinforce the division by 2. Provide support when pupils are using this reformatted formula to complete the missing values in the following table.

	Base	10 m	25 cm	5.4 m	8.5 cm
Triangle	Height	8 m	6 cm	10 m	20 cm
	Area				

Same-day enrichment

- Display three rows of numbers:

3	26	6.4	9	18
42	7.5	109.2	48	14
15	8.4	12	33.75	294

Explain that the numbers are sets of base, height and area measurements for five triangles that have been mixed up. Ask pupils to sort the sets into base, height and area for each triangle.

Question 2

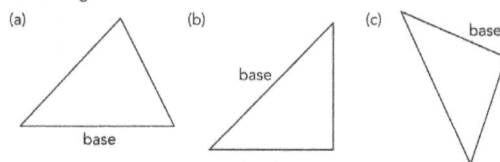

2 In each figure, use a set square to draw the height to the given base of each triangle.

(a) (b) (c)

What learning will pupils have achieved at the conclusion of Question 2?

- Pupils will know that the height of a triangle is given by the perpendicular distance from the base to the opposite vertex and will be able to determine and mark the height on any triangle, given the base, using a set square.

Activities for whole-class instruction

- Draw around a large triangle on the board three times and mark a different side to be the base for each triangle.

  Remind pupils that, as there are three sides and three angles to any triangle, it follows that there are three heights to any triangle depending on which side we choose as the base.

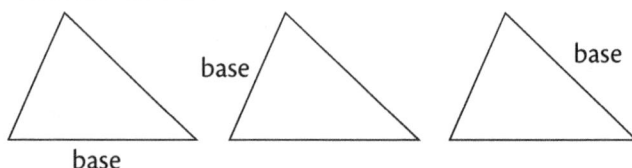

All say ...

The height of a triangle is the perpendicular distance from the base to the opposite vertex.

Explain that one of the easiest methods for marking the height is to use a set square, as one of its vertices is 90 degrees.

Demonstrate how to place the base of the set square exactly on the base of the triangle. Adjust the left edge of the set square so that it forms a right angle from the base to the opposite vertex. Making sure that the set square does not move, press it firmly with one hand and draw a line along the left edge, from the vertex up/down to the base.

Demonstrate how to turn the set square so that it lines up with the base for the two remaining triangles. Draw the heights for each as shown below.

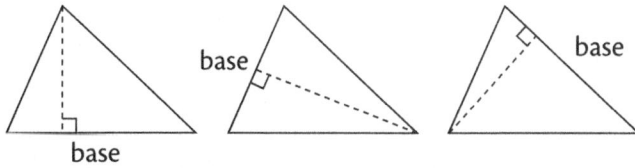

base

base

base

- Pupils should complete Question 2 in the Practice Book.

Same-day intervention

- Give pupils some paper triangles. Provide support as pupils mark the height using a set square.

Same-day enrichment

- Provide each pupil with a set square and a copy of **Resource 6.4.6** Heights of triangles. Ask them to use the set square to mark the three heights for each triangle.

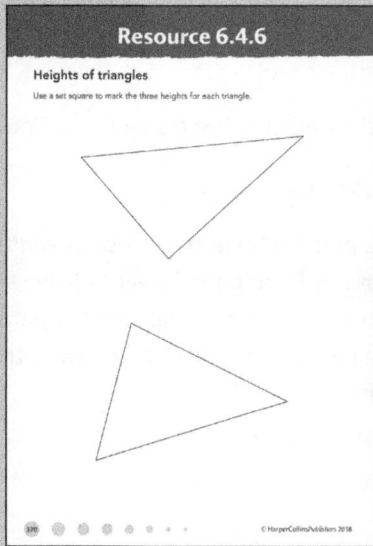

Resource 6.4.6

Heights of triangles
Use a set square to mark the three heights for each triangle.

© HarperCollinsPublishers 2018

Question 3

3 Complete each statement.

The figure on the right shows △ABC with three sides and three heights. Three pairs of corresponding base and height are

base AC and height _____,

base _____ and height AD,

and base _____ and height _____.

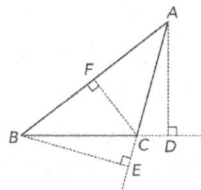

What learning will pupils have achieved at the conclusion of Question 3?

- Pupils will know that the height of a triangle is given by the perpendicular distance from the base to the opposite vertex and will be able to determine and mark the height on any triangle, given the base, using a set square.

Activities for whole-class instruction

- Draw an obtuse scalene triangle as in figure a) below, and mark the base.

a)

b)

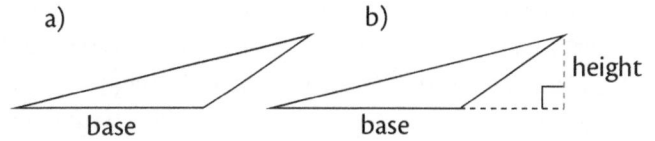

base

base

height

Ask: *How would you find and mark the height for the base given?* Share ideas. Explain that sometimes the height will need to be drawn outside the triangle. In this case, you need to extend the base of the figure so that it intersects the height at a right angle. Demonstrate this by extending the base as shown in figure b). Then draw the height perpendicular to the extended base to meet the vertex.

- Display the following triangle:

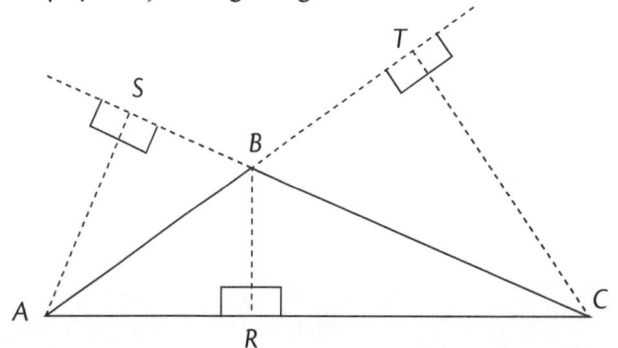

Ask: *If the base of the triangle is AC, what is the height?* Agree *BR*, the perpendicular distance from the base *AC* to the opposite vertex *B*.

Ask: *If the height is given by the line AS, what is the base?* Agree *BC*. Ask: *How do you know?* Try to ensure pupils can explain or demonstrate that to establish a perpendicular from the base *BC* with the vertex *A*, the height will fall outside the triangle and the base *BC* must be extended. Use a ruler and set square to reinforce how the base was extended and the perpendicular to the vertex was drawn.

Ask: *If the base is AB, what is the height?* Agree *CT*.

- Pupils should complete Question 3 in the Practice Book.

Same-day intervention

- With support, pupils should practise finding the height of triangles drawn on squared paper, using the gridlines as the base. Encourage pupils to use both gridlines and set square together to find the perpendicular line that joins the base to the opposite vertex.

Same-day enrichment

- Ask pupils to draw an obtuse triangle and then find the heights using all three possible bases. They will need to extend two of the bases to draw heights, using a ruler and a set square. They label the vertices of the triangle and the intersection of each height and base (or extended base) and then swap papers with a partner to name the three pairs of bases and heights.

Question 4

4 Look at each figure and find the area of the triangle. (Unit: cm)

(a)

5
8

(b)

14 / 12
15

(c)

4
3
5

What learning will pupils have achieved at the conclusion of Question 4?

- Pupils will be able to find the area of triangles, given base and height.

Activities for whole-class instruction

- Show the triangles:

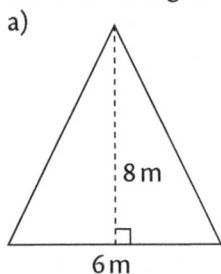

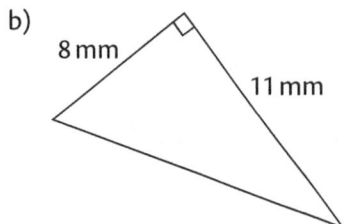

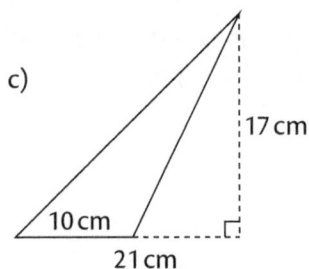

a)

8 m
6 m

b)

8 mm
11 mm

c)

17 cm
10 cm
21 cm

Point to diagram a). Ask: *What is the length of the base?* (6 m) *The height?* (8 m) *How do you know?* Pupils should explain that the height is given by the perpendicular distance from the base to the opposite vertex. Ask: *What is the area? How did you calculate it?* ($\frac{1}{2}$ (8 × 6) = 24 m^2)

Point to diagram b). Ask: *How do we decide which side is the base in this triangle?* Agree that there is no dotted line to show height, so the height must be one of the sides. Agree that either of the perpendicular sides of a right angle could be the base. And the other must be the height. Ask pupils to calculate the area. (44 mm^2; $\frac{1}{2}$ of 8 × 11 = $\frac{1}{2}$ of 88)

Point to diagram c). Ask: *How do we decide which measurements give the base and height in this triangle?* Share ideas. Establish that the base and height must be perpendicular to one another and therefore the base is 10 cm and the height 17 cm. The triangle is obtuse and the base gives a height that is shown outside the triangle. Ask pupils to calculate the area. (85 cm^2; $\frac{1}{2}$ of 10 × 17 = $\frac{1}{2}$ of 170)

- Pupils should complete Question 4 in the Practice Book.

Same-day intervention

Look out for … pupils who find the area by multiplying base by height and forget to halve the answer. Remind pupils that since a triangle is not a parallelogram the formula for its area will be different from that for a parallelogram.

- Show the triangle below:

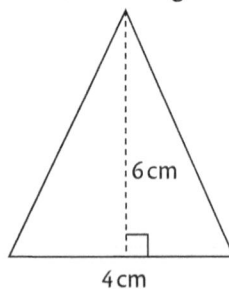

6 cm
4 cm

On the board, model how to compose a rectangle from the triangle. Establish that the area of a triangle is half the area of a rectangle with the same base and height, and develop this as a general formula.

Ask pupils to find the area of the triangle by using the area formula. Develop thinking by asking the following questions:

- *How did you decide which values to use when calculating the area? Identify these values by pointing to them on the diagram.*

- *What does each variable represent in the formula?*

– *How did you complete the calculation?*

Ensure pupils label the answer with the appropriate unit.

Same-day enrichment

- Display this diagram.

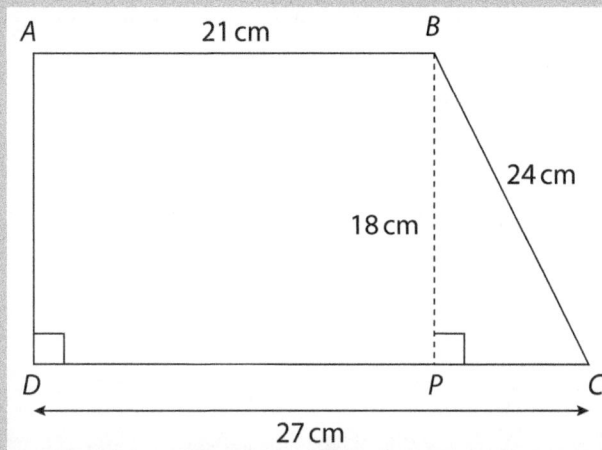

Ask pupils to find the area of shape *ABCD*. Discuss answers and reasons.

Answer: $(21 \times 18) + \frac{1}{2}(6 \times 18) = 432 \, cm^2$

Question 5

5 True or false? (Put a ✓ for true and a ✗ for false in each box.)

(a) If a triangle and a parallelogram share one common base, then the area of the triangle is half of the area of the parallelogram. ☐

(b) There is only one height in an obtuse triangle. ☐

(c) There are three pairs of corresponding base and height in a triangle. ☐

(d) In a right-angled triangle, if the lengths of the two sides of the right angle are given, then its area can be found. ☐

What learning will pupils have achieved at the conclusion of Question 5?

- By dissecting a parallelogram into two congruent triangles, pupils will be able to recognise the area of a triangle as half the area of a related rectangle.
- Pupils will be able to solve simple word problems that involve finding the area of a triangle.

Activities for whole-class instruction

- Display these statements.

1. If a triangle and parallelogram are on the same base and have identical heights then the area of the parallelogram is double the area of the triangle.
2. An acute triangle has only one height.
3. If the height of a rectangle equals the base of a parallelogram, and the base of the rectangle equals the height of the parallelogram, then the rectangle and parallelogram have the same area.
4. If the base of a triangle doubles, then its area increases by four times.

Work through each statement, with pupils assisting, to consider whether each statement is true or false. Invite pupils to share their views and state the reason for their decision.

- Show pupils this diagram.

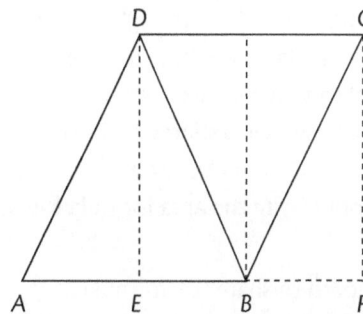

- Remind pupils that if a triangle and a parallelogram are on the same base and between the same pair of parallel lines, then the area of triangle is equal to half the area of the parallelogram. In other words, the area of the parallelogram is double that of the triangle. Use the diagram to illustrate this. Explain that parallelogram *ABCD* and $\triangle ABD$ are on the same base, *AB*, and between the same parallels, *AF* and *DC*. Therefore:

area of $\triangle ABD = \frac{1}{2}$ area of parallelogram *ABCD*

$= \frac{1}{2}(AB \times DE)$ where *AB* is the base and *DE* is the height of $\triangle ABD$ (Since, *DE* is the height of parallelogram *ABCD*.)

Agree that statement 1 is true.

- Draw a triangle on the board and invite a pupil to mark all the pairs of corresponding base and heights. Agree that there are three pairs. Ask pupils if this number of pairs would change for different types of triangles, for example obtuse or acute. Agree that the number does not change and that statement 2 is false.

- Read statement 3 aloud. Ask pupils what they know about the areas of rectangles and parallelograms. Agree that the area is found using the same formulae for both shapes. Remind pupils of the commutative property of multiplication and establish both base multiplied by height for one shape will be equal to height multiplied by base for the other shape. Agree that statement 3 is true.

- Refer to statement 4 and ask pupils to state the formulae for the area of a triangle (half base multiplied by height). Write the formula on the board and invite pupils to substitute values for base and height and calculate the area. They double the base and calculate the area noting that the area doubles. Agree that statement 4 is false.

Same-day intervention

- Display the following statement on the board and ask pupils to decide whether it is true or false.

  Two triangles, X and Y, share the same base. If the area of triangle Y is three times that of triangle X, then the height will also be three times larger than that of triangle X.

  Ask pupils to work in pairs and draw triangles X and Y. Discuss how they should label the base and height of each triangle. Establish that the same letter code should be used for the base as it is shared by both triangles and that $h1$ and $h2$ could be used to represent the heights. Pupils should write the area formula for each triangle.

  Invite a pupil to the board to share the formulae. Expect: A (X) = $\frac{1}{2}bh1$, A (Y) = $\frac{1}{2}bh2$. Establish that $\frac{1}{2}b$ is common to both expressions and will not change. Therefore, if the area was to increase by three times then $h2$ would need to be three times larger than $h1$. If necessary, give pupils the opportunity to substitute values into the expression to check this.

Same-day enrichment

- Instruct pupils to work in pairs to write three or four statements that relate to the properties of a triangle, particularly the calculation of area. At least one of these statements should be false. Pupils then swap statements with other pairs and deduce which of the statements are false. They return their papers for marking.

Question 6

6 Solve these problems.

(a) The height of a triangle is 24 cm and its base is 3 cm more than three times its height. Find its area.

(b) The base of a triangle is 32 cm, which is 7 cm more than its height. What is its area?

(c) The base of a triangle is 0.18 m, which is $\frac{1}{5}$ of its height. Find its area.

What learning will pupils have achieved at the conclusion of Question 6?

- Pupils will be able to solve simple word problems that involve finding the area of a triangle.

Activities for whole-class instruction

- Show this problem:

  The height of a triangle is 15 cm and its base is 5 cm more than four times its height. Find its area.

Ask: *What is the key information here that you need for the calculation? What calculation will you do? What rules about finding the area of a triangle do you need to think about?* Pupils discuss with a partner and share ideas with the class.

Answer: $(4 \times 15) + 5 = 65$, $\frac{1}{2}(15 \times 65) = 487.5 \, \text{cm}^2$

- Show this problem:

  The base of a triangle is 49 cm, which is 11 cm more than its height. What is its area?

Ask: *What is the key information here that you need for the calculation? What calculation will you do? What rules about finding the area of a triangle do you need to think about?* Pupils discuss with a partner and share ideas with the class.

Answer: $49 - 11 = 38$, $\frac{1}{2}(49 \times 38) = 931 \, \text{cm}^2$

● Show this problem:

> The base of a triangle is 0.05 cm, which is $\frac{1}{8}$ of its height.
> Find its area.

Ask: *What is the key information here that you need for the calculation? What calculation will you do? What rules about finding the area of a triangle do you need to think about?* Pupils discuss with a partner and share ideas with the class.

Answer: $0.05 \times 8 = 0.4$, $\frac{1}{2}(0.05 \times 0.4) = 0.01 \, cm^2$

● Pupils should complete Question 6 in the Practice Book.

Same-day intervention

● Provide a guided example for pupils to follow, for example display the following:

> The base of a triangle is 20 cm and its height is 10 cm more than five times its base. Find its area.

Invite a pupil to the board to draw a diagram of the triangle. Ask: *Will the height be bigger than the base? How much greater?* (five times plus 10 cm) They draw an approximately proportional triangle and label the base 20 cm and the height.

● Ask: *Which expression will give the height?* Confirm: $5 \times 20 \, cm + 10 \, cm$. Ask pupils to calculate the height. (110 cm)

● Ask: *What do we do next?* (multiply the base and height) *Why?* Remind pupils that the area formula is half base times height. Ask: *What is the product of base times height?* ($2200 \, cm^2$) Discuss the mental or written strategies employed by pupils. Ask: *Have we found the area of the triangle?* (no) *What else do we need to do?* (halve the answer; divide by 2) *What is the answer?* ($1100 \, cm^2$)

Same-day enrichment

● Show this problem:

> The manager of a construction company is planning to build on a plot of land in the shape of a right-angled triangle. She measures one of the shorter sides of the triangle. The area of the land is 90 000 square metres. If the side measures 360 metres, what is the length of the other shorter side?

Answer: $90\,000 \times 2 = 180\,000$, $360 \times ? = 180\,000$, $180\,000 \div 360 = 500$. Check: $\frac{1}{2}(500 \times 360 = 90\,000 \, m^2$

Challenge and extension questions

Question 7

> **7** In a right-angled triangle *ABC*, ∠*A* = 45°
> and *BC* = 6 cm. Find its area.
> (Drawing not to scale.)

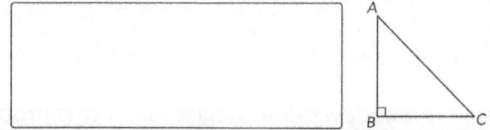

Pupils are presented with a right-angled triangle, given the length of the base and are asked to calculate the area. They are also told that one of the acute angles is 45 degrees. To answer the question, pupils need to recognise that a right-angled triangle with one angle of 45 degrees is an isosceles triangle, and therefore the height is equal to the base.

Question 8

> **8** In a right-angled triangle, the side lengths
> are 3.6 cm, 4.8 cm and 6 cm, respectively.
> Find its area.

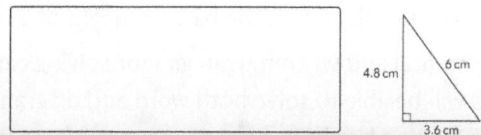

Pupils are given the side lengths of a right-angled triangle and are asked to find the area. To answer the question, pupils must recognise that the longest side given is that of the side opposite the right angle, and is therefore not the base or height. They must calculate the area using the formula with the other two measurements as base and height.

Unit 4.7
Area of a triangle (2)

Conceptual context

In this unit pupils develop strategies for solving problems using the area formula for a triangle that they learned in the previous unit, for example finding a missing base or height when given the area. Some of the problems will be multi-step, for example finding the increase in area given an extension to the base, height (or both) of a triangle. Other problems will involve diagrams where one or more triangles are part of a larger shape, for example a rectangle. Pupils will need to apply mental and written strategies for solving calculations involving the four basic operations, together with problem-solving skills to determine the area of component shapes of representations.

Learning pupils will have achieved at the end of the unit

- Pupils will be able to find the area of a triangle, given the base and height (Q1)
- Pupils will be able to find the base or height of a triangle when given the other and the area (Q2)
- Using mental and written strategies for solving calculations involving the four basic operations, pupils will be able to solve both word and diagrammatic problems that involve the calculation of area, a missing height or base, or the area of a component of a larger geometric structure (Q3, Q4)

Resources

interlocking cubes

Vocabulary

height, base, perpendicular, commutative property of multiplication, equation, 'balancing' an equation

Question 1

1 Look at the figures and calculate the areas of the triangles. (Unit: cm)

(a)

6 7

8

(b)

5 9

12

(c)

9 15

12

What learning will pupils have achieved at the conclusion of Question 1?

● Pupils will be able to find the area of a triangle, given the base and height.

Activities for whole-class instruction

● Display the following diagrams:

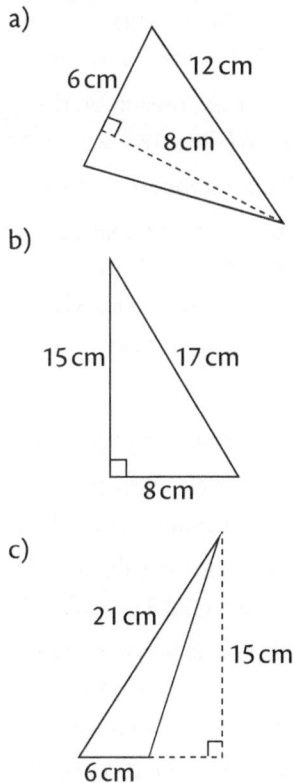

a)

6 cm 12 cm

8 cm

b)

15 cm 17 cm

8 cm

c)

21 cm

15 cm

6 cm

Explain that given the base and height, we need to find the area of each triangle. Give pupils time to answer the problems then discuss solutions.

● Point to diagram a). Ask:

 – *What is the length of the base?* (6 cm)

 – *The height?* (8 cm)

 – *How do you know?* (The height is given by the perpendicular distance from the base to the opposite vertex.)

 – *How do we calculate the area?* (Use the area formula: area = $\frac{1}{2}$ base × height). Ask pupils to calculate the answer. (24 cm^2; $\frac{1}{2}$ of 6 × 8 = $\frac{1}{2}$ of 48)

● Point to diagram b). Ask: *How do we decide which side is the base in this triangle?* Share ideas. Agree that either of the perpendicular sides of a right-angled triangle can be the base. Remind pupils of the commutative property of multiplication and that 8 × 15 will give the same product as 15 × 8. Ask pupils to calculate the area. (60 cm^2; $\frac{1}{2}$ of 8 × 15 = $\frac{1}{2}$ of 120)

● Point to diagram c). Ask: *How do we decide which measurements give the base and height in this triangle?* Share ideas. Establish that as the triangle is obtuse, the height is shown outside the triangle; the height marked by the dashed line that meets the extended base at right angles (15 cm). Ask pupils to calculate the area. (45 cm^2; $\frac{1}{2}$ of 6 × 15 = 3 × 15)

● Pupils should complete Question 1 in the Practice Book.

Same-day intervention

● Look out for pupils who find the area by multiplying base by height and forget to halve the answer. Remind pupils that since a triangle is not a parallelogram the formula for its area will be different to that for a parallelogram.

Same-day enrichment

● Display the following diagram. Ask pupils to find the area of the 'house' shape.

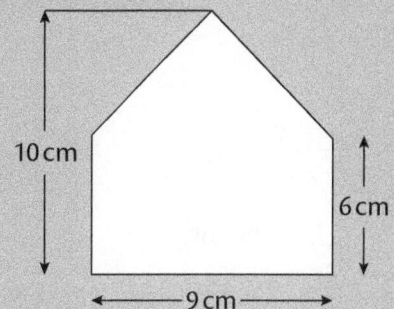

10 cm

6 cm

9 cm

Answer: 9 × 6 = 54, $\frac{1}{2}$(9 × 4) = 18, 54 + 18 = 72 cm^2

Question 2

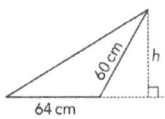

c)

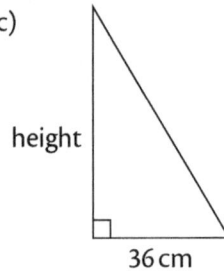

Area = 900 cm²

- Explain that given the area and base or height, we need to find the missing measurement. Give pupils time to answer the problems then discuss solutions.

- Point to diagram a). Ask:
  - *What is the area?* (42 cm²)
  - *The height?* (12 cm)
  - *How do you know?* (The height is given by the perpendicular distance from the base to the opposite vertex.)

Invite a pupil to the board to write the formula for the area of a triangle. Expect: $A = b \times h \div 2$. Substitute the values for A and h in the formula:
$42 = b \times 12 \div 2$ and ask: *How do we find b?* Share ideas.

Demonstrate that the expression on the right can be simplified: $42 = b \times 6$ (since $12 \div 2 = 6$). Ask:
  - *Since we now know 6 times b is 42, what is b?* (7)
  - *How do you know?* Expect pupils to use the multiplication fact $6 \times 7 = 42$ or to comment on the inverse operation: 42 divided by 6 is 7.
  - *What length is the base?* (7 cm)

- Point to diagram b). Ask:
  - *What measurements are we given?* (Area and base)
  - *How do you know which side is the base?* (The extended side 4 cm is perpendicular to the height.)

Invite a pupil to the board to substitute known values in the area formula. Expect: $28.8 = 4 \times h \div 2$.

Ask: *Can we simplify the expression to the right?* Agree $4 \times h \div 2$ can be rewritten as $h \times 4 \div 2$.
Write: $28.8 = h \times 4 \div 2 = h \times 2$ (solving for $4 \div 2$).

Ask: *What is h?* (14.4) *How do you know?*

- Point to diagram c). Ask:
  - *What measurements are we given?* (Area and base)

Invite a pupil to the board to substitute known values in the area formula. Expect: $900 = 36 \times h \div 2$.

Solve for $36 \div 2$ and simplify: $900 = 18 \times h$. Ask: *How do we find h?* (divide by 18) Give pupils time to calculate the answer then confirm $h = 50$ cm.

What learning will pupils have achieved at the conclusion of Question 2?
- Pupils will be able to find the base or height of a triangle when given the other and the area.

Activities for whole-class instruction

- Display the following triangles:

a)

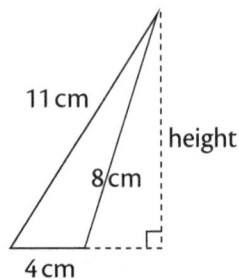

base

12 cm

Area = 42 cm²

b)

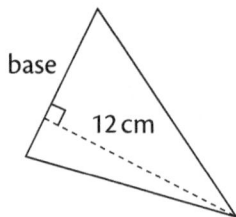

11 cm

height

8 cm

4 cm

Area = 28.8 cm²

• Pupils should complete Question 2 in the Practice Book.

Same-day intervention

• For pupils who find it difficult to recall or apply inverse operations to finding an unknown value in a formula, review the four basic operations (that is, add, subtract, multiply and divide) and give them opportunities to determine the inverse of each by providing example equations: $a + 3 = 7$, $b - 5 = 14$, $3c = 15$, $\frac{d}{4} = 5$. Provide feedback as needed.

• Use manipulatives such as cubes to model the equation $20 = 2 \times 10$. Demonstrate that dividing by 10 on both sides keeps the equation equal, or 'balanced'. Help pupils apply this understanding to the equation $20 = b \times 10$.

Repeat for other examples: $42 = 6 \times 7$ ($42 = 6 \times h$).

Same-day enrichment

• Display the following diagram. Explain that pupils must work out the unknown value y, the area of the rectangle, given the area of the triangle is 180 square centimetres.

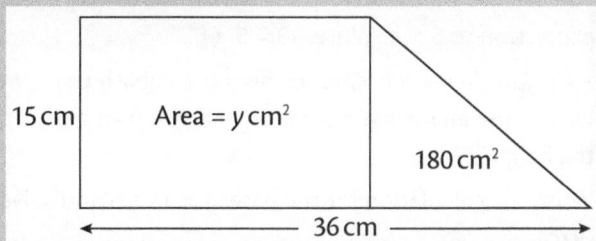

Answer: $180 = \frac{1}{2}(15 \times ?)$, $180 \div 15 = 12 \times 2 = 24$, $36 - 24 = 12$, $12 \times 15 = 180\,\text{cm}^2$, $y = 180$

Question 3

3 Solve these problems.

(a) A flowerbed is shaped like a triangle. The height of this triangle is 18 m which is 8 m less than its corresponding base. What is the area of the triangle?

(b) A triangular-shaped vegetable plot has a base of 24 m and a height of 16 m. If the base is increased by 6 m and the height is increased by 3 m, by how much will the area of the plot be increased?

(c) The figure shows a rectangle *ABCD* with an area of 6600 cm². *AB* is 60 cm and *BE* is 40 cm. Find the area of triangle *CDE*.

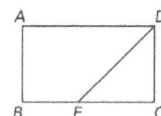

(d) The area of triangle *ABD* in the figure is 24 cm², *BD* is 6 cm and *DC* is 5 cm. Find the area of triangle *ABC*.

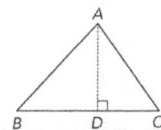

What learning will pupils have achieved at the conclusion of Question 3?

• Using mental and written strategies for solving calculations involving the four basic operations, pupils will be able to solve both word and diagrammatic problems that involve the calculation of area, a missing height or base, or the area of a component of a larger geometric structure.

Activities for whole-class instruction

• Display these problems. Pupil pairs should copy the questions and agree which pieces of information are important, before solving the problems.

(a) The base of a triangular-shaped wall is 20 m, which is 4 m less than its height. What is the area of the wall?

(b) When viewed from above, the floor of an animal enclosure at a zoo has the shape of a triangle. The base of this triangle is 24 m long and its height is 28 m. If the base of the triangle is increased by 4 m and the height of the triangle is increased by 6 m, by how much will the area of the triangle be increased?

(c) The figure shows a rectangle *ACDE* with an area of 4200 cm². *AE* is 50 cm and *BC* is 30 cm. Find the area of the triangle *ABE*.

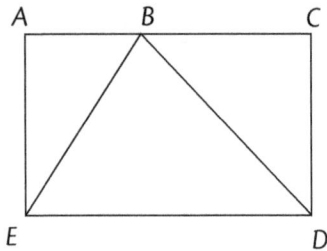

- Discuss question a). Ask:
  - *What is the length of the base of the wall?* Agree, 20 m.
  - *What is the height of the wall?* Agree, 24 m.
  - *How do we work out the area of the wall?* Invite a pupil to the board to substitute the known values in the area formula. Expect: A = 20 × 24 ÷ 2.
  - *What is the most efficient strategy for solving this calculation?* (Divide 20 by 2 (10) then proceed.) A = 10 × 24 = 240.
  - *What is the answer to the question?* Agree the area of the wall is 240 m²
- Discuss question b). Explain that the new area is called *x* and the original area *y*. Invite a pupil to come to the board to substitute values in the area formula to give the area of the new larger enclosure.

  Agree the original area is found by finding the difference between *x* and *y*, and that:

  x = (24 × 28) ÷ 2

  y = [(24 + 4) × (28 + 6)] ÷ 2

  Ask pupils to calculate the answer, simplifying where useful. Agree x = 336, and y = 476 so the increase is 140 m².
- Discuss question c), inserting measurements as they are agreed. Ask: *Do we know the base or height of ABE?* Agree height *AE* is given (50 cm) and base *AB* is not.

  Explain that in diagrammatic problems where we are given triangles inside a rectangle, missing side measurements for triangles are usually found by first finding the dimensions of the outer rectangle.
- Ask: *What other measurements can we calculate?* Agree the height and area of the rectangle are known so the width can be calculated (84 cm) and so *AB* can be found. (54 cm)
- Now the base and height of triangle *ABE* are known so the area can be calculated:

  54 × 50 ÷ 2 = 54 × 25 = 1350 cm².

- Pupils should complete Question 3 in the Practice Book.

Same-day intervention

- Display the following problem on the board:

  A triangle-shaped lawn has the following measurements: base 10 m and area 45 m². What is the height of the triangle given the area of the triangle and its base?

  Ask pupils to draw a diagram of the lawn and to mark and label the base, area and height. Have them share their diagrams and confirm that the measurements are correct and marked appropriately. Reinforce that the height is the perpendicular distance from the base to the opposite vertex.

  Ask: *Which formula would you use to find the height of the triangle?* Agree that the formula for the area of a triangle should be used. Write: A = b × h ÷ 2. Ask: *Which values have we been given?* (Area and base) Invite a pupil to the board to substitute the values in the formula: 45 = 10 × h ÷ 2.

  Point to the expression 10 × h ÷ 2. Ask: *Can we simplify the expression to the right?* Accept comments and establish that since 10 ÷ 2 is 5 we can simply the expression to 5 × h. Write: 45 = 5 × h.

  Ask: *How do we calculate the height?* Establish that we can use an inverse operation of division to give the height.

  Write the calculation for the base: h = 45 ÷ 5 and solve. (9 m)

Same-day enrichment

- Display the following diagram. Ask pupils to work out the area of the triangular head of the arrow.

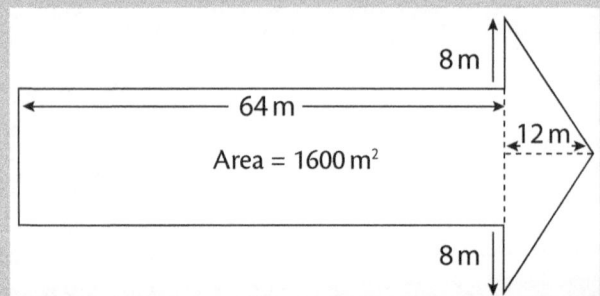

Answer: 1600 ÷ 64 = 25, 25 + 8 + 8 = 41, $\frac{1}{2}$(12 × 41) = 246 m²

Question 4

4 Complete each statement.

(a) The area of a parallelogram is 10 m². If a triangle has its base and height equal to the base and height of the parallelogram, then the area of the triangle is ☐ m².

(b) If the base of a triangle is increased to twice its original length and the height is increased to three times its original length, then the area is increased to ☐ times its original area.

(c) The area of a triangle is the same as the area of a parallelogram and their heights are also equal. If the base of the parallelogram is 100 cm, then the base of the triangle is ☐ cm.

(d) The figure shows a right-angled triangle ABC. If AB = 3 cm, BC = 4 cm and AC = 5 cm, then BD = ☐ cm.

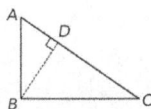

What learning will pupils have achieved at the conclusion of Question 4?

- Using mental and written strategies for solving calculations involving the four basic operations, pupils will be able to solve both word and diagrammatic problems that involve the calculation of area, a missing height or base, or the area of a component of a larger geometric structure.

Activities for whole-class instruction

- Display these problems. Pupil pairs should copy the questions and agree which pieces of information are important, before solving the problems.

a) The area of a parallelogram is 20 m². If a triangle has its base and height equal to the base and height of the parallelogram, then the area of the triangle is ___.

b) If the base of a triangle is increased to four times its original length and the height is increased to six times its original length, then the area is increased to __ times its original area.

c) The area of a triangle is the same as the area of a parallelogram and their heights are also equal. If the

base of the parallelogram is 50 cm, then the base of the triangle is ___ cm.

d) The figure shows a right-angled triangle ABC. If AB = 9 cm, BC = 12 cm and AC = 15 cm, then BD = ___ cm.

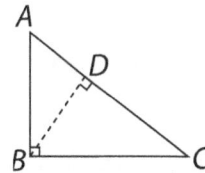

- Discuss question a). Ask: *If a parallelogram and a triangle share the same base and height, what does this tell us?* Accept comments and establish that the area of the triangle will be half that of the parallelogram, that is 10 m².

- Discuss question b). On the board, write the formula for the area of a triangle (A = b × h ÷ 2). Ask:
  - *If the base is increased to four times its original length and the height is increased to six times its original length, how would we represent this?* Agree that if b and h are the original measurements then after enlargement the base would become 4b and the height would become 6h. Ask a pupil to write the calculation for the area of the enlarged triangle. Expect: A = 4b × 6h ÷ 2.
  - *How much bigger will the area of the new triangle (4b × 6h ÷ 2) be?* Together, expand the calculation to give 4 × b × 6 × h ÷ 2 = 24 × b × h ÷ 2. Agree the new area is 24 times bigger.

- Discuss question c) Establish that the area calculation for both the parallelogram and the triangle must give the same answer. Write: l × w = b × h ÷ 2.

  Explain that since the heights of the parallelogram and triangle are equal we can rewrite the equation as l × h = b × h ÷ 2. Demonstrate that dividing both sides by h gives l = b ÷ 2. Agree the base of the triangle is twice that of the base of the parallelogram, that is 100 cm.

- Discuss question d) Establish that:
  - BD is the perpendicular distance from AC to B. Therefore, AC is the base of the triangle and the height must be found.
  - The area of the triangle area is half that of the rectangle and we can calculate the area of the rectangle because we know the two sides (AB = 9 cm and BC = 12 cm).
  - Agree the area of the triangle is half of 9 × 12, that is 54 cm².
  - Once the area and base are known, the height can be calculated. So:

$54 = b \times h \div 2$

$54 = \frac{b}{2} \times h$ or $b \times \frac{h}{2}$

$54 = 7.5 \times h$

$h = 7.2\,\text{cm}.$

Same-day intervention

● Show this problem:

> The area of a triangle is the same as the area of a parallelogram and their bases are also equal. If the height of the parallelogram is 80 cm, then the height of the triangle is ___ cm.

Work through the calculation as a guided example. Ask the following questions to elicit thinking:

- *Which measurements do both shapes have in common?*

- *Using area formulas, how would you write a number sentence to represent this equivalence in area?*

- *Show me how you would substitute known values into the equivalent expressions.* Write: $80 \times b = b \times h \div 2$.

- *How would you simplify both sides of the equation to give just the height of the triangle?* (Divide both sides of the equation by b.) Write: $80 = h \div 2$.

- *How would you use an inverse operation to give h?* (Use the inverse operation of multiplication to give h.) Write: $h = 80 \times 2 = 160$.

- *What is the height of the triangle?* (160 cm)

Same-day enrichment

● Display the following problem for pupils to solve:

> An isosceles triangle is drawn inside a rectangle and both share the same base and height. If the two congruent sides of the triangle are 13 cm, its perimeter is 36 cm and its height is 15 cm, how much bigger is the area of the rectangle than that of the triangle?

Challenge and extension questions

Question 5

5 What is the sum of the areas of the shaded parts in the figure?

Pupils are presented with three triangles inscribed in a rectangle. All three triangles are the same height as the rectangle and divide the length of the rectangle between their bases. Pupils are asked to find the combined area of the three triangles. To answer the question, pupils must recognise that the area of a single triangle can be split into smaller triangles that have the same height and combined base length, according to the distributive property of multiplication over addition.

Question 6

6 The area of triangle *ABC* in the figure on the right is 48 cm² and the length of *BD* is twice that of *DC*. Find the area of triangle *ABD*.

Pupils are presented with a triangle divided into two by a line segment from the vertex to a point on the base that divides the base by a ratio of 2 : 1. Given the area of the whole triangle, pupils must find the area of the larger of the two component triangles. To answer the question, pupils must recognise that area and base are in a proportional relationship: dividing the base by a 2 : 1 ratio will divide the area by a 2 : 1 ratio.

Unit 4.8
Practice and exercise (2)

Conceptual context

This unit uses and extends pupils' geometrical reasoning skills in the following areas: parallel and perpendicular lines, properties of parallelograms and the area of parallelograms and triangles. The questions test pupils' problem-solving strategies and their ability to visualise geometrical objects and work with them mentally or on paper.

Learning pupils will have achieved at the end of the unit

- Pupils will have applied their knowledge of the properties of parallel and perpendicular lines to identify them in geometrical objects, including triangles and parallelograms, and infer information (Q1, Q2)
- Pupils will be able to solve both multi-step word and diagrammatic problems that involve the calculation of the area of a shape or the component of a larger geometric structure (Q3, Q4)

Resources

squared or dotted paper; paper shape tiles (cut-outs of parallelograms, rectangles, squares and triangles)

Vocabulary

parallel lines, perpendicular lines, congruent, height, base, area

Questions 1 and 2

1 Complete each statement.

(a) When two lines intersect to form a right angle, the two lines

are _____ to each other.

(b) A parallelogram has ☐ pairs of parallel lines.

(c) A triangle has ☐ pairs of parallel lines.

(d) In a rectangle, there are ☐ pairs of sides perpendicular to each other and ☐ pairs of sides parallel to each other.

(e) A parallelogram and a triangle have the same area and the same height. The base of the parallelogram is 2a. The base of the triangle is ☐ .

2 Multiple choice questions. (For each question, choose the correct answer and write the letter in the box.)

(a) There are ☐ perpendicular line(s) between two parallel lines.

   A. 0   B. 1

   C. 2   D. infinitely many

(b) In the following statements, the correct one is ☐ .

   A. There are four pairs of parallel lines in a parallelogram.

   B. The four sides of a square are perpendicular to each other.

   C. The four sides of a square are parallel to each other.

   D. Both squares and rectangles are special parallelograms.

(c) In the figure below, a // b. The areas of △ABC, △EBC, and △FBC are denoted by $S_{\triangle ABC}$, $S_{\triangle EBC}$ and $S_{\triangle FBC}$, respectively.

   The correct statement is ☐ .

   A. $S_{\triangle ABC}$ is the largest.

   B. $S_{\triangle EBC}$ is the largest.

   C. $S_{\triangle FBC}$ is the largest.

   D. The areas are all the same.

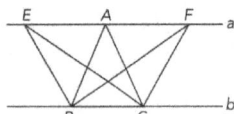

What learning will pupils have achieved at the conclusion of Questions 1 and 2?

- Pupils will have applied their knowledge of the properties of parallel and perpendicular lines to identify them in geometrical objects, including triangles and parallelograms, and infer information.

Activities for whole-class instruction

- Provide pupils with squared or dotted paper. Ask them to draw the following geometrical objects: a right angle, a triangle, a non-rectangular parallelogram, a rectangle and a square.

  Ask pupils to look at the two lines that intersect to form a right angle. Ask: *What is the relationship between the lines?* Agree they are perpendicular to each other.

Referring to the parallelogram, ask: *How many pairs of parallel lines does a parallelogram have?* Pupils should mark them on the shape. Tell pupils that when we draw a pair of parallel lines, we use an arrow mark (>) on each of the lines to show that the lines are parallel.

Ask: *How many pairs of parallel lines does a triangle have?* Agree none.

Referring to the rectangle, ask pupils to tell a partner about the relationships between the sides. Share ideas. Draw a rectangle and confirm that the shape has two pairs of parallel sides and two pairs of perpendicular sides.

Repeat this for a square and confirm that, like a rectangle, a square has two pairs of parallel sides and two pairs of perpendicular sides. Remind pupils that a square is a special example of a rectangle and that both shapes are special examples of a parallelogram because they all have two pairs of parallel sides.

- Draw a parallelogram and a triangle. Tell pupils that both have the same height and area. Mark and label the height (*h*) of both shapes. Mark the base of the parallelogram, 4*a* and the base of the triangle, *b*. Pupil pairs should work out the length of the base of the triangle given the length of the base of the parallelogram. Share ideas.

  Together, use the formula for the area of the parallelogram, to agree that the base is 4*a*, so the area of the parallelogram as 4*a* × *h*. Write 4*a* × *h* below the parallelogram.

  Together, label the triangle to show *h* and *b* and write the formula for the area of the triangle below it. Pupils should write an expression that shows what is known about the two shapes that will help work out the base of the parallelogram (the original question). Agree:

  $4a \times h = \frac{(h \times b)}{2}$

  Ask: *How can we simplify both expressions?* (Divide both sides by *h*.) Write: $4a = \frac{b}{2}$. Agree that *b* must be 8*a*.

- Draw a pair of parallel lines. Invite a pupil to the board to draw a perpendicular line between them. Ask: *How many more could be drawn?* Agree that an infinite number can be drawn.

- Draw three triangles that share the same base and height. Ask: *Given that these triangles all have the same base and height, is there another measurement that they all share?* Agree, area.

Same-day intervention

- On a large piece of squared paper, draw a right angle, a triangle, a non-rectangular parallelogram and a rectangle. Draw the shapes so that parallel sides lie on the grid lines. Together, mark right angles with the appropriate symbol (a small box). Ask: *What do we call lines that meet at a right angle?* Agree, perpendicular.

  Ask: *Which lines are parallel?* Pupils should mark pairs of parallel lines. Ask: *How do you know the lines are parallel?* Ensure pupils can explain that they follow the grid lines which remain the same distance apart along their lengths and never meet.

- Draw a parallelogram divided into two triangles along one diagonal. Together, write the area formulae for a parallelogram and a triangle. Confirm that for the same base and height, the triangle is half the area of the parallelogram.

Same-day enrichment

- Pupil pairs should sit on opposite sides of a barrier, each with a tray of shape tiles (paper cut-outs): parallelograms, rectangles, squares and triangles. Pupils take turns to describe a 'secret' shape to their partner. They must use geometrical language in their description that includes reference to perpendicular and parallel sides, angle size and side length. Pupils score five points if they guess after the first clue; four points after the second clue, three points after the third, and so on.

Questions 3 and 4

3 The figure shows a piece of rectangular lawn with a length of 40 m and a width of 30 m. There are two paved paths through it. The width of each path is 2 m. Find the area of the lawn.

4 To cut out an acute-angled triangle with a base of 3 cm from a rectangle of 4 cm × 6 cm, the greatest possible area of the acute-angled triangle that could be

cut out is [ ] cm².

(Hint: the base of the triangle can be horizontal or vertical or in another position. You may use a drawing to help find the answer.)

What learning will pupils have achieved at the conclusion of Questions 3 and 4?

- Pupils will be able to solve both multi-step word and diagrammatic problems that involve the calculation of the area of a shape or the component of a larger geometric structure.

Activities for whole-class instruction

- Show the following:

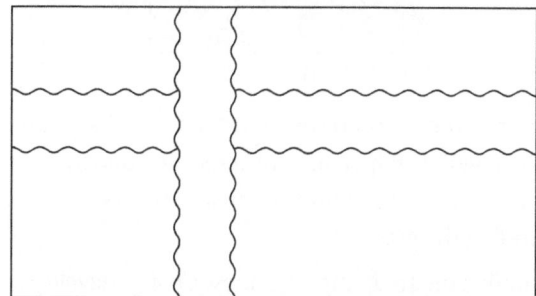

- Explain that a farmer has divided a field into four sections by planting two long hedges perpendicular to each other and parallel with the sides of the field. The length of the field is 60 m, its width is 40 m and the width of each hedge is 2 m. Ask pupils to find the area of field that is not planted with hedges.

  Give pupils time to discuss the problem then accept solutions. Establish that the four sections can be considered as one rectangle with dimensions (60 m – 2 m) by (40 m – 2 m). The area can be found by the formula, A= $b \times h$ (58 m × 38 m = 2204 m^2).

- Display the following rectangle on the board:

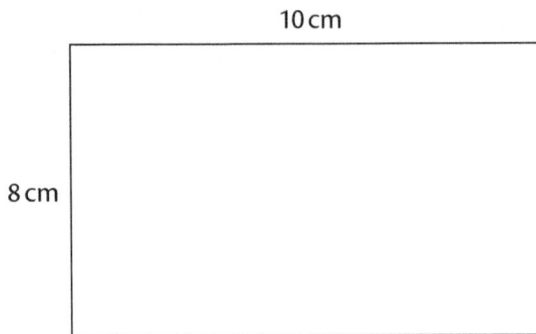

10 cm

8 cm

Ask pupils to copy the rectangle. Explain that you want them to draw an acute-angled triangle with a base of 5 cm anywhere inside the rectangle. The triangle should be drawn so that it has the maximum possible area.

- Give pupils time to discuss the problem then share ideas. Establish that the height needs to be as great as possible. This is done by positioning the base on the shorter side and drawing a triangle with height equivalent to the length of the longer side. Ask: *What is the area of the triangle?* (25 cm^2; (5 × 10) ÷ 2)

Same-day intervention

- Display the following image:

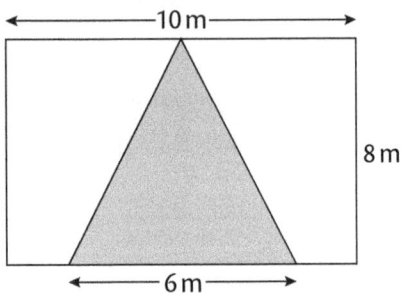

10 m

8 m

6 m

Explain that the diagram shows a plan view of a garden, with a triangular-shaped area of grass surrounded by stones. Ask pupils to find the area of stones surrounding the grass.

Give pupils time to discuss the question and develop a strategy to solve the problem. Ask:

- *The area of stones is the difference between the areas of which two shapes?*
- *How would you find the area of the grassy triangle?*
- *How would you find the area of the rectangle?*
- *Tell me the calculation that would give the area of stones.*

Work through the problem as a class. Establish that the area of stones is the difference between the area of the rectangle and the triangle. Invite pupils to the board to calculate the areas of each shape using the appropriate formulae (Rectangle: 10 m × 8 m = 80 m^2; Triangle: 6 m × 8 m ÷ 2 = 24 m^2) and then determine the difference. (80 m^2 – 24 m^2 = 56 m^2)

Same-day enrichment

- Display the following diagram:

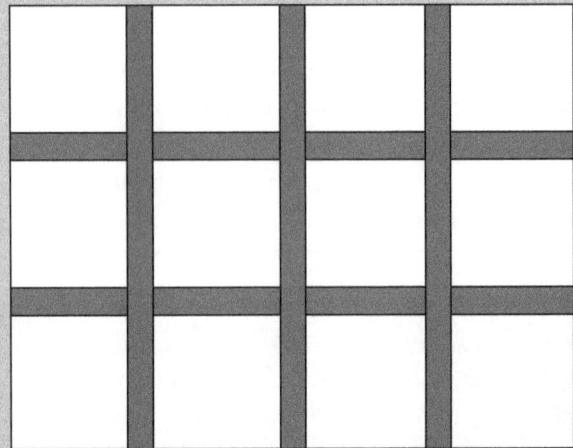

Explain that five pieces of timber divide the glass in a large window into twelve sections. The five pieces of wood are perpendicular to each other and parallel with the sides of the window frame. The length of the window is 12 m, its width is 7 m and the width of each piece of wood is 0.5 m. Ask pupils to find the combined area of the glass panels.

Answer: Establish that the twelve sections can be considered as one rectangle with dimensions (12 m – (3 × 0.5 m)) by (7 m – (2 × 0.5 m)). The area can be found by the formula, A = $b \times h$ (10.5 m × 6 m = 63 m^2).

Challenge and extension question

Question 5

5　The figure shows a rectangle ABCD. AD is 18 cm and AB is 15 cm. E is the midpoint of BC (that is, BE = EC) and F is the midpoint of CD. Find the area of triangle AEF.

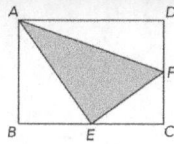

Pupils are presented with a triangle inscribed in a rectangle. The dimensions of the rectangle are given. Also, one vertex is shared between the rectangle and the triangle while the other two vertices of the triangle are positioned at the midpoint of two sides of the rectangle. Pupils are asked to work out the area of the inscribed triangle. To do so, they must recognise that the area of the triangle is found by subtracting the area of the three surrounding triangles from that of the rectangle.

Chapter 4 test (Practice Book 6A, pages 136–140)

Test Question number	Relevant Unit	Relevant questions within unit
1	Unit 4.2	Q1, Q2, Q3, Q4, Q5, Q6
	Unit 4.1	Q1, Q2, Q3, Q4, Q5, Q6
	Unit 4.3	Q1, Q2, Q3, Q4, Q5, Q6
	Unit 4.4	Q1, Q2, Q3, Q4, Q5, Q6
2	Unit 4.5	Q1, Q2, Q3
	Unit 4.6	Q1, Q2, Q3
	Unit 4.7	Q1, Q2, Q3
3	Unit 4.5	Q1, Q2, Q3, Q4
	Unit 4.6	Q1, Q2, Q3, Q4
	Unit 4.7	Q1, Q2, Q3, Q4
4	Unit 4.5	Q1, Q2
	Unit 4.6	Q1, Q2
	Unit 4.7	Q1, Q2
5	Unit 4.6	Q1
	Unit 4.7	Q1
6	Unit 4.5	Q1
7	Unit 4.6	Q1
	Unit 4.7	Q1
8	Unit 4.5	Q1
	Unit 4.6	Q1
	Unit 4.7	Q1
9	Unit 4.5	Q1
	Unit 4.6	Q1
	Unit 4.7	Q1
10	Unit 4.6	Q1
	Unit 4.7	Q1

Chapter 5
Consolidation and enhancement

Chapter overview

Area of mathematics	National Curriculum statutory requirements for Key Stage 2	Shanghai Maths Project reference
Number – multiplication and division	Year 5 Programme of study: Pupils should be taught to: ■ solve problems involving addition, subtraction, multiplication and division and a combination of these, including understanding the meaning of the equals sign.	Year 6, Units 5.3, 5.4, 5.5
Measurement	Year 5 Programme of study: Pupils should be taught to: ■ measure and calculate the perimeter of composite rectilinear shapes in centimetres and metres.	Year 6, Unit 5.5
Measurement	Year 6 Programme of study: Pupils should be taught to: ■ solve problems involving the calculation and conversion of units of measure, using decimal notation up to two decimal places where appropriate ■ use, read, write and convert between standard units, converting measurements of length, mass, volume and time from a smaller unit of measure to a larger unit, and vice versa, using decimal notation to up to three decimal places.	Year 6, Unit 5.7 Year 6, Unit 5.7
Geometry – properties of shapes	Year 5 Programme of study: Pupils should be taught to: ■ use the properties of rectangles to deduce related facts and find missing lengths and angles.	Year 6, Unit 5.5

Algebra	Year 6 Programme of study: Pupils should be taught to: ■ express missing number problems algebraically.	Year 6, Units 5.3, 5.4, 5.5
Geometry – properties of shapes	Year 6 Programme of study: Pupils should be taught to: ■ illustrate and name parts of circles, including radius, diameter and circumference and know that the diameter is twice the radius ■ recognise angles where they meet at a point, are on a straight line, or are vertically opposite, and find missing angles.	Year 6, Unit 5.6
Number – fractions (including decimal and percentages)	Year 6 Programme of study: Pupils should be taught to: ■ multiply one-digit numbers with up to two decimal places by whole numbers ■ use written division methods where the answer has up to two decimal places ■ solve problems which require answers to be rounded to specified degrees of accuracy.	Year 6, Units 5.1, 5.2 Year 6, Unit 5.1, 5.2 Year 6, Unit 5.1

Pre-requisite knowledge

For pupils to be successful with the work in this chapter, they will need to have achieved mastery in their learning in previous relevant units. Teaching there will have introduced and developed concepts and skills that are necessary to work with the content in this chapter. A summary of pre-requisite knowledge is set out in the table below. If you believe that some pupils need to revisit particular areas, the units in which it was taught are also shown in the table so that you can locate appropriate guidance in Teacher's Guides and Practice Books. Guidance provided for Chapter 5 on the following pages will therefore focus on new learning.

Pre-requisite knowledge, understanding or skill	Where this was taught in The Shanghai Maths Project
Pupils recognise the number of minutes in one hour and the number of seconds in one minute, and can apply these facts to calculations and problems involving time.	Year 2, Unit 7.1 Year 3, Unit 5.1
Pupils are able to calculate intervals of time as well as using known information to derive an unknown start or end time.	Year 2, Unit 7.3 Year 3, Unit 5.4
Pupils can read and understand 24-hour digital clock times.	Year 3, Unit 5.2
Pupils understand and apply the laws of operation.	Year 1, Unit 3.6 Year 2, Units 4.6, 5.4, 5.5 Year 4, Units 10.11, 10.12, 10.13, 10.14 Year 6, Unit 2.4
Pupils understand and apply brackets appropriately.	Year 4, Units 10.3, 10.5, 10.6 Year 5, Units 5.3, 5.4, 5.5, 5.6
Pupils can apply their understanding of the perimeter of rectangles.	Year 3, Units 10.6, 10.7 Year 4, Units 9.2, 9.3
Pupils understand and apply ratio in context.	Year 5, Units 3.1, 3.2
Pupils understand the concept of negative numbers.	Year 5, Units 7.1, 7.2, 7.3, 7.4
Pupils understand how to calculate with decimals.	Year 5, Units 6.3, 6.4, 6.5, 6.6, 6.7 Year 6, Units 1.2, 1.3, 2.1, 2.2, 2.3, 2.4, 2.5, 2.6, 2.7, 2.8, 2.11
Pupils can simplify algebraic expressions with understanding.	Year 6, Units 3.3, 3.4
Pupils can evaluate algebraic expressions with understanding.	Year 6, Units 3.3, 3.4
Pupils apply their understanding to solving equations.	Year 6, Units 3.1, 3.2, 3.3, 3.4, 3.5, 3.6, 3.7, 3.8, 3.9, 3.10
Pupils apply their understanding to establishing equations and solving them.	Year 6, Units 3.2, 3.3, 3.4, 3.5, 3.6, 3.7, 3.8, 3.9, 3.10
Pupils can measure and calculate the perimeter of a rectilinear figure (including squares) in centimetres and metres.	Year 4, Units 9.2, 9.3
Pupils are able to find the area of rectilinear shapes by counting squares.	Year 4, Unit 9.4
Pupils can calculate the area of parallelograms and triangles.	Year 6, Units 4.5, 4.6, 4.7

Unit 5.1
Operations of decimals (1)

Conceptual context

In this unit, pupils will revisit calculations with decimal numbers. Their concepts of laws of operations are applied increasingly fluently as they make decisions about efficient ways to calculate with decimals.

Learning pupils will have achieved at the end of the unit

- Conceptual understanding about calculation methods will have been strengthened through working in the context of decimal numbers (Q1, Q2, Q3)
- Pupils will be able to use known facts and relationships to infer other facts (Q4, Q5)
- Pupils will be able to calculate accurately with decimal numbers (Q1, Q2, Q3, Q4, Q5)

Resources

place value sliders; **Resource 6.5.1** Making connections

Vocabulary

relationship, decimal, quotient, product

Questions 1, 2 and 3

1 Work these out mentally. Write the answers.

(a) 2.7 + 7.2 = ☐

(b) 7.1 − 2.9 = ☐

(c) 5.25 × 4 = ☐

(d) 40 ÷ 25 = ☐

(e) 10.6 − 0.6 × 15 = ☐

(f) 1.4 ÷ 8 × 12 = ☐

2 Choose the column method to calculate the following.

(a) 24 × 10.5   (b) 4.35 × 328   (c) 49 + 14   (d) 77.55 ÷ 33

3 Work these out step by step. (Calculate smartly if possible.)

(a) 7.25 ÷ 25 + (4.38 − 2.61)

(b) 1.25 × 56 ÷ 7

(c) (172.5 − 72.5) × 0.12 ÷ 10

(d) 48 × 7.6 + 3.4 × 48 − 48

What learning will pupils have achieved at the conclusion of Questions 1, 2 and 3?

- Conceptual understanding about calculation methods will have been strengthened through working in the context of decimal numbers.
- Pupils will be able to calculate accurately with decimal numbers.

Activities for whole-class instruction

- Display on the board:

  a) 28 + 42
  b) 453 ÷ 3
  c) 108 − 97
  d) 13 × 16

  Ask pupils to calculate the results mentally. Discuss strategies. Pupils should explain:

  - how they partitioned the numbers
  - what connections and inferences they made
  - what 'facts' they used.

- Alongside the first list of calculations, display:

  e) 2.8 + 4.2
  f) 45.3 ÷ 3
  g) 10.8 − 9.7
  h) 1.3 × 16

  Ask pupils to calculate the results mentally. Discuss strategies. Pupils should explain:

  - how they partitioned the numbers
  - what connections and inferences they made
  - what 'facts' they used
  - how they used the first list to help with the second.

  Agree that strategies used with whole numbers can also be used with decimal numbers.

- Ask pupils to use the column method to calculate: 371 × 15, 371 × 1.5 and 371 × 0.15. Allow time for completion and share ideas. Pupils should see the similarities between calculating with integers and with decimal numbers. (5565; 556.5; 55.65)

- Pupils should complete Questions 1, 2 and 3 in the Practice Book.

Same-day intervention

- Use **Resource 6.5.1a** Making connections, to support pupils in perceiving the relationship between integer and decimal calculation strategies.

Answers: **1.** 155, 310, 465; 15.5, 31.0, 46.5; **2.** 270, 900, 1170; 27.0, 90.0, 117.0; **3.** 135, 1350, 1485; 1.35, 13.50, 14.85; **4.** 063 (or 63), 630, 693; 06.3 (or 6.3), 63.0, 69.3

Same-day enrichment

- Show pupils the following.

> **Words and pictures**
>
> In Question 2(a) you used the column method to work out 24 × 10.5.
>
> Sarah says, 'I don't need to use the column method for that. I can do it in my head.'
>
> How do you think Sarah might have worked out the product mentally?
>
> Draw a picture to explain why your method works.
>
> Matilda says, 'I worked out 12 × 21 because I knew that would give the answer to 2(a).'
>
> Why does Matilda's strategy work? Draw a picture to explain why her method works.

Working in pairs, pupils should work through the problem and explain their pictures to each other.

Questions 4 and 5

4　Complete each statement.

(a) If 7.6 × 237 = 1801.2, then 0.76 × 2370 = ☐

and 1801.2 ÷ 76 = ☐ .

(b) 3.89 × 20 = 38.9 × ☐   23 ÷ 110 = 2.3 ÷ ☐

2.8 × 34 = ☐ × 17

0.9 ÷ 15 = 9 ÷ ☐ = 3 ÷ ☐ = ☐ ÷ 100

(c) If A × 1.5 = B × 1.1 = C × 0.3 = D × 0.1 (A, B, C and D are all greater than 0), then the greatest of these four numbers is ☐ and the least number is ☐ .

(d) 54 × 3.2 + 32 + 32 × ☐ = 320

5　Multiple choice questions. (For each question, choose the correct answer and write the letter in the box.)

(a) When a = 128 × 0.25, and b = 128 × 0.2, the relationship between a and b is ☐ .

A. a > b   B. a = b   C. a < b   D. uncertain

(b) In all the decimal numbers with three decimal places that are rounded to 0.80, the difference between the greatest and the least is ☐ .

A. 0.004   B. 0.005   C. 0.009   D. 0.01

What learning will pupils have achieved at the conclusion of Questions 4 and 5?

- Pupils will be able to use known facts and relationships to infer other facts.
- Pupils will be able to calculate accurately with decimal numbers.

Activities for whole-class instruction

- Use a spider diagram to explore the relationships between different calculations.

Write 11 × 12 = 132 in the centre of a spider diagram.

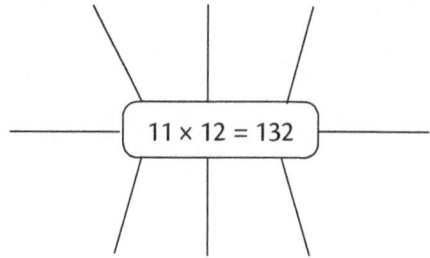

Ask pupils, working in pairs, to record as many related calculations on the diagram as possible. They should include decimal numbers and division calculations.

Share ideas, asking some pupils to record theirs on the board. Talk about the connections between the integer calculations and the decimal calculations. Agree that the calculations and thinking used with integers can also be used with decimal numbers.

- Pupils should complete Questions 4 and 5 in the Practice Book.

Same-day intervention

- Use three place value sliders alongside a spider diagram. Write each of the numbers on different place value sliders and arrange the sliders with the operator between them like this:

☐1 6.☐☐☐ × ☐2 3.☐☐☐ = ☐3 6 8.☐☐☐

Work with pupils to adjust one slider at a time and notice the adjustments that are needed on the other slider (or sliders) to ensure that the calculation is correct.

Record the results in a spider diagram.

Same-day enrichment

- Tell pupils that 1 × 2 × 3 × 4 × 5 × 6 × 7 × 8 × 9 × 10 = 3 628 800 and ask them to use this to calculate 0.1 × 0.2 × 0.3 × 0.4 × 0.5 × 0.6 × 0.7 × 0.8 × 0.9 × 1.0. (0.000 362 88)

Challenge and extension questions

Question 6

> 6 A lorry travelled 18 km in 0.6 hours. How many kilometres did the lorry travel in one minute? How many minutes would it take the lorry to travel 1 km?

It is likely that pupils will need support in working with time as a decimal. You might like to ask them how many minutes make up 0.5 of an hour, then move on to asking how many minutes make up 0.6 of an hour to support them in understanding the need for conversion.

Question 7

> 7 Short division is a shorthand method for long division. Observe the following example carefully and complete the short division as indicated below. (For question (b), express the answer as a whole number plus a remainder.)
>
> Example: 123.5 ÷ 5   (a) 279.6 ÷ 12   (b) 923 ÷ 7
>
> ```
>      2 4 . 7
>   5 ) 1 2²3³. 5          12) 2 7 9 . 6      7 ) 9 2 3
> ```
>
> Answer: 24.7   Answer: [ ]   Answer: [ ]

This question introduces short division to pupils, offering a simple example and then two questions for pupils to work on. Challenge pupils to make sense of the example (working in pairs will allow for discussion). Pupils may find that working through the example using the column method will support them in making sense of it.

Unit 5.2
Operations of decimals (2)

Conceptual context

In this unit, pupils revisit the use of the order of operations with decimal numbers.

Learning pupils will have achieved at the end of the unit

- Pupils will have revisited and deepened their understanding of the order of operations (Q1, Q2, Q3, Q4)
- Pupils will have built fluency in calculating with decimal numbers (Q1, Q2, Q3, Q4)
- Pupils will be able to look for connections to support them in calculating smartly (Q3)

Resources

Resource 6.5.2a Tree diagrams; **Resource 6.5.2b** Pairs

Vocabulary

decimal number, product, quotient, order of operations

Questions 1 and 2

1 Work these out mentally. Write the answers.

(a) $2 - 0.55 + 0.45 = \boxed{}$

(b) $14.4 + 4.4 \times 6 = \boxed{}$

(c) $0.4 + 0.6 \div 5 = \boxed{}$

(d) $1.8 \div 5 \times 20 = \boxed{}$

2 Work these out step by step.

(a) $21.45 - 2.45 \times 4 + 7.8$

(b) $(2.82 + 2.8 \times 9) \div (0.6 + 2.4)$

(c) $72 \times 0.75 - 36.36 \div 18$

(d) $5.5 \div 5 \times 2 \div (2.82 + 2.18)$

(e) $16.73 + 3.75 \div 75 \times 48$

(f) $(4.5 - 0.45) \div (0.1 + 0.3 \times 3)$

(g) $7.85 + (3.9 - 3.51) \div 3$

(h) $(36 \times 1.25 + 3) \times 0.25 - 1.28$

What learning will pupils have achieved at the conclusion of Questions 1 and 2?

- Pupils will have revisited and deepened their understanding of the order of operations.
- Pupils will have built fluency in calculating with decimal numbers.

Activities for whole-class instruction

- On the board, write: $0.7 + 1.4 \div 7 \times 2$. Ask pupils: *How should we do this calculation?*

  Discuss strategies. Pupils should be able to explain the order of operations and the use of brackets.

- Now show pupils these calculations:

$0.7 + 1.4 \div 7 \times 2 = 0.6$
$0.7 + 1.4 \div 7 \times 2 = 1.8$
$0.7 + 1.4 \div 7 \times 2 = 1.1$
$0.7 + 1.4 \div 7 \times 2 = 0.15$

  Working in pairs, ask pupils to copy the calculations and add brackets so that each answer is correct. Discuss responses and use them to remind pupils of the order of operations.

Answers:

$(0.7 + 1.4) \div 7 \times 2 = 0.6$

$(0.7 + 1.4 \div 7) \times 2 = 1.8$

$0.7 + 1.4 \div 7 \times 2 = 1.1$

$(0.7 + 1.4) \div (7 \times 2) = 0.15$

- Pupils complete Questions 1 and 2 in the Practice Book.

Same-day intervention

- Provide pupils with **Resource 6.5.2a** Tree diagrams, which shows the number sentences used in the whole-class task represented as tree diagrams.

  Together, relate the tree diagrams to the number sentences, drawing attention to the hierarchy of operations and the way that the use of brackets can change this.

  Work with pupils to write the last two tree diagrams as number sentences and evaluate the calculations.

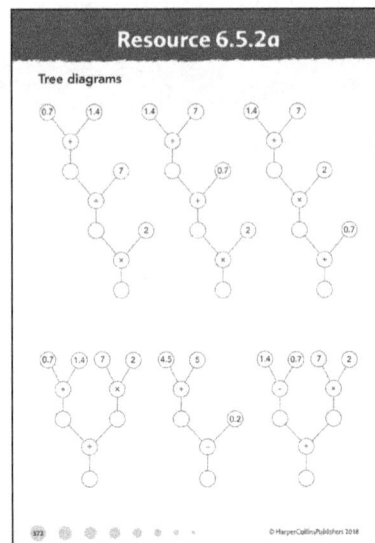

Resource 6.5.2a

Tree diagrams

Answers: 2.1, 0.3, 0.6; 0.2, 0.9, 1.8; 0.2, 0.4, 1.1; 2.1, 14, 0.15; 0.9, 0.7; 0.7, 14, 0.05

Same-day enrichment

- Show pupils this tree diagram.

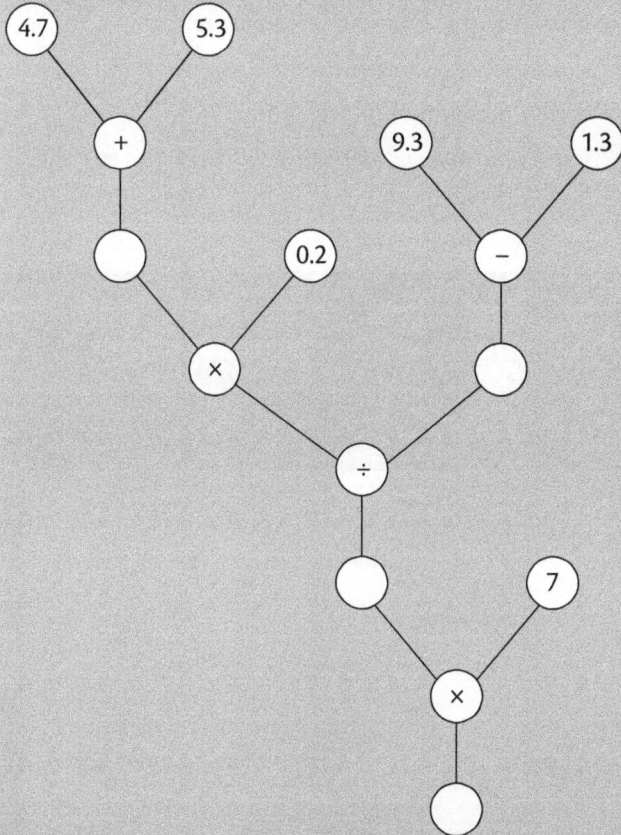

Working in pairs, ask pupils to use the order of operations to write this as a single number sentence, and to find the answer.

Questions 3 and 4

3 Calculate smartly.

(a) $28.7 - 4.32 - 2.68$

(b) $82.6 - 22.6 - 41.19 + 1.19$

(c) $0.5 \times 1.25 \times 2.5 \times 64$

(d) $79 \times 1.25 + 1.25$

(e) $4.75 \div 3 + 2.3 \div 3$

(f) $4.8 + 4.8 \times 7 - 4.8 \times 6$

(g) $1.64 + 99 \times 4.5 + 2.86$

(h) $5.5 \times 7 - 2 \times 5.5 + 4.5 \times 5$

4 A factory is contracted to produce work suits. According to its original plan, it needs 24 workers for 12.5 days to finish the job, and each worker will process 140 suits every day. How many suits are there in this contract?

Now, under the new plan, each worker processes 10 more suits every day so the task can be completed 2.5 days earlier than the original plan. How many more workers are needed?

What learning will pupils have achieved at the conclusion of Questions 3 and 4?

- Pupils will have revisited and deepened their understanding of the order of operations.
- Pupils will be able to look for connections to support them in calculating smartly.
- Pupils will have built fluency in calculating with decimal numbers.

Activities for whole-class instruction

- Show pupils a game in which they take turns to complicate a calculation. Start by writing on the board: $0.8 = 0.8$.

Invite a pupil to play the game at the board with you. Underline one of the numbers and write it in a more complex way.
For example:

$0.8 = \underline{0.8}$

$0.8 = 0.3 + 0.5$

Now another player underlines a number and writes that in a more complex way.

0.8 = <u>0.8</u>

0.8 = <u>0.3</u> + 0.5

0.8 = (0.6 ÷ 2) + 0.5

Repeat, creating increasingly complex calculations.

In pairs, pupils should play the game, using the same starting calculation but expanding it in their own ways.

Discuss how calculations are often not as complex as they might at first appear to be.

Remind pupils that looking for connections such as numbers that add or multiply to whole numbers is a useful strategy when calculating with decimal numbers.

- Pupils should complete Questions 4 and 5 in the Practice Book.

Same-day intervention

- Use **Resource 6.5.2b** Pairs to work with pupils to match the equivalent calculations.

  While working, discuss with pupils the clues that they are looking for to identify the matching calculations.

Resource 6.5.2b

Answers: **1.** a) and b). They are both equal to 10 lots of 3.2; **2.** a) and c). 2.96 + 1.04 = 4, so they are both equal to the total of 4.67 and 4; **3.** b) and c). 4.8 + 1.1 equals 5.9, so they are both equal to 5.9 ÷ 2; **4.** a) and b). 2.5 × 4 = 10, so they are both equal to 10 × 2 × 1.7.

Same-day enrichment

- Pupils play the game used in the whole-class task but add some extra restrictions. For example:
  - insist that all numbers used are decimal numbers
  - do not allow addition
  - insist that all expansions use numbers with at least two decimal places.

Challenge and extension question

Question 5

5 The table shows a summary of the gas and electricity bill of Jason's family for the last quarter of 2018. Answer the questions below based on the table (excluding other charges, such as standing charges and VAT).

	Usage	Unit price
Gas (Unit: m³)	764	44.21p
Electricity (Unit: kWh)	963	12.02p

(a) How much was the monthly charge for the usage of gas?

(b) How much was the monthly charge for the usage of electricity?

(c) How much was the total charge for the family to pay for the use of gas and electricity in the quarter?

(d) Can you pose a question based on the information given in the table? Write it down and give your answer.

This question uses a utilities bill to provide a context for pupils to calculate with decimals. Pupils may need support in interpreting the bill and knowing how the monthly charge is calculated.

Unit 5.3
Simplification and equations (1)

Conceptual context

This unit revisits simplification of algebraic expressions and the use of equations to solve problems. Pupils will deepen their understanding of simplification and consolidating methods for solving equations. There are also opportunities to solve application problems.

Learning pupils will have achieved at the end of the unit

- Pupils will have deepened their understanding of simplification (Q1)
- Fluency in solving equations will have been developed through practice with equations presented in different ways (Q2, Q3)
- Pupils will be able to establish and solve equations based on information presented in descriptions of real-life scenarios and application problems (Q4, Q5)

Resources

mini whiteboards; 0–100 number cards; lettered flashcards; blank cards; counters; **Resource 6.5.3a** Match expressions; **Resource 6.5.3b** Find solutions; **Resource 6.5.3c** Equations and solutions; **Resource 6.5.3d** Problem solving (1)

Vocabulary

simplify, expression, algebra, equation, solve, solution, expansion

Question 1

> 1 Simplify the following expressions.
>
> (a) $3a + 2a =$ _____
> (b) $12y \div 3 =$ _____
>
> (c) $8b - 7b =$ _____
> (d) $7x - 4x \div 2 =$ _____
>
> (e) $2x \times 8 - x =$ _____
> (f) $4a - 7b - 3a - 5b =$ _____

What learning will pupils have achieved at the conclusion of Question 1?

- Pupils will have deepened their understanding of simplification.

Activities for whole-class instruction

- Show each of these expressions separately and ask pupils to simplify them:

> $8t + 3t$
> $3s - 2s$
> $14h \div 2$
> $20p - 10p \div 2$
> $8t \times 3$
> $4 \times 4h - h$

Answers: $11t$; $1s$; $7h$; $5p$; $24t$; $15h$

Ask pupils to draw a bar model to represent each expression.

In pairs, pupils should generate eight of their own expressions for their partner to simplify.

- Show each of these equations separately and ask pupils to decide if they are true or false.

> $4t + 2t = 7t$
> $4s - 4s = 0$
> $21d \div 3 = 7$
> $25h - 16h \div 2 = 17h$
> $10k \times 4 = 40k$
> $6 \times 3g - h = 18gh$

Answers: False; True; False; True; True; False

- Now show pupils these equations:

> $c + c + c - c + d + d = 2c + 3d$
> $12z \div 4 + r + 3z + r = 2r + 6z$
> $4x + y - 2x \div 2 + y = 3x + 2y$
> $5r - 3r + t + t + r = 4r + 2t$
> $8s - s + y - 3s - 3y = 4s - 2y$
> $2r \times 5 + r - s = 10r - s$

Answers: False; True; True; False; True; False

In pairs, pupils decide if the equations are true or false. Discuss conclusions.

- Pupil pairs should generate eight of their own true/false equations. Then swap with another pair who should decide whether they are true/false and explain their reasoning.

- Pupils should complete Question 1 in the Practice Book.

Same-day intervention

- Show pupils these calculations:

> $5 \times 4 + 12$
> $7 \times 7 - 5 \times 3$
> $20 \div 5 + 4 - 3$

Answers: 32; 34; 5

Ask pupils to find the answers to the calculations. Share answers.

- Show pupils these equations and together, decide if they are true or false.

> $3a + 2a = 5a$
> $5a + a - b - b = 6a - 3b$
> $4a \div 2 + 4 = 2a + 4$

Answers: True; False; True

- Use bar modelling to support pupil understanding.

Same-day enrichment

- Show pupils the following.

> $3t - 4r - 3t - 5r$

- Ask them to make a spider diagram by drawing lines from the shape and write equivalent expressions at the end of them. Remind them that they could use (,) , $+, -, \times, \div$, zero, integers, decimals and fractions.

Questions 2 and 3

---

2 Use different methods to solve the equations.

(a) $9x \div 5 = 3.6$

Method 1:

Method 2:

(b) $10(x + 0.15) = 5$

Method 1:

Method 2:

---

3 Solve the equations. (Check the answers to the questions marked with *.)

(a) $6(x - 1.5) = 15$

(b) $5(x + 0.24) = 2.65$

(c) $13x - 27 = 10x$

(d) $17x - 4 \times 2.7 = 57.2$

(e) $*3(2x - 5) \div 12 = 2.5$

(f) $*11(x - 3) = 5.5 \times 4$

What learning will pupils have achieved at the conclusion of Questions 2 and 3?

- Fluency in solving equations will have been developed through practice with equations presented in different ways.

Activities for whole-class instruction

- Write on the board: $5(2a + t) = 5 \times 2a + 5 \times t$. Ask: *Is the equation true or false?* Agree true. Ask: *What could be written after $5 \times 2a + 5 \times t$?* Agree $10a + 5t$.

- Write on the board: $3s + 5s - 6t - 2t = 8s - 8t$. Ask: *Is the equation true or false?* Agree true. Ask: *What could be written after $8s - 8t$?* Agree $8(s - t)$.

Look out for ... pupils who do not understand expansion of brackets. Use this array to support understanding:

	5
$2a$	$10a$
t	$5t$

$5 \times (2a + t) = 5 \times 2a + 5 \times t$

$5 \times (2a + t) = 10a + 5t$

$5 \times (2a + t) = 2a + 8a + 5t$

- Write on the board: $\_\_(e + 2.5t) = 3\_\_ + \_\_.5t$. Ask: *What is missing from the equation?* Pupils discuss in pairs. Can they show $3(e + 2.5t) = 3e + 7.5t$?

Share ideas.

- Show pupils these incomplete equations and ask pupils to work in pairs to complete them.

$4(d + 0.5r) = 4d + \_\_$

$3e - 4r + \_\_ = 2(5e - 2\_\_)$

$\_\_ + 5(e + 2f) \div 5 = 5 + \_\_ + \_f$

$4(0.5a - \_\_b + 3a) - 2 \times \_\_ = \_\_a - b - 6$

Answers: $4(d + 0.5r) = 4d + 2r$; $3e - 4r + 7e = 2(5e - 2r)$; $5 + 5(e + 2f) \div 5 = 5 + e + 2f$; $4(0.5a - 0.25b + 3a) - 2 \times 3 = 14a - b - 6$

Share responses.

- Working in pairs, ask pupils to complete **Resource 6.5.3a** Match expressions, matching expressions with simplified versions. Explain that there are missing answers and one mistake to correct. Pupils match the cards and share their solutions.

Resource 6.5.3a

Match expressions

$3n + p - 2n + 4p$	$n + 5p$	$3(4x + 5y - 2y)$
$12x + 13y$	$4a \div 2 \times 11$	_____
$10 \times 4a + 8 - 9a$	_____	$7e \times 5 - 3e$
$32e$	$2(4r + 2r - 4y + 2)$	$\_(3\_ -y)$

Answers: Correction: $12x + 13y$ should be $12x + 9y$; Missing answers: $22a$; $-4a$; $4(3r - y)$.

- Show pupils these equations:

$H + 5 = 18$

$J - 7.5 = 3.5$

$4h = 20$

$10x \div 2 = 20$

Answers: $H = 13$; $J = 11$; $h = 5$; $x = 4$

For each equation ask: *What is the solution of this equation?* Discuss responses.

- Show pupils these equations:

$$3e + 9 = 12$$
$$4b = 13b - 4.5$$
$$10c \div 4 = 7.5$$
$$4(d - 4.5) = 6$$

For each equation ask:

- *What steps are needed to solve this equation?*
- *Is there more than one way to solve it?*
- *How can the solution be checked?*

Pupils discuss responses in pairs. Encourage the use of bar models to support their understanding. Discuss conclusions.

Can they show, for example:

$$3e + 9 = 12$$
$$3e = 12 - 9$$
$$3e = 3$$
$$e = 3 \div 3$$
$$= 1$$

Check: $3 \times 1 + 9 = 12$.
It checks.

$$4b = 13b - 4.5$$
$$13b - 4b = 4.5$$
$$9b = 4.5$$
$$b = 4.5 \div 9$$
$$= 0.5$$

Check: $4 \times 0.5 = 13 \times 0.5 - 4.5$.
It checks.

- Or

$$4b = 13b - 4.5$$
$$130b - 40b = 45$$
$$90b = 45$$
$$b = 45 \div 90$$
$$= 0.5$$

Check: $4 \times 0.5 = 13 \times 0.5 - 4.5$.
It checks.

$$10c \div 4 = 7.5$$
$$10c = 7.5 \times 4$$
$$10c = 30$$
$$c = 30 \div 10$$
$$= 3$$

Check: $10 \times 3 \div 4 = 7.5$.
It checks.

- Or

$$10c \div 4 = 7.5$$
$$100c = 75 \times 4$$
$$100c = 300$$
$$c = 300 \div 100$$
$$= 3$$

Check: $10 \times 3 \div 4 = 7.5$.
It checks.

$$4(d - 4.5) = 6$$
$$d - 4.5 = 6 \div 4$$
$$d - 4.5 = 1.5$$
$$d = 1.5 + 4.5$$
$$= 6$$

Check: $4(6 - 4.5) = 6$.
It checks.

- Or

$$4(d - 4.5) = 6$$
$$4d - 18 = 6$$
$$4d = 6 + 18$$
$$4d = 24$$
$$d = 24 \div 4$$
$$= 6$$

Check: $4(6 - 4.5) = 6$.
It checks.

- Show pupils these equations:

$$7c \div 6 = 3.5$$
$$2.8 = 10d \div 4 - 3$$
$$8(y - 1.5) = 4$$
$$5 = 6(2z - 5) \div 6$$

Answers: $c = 3$; $d = 2.32$; $y = 2$; $z = 5$

In pairs, ask pupils to solve each equation in as many different ways as they can. Discuss responses.

- Give pupils **Resource 6.5.3b** Find solutions, and ask them to complete section A in pairs, finding the solutions to the given equations. Two methods need to be used for the starred questions.

Answers: **1.** 6.35; **2.** 2.75; **3.** 5; **4.** 1.75; **5.** 2.8; **6.** 0.75; **7.** 7.5; **8.** 1.6; **9.** 5.5; **10.** 0.05; **11.** 1.5; **12.** 2.5

- Pupils should complete Questions 2 and 3 in the Practice Book.

Same-day intervention

- Write on the board: $5x - 4 = 6$. Represent the equation using counters and cards. Together, draw a bar model of the equation:

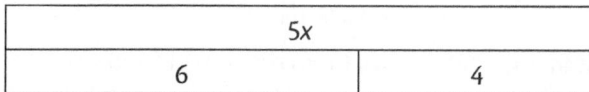

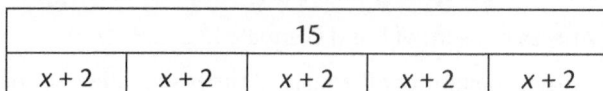

5x	
6	4

Then together set out the working, moving counters to show the step, as each line is written:

$$5x - 4 = 6$$
$$5x = 6 + 4$$
$$5x = 10$$
$$x = 10 \div 5$$
$$= 2$$

Check: $5 \times 2 - 4 = 6$.
It checks.

- Write on the board: $5(x + 2) = 15$. Ask pupils: *What operation is not shown between 5 and the first bracket?* Agree ×.

Together, draw a bar model of the equation:

15				
x + 2	x + 2	x + 2	x + 2	x + 2

Set out the working:

$$5(x + 2) = 15$$
$$x + 2 = 15 \div 5$$
$$x + 2 = 3$$
$$x = 3 - 2$$
$$= 1$$

Check: $5(1 + 2) = 15$.
It checks.

Together, draw an array to show expansion of brackets:

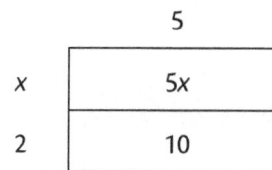

	5
x	5x
2	10

Then together, set out the working

$$5(x + 2) = 15$$
$$5x + 10 = 15$$
$$5x = 15 - 10$$
$$5x = 5$$
$$x = 5 \div 5$$
$$= 1$$

Check: $5 (1 + 2) = 15$.
It checks.

Same-day enrichment

- Pupils complete section B of **Resource 6.5.3b** Find solutions, using the given answers to create their own equations. They can use section A for examples.

Question 4

4 In each question below, write the equation and then find the solution.

(a) Three times a number is divided by 2 and the quotient is 2.4. Find this number.

(b) Five times the sum of Number A and Number B is 19.25. Number B is 1.28. Find Number A.

(c) Number A is 1.5. Twelve times Number A equals 24 times the difference between Number B and 2.25. Find Number B.

What learning will pupils have achieved at the conclusion of Question 4?

- Pupils will be able to establish and solve equations based on information presented in descriptions of real-life scenarios and application problems.

Activities for whole-class instruction

- Give pupils **Resource 6.5.3c** Equations and solutions, to complete. They use shading to match equations with their solutions.

Answers: $H = 3$; $x = 1.5$; $a = 3$; $b = 7.5$; $c = 3$; $d = 5.5$; $e = 0.75$; $f = 5$

Discuss responses.

- Check pupils' understanding of establishing an equation by asking quickfire questions, for example:

  Show me three times a number.
  Change $4 \div x = 5$ into words and include the word 'quotient'.
  Show me 6 times the sum of a and b.
  Change $24 = g(v - 2)$ into words and include the word 'difference'.

- Show pupils two lists:

Equation	Word form
$4x + 5y = 25$	Seven times a number equals 4 times the difference of g and 5.25.
$23s = 5 - 5t$	Fourteen is the quotient of 7 times $7c$ and a letter.
$7 \times 7c \div z = 14$	The sum of four times a number and five times a number is 25.
$5(4d + f) = 30$	The difference of 5 and 5 times a number equals 23 times a number.
$7a = 4(g - 5.25)$	Five times the sum of f and 4 times a number is 30.

In pairs, pupils should match corresponding equations with the word form.

Equation	Word form
$4x + 5y = 25$	The sum of four times a number and five times a number is 25.
$23s = 5 - 5t$	The difference of 5 and 5 times a number equals 23 times a number.
$7 \times 7c \div z = 14$	Fourteen is the quotient of 7 times $7c$ and a letter.
$5(4d + f) = 30$	Five times the sum of f and 4 times a number is 30.
$7a = 4(g - 5.25)$	Seven times a number equals 4 times the difference of g and 5.25.

Share ideas.

- In pairs, pupils should generate eight of their own equations and their equivalent word forms. Each pair then matches the equations for another pair. They should explain their reasoning.

- Show pupils these statements:

Five times a number divided by 4 equals 3.5.
Three times a number D is the difference of six and three times a number T, $T = 1.25$.
2.8 is the quotient of six times a number and 3.
7 times the sum of F and G equals 12.6, $G = 1.34$.
8 times the number R equals 12 times the difference of a number S subtracted by 4.5, $R = 2.25$.

Answers: 2.8; 0.75; 1.4; 0.46; 6

In pairs pupils, write the equations and then solve them. Share responses.

- Pupil pairs should generate eight of their own equations in word form and solve them. Each pair then solves the equations for another pair. They should explain their reasoning.

● Pupils should complete Question 4 in the Practice Book.

Same-day intervention

● Show pupils these statements:

> The sum of 7 times x and 6 is 20.
>
> 5 is 3 less than 4 times r.
>
> 7 times the difference of 6 and R is 28.
>
> The quotient of T and 6 is 3 times 1.5.

Together, focus on the meanings of the words and use bar modelling/arrays to represent the statements. Then establish the equations, using counters and cards. Solve the equations.

Answers: $7x + 6 = 20$, $x = 2$; $4r - 3 = 5$, $r = 2$; $7(6 - R) = 28$, $R = 2$; $T \div 6 = 3 \times 1.5$, $T = 27$

Same-day enrichment

● Show pupils these solutions to equations:

> 4
> 1.5
> 3.25
> 2.2

Ask pupils to create statements and equations with these solutions.

Question 5

> **5** Solve these problems.
>
> (a) A family in a village cultivated 1580 m² of potato crop last year, which was 120 m² less than twice that of the area the year before last. How many square metres was the area of potatoes cultivated by the family the year before last?
>
> (b) A school bought 22 footballs, which was 8 more than half the number of the basketballs it bought. How many basketballs did the school buy?

What learning will pupils have achieved at the conclusion of Question 5?

● Pupils will be able to establish and solve equations based on information presented in descriptions of real-life scenarios and application problems.

Activities for whole-class instruction

● Show pupils these equations:

> $5s - 25 = 20$
>
> $0.5x = 7.5$
>
> $6p + 4f = 15$, $p = 1.5$
>
> $4y \div 2 = 4.8$
>
> $12A = 2.5(C - 3.25)$, $A = 3$

Answers: 9; 15; 1.5; 2.4; 17.65

Ask pupil pairs to create word forms and solve each equation. They should explain their reasoning to each other. Discuss responses.

● Show pupils this problem:

> An office received 25 kg of paper on Tuesday. This was 7 kg less than two times the amount of paper it received on Monday.
>
> How much paper was received on Monday?

Ask questions such as:

- *What is the question asking?*
- *What is the problem that needs to be solved?*
- *What do we need to find out/work out?*
- *Is the problem about a whole and its parts?*
- *Is it a problem about something being a number of times bigger or smaller than something else? Is it about something else? How do we know?*
- *What operations are going to be used?*
- *What is the calculation that needs to be done? If there is more than one step, in what order should the steps be carried out?*

Together, draw a bar model to represent the problem:

2x	
25	7

Ask: *What equation should be established?*
Agree: $2x - 7 = 25$ or $2x - 25 = 7$.

Ask: *Using 2x – 7 = 25, how is the working and check set out? Agree:*

$$2x - 7 = 25$$
$$2x = 25 + 7$$
$$2x = 32$$
$$x = 32 \div 2$$
$$= 16$$

Check: $2 \times 16 - 7 = 25.$
It checks.

● Show this problem:

> A road sweeper drove 35 km on Monday morning. This was 7 km more than half the distance it drove on Friday. How many km did the road sweeper travel on Friday?

Ask pupils questions as in the previous problem.

Together, draw a bar model to represent the problem:

35	
0.5x	7

Ask: *What equation should be established? Agree:*

$0.5x + 7 = 35$ or $35 - 0.5x = 7.$

Ask: *Using 0.5x + 7 = 35, how could the working and check be set out? Agree, for example:*

$$0.5x + 7 = 35$$
$$0.5x = 35 - 7$$
$$0.5x = 28$$
$$x = 28 \div 0.5$$
$$= 56$$

Check: $0.5 \times 56 + 7 = 35.$
It checks.

● In pairs, ask pupils to complete section A of **Resource 6.5.3d** Problem solving (1), creating equations to solve the real-life problems.

Answers: **1.** 4 kg; **2.** 32 km; **3.** 7600 litres;
4. 6000 customers; **5.** 42 km; **6.** 50 hours; **7.** 3040 miles;
8. 4500 tonnes

● Pupils should complete Question 5 in the Practice Book.

Same-day intervention

● Display on the board:

> Josef walked 5 km today. This is 4 km less than the distance he walked yesterday.

Ask: *How many kilometres did Josef walk yesterday? Use counters to agree 9 km.*

● Display on the board:

> Fatima walked 6 km yesterday. This is 5 km more than she walked today.

Ask: *How many kilometres did Fatima walk today? Use counters to agree 1 km.*

● Display on the board:

> Muhammed walked 6 km this afternoon. This is 2 km less than twice the distance he walked this morning.

Together, draw a bar model to represent the problem and establish its equation:

x		x	
6			2

Agree: $2x - 2 = 6$ or $2x - 6 = 2.$

Together, solve the equation, asking pupils to explain the different steps:

$$2x - 2 = 6$$
$$2x = 6 + 2$$
$$2x = 8$$
$$x = 8 \div 2$$
$$= 4$$

Check: $2 \times 4 - 2 = 6.$
It checks.

● Repeat with a problem that creates $0.5P + 4 = 10.$

Same-day enrichment

● Ask pupils to complete section B of **Resource 6.5.3d**
Problem solving (1), creating equations to solve the
real-life problems.

Resource 6.5.3d 3 of 3

B

1. A recycling centre collected 3000 tonnes of rubbish in 2016 and again in 2017. In
2018 it collected 250 tonnes less than three quarters the total for 2016 and 2017.
How many tonnes of rubbish were collected in 2016, 2017 and 2018 altogether?

2. A petrol station served 250 motorists every day last week. This week it predicts it
will serve 1.2 times last week's total amount.
If the prediction is correct, how many motorists would be served over the
two weeks?

© HarperCollinsPublishers 2018

Answers: **1.** 6750 tonnes; **2.** 3850 motorists

Challenge and extension question

Question 6

6 Fill in the missing numbers.

(a) (☐ − 3.6) ÷ 5 × 7 + 4.8 = 7.6

(b) [12 × (☐ + 6) − 1.5] ÷ 4 = 102

This question provides further opportunity for
rearranging an equation to find an unknown number. It
consolidates the use of inverse operations.

Unit 5.4
Simplification and equations (2)

Conceptual context

This is the second unit of two units consolidating simplification and equations. Pupils will reinforce their understanding of evaluation, consolidate methods for solving equations and solve application problems.

Learning pupils will have achieved at the end of the unit

- Pupils' understanding of evaluation of algebraic expressions and methods for solving equations will have been reinforced (Q1, Q2)
- Pupils will be able to apply their knowledge about algebra to solve real-world problems (Q3)

Resources

0–100 number cards; lettered flashcards; blank cards; counters; **Resource 6.5.4a** Card match; **Resource 6.5.4b** Create equations; **Resource 6.5.4c** Problem solving (2)

Vocabulary

simplify, expression, algebra, equation, solve, solution, expansion, evaluate

Questions 1 and 2

1 Simplify and then evaluate.

(a) When $x = 3.5$, find the value of $5x + 3x \times 5$.

(b) When $m = 10$ and $n = 4.8$, find the value of $8m + 3n \div 2 - 5m$.

2 Solve the equations. (Check the answers to the questions marked with *.)

(a) $25x \div 5 + 14 = 24$

(b) $3(8 + x) \div 2 = 18$

(c) $35 - x = 4x$

(d) $5(2x + 3) = 20$

(e) $(4x + 6) \div 3 = 7$

(f) $90 - 4(x + 1) = 10$

(g) $*3(9x - 5x) = 27$

(h) $*9.6 \div (6x - 1.6) = 4.8$

What learning will pupils have achieved at the conclusion of Questions 1 and 2?

- Pupils' understanding of evaluation of algebraic expressions and methods for solving equations will have been reinforced.

Activities for whole-class instruction

- Discuss these equations. Pupils should decide if the equations are true or false, explaining their reasoning.

$5t + 3t + 3e - 5t = 13t + 3e$

$3s - 4 \times 2r + s + r = 4s - 7r$

$14h \div 2 + h - 3 \times h = 5h$

$2 \times 5p + 3q - 10p \div 2 - 2q = 6pq$

$3e - 7 \times c + 2e - 12c \div 6 = 5e - 9c$

$3(3t + q) - 9t - 3q = 0$

Answers: False; True; True; False; True; True

Discuss responses.

- Write on the board: $4s - 7r$.

  Ask: *How is the value of 4s − 7r found if s = 4 and r = 2?* Can pupils see:

  $4 \times 4 - 7 \times 2 = 2$

  Discuss conclusions.

- Write on the board: $14h \div 2 + h - 3 \times h$.

  Ask: *How is the value of 14h ÷ 2 + h − 3 × h found if h = 4?* Pupils should see:

  - the expression needs to be simplified to $5h$ first

  - $5 \times 4 = 20$.

  Discuss conclusions.

- Write on the board:

  $3e - 7 \times c + 2e - 12c \div 6$.

  Ask: *How is the value of 3e − 7 × c + 2e − 12c ÷ 6 found if c = 2 and e = 4?* Pupils should see:

  - the expression needs to be simplified to $5e - 9c$

  - $5 \times 4 - 9 \times 2 = 2$.

  Discuss conclusions.

- Working in pairs, pupils should find the values of the following expressions.

$2c + 3c + 2d + 4d$, where $c = 1$ and $d = 2$
$4x + 2y - 2x + y$, where $x = 4$ and $y = 2$
$12z \div 4 + 3z$, where $z = 2$
$2 \times 6p + 3q - 12p \div 2 + 3q$, where p = 1.5 and $q = 2$
$2e - 5 \times c + 3e - 10c \div 5$, where $c = 1.1$ and $e = 2.5$

  Answers: $5c + 6d$, 17; $2x + 3y$, 14; $6z$, 12; $6p + 6q$, 21; $5e - 7c$, 4.8

  Share ideas.

- Ask pupil pairs to generate eight of their own expressions that they can evaluate. Each pair then evaluates the expressions for another pair. They should explain their reasoning.

- Show these equations and for each equation, ask: *How can the equation be solved? How can the solution be checked?* Pupil pairs should discuss.

$45 - y = 4y$
$14x \div 2 + 12 = 26$
$4(2.5 + c) \div 2 = 14$
$6.2 \div (4x - 3.2) = 3.1$

  Encourage the use of bar models to support their understanding.

  Can they see, for example:

  $45 - y = 4y$

  $4y + y = 45$

$5y = 45$

$y = 45 ÷ 5$

$= 9$

Check: 45 − 9 = 4 × 9.

It checks.

$14x ÷ 2 + 12 = 26$

$7x + 12 = 26$

$7x = 26 − 12$

$7x = 14$

$x = 14 ÷ 7$

$= 2$

Check: 14 × 2 ÷ 2 + 12 = 26.

It checks.

Or

$14x ÷ 2 + 12 = 26$

$14x ÷ 2 = 26 − 12$

$14x ÷ 2 = 14$

$7x = 14$

$x = 14 ÷ 7$

$= 2$

Check: 14 × 2 ÷ 2 + 12 = 26

It checks.

$4(2.5 + c) ÷ 2 = 14$

$4(2.5 + c) = 14 × 2$

$4(2.5 + c) = 28$

$(2.5 + c) = 28 ÷ 4$

$2.5 + c = 7$

$c = 7 − 2.5$

$= 4.5$

Check: 4(2.5 + 4.5) ÷ 2 = 14.

It checks.

Or

$4(2.5 + c) ÷ 2 = 14$

$4(2.5 + c) = 14 × 2$

$4(2.5 + c) = 28$

$10 + 4c = 28$

$4c = 28 − 10$

$4c = 18$

$c = 18 ÷ 4$

$= 4.5$

Check: 4(2.5 + 4.5) ÷ 2 = 14.

It checks.

$6.2 ÷ (4x − 3.2) = 3.1$

$4x − 3.2 = 6.2 ÷ 3.1$

$4x − 3.2 = 2$

$4x = 2 + 3.2$

$4x = 5.2$

$x = 5.2 ÷ 4$

$= 1.3$

Check: 6.2 ÷ (4 × 1.3 − 3.2) = 3.1.

It checks.

Discuss conclusions.

- In groups of four, pupils should cut out cards from **Resource 6.5.4a** Card match to complete the 'follow me' cards, creating a loop. The answer to each question is on a different card.

Answers: $2x − 4 = 5$, $x = 4.5$; $32c ÷ 8 + 15 = 40$, $c = 6.25$; $52 − d = 7d$, $d = 6.5$; $(5x + 7) ÷ 3 = 8$, $x = 3.4$; $4(2x − 3) = 30$, $x = 5.25$; $80 − 7(x+1) = 20.5$, $x = 7.5$; $2(11x − 6x) = 34$, $x = 3.4$; $8.2 ÷ (5x − 1.4) = 4.1$, $x = 0.68$; $42 − 8d = 12$, $d = 3.75$; $24e ÷ 6 + 15 = 60$, $e = 11.25$; $8.1 ÷ (9x − 1.5) = 2.7$, $x = 0.5$; $60 − 3(2x − 4) = 7.8$, $x = 10.7$

- Pupils should complete Questions 1 and 2 in the Practice Book.

Same-day intervention

- Show pupils these expressions:

> $4v$
> $5w$
> $4v + 5w$

Make two sets of 'cards' labelled v and w.

Represent each expression using cards and ask: *What does the expression mean if $v = 3$ and $w = 5$? How do we find the value of the expression?*

Repeat for $7r - 5t$, $14t \div 2 + 2w$, and so on.

- Show these equations:

> $4 - 3e = 2e$
> $3(x + 2) = 6$
> $10a \div 2 + 1 = 4$

Represent each equation using counters and cards, and a bar model.

Together, set out the working for each equation, moving counters to show the step, as each line is written.

Same-day enrichment

- Ask pupils to create their own set of 'follow me' cards about solving equations, using **Resource 6.5.4b** Create equations.

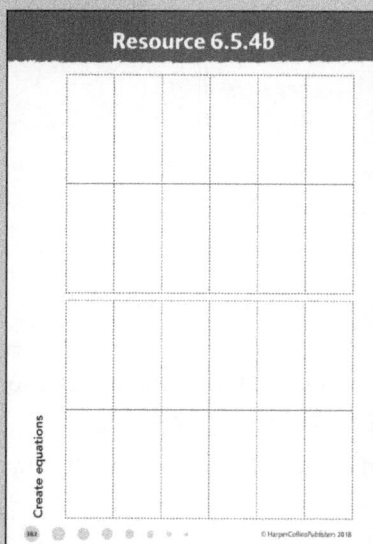

Resource 6.5.4b

Question 3

3 Use equations to solve these problems.

(a) A pigeon can fly 4.8 km in 0.4 hours. Based on this speed, how many hours does the pigeon need to fly 18 km?

(b) A shop received a batch of apples and pears. The weight of apples was 270 kg, which was 24 kg more than 1.5 times that of the pears. How many kilograms of pears did the shop receive?

(c) There are two bags of corn. The first bag weighs 150 kg. If 30 kg of corn is taken out of the first bag and put into the second bag, then the remaining corn in the first bag will be 10 kg more than the second bag. How many kilograms of corn were in the second bag to begin with?

(d) There are 6 boxes of sweets of equal mass. If 0.45 kg of sweets are taken out of each box, then the remaining sweets in the 6 boxes weigh 3.3 kg in total. How many kilograms of sweets were in each box to begin with?

What learning will pupils have achieved at the conclusion of Question 3?

- Pupils will be able to apply their knowledge about algebra to solve real-world problems.

Activities for whole-class instruction

- Show pupils these expressions and equations. Working in pairs, pupils find the values and solve the equations.

> $32y \div 4 + 12$, where $y = 2$
> $3(8x - 1.5x)$, where $x = 0.4$
> $100 - 5(a + 2) - 20$, where $a = 4$
> $5(3x + 2) = 34$
> $9.7 \div (3x - 1.6) = 19.4$

Answers: 28; 7.8; 50; 1.6; 0.7

Discuss responses.

- Show pupils this problem:

> A recipe needs 1.6 litres of milk for 0.5 kg of flour. How many kilograms of flour are needed for 2.4 litres of milk?

Ask questions such as:

What is the question asking?

What is the problem that needs to be solved?

What do we need to find out/work out?

Is the problem about a whole and its parts?

Is it a problem about something being a number of times bigger or smaller than something else? Is it about something else? How do we know?

What operations are going to be used?

What is the calculation that needs to be done? If there is more than one step, in what order should the steps be carried out?

Together, draw bar models to represent the problem:

0.5 kg	
1 l	0.6 l

?		
1 l	1 l	0.4 l

Ask pupils: *What equations should be established?* Agree:

  1.6 l = 0.5 kg

  2.4 l = 1.6 l + 0.8 l

  2.4 l = 0.5 kg + 0.25 kg

  2.4 l = 0.75 kg

2.4 ÷ 1.6 = 1.5 times greater

1.5 × 0.5 = 0.75 kg

- Show pupils this problem:

> There are two bags of nuts. The first bag weighs 25 kg. If 7 kg of nuts is taken out of the first bag and put into the second bag, then the remaining nuts in the first bag will be 5 kg more than the second bag.

How many kilograms of nuts were in the second bag to begin with?

Ask questions as in the previous problem.

Together, draw a bar model to represent the problem:

25 – 7		
B	7	5

- Ask: *What equation should be established?* Agree:
$B + 7 + 5 = 25 - 7$ or $B + 7 = 25 - 7 - 5$. Say: *Using*
$B + 7 + 5 = 25 - 7$, *how is the working and check set out?*
Agree:

$B + 7 + 5 = 25 - 7$

$B + 7 + 5 = 18$

  $B + 12 = 18$

    $B = 18 - 12$

      $= 6$

Check: $6 + 7 + 5 = 25 - 7$.
It checks.

- Show pupils this problem:

> There are 4 boxes of sweets of equal weight. If 0.3 kg of sweets are taken out of each box, then the remaining sweets in the 4 boxes weigh 6 kg in total.
>
> How many kilograms of sweets were in each box to begin with?

Ask questions as in the previous problem.

Together, draw a bar model to represent the problem:

6			
s – 0.3	s – 0.3	s – 0.3	s – 0.3

Ask: *What equation should be established?* Agree:
$4(s - 0.3) = 6$.

Ask: *How is the working and check set out?* Agree, for example:

$4(s - 0.3) = 6$

  $s - 0.3 = 6 \div 4$

  $s - 0.3 = 1.5$

      $s = 1.5 + 0.3$

        $= 1.8$

Check: $4(1.8 - 0.3) = 6$.
It checks.

- In pairs, pupils now solve word problems in section A of **Resource 6.5.4c** Problem solving (2).

Answers: **1.** 0.75 hours; **2.** 27.5 minutes; **3.** 216; **4.** 62.5 kg; **5.** 110; **6.** 100 kg; **7.** 153 g; **8.** 1.2; **9.** 225.5 g

- Pupils should complete Question 3 in the Practice Book.

Same-day intervention

- Display on the board:

  > A recipe uses 1 litre of water for 0.5 kg of flour.

- Ask pupils: *How many kilograms of flour are needed for 2 litres of water?*

  Together, draw bar models to represent the problem:

0.5 kg
1 l

?	
1 l	1 l

  Ask: *What equations should be established?* Agree:

  $1 l = 0.5 kg$

  $2 l = 0.5 kg + 0.5 kg$

  $2 l = 1 kg$

  $2 \div 1 = 2$ times greater

  $2 \times 0.5 = 1 kg$

  Repeat for more difficult ratios, for example, multiplying by 1.5 and 2.5.

- Show pupils this problem:

  > There are two bags of carrots. The first bag weighs 15 kg. If 5 kg of carrots is taken out of the first bag and put into the second bag, then the remaining carrots in the first bag will be 3 kg more than the second bag.
  > How many kilograms of carrots were in the second bag to begin with?

  Represent the problem using counters and cards, moving counters to show how to find the answer. Then together, draw a bar model to represent the problem:

15 − 5		
B	5	3

  Ask: *What equation should be established?* Agree:
  $B + 5 + 3 = 15 − 5$ or $B + 5 = 15 − 5 − 3$.

  Ask: *Using $B + 5 + 3 = 15 − 5$, how is the working and check set out?* Agree:

  $B + 5 + 3 = 15 − 5$

  $B + 5 + 3 = 10$

  $B + 8 = 10$

  $B = 10 − 8$

  $= 2$

  Check: $2 + 5 + 3 = 15 − 5$.
  It checks.

  Repeat for higher numbers of kilograms.

Same-day enrichment

- Ask pupils to complete section B of **Resource 6.5.4c** Problem solving (2).

Answers: **1.** yes, 875 words in 25 minutes; **2.** 2905 m; **3.** 21 kg; **4.** a) $4(x − 25.5) + 0.5x + 0.5x = 150$; b) 4×50.4 g of sweets, 2×25.2 g of sweets

Challenge and extension questions

Question 4

> 4   If $a \blacktriangle b$ represents $(2a − b) \times b$, for example, $4 \blacktriangle 5 = (2 \times 4 − 5) \times 5 = 3 \times 5 = 15$, then, when $a \blacktriangle 3 = 24$, what is a?

This question provides further opportunity for rearranging an equation to find an unknown number through the context of a puzzle. Substitution is needed as a first step for solving the puzzle.

Question 5

> 5   Some Year 6 pupils participated in a mathematics competition. Among the winners, the number of boys is 3 more than 1.5 times the number of girls. The number of boys is also 2 less than twice the number of girls. How many winners are there altogether?

This provides further opportunity for establishing and solving equations. Two equations have to be established and then equated to find the value one of the unknowns.

Unit 5.5
More equation problems

Conceptual context

This unit reinforces solving equations and provides opportunities to solve application problems. Pupils' knowledge will become even more secure and their algebraic reasoning will become more fluent.

Learning pupils will have achieved at the end of the unit

- Fluency will have been developed through further practice in solving equations (Q1)
- Pupils will have further strengthened their conceptual understanding through using algebra to solve real-world problems (Q2, Q3, Q4, Q5)
- Pupils will have further strengthened their conceptual understanding through using algebra to solve more complex real-world problems (Q6, Q7, Q8, Q9)

Resources

0–100 number cards; lettered flashcards; blank cards; counters; **Resource 6.5.5a** Problem solving (3); **Resource 6.5.5b** Problem solving (4)

Vocabulary

algebra, equation, solve, solution, simplify

Question 1

> **1** Solve the equations.
>
> (a) $24x - 3.6 = 7.2$
>
> (b) $0.4 + 5x = 2.4$
>
> (c) $x + 5.8 - 2.5 = 9.4$
>
> (d) $15x - 1.2 = 4.8$

What learning will pupils have achieved at the conclusion of Question 1?

- Fluency will have been developed through further practice in solving equations.

Activities for whole-class instruction

- Show these equations. Pupils should explain to their partner how each equation can be solved.

  $40 - h = 3h$

  $15x \div 3 + 12 = 22$

  $4(2w + 5) = 24$

  $3(4.5 + c) \div 3 = 12$

  $5.2 \div (3z - 2.5) = 2.6$

  Answers: $h = 10$; $x = 2$; $w = 0.5$; $c = 7.5$; $z = 1.5$

  Discuss responses.

- Show pupils these equations.

  $4s - 3.4 - 3.4 = 6$

  $6h - 2.4 + 3h + 4.7 = 10.4$

  $12.2 = 3.5e - 4 + 5.2 - 2.5e$

  Ask: *For each equation, what can we do before solving it?* Agree that each equation can be simplified.

  Ask: *Can you find the smallest number of steps needed to solve each equation?* Pupil pairs discuss. They should see that:

  $4s - 3.4 - 3.4 = 6$

  3 steps

  $3.4 + 3.4 = 6.8$

  $6 + 6.8 = 12.8$

  $12.8 \div 4 = 3.2$

  $6h - 2.4 + 3h + 4.7 = 10.4$

  4 steps

  $4.7 - 2.4 = 2.3$

  $6h + 3h = 9h$

  $10.4 - 2.3 = 8.1$

  $8.1 \div 9 = 0.9$

  $12.2 = 3.5e - 4 + 5.2 - 2.5e$

  3 steps

  $3.5e - 2.5e = e$

  $5.2 - 4 = 1.2$

  $12.2 - 1.2 = 11$

  Share ideas.

  Working in pairs, pupils should generate eight of their own equations that need simplifying and that they can solve in the minimum number of steps. Each pair then solves the equations for another pair. They should explain their reasoning.

- Pupils should complete Question 1 in the Practice Book.

Same-day intervention

- Show pupils these equations:

  $4s - 4 - 2 = 6$

  $6h + 3.5 = 9.5$

  $10x - 1.5 = 2.5$

  Represent each equation using bar models, counters and cards. For each equation, ask: *How many steps are needed to solve the equation?*

  Together, set out the working for each equation, moving counters to show the step, as each line is written.

Same-day enrichment

- Show these solutions to equations:

  5

  1.5

  3.8

  2.4

  Ask pupils to create equations with these solutions that need simplifying.

Questions 2, 3, 4 and 5

> **2** Shanee bought 4 notebooks in a stationery shop with £50 and received £6 in change. How much did each notebook cost?

> **3** Mr Webb would like to buy 80 ropes in a sports shop with £200, but he is short of £40 to buy them. How much does each rope cost?

> **4** A gas company has 1240 employees, which is 40 more than 6 times the number of employees it had 5 years ago. How many employees did the company have 5 years ago?

> **5** An orchard has 370 peach trees, which is 32 fewer than 3 times the number of apricot trees it has. How many apricot trees are there in the orchard?

What learning will pupils have achieved at the conclusion of Questions 2, 3, 4 and 5?

- Pupils will have further strengthened their conceptual understanding through using algebra to solve real-world problems.

Activities for whole-class instruction

- Show these equations. Working in pairs, pupils solve the equations.

$4y + 5 = 40$
$200 = 40z + 50$
$D + 2 \times 7.20 = 40$
$700 = 15 \times 24.50 + 14n$

Answers: $y = 8.75$; $z = 3.75$; $D = 25.6$; $n = 23.75$

Discuss responses.

- Show pupils this problem:

> Peter bought 5 pens in a stationery shop with £10 and received £2 change.
>
> How much did each pen cost?

Discuss the problem. Ask questions such as:

What is the question asking?

What is the problem that needs to be solved?

What do we need to find out/work out?

Is the problem about a whole and its parts?

Is it a problem about something being a number of times bigger or smaller than something else? Is it about something else? How do we know?

What operations are going to be used?

What is the calculation that needs to be done? If there is more than one step, in what order should the steps be carried out?

Together, draw a bar model to represent the problem:

10					
p	p	p	p	p	2

Ask: *What equation should be established?* Agree: $5p + 2 = 10$.

Ask: *How is the working and check set out?* Agree:

$$5p + 2 = 10$$
$$5p = 10 - 2$$
$$5p = 8$$
$$p = 8 \div 5$$
$$= 1.6$$

Check: $5 \times 1.6 + 2 = 10 - 2$.
It checks.
So, a pen costs £1.60.

- Say to pupils:

> Catherine was given a £20 note to spend. She bought a book and the change she got was exactly enough to buy 2 DVDs at £5.40 each.
>
> How much did Catherine pay for the book?

Ask questions: *What bar model would represent the problem? What equation should be established? How is the working and check set out?* Pupils discuss in pairs. They should show:

20		
b	5.4	5.4

$$b + 2 \times 5.4 = 20$$
$$b + 2 \times 5.4 = 20$$
$$b + 10.8 = 20$$
$$b = 20 - 10.8$$
$$= 9.2$$

Check: $9.2 + 2 \times 5.4 = 20$.
It checks.
So, a book costs £9.20.

- Give pupil pairs **Resource 6.5.5a** Problem solving (3) and ask them to complete section A, creating equations to solve real-world problems.

Answers: **1.** £11; **2.** £2.90; **3.** £5.50; **4.** £7.99; **5.** £33.20;
6. £25.25; **7.** £21; **8.** £37

- Pupils should complete Questions 2, 3, 4 and 5 in the Practice Book.

Same-day intervention

- Display the following:

Anita bought 3 pens at a shop with £5.00. She got £2 in change. How much did a pen cost?

Represent the problem using counters and cards.
Together, draw a bar model to represent the problem:

5			
p	p	p	2

Ask: *What equation should be established?* Agree:
$3p + 2 = 5$.

Ask: *How is the working and check set out?* Agree:

$3p + 2 = 5$

$\quad 3p = 5 - 2$

$\quad 3p = 3$

$\quad\quad p = 3 \div 3$

$\quad\quad\quad = 1$

Check: $2 + 5 + 3 = 15 - 5$.
It checks.

Repeat for other combinations of products and costs.

Same-day enrichment

- Ask pupils to complete section B of **Resource 6.5.5a** Problem solving (3), creating equations to solve real-wold problems.

Answers: **1.** £18.84; **2.** a) $2 \times 8.99 + s + c = £34.50$;
b) various

Questions 6, 7, 8 and 9

6 The perimeter of a rectangle is 32 cm and its length is 9.5 cm. Find the width of the rectangle.

7 Ahmed had £30 and he first bought a pack of chocolate truffles. The change he got was exactly enough to buy 2 packs of cashew nuts at £6.80 each. How much did he pay for the pack of chocolate truffles?

8 Mr Kumar bought 16 pairs of table tennis bats and 12 basketballs for £800. Each pair of table tennis bats was £27.50. How much did one basketball cost?

9 Factory A has 148 tonnes of steel and Factory B has 112 tonnes of steel. If Factory A uses 18 tonnes per day and Factory B uses 12 tonnes per day, after how many days will the two factories have the same quantity of steel?

What learning will pupils have achieved at the conclusion of Questions 6, 7, 8 and 9?

- Pupils will have further strengthened their conceptual understanding through using algebra to solve more complex real-world problems.

Activities for whole-class instruction

- Show these equations. Ask pupils to solve the equations in pairs.

$$8y + 30 = 182$$
$$200 = 4s - 35$$
$$2(x + 2.5) = 12$$
$$20 - 5z = 15 - 3z$$

Answers: $y = 19$; $s = 58.75$; $x = 3.5$; $z = 2.5$

Discuss responses.

- Show pupils this problem:

> Pierre employs 100 people, which is 25 more than 5 times the number of people he employed 5 years ago.
>
> How many people did Pierre employ 5 years ago?

Ask questions, such as:

What is the question asking?

What is the problem that needs to be solved?

What do we need to find out/work out?

Is the problem about a whole and its parts?

Is it a problem about something being a number of times bigger or smaller than something else? Is it about something else? How do we know?

What operations are going to be used?

What is the calculation that needs to be done? If there is more than one step, in what order should the steps be carried out?

Together, draw a bar model to represent the problem:

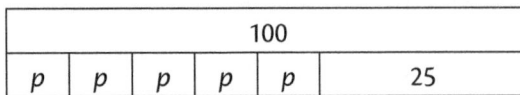

100					
p	p	p	p	p	25

Ask: *What equation should be established?* Agree:
$5p + 25 = 100$.

Ask: *How is the working and check set out?* Agree:

$$5p + 25 = 100$$
$$5p = 100 - 25$$
$$5p = 75$$
$$p = 75 \div 5$$
$$= 15$$

Check: $5 \times 15 + 25 = 100$.
It checks.
So, 15 people.

- Show pupils this problem:

> Supermarket A has 165 loaves of bread and supermarket D has 125 loaves of bread. Supermarket A sells 21 loaves per day and supermarket D sells 17 loaves per day.
>
> After how many days will the supermarkets have the same number of loaves?

Ask questions as in previous problems. Together, draw a bar model to represent the problem:

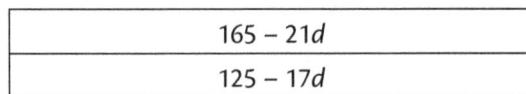

$165 - 21d$
$125 - 17d$

Ask: *what equation should be established?* Agree:
$165 - 21d = 125 - 17d$ or $125 - 17d = 165 - 21d$.

Ask: *Using $125 - 17d = 165 - 21d$, how is the working and check set out?* Agree:

$$125 - 17d = 165 - 21d$$
$$125 - 17d + 21d = 165$$
$$125 + 4d = 165$$
$$4d = 165 - 125$$
$$4d = 40$$
$$d = 40 \div 4$$
$$= 10$$

Check: $125 - 17 \times 10 = 165 - 21 \times 10$.
It checks.
So, 10 days.

- Ask pupils, in pairs, to complete section A of **Resource 6.5.5b** Problem solving (4), using equations to solve more complex real-world problems.

Answers: **1.** 15 km; **2.** 70 people; **3.** 77 cows; **4.** 58 CDs; **5.** 12.5 cm; **6.** 18.4 cm; **7.** 6 days; **8.** 10 days

- Pupils should complete Questions 6, 7, 8 and 9 in the Practice Book.

Same-day intervention

- Show pupils this problem:

> 10 people went to a café on Monday. This is 2 more than 2 times the number that went on Tuesday. How many went on Tuesday?

Represent the problem using counters and cards.

Together, draw a bar model to represent the problem:

10		
p	p	2

Ask: *What equation should be established?* Agree that p is the number of people on Tuesday.

Agree: $2p + 2 = 10$.

Ask: *How is the working and check set out?* Agree:

$2p + 2 = 10$
$\quad 2p = 10 - 2$
$\quad 2p = 8$
$\quad\ p = 8 \div 2$
$\quad\quad = 4$

Check: $2 \times 4 + 2 = 10$.
It checks.
So, 4 people.

- Show pupils this problem:

> The perimeter of a rectangle is 20 cm and its length is 8 cm. What is the width of the rectangle?

Together, draw a rectangle to represent the problem:

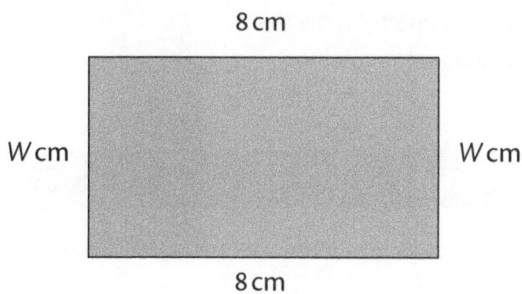

8 cm

W cm $\qquad\qquad\qquad\qquad$ W cm

8 cm

With help from pupils, write on the board:
$20 = 8 + 8 + W + W = 16 + 2W$.

Agree that $2W + 16 = 20$ is the equation that needs to be established.

Together, draw a bar model to represent the problem:

20		
W	W	16

Ask: *How is the working and check set out?* Agree:

$2W + 16 = 20$

$2W = 20 - 16$
$2W = 4$
$W = 4 \div 2$
$W = 2$
Check: $2 \times 2 + 16 = 20$.
It checks.
So, the width is 2 cm.

Same-day enrichment

- Ask pupils to complete section B of **Resource 6.5.5b** Problem solving (4).

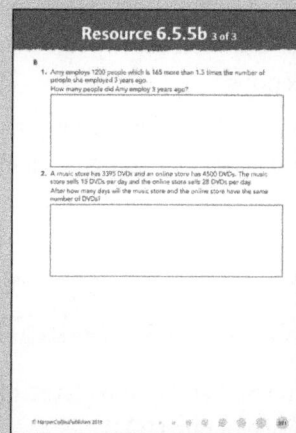

Resource 6.5.5b 3 of 3

Answers: **1.** 690 people; **2.** 85 days

Challenge and extension question

Question 10

> 10 A school bought 5 tables and 8 chairs for £375. A table costs £10 more than a chair. How much does each table cost? How much does each chair cost?

This question provides further opportunity for establishing and solving equations. The relationship between two unknowns has to be established to create an equation in one unknown that can then be solved.

Unit 5.6
Calculating the areas of shapes

Conceptual context

The aim of this unit is to consolidate what pupils know about calculating the area of triangles and parallelograms, and then use this knowledge to extend familiar concepts to less familiar geometric constructions.

The questions test pupils' problem-solving strategies and their ability to decompose composite shapes into simple shapes, such as right-angled triangles. They use a process of decomposition to calculate the areas of irregular polygons.

Learning pupils will have achieved at the end of the unit

- Pupils will have revised and consolidated identification and marking of the base and height of triangles and parallelograms (Q1)
- Pupils will have revised and consolidated use of area formulae to calculate the area of triangles and parallelograms, given the base and height of shapes (Q2)
- Given a base or height and the area of a parallelogram, pupils will be able to use the area formula to calculate the missing measurement (Q3)
- Using mental and written strategies, pupils will have revised solving multi-step problems that involve the calculation of area by decomposition of composite shapes and rectangles into right-angled triangles (Q4, Q5)

Resources

set squares; rulers; mini whiteboards; **Resource sheet 6.5.6** Triangles and parallelograms

Vocabulary

base, height, area, perpendicular, partition (decompose)

Question 1

> **1** The figures below show a triangle and a parallelogram. Draw the height corresponding to the base indicated in each figure.
>
> base
>
> base

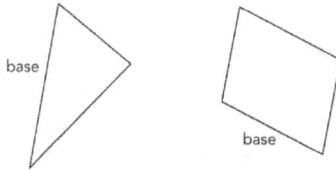

What learning will pupils have achieved at the conclusion of Question 1?

- Pupils will have revised and consolidated identification and marking of the base and height of triangles and parallelograms.

Activities for whole-class instruction

- Draw around a large triangle on the board similar to the diagram below:

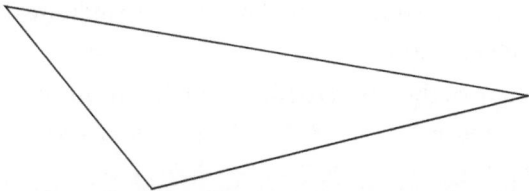

Ask: *Which side of the triangle is the base?* Accept answers. Remind pupils that there are three possible heights to any triangle, depending on which side is chosen as the base.

Label the longest side as the base. Ask: *Given this base, how would you mark the height?* Accept suggestions. Remind pupils that the height of a triangle is the perpendicular distance from the base to the opposite vertex.

Ask: *Which tool could you use to draw the height accurately?* Agree that a set square can be used to find and mark the height as it already carries a 90 degree angle.

Remind pupils how to place the base of the set square exactly on the base of the triangle. Adjust the left edge of the set square so that it forms a right angle from the base to the opposite vertex. Draw a dashed line along the left edge, from the vertex up/down to the base. Label the height. Include a right angle symbol to show that the height is perpendicular to the base.

Provide pupils with paper, set squares and rulers. Ask them to draw a triangle, label the base and draw the height using the set square.

- Draw a parallelogram on the board similar to the one below.

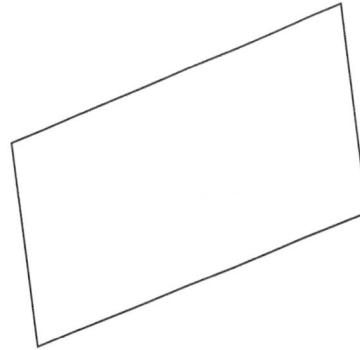

Ask: *Which side is the base?* Share ideas. Remind pupils that any side of a parallelogram can be its base, and a line segment drawn from a vertex perpendicular to the opposite base is called the height.

Use a set square to draw the height of the parallelogram by marking a dashed line segment from a vertex perpendicular to the opposite base. Remind pupils that this is the shortest distance between the base and the side opposite. Label the height.

Ask pupils to draw a parallelogram and to label the base and draw the height using a set square. They should include a right angle symbol to show that the height is perpendicular to the base.

- Pupils should complete Question 1 in the Practice Book.

Same-day intervention

- Provide pupils with rulers and squared paper, and ask them to draw a triangle and a non-rectangular parallelogram so that each shape has a horizontal base. Remind pupils of the definition of height for each shape. Ask pupils to label the base on each shape and use a ruler to mark the height.

Same-day enrichment

- Provide pupils with copies of **Resource 6.5.6** Triangles and parallelograms. Explain that the base of each parallelogram has been highlighted. Pupils must mark and label the height.

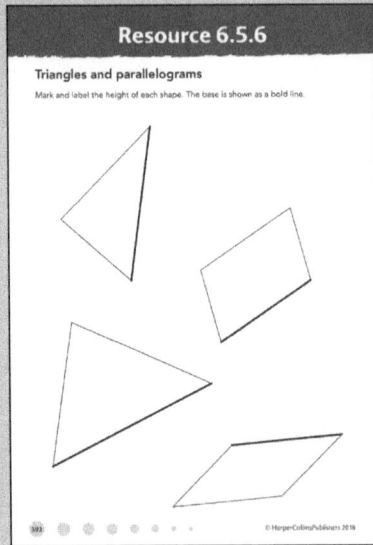

Resource 6.5.6

Triangles and parallelograms

Mark and label the height of each shape. The base is shown as a bold line.

© HarperCollinsPublishers 2018

Question 2

2 Calculate the area of each figure. (Unit: cm)

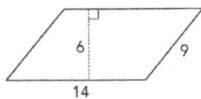

6   9   10.5   14

14

Area = [ ]   Area = [ ]

What learning will pupils have achieved at the conclusion of Question 2?

- Pupils will have revised and consolidated use of area formulae to calculate the area of triangles and parallelograms, given the base and height of shapes.

Activities for whole-class instruction

- Display the following parallelogram:

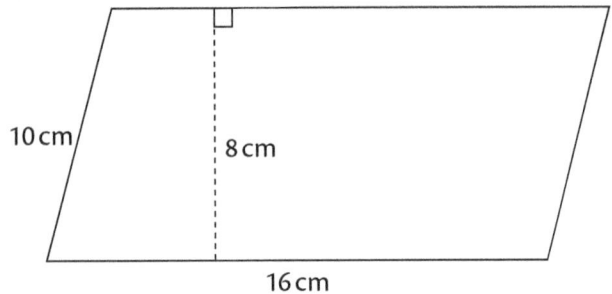

10 cm   8 cm

16 cm

Ask: *How would you find the area of the parallelogram?* Share ideas. Remind pupils to use the area formula for a parallelogram. Invite a volunteer to the board to write the formula: A = *b* × *h*.

Ask: *What do b and h stand for?* (base and height) *What are the base and height for the parallelogram?* (In this case, the base is 16 cm and the height is 8 cm.) *Why is the base not 10 cm?* Agree that, if the shorter side was the base, a perpendicular line from it would be shown to indicate the height – there is no such line.

Invite a pupil to the board to substitute the known values into the formula: A = 16 × 8. Ask: *What is the answer?* (128 cm^2)

- Display the following triangle:

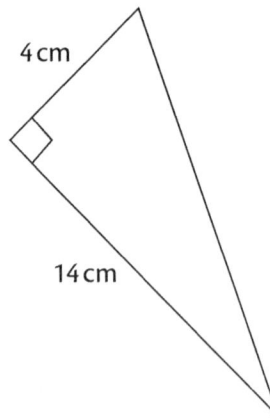

4 cm

14 cm

Ask: *How would you find the area of the triangle?* Share ideas. Remind pupils to use the area formula for a triangle. Invite a volunteer to the board to write the formula: A = (*b* × *h*) ÷ 2.

Ask: *What is the base for this triangle?* Agree that either of the perpendicular sides of a right angle can be the base. Pupils should substitute the known values in the formula and calculate the solution. Agree: A = (14 × 4) ÷ 2.

- Pupils should complete Question 2 in the Practice Book.

Same-day intervention

- Display the diagrams below and solve the problems as guided examples. For pupils who make conceptual errors when calculating the area of a parallelogram or triangle, use questioning to develop thinking.

How did you decide which values to use when calculating the area of each shape?

Can you show me the base and height of the figure?

What is the area formula for a parallelogram/triangle? What does each variable represent?

Can you show me how to substitute these values in the formula?

14 cm · 12 cm · 20 cm

5 cm · 15 cm

Same-day enrichment

- Display the diagram below. Ask pupils to work out the area of the shaded region.

Do they see that the area of the triangle (half of 9 m × 8 m) must be subtracted from the area of the whole rectangle (14 m × 8 m)?

14 m · 8 m · 9 m

Answer: 76 m^2

Question 3

3 The area of a parallelogram is 36 cm^2. The base is 4.5 cm. Find the height of the parallelogram.

What learning will pupils have achieved at the conclusion of Question 3?

- Given a base or height and the area of a parallelogram, pupils will be able to use the area formula to calculate the missing measurement.

Activities for whole-class instruction

- Show pupils this problem:

The area of a parallelogram is 78 m^2. The base is 6.5 m. Find the height of the parallelogram.

Answer: 12 m

Explain that, given the area and base, we need to find the missing measurement: the height of the parallelogram. Ask pupils to draw a diagram for the problem on their whiteboards. Check that the diagrams match the problem by asking pupils to hold up their drawings. Share solutions.

● Pupils should complete Question 3 in the Practice Book.

Same-day intervention

● For pupils who find it difficult to recall or apply inverse operations for finding an unknown value in a formula, use manipulatives, such as cubes, to model an equation, for example $40 = 5 \times 8$. Demonstrate that dividing by 5 on both sides keeps the equation equal, or 'balanced'. Help pupils apply this understanding to solving the equation $40 = 5 \times h$.

Same-day enrichment

● Ask pupils to write their own problems based on the one in the main activity, for example 'The area of a parallelogram is $56\,m^2$. The height is 3.5 m. Find the base of the parallelogram.' Pupils write five such problems then swap with a partner. They solve the calculation then return the paper for marking. Pupils should write problems where the base or height is a whole number and the missing measurement is a number with one decimal place.

Questions 4 and 5

4 Find the area of the shaded parts in the figure. (Unit: cm)

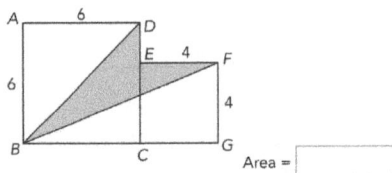

Area =

5 The perimeter of square ABCD is 24 cm. CEGF is a rectangle, EC = 2BE and DF = 2FC. Find the area of the shaded part.

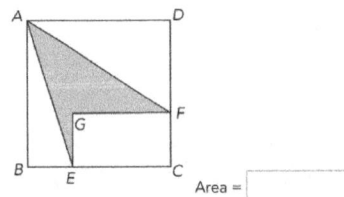

Area =

What learning will pupils have achieved at the conclusion of Questions 4 and 5?

● Using mental and written strategies, pupils will have revised solving multi-step problems that involve the calculation of area by decomposition of composite shapes and rectangles into right-angled triangles.

Activities for whole-class instruction

● Display the diagram below:

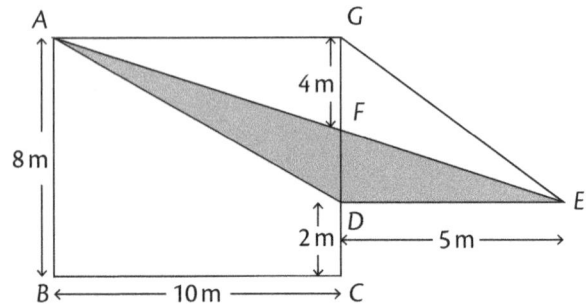

Pupils should calculate the area of the shaded parts of the shape. Remind them to try to partition the shape into rectangles, parallelograms and triangles because they know how to find the area of those.

Give pupils time to discuss the problem, then invite a volunteer to the board to separate the irregular shape into recognisable non-overlapping triangles, parallelograms and rectangles. Together, compute the length of the line segment DF (8 m – [4 m + 2 m] = 2 m) and establish that the composite figure can be separated as below:

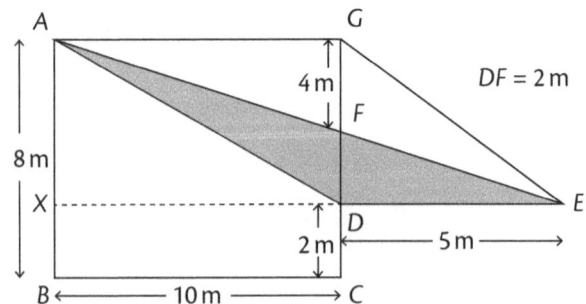

Ask: *How do we find the area of triangle ADF?* Together, agree that the area of ADF is the difference between the area of rectangle ABCG and shape ABCD and triangle AFG.

Ask: *How do we calculate the area ABCD?* Accept suggestions. Establish that ABCD is a composite of a rectangle BCDX (10 m by 2 m) and a triangle AXD (6 m [8 m – 2 m] by 10 m).

Ask pupils to substitute values into the area formulae:

Area $BCDX = 10\,m \times 2\,m = 20\,m^2$

Area $AXD\ \ = (10\,m \times 6\,m) \div 2 = 30\,m^2$

Area $AFG\ \ = (10\,m \times 4\,m) \div 2 = 20\,m^2$

Area $ADF\ \ = \dfrac{Area}{ABCG} - \dfrac{Area}{BCDX} - \dfrac{Area}{AXD} - \dfrac{Area}{AFG}$

$\qquad\qquad = (10\,m \times 8\,m) - 20\,m^2 - 30\,m^2 - 20\,m^2$

$\qquad\qquad = 80\,m^2 - 70\,m^2 = 10\,m^2$

Area $DEF\ \ = (5\,m \times 2\,m) \div 2 = 5\,m^2$

Area $ADEF = $ Area $ADF + $ Area $DEF = 10\,m^2 + 5\,m^2$

$\qquad\qquad\qquad\qquad\qquad\qquad = 15\,m^2$

Some pupils may notice that the area of triangle $ADEF$ could be obtained directly using base 5 m and height 6 m, so Area $= 5 \times 6 \div 2 = 15\,m^2$.

- Pupils should complete Questions 4 and 5 in the Practice Book.

Same-day intervention

- Show pupils the following:

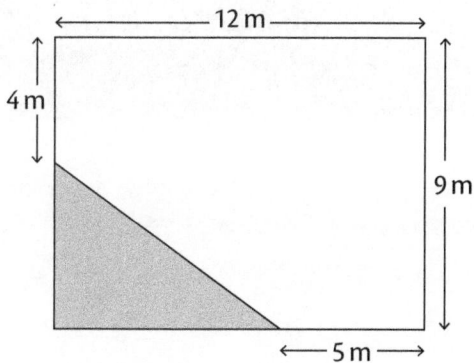

Ask pupils to calculate the area of the shaded section. Remind them to divide the shape into more manageable parts. Pupil pairs should sketch and discuss. Share ideas.

Agree that the shape can be partitioned as follows:

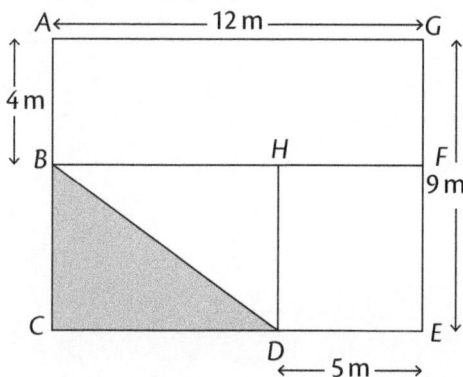

Label the vertices of the shape and the intersection of the internal line segments. Ask: *How would you work out the length of the line segment HF?* Share ideas. Establish that since *DEFH* is a rectangle, *HF* equals *DE*. (5 m)

- Ask: *How would you work out the length of the line segment BH?* Establish that since $BF = AG = 12\,m$ and $BF = BH + 5\,m$ then BH must be $12\,m - 5\,m = 7\,m$.

Ask: *What is the length of line segment DH?* Agree that $DH = EF$ and $GF = AB$ so $HD = EG - AB = 9\,m - 4\,m = 5\,m$.

Label the shape with the calculated measurements.

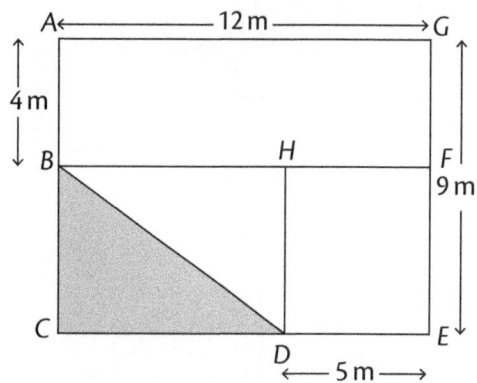

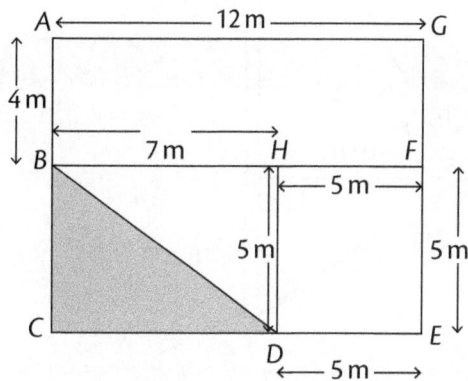

Ask: *How do we use these measurements to calculate the shaded section?* Agree that the area of the shaded section is the difference between area *ACEG* and the sum of the areas of rectangle *ABFG*, square *DEFH* and triangle *BDH*.

Together, calculate the area of *BCD*.

Area $BCD = $ Area $ACEG - $ (Areas: $ABFG + DEFH + BDH$)

$\qquad\quad = (9\,m \times 12\,m) - [(4\,m \times 12\,m) + (5\,m \times 5\,m)$
$\qquad\qquad\qquad\qquad\qquad\qquad\qquad + (7\,m \times 5\,m \div 2)]$

$\qquad\quad = 108\,m^2 - (48\,m^2 + 25\,m^2 + 17.5\,m^2)$

$\qquad\quad = 108\,m^2 - 90.5\,m^2$

$\qquad\quad = 17.5\,m^2$

Pupils may also note that they can also find the answer using a quicker method; by finding half of the area of the rectangle *BCDH*:

Area $BCD = \frac{1}{2}$ of area *BCDH*

$= (7 \times 5) \div 2$

$= 17.5 \, \text{m}^2$

Same-day enrichment

- Ask pupils to find the area of the shaded regions on these diagrams.

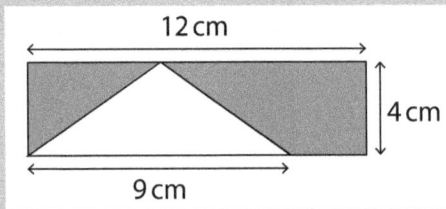

Answer: $12 \times 4 = 48$, $9 \times 4 \div 2 = 18$, $48 - 18 = 30 \, \text{cm}^2$

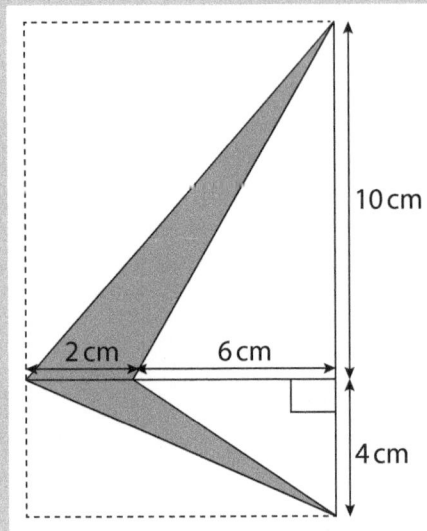

Answer: $2 \times 10 \div 2 = 10$, $2 \times 4 \div 2 = 4$, $10 + 4 = 14 \, \text{cm}^2$

Challenge and extension question

Question 6

6 The figure below shows a square *ABCD* with a side length 20 cm, $DE = 3AE$, and $BF = 4AF$. Find the area of triangle *CEF*.

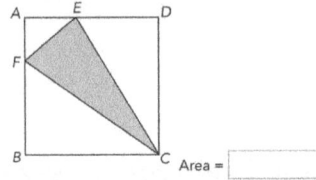

Area =

In this question, pupils are presented with a triangle inscribed in a square, where the triangle partitions the shape into three right-angled triangles. The two shapes have one common vertex. The other two vertices of the triangle touch the sides of the square, dividing them in ratios that are also given. To work out the area of the triangle, pupils must use the ratios given to deduce the base and height of the right-angled triangles, calculate the sum of their individual areas and subtract this from the area of the square.

Unit 5.7
Mathematics plaza – calculation of time

Conceptual context

This is the final unit in a chapter that provides the opportunity for pupils to strengthen and extend previous knowledge. The focus for this unit is on problems involving calculating differences in time. In particular, pupils will consolidate their understanding of time-based number sentences, calculating start and end times, finding the total of several durations and solving multi-step time problems.

Pupils are given opportunities to investigate, explore and apply previously learned concepts of time in different real-life, problem-solving contexts.

Learning pupils will have achieved at the end of the unit

- Mental methods will have been used to solve problems – finding totals of and differences between durations (Q1)
- Knowledge about duration will have been applied in a real-life context (Q2, Q3, Q4)
- Problem-solving skills will have been extended to tackle multi-step problems (Q3, Q4)

Resources

mini whiteboards; analogue clocks; **Resource 6.5.7a** Think about duration; **Resource 6.5.7b** Duration challenge!

Vocabulary

minutes, seconds, hours, days, duration, start time, end time, difference, a.m., p.m.

Question 1

> **1** Calculate the answers.
>
> (a) 36 minutes – 13 minutes 30 seconds = _____
>
> (b) 5 hours 28 minutes + 3 hours 32 minutes = _____
>
> (c) 9 minutes 14 seconds – 5 minutes 48 seconds + 1 minute 25 seconds
>
> = _____

What learning will pupils have achieved at the conclusion of Question 1?

- Mental methods will have been used to solve problems – finding totals of and differences between durations.

Activities for whole-class instruction

- Write on the board: 50 + 24 = ?

  Briefly discuss the answer, then alter the calculation to 50 cm + 24 cm. Again, briefly note that the calculation is the same and alter it once more to 50 minutes + 24 minutes = ?

  Ask: *Why does this particular calculation need a bit more thought?* Establish that, although pupils could just work out the answer as 74 minutes, they are dealing with units of measurement that alter when they get to 60 (60 minutes = 1 hour) and so 50 minutes + 24 minutes can also be expressed as 1 hour 14 minutes.

- Write on the board:

  3 minutes 45 seconds + 2 minutes 27 seconds = ?

  Give pupils time to work out the answer. Share ideas.

  Look out for … pupils who find the answer by adding each unit of measurement separately and then express their answer by continuing to keep the units separate. For example: 3 minutes 45 seconds + 2 minutes 27 seconds = 5 minutes 72 seconds. Strictly speaking, this is mathematically correct (it is the equivalent of equating 4 metres with 3m 100 cm). However, not combining the parts of their answer does imply that pupils may not recognise that it is possible to do so. They can convert the 72 seconds into 1 minute and 12 seconds. Although they may choose to deal with each unit separately as they perform the calculation, it is essential that they combine their answers at the end.

- Choose pupils to model their answer using an analogue clock face. Ask: *If this number sentence was based on a real-life situation, what might it represent?* For example,

the total cooking time to heat soup if it is cooked 3 minutes 45 seconds before stirring and then another 2 minutes 30 seconds afterwards.

- Display further time-based addition and subtraction calculations, including those that cross the minute or hour barrier. For example:

> 6 hours 18 minutes – 2 hours 38 minutes = ?
>
> 14 minutes – 1 minute 26 seconds = ?
>
> 5 hours 54 minutes + 1 hour 37 minutes = ?
>
> 10 minutes 8 seconds – 4 minutes 12 seconds + 1 minute 30 seconds = ?

Answers: 3 hours 40 minutes; 12 minutes 34 seconds; 7 hours 31 minutes; 7 minutes 26 seconds

For each example, ask pupils to share the strategies they used to find the answer with a partner (for example, deal with each unit separately before recombining or partition the larger units to help). Encourage pupils to use analogue clock faces to talk through the answer if they are unsure about crossing an hour or minute boundary.

Give them opportunities to contextualise each number sentence by suggesting real-life scenarios when each calculation might be used. Share ideas.

- Pupils should complete Question 1 in the Practice Book.

Same-day intervention

- Briefly ask pupils to count in seconds from 40 seconds. Listen to see what happens when they reach 60 and begin counting beyond. Some will continue 61, 62, 63, and some might say 1 minute, 1 minute 1 second, 1 minute 2 seconds, 1 minute 3 seconds, and so on. Ask: *Are both ways correct?* Agree, yes.

- Show a series of additions using a single unit of measurement of time (either minutes or seconds). For example:

> a) 45 seconds + 34 seconds
>
> b) 35 minutes + 35 minutes
>
> c) 24 minutes + 19 minutes

Ask pupils to identify those calculations that will give an answer that crosses the hour or minute barrier. Ask: *How do you know this? Can you show this on a clock-face? Does this affect how you write your answer?*

• Extend the activity to include times expressed using two units of measurement and subtractions. For example:

> a) 5 minutes 30 seconds – 1 minute 15 seconds
>
> b) 12 hours 14 minutes – 5 hours 49 minutes
>
> c) 7 minutes 20 seconds + 2 minutes 40 seconds

Answers: 4 minutes 15 seconds; 6 hours 25 minutes; 10 minutes

Pupils should explain their predictions. Ask: *What would you do to work out the answer? Can you show it on a clock-face?*

• Remind pupils that a clock-face can be thought of as simply a circular number line (from 0 to 60) and so when they count back to zero (for example, when subtracting 49 minutes from 14 minutes in example (b) above) they simply break through into the previous minute and start counting back from 60 again. With addition, as soon as they reach 60 on the 'number line', they break through into the next minute and start counting forwards from 0 again.

Same-day enrichment

• Pupils should work in small groups and write times on a series of blank cards. These may be expressed using one unit of measurement ('7 minutes', '2 hours', '45 seconds') or two ('3 hours 19 minutes', '25 minutes 12 seconds'). Pupils should complete four or five of these cards each and place them in the centre of the table. In turn, each pupil should choose two of the cards (featuring similar units) and use them to create a number sentence for the others in the group to solve.

• As an extension, pupils may wish to choose three of the times and use them to make a number sentence containing two steps.

Question 2

2 (a) Jet arrived at a Community Youth Club at 10:45 a.m. and stayed there for 48 minutes. At what time did Jet leave the club?

(b) It takes 83 minutes to travel from Southampton Central Station to London Waterloo Station by train. If the train reaches London Waterloo Station at 9:53 a.m., at what time did the train leave Southampton Central Station?

What learning will pupils have achieved at the conclusion of Question 2?

• Knowledge about duration will have been applied in a real-life context.

Activities for whole-class instruction

• Give pupils different scenarios to encourage them to consider the information required to be able to find either the start or end point of a duration. For example, what information do you need to know to be able to work out …

… the time a film is going to end?

… the time that a train started on its journey?

… the time that a pizza needs to be taken out of the oven?

Establish that in each case, pupils need to know the length of time the activity takes (the duration) and either the start or the end time. For example, to work out the time that a train started on its journey, they would need to know the time it arrived at its destination and the time it took to get there. For each example, ask: *What would you then do to work out the answer?*

```
START                              END
TIME                               TIME
 ●<------------------------------->●
            DURATION
```

Clarify what the diagram shows and discuss how, as long as two of the three variables are known, the other can be inferred. Spend some time covering up different labels on the diagram and discussing how pupils would use the remaining two pieces of information to find the answer.

- Display the following problem:

> Otis clicks the download button on his computer screen at 5:50 p.m. A message appears saying 'Download time 36 minutes'. At what time will his download have completed?

Answer: 6:26 p.m.

Refer pupils back to the START/END diagram and ask them which of the three parts they know already (the start time and the duration) and which they need to find out (the end time). Ask: *What would you do with these two pieces of information to find the answer?*

Repeat for further problems about duration. For example:

> When Afia hangs up her mobile phone, it says that the call has lasted 12 minutes. The time now is 10:04 a.m. What time did she make the call?
>
> It takes 25 minutes to cook a chicken chow mein meal in the oven. Josh's mum put it in at 6:52 p.m. What time will dinner be ready?

Answers: 9:52 a.m.; 7:17 p.m.

- Pupils should complete Question 2 in the Practice Book.

Same-day intervention

- Share a number of single-step problems. Ask pupils whether they think they have to count forwards or backwards in time to find the answer. (These will be to find the end time or start time, respectively.)

- Display this problem:

> An oven timer has 90 minutes showing on it. The time is 12:45 p.m. What time will the timer go off?

Ask: *Are you being asked to find the start or the end time? Does this mean you need to count forwards or backwards?* Choose pupils to make the start time on analogue clocks and then begin to count up to 90, moving the minute hand for each minute. After counting through a few numbers, ask: *Is there a quicker way to count forwards 90 minutes?* Remind pupils that 90 minutes is equal to 1 hour 30 minutes. Agree they can simply move the hands one hour (to 1:45 p.m.) and then 30 minutes (to 2:15 p.m.).

Repeat for further problems, ensuring pupils familiarise themselves with the strategies needed to find the start or end time, and how to convert durations given in minutes into hours and minutes.

Same-day enrichment

- Pupils should work in small groups. Instructions for the following activity are found on **Resource 6.5.7a** Think about duration, which should be provided to each group.

Pupils should all have analogue clocks with movable hands. One member of the group chooses a scenario (for example, someone cooking an apple pie), a duration (for example, 65 minutes) and then models a start time on their clock-face. Each of the others in the group should use the information they have been given to model the end time on their clock-faces, before comparing their answers.

Pupils should swap roles and include examples of problems where they are also required to work backwards from a known end time and find the start time.

Question 3

> **3** (a) Fatima arrives at school at five to nine in the morning. The first lesson starts at a quarter past nine. She has four lessons to attend, each lasting 45 minutes. There is a 20-minute break between the second and third lessons, and the last lesson is followed by lunch for 30 minutes. At what time does lunch break end?
>
> (b) One day, Maria went hiking. It took her 1 hour and 45 minutes to walk up to the top of a hill. After a half-hour break she walked back, which took 1 hour and 26 minutes. How much time did the whole hike take?

What learning will pupils have achieved at the conclusion of Question 3?

- Knowledge about duration will have been applied in a real-life context.
- Problem-solving skills will have been extended to tackle multi-step problems.

Activities for whole-class instruction

- Remind pupils of the diagram they have already used to consider duration problems (see above). Display the following diagram and ask what this shows.

●◀- - - - - - - - - - - - - ->●◀- - - - - - - - - - - - - ->●◀- - - - - - - - - - - ->●

Establish that the diagram shows a series of durations. Ask: *If this shows a number of lessons in school, what would you need to know to find out the end time?* Display the following problem where numbers are introduced to the scenario:

> Every morning, Year 6's school day begins at 9:05 a.m. They have three short lessons before break time. Each lesson is 40 minutes long. What time is break-time?

Together, label the diagram with the information they are given in the question. Initially, this will just show the start time and the durations:

9:05 a.m.   ?

●- - - - - - - - - - - - - ->●- - - - - - - - - - - - - - ->●- - - - - - - - - - - ->●
   40 minutes   40 minutes   40 minutes

Provide pupils with an analogue clock-face and ask them to model the three durations using the clock. Some pupils may find the addition of 40 minutes onto various times is a lot easier when they are able to visualise the times and physically move the hands.

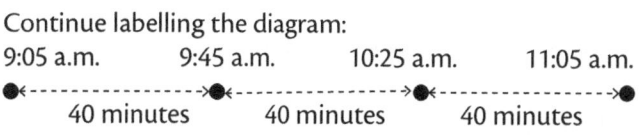

Continue labelling the diagram:

9:05 a.m.   9:45 a.m.   10:25 a.m.   11:05 a.m.

●- - - - - - - - - - - ->●- - - - - - - - - - - ->●- - - - - - - - - - - ->●
   40 minutes   40 minutes   40 minutes

Another strategy might be to find the total of the durations (in this case 40 minutes × 3 = 120 minutes = 2 hours) and then add this to the start time to find the answer. Ask: *Which method do you find most efficient? Why? How would you write your method as a number sentence?* This may involve pupils considering times in terms of hours and minutes (for example: 9 hours 5 minutes + 2 hours = 11 hours 5 minutes).

- Provide pupils with further opportunities to solve and discuss problems of duration containing several steps. For example:

> Underground stations are 3 minutes apart. Trains stop for 2 minutes at each station before continuing. A train leaves Central station at 8:14 a.m. It stops at 4 different stations and then finally it reaches its destination – High Street. What time does it reach High Street station?
>
> Here is the recipe for a chicken casserole:
> 1) Prepare vegetables (this should take around 8 minutes).
> 2) Lightly fry meat in a pan for 6 minutes.
> 3) Place meat and vegetables in the oven with sauce and cook for 1 hour and 12 minutes.
> 4) Stir the casserole and cook for a further 55 minutes.
>
> How long will the whole casserole take to prepare and cook?

Answers: 8:37 a.m.; 2 hours 21 minutes

For each example, ensure that pupils can identify the key information from the text and can describe what they need to do to find the answer, expressing each calculation as a number sentence where appropriate.

- Pupils should complete Question 3 in the Practice Book.

Same-day intervention

● Show pupils the following:

> A football match ends at 6 p.m. Both halves were
> 45 minutes long and there was a 15 minute break for
> half-time. What time did the match kick-off?

Ask: *How would you show this problem using a diagram
similar to the one we have used already? How many
parts are there to the diagram? Do you know the start or
the end time? Are we working forwards or backwards?*

Challenge pupils to make physical representations of
the duration diagram by placing clocks on a table and
pieces of string connecting them, labelled with each
duration. They should start at one end with the time
they already know and adjust the other clocks so that
they work out the final answer.

Repeat for similar examples and, after each one,
encourage pupils to consider how they might 'read
through' their diagram in the opposite direction to
check that their answer is correct.

Same-day enrichment

● Challenge pupils to write their own duration-
based story problems that are based on multi-step
calculations they need to do in their own lives. For
example, when working out when the final whistle in a
football match will end or the time they need to leave
home to get somewhere by a given time. If time allows,
pupils should share their problems for peers to solve.

Questions 4, 5 and 6

4 It takes 45 minutes to bake a cake. If a cake has been baking for 6 minutes
and 32 seconds, how much time is still needed?

5 Kim has a good habit of reading from half past six to twenty past eight
every evening. Accordingly, how much time does she spend on reading in
the evenings in a week (7 days) in total?

6 Jack is going to a concert, which starts at 19:30 and ends at 21:30. It takes
45 minutes to get there and 40 minutes to get back home. At what time
should he leave home for the concert if he needs to arrive 10 minutes
before it starts? At what time will he arrive at home if he goes home
immediately after the concert?

What learning will pupils have achieved at the conclusion of Questions 4, 5 and 6?

● Knowledge about duration will have been applied in a
real-life context.

● Problem-solving skills will have been extended to tackle
multi-step problems.

Activities for whole-class instruction

● Draw a series of steps on the board. Explain to pupils that
they will be thinking about time problems where there
is more than one step to find the answer and so it is a
reminder that, with each problem they face, they need to
be considering: 'What do I need to do first to find out the
answer? What next?'

● Show pupils this problem:

> A local amateur football team trains four evenings a
> week. Their training sessions start at 7:30 p.m. and end
> at 8:50 p.m. How much time do they spend a week in
> training?

Refer pupils back to the pictorial model they have
considered already. Agree that they know the start and
end times, but do not know the duration. Ask: *What do
you need to do first to find out the answer? What next?*

Pupils should recognise that they first need to work out
the duration of one training session, and then multiply

this by 4 to find out the time that the team spends training in a week.

Ask: *What do you need to think about when multiplying a time?* Give pupils time to consider the answer in pairs and then to share their methods as a series of steps. Some may have chosen to express the training session in minutes and worked out and then converted the answer into hours and minutes at the end:

    1 training session = 80 minutes

    80 × 4 = 320 minutes per week which is the same as
    5 hours 20 minutes

Others may have chosen to think of the training session in hours and minutes and then worked out each part individually before recombining to find the final total:

    1 training session = 1 hour 20 minutes

    1 hour 20 minutes × 4 = 4 hours 80 minutes per week
    which is the same as 5 hours 20 minutes

- Display further multi-step duration problems for pupils to consider. For example:

> Sue is going on holiday. Her plane takes off at 7:30 a.m., but she needs to check in 1 hour and 15 minutes before take-off. Her local taxi firm say it will take 55 minutes to get from her house to the airport. What time should she book the taxi for?
>
> A group of friends go to the cinema to watch an 85-minute film that starts at 1:20 p.m. They are going to be picked up by a parent 10 minutes after the film ends. What time will they be picked up?
>
> Kieran wants to record a football programme onto his TV as it is after his bedtime. The programme starts at 10:20 p.m. and ends at 11:35 p.m. He only has space left to record 80 minutes of television. Does he have enough space to record the programme?

Answers: 5:20 a.m.; 2:55 p.m.; yes

It is important to get pupils to look for connections between the problems. For each new problem, ask pupils: *What is the same about this problem and the last one?* Move pupils beyond: 'They are both questions about time' towards a deeper understanding (perhaps, 'I had to convert a time in minutes into a time in hours and minutes in both questions.') Similarly, ask them to consider: *What is different about this problem and the last one? What pieces of information were you given and what did you need to do to find the missing information?*

- Pupils should complete Questions 4, 5 and 6 in the Practice Book.

Same-day intervention

- Practise modelling chains of events using analogue clocks and whiteboards to describe durations. For example:

45 mins
Sam plays in park

10 mins
Sam walks home

Encourage children to cover up some of the information. Ask: *How would you use the information you can see to find the hidden information?* Pupils should write their own word problems based on the scenarios they have modelled.

Same-day enrichment

- Give pupils **Resource 6.5.7b** Duration challenge!

Pupils should cut out the cards and play the game about durations, working out the missing time in each case.

Challenge and extension question

Question 7

7 A film lasts 95 minutes. A cinema plans to start the film at 9 o'clock in the morning. The interval between two shows is 20 minutes for the films shown before 16:00 and 15 minutes for those after 16:00. Based on this plan, answer the following questions.

(a) The cinema closes at 22:00. Work out at what time the last film should end.

(b) The ticket price of a show varies depending on the show time. Each ticket is £8 for shows before 16:00 and £10 for those after 16:00. The cinema has a total of 600 seats and, on average, there are 100 seats unsold for each show. If a film is on show for one week (7 days), how much money does the cinema earn by selling the tickets?

Pupils are given a scenario based on a cinema's showings of a film from 9 o'clock in the morning, through until the evening when the cinema closes at 22:00. They are provided with the cinema's interval times and should use this information to calculate the time the final showing will end, given the closing time of the cinema. In the second part of the question, pupils are required to use multiplication to calculate the total amount of money the cinema earns, given the number of shows they have already calculated, the price for different show times and the average number of seats that are sold.

Chapter 5 test (Practice Book 6A, pages 162–166)

Test question number	Relevant unit	Relevant questions within unit
1	Unit 5.1	Q1
	Unit 5.2	Q1
2	Unit 5.1	Q2
3	Unit 5.3	Q2, Q3
	Unit 5.4	Q2
	Unit 5.5	Q1
4	Unit 5.1	Q3
	Unit 5.2	Q2, Q3
5	Unit 5.3	Q2, Q3, Q4, Q5
	Unit 5.4	Q2, Q3
	Unit 5.5	Q1, Q2, Q3, Q4, Q5, Q6, Q7, Q8, Q9
6	Unit 5.3	Q2, Q3, Q4, Q5
	Unit 5.4	Q2, Q3
	Unit 5.5	Q1, Q2, Q3, Q4, Q5, Q6, Q7, Q8, Q9
7	Unit 5.3	Q2, Q3, Q4, Q5
	Unit 5.4	Q2, Q3
	Unit 5.5	Q1, Q2, Q3, Q4, Q5, Q6, Q7, Q8, Q9
8	Unit 5.3	Q2, Q3, Q4, Q5
	Unit 5.4	Q2, Q3
	Unit 5.5	Q1, Q2, Q3, Q4, Q5, Q6, Q7, Q8, Q9
9		
10	Unit 5.6	Q1
11	Unit 5.3	Q1, Q2
	Unit 5.4	Q1, Q2
	Unit 5.5	Q1, Q6
	Unit 5.6	Q1, Q2
12	Unit 5.1	Q5
13	Unit 5.1	Q5
14	Unit 5.6	Q1
15	Unit 5.6	Q1
16	Unit 5.3	Q2, Q3
	Unit 5.4	Q2
	Unit 5.5	Q1
	Unit 5.7	Q2
17	Unit 5.1	Q4
18	Unit 5.1	Q4
	Unit 5.3	Q2, Q3
	Unit 5.4	Q2
	Unit 5.5	Q1
19	Unit 5.6	Q1
20	Unit 5.3	Q2, Q3, Q4, Q5
	Unit 5.4	Q1, Q2, Q3
	Unit 5.5	Q1, Q2, Q3, Q4, Q5, Q6, Q7, Q8, Q9

Number sequences

Here are some number sequences. Deduce the value of each symbol.

Tip: Work out the differences.

1. 1, 7, 13, ☆, 25, 31, ✳, …

☆ = ☐   ✳ = ☐

2. 0.2, 0.4, ◇, 0.8, 1.0, 1.2, ✦, …

◇ = ☐   ✦ = ☐

3. 1, 4, ✕, 16, ♥, 36, 49, …

✕ = ☐   ♥ = ☐

4. 3, 4, 6, 9, ⬡, 18, 24, ✳, 39, 48, …

⬡ = ☐   ✳ = ☐

Tip: In these number patterns, there are two number sequences.

5. 7, 100, 10, 98, ☆, 96, 16, ✳, 19, 92, 22, …

☆ = ☐   ✳ = ☐

6. 5, 5, ◇, 10, 125, 15, 625, ✦, …

◇ = ☐   ✦ = ☐

Resource 6.1.1b

Number sequences with unknowns

Here are some number sequences. Deduce the value of each symbol.

1. 6, 18, ☆, 162, 486, …

☆ = ▢

2. 1, ◇, 27, 64, ✦, …

◇ = ▢   ✦ = ▢

3. 2, 0.3, 4, 0.6, ✕, 0.9, 16, ♥, 32, 1.5, …

✕ = ▢   ♥ = ▢

4. 10, 0.4, 5, 0.8, 0, ⬡, −5, 1.6, ✳, 2.0, −15, …

⬡ = ▢   ✳ = ▢

Sequences that have the rule 'add the previous two numbers' are known as Fibonacci sequences. Deduce the value of each symbol.

5. 0.1, 0.1, 0.2, 0.3, ◎, 0.8, 1.3, ☆, 3.4

◎ = ▢   ☆ = ▢

6. 2, 2, 4, ◁, 10, 16, 26, ❖, 68

◁ = ▢   ❖ = ▢

Find out about Fibonacci numbers.

Working forwards and backwards

Work forwards.

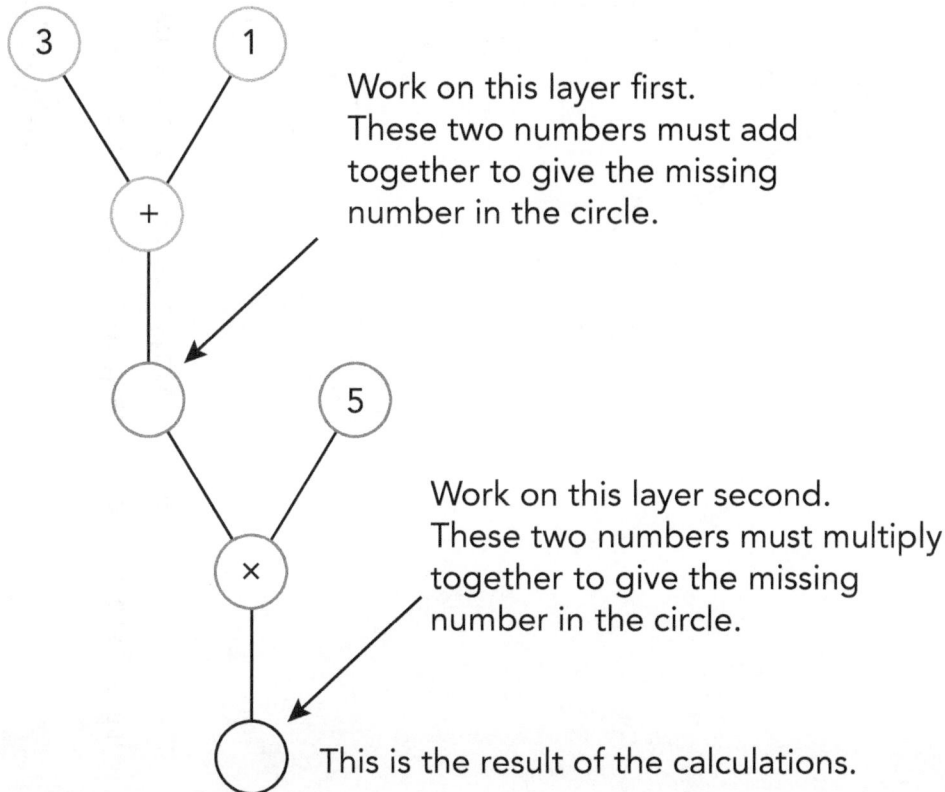

3   1

+

Work on this layer first.
These two numbers must add
together to give the missing
number in the circle.

5

×

Work on this layer second.
These two numbers must multiply
together to give the missing
number in the circle.

This is the result of the calculations.

Now work backwards.

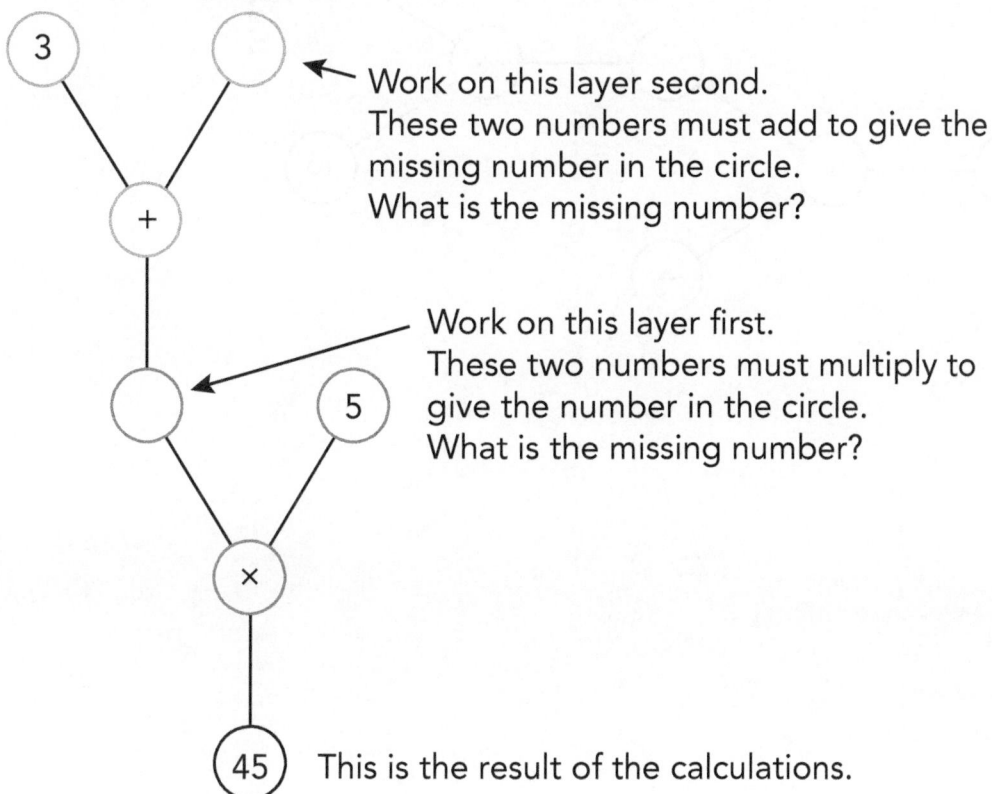

3

+

Work on this layer second.
These two numbers must add to give the
missing number in the circle.
What is the missing number?

5

Work on this layer first.
These two numbers must multiply to
give the number in the circle.
What is the missing number?

×

45   This is the result of the calculations.

Resource 6.1.3b

Tree stories

Write a story to go with each of these two tree diagrams.
Can you write more than one story for each?

Diagram 1

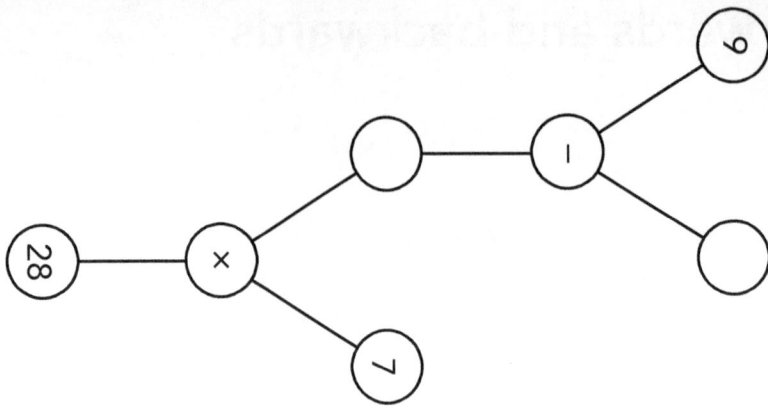

Diagram 2

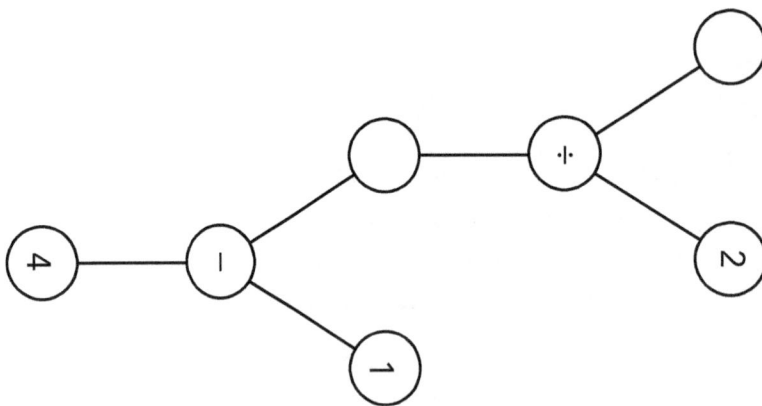

Rounding numbers

For each question, use the number line to help you round the number to:

   a. 2 decimal places

   b. 1 decimal place.

Record your answers on a separate sheet.

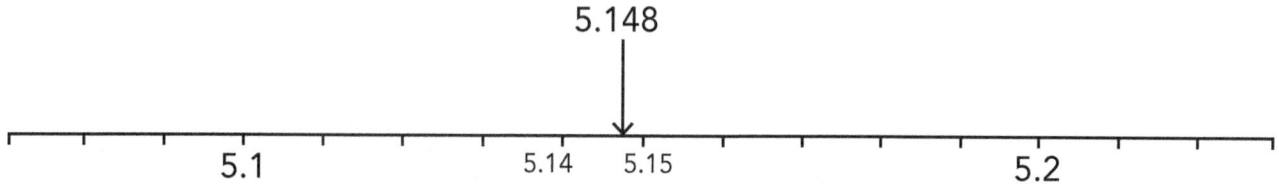

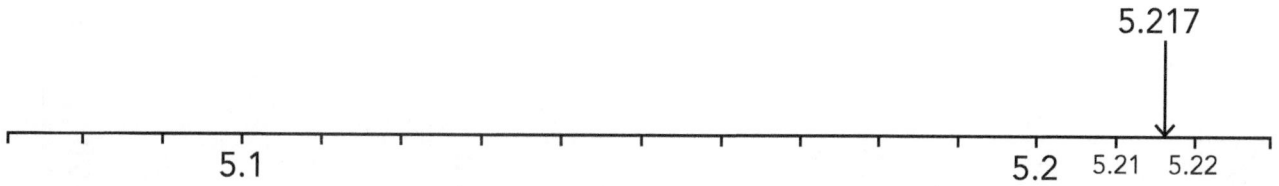

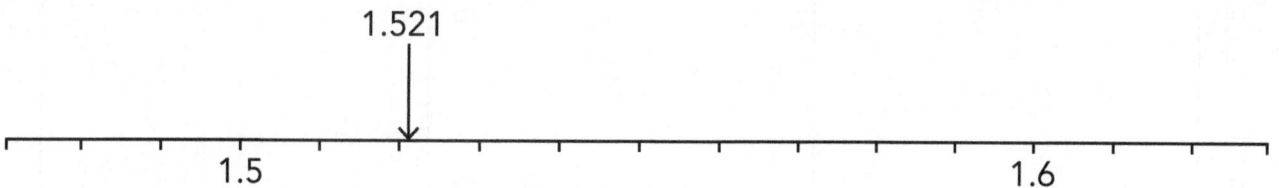

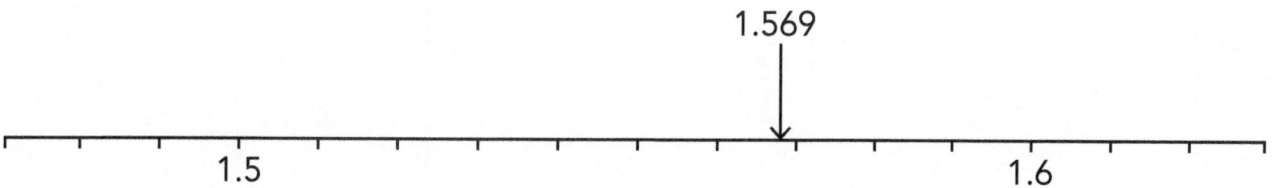

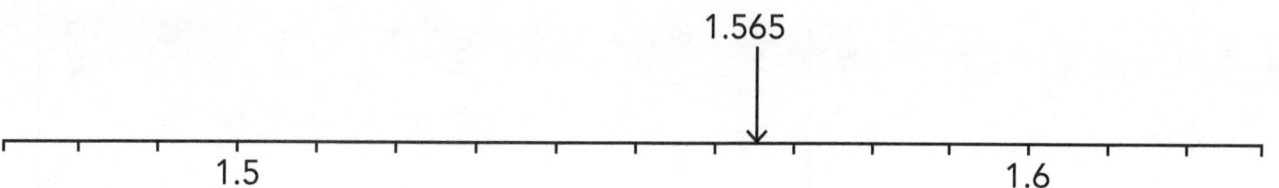

5.148

```
├──┬──┬──┬──┬──┬──┬──┬──┬──┬──┬──┬──┬──┤
   5.1           5.14  5.15           5.2
```

5.217

```
├──┬──┬──┬──┬──┬──┬──┬──┬──┬──┬──┬──┬──┤
   5.1                          5.2  5.21  5.22
```

1.521

```
├──┬──┬──┬──┬──┬──┬──┬──┬──┬──┬──┬──┬──┤
   1.5                          1.6
```

1.569

```
├──┬──┬──┬──┬──┬──┬──┬──┬──┬──┬──┬──┬──┤
   1.5                          1.6
```

1.565

```
├──┬──┬──┬──┬──┬──┬──┬──┬──┬──┬──┬──┬──┤
   1.5                          1.6
```

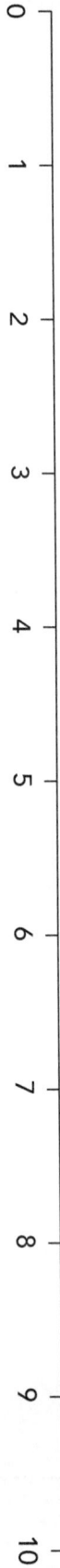

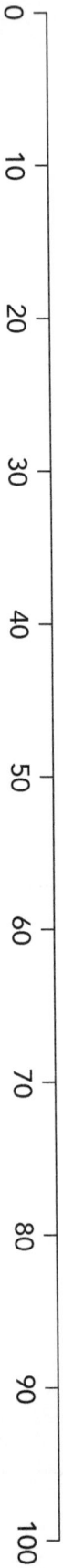

Number lines

0	0	0	0
10	1	0.1	0.01
20	2	0.2	0.02
30	3	0.3	0.03
40	4	0.4	0.04
50	5	0.5	0.05
60	6	0.6	0.06
70	7	0.7	0.07
80	8	0.8	0.08
90	9	0.9	0.09
100	10	1	0.1

Rounding first or last?

Zeb and Lindi are working on this maths question.

> Calculate 3.988 + 2.855.
> Give your answer to 2 decimal places.

Zeb says, 'I'm going to add the numbers first, then round the answer to 2 decimal places.'

Lindi says, 'I'm going to round the numbers to 2 decimal places first to make the addition easier.'

Does it matter whether the rounding is done first or last? _____

Explain how you know.

_____

_____

_____

_____

Yin Yang symbol

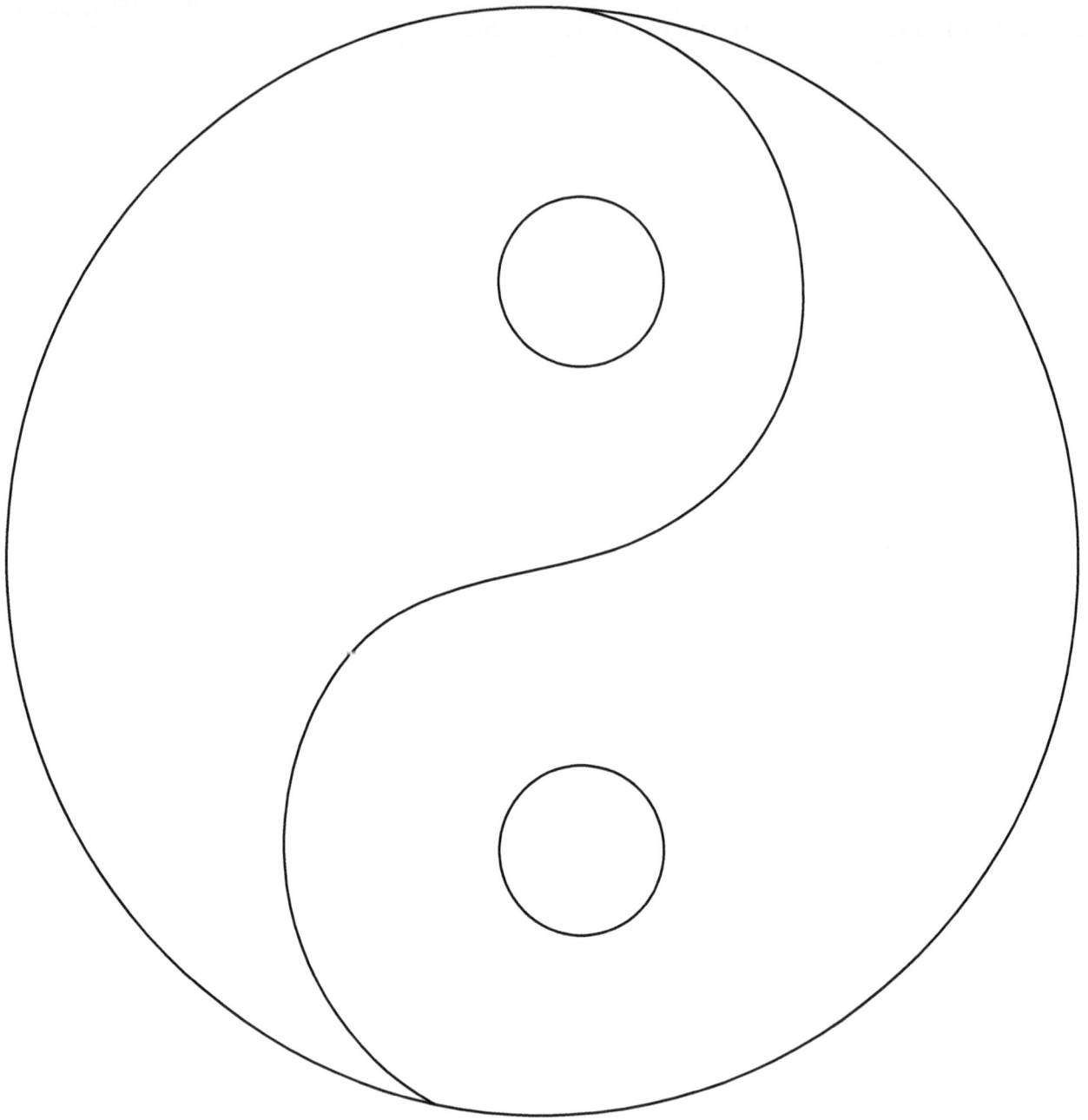

Resource Sheet 6.1.6b

Missing angle problems

1.

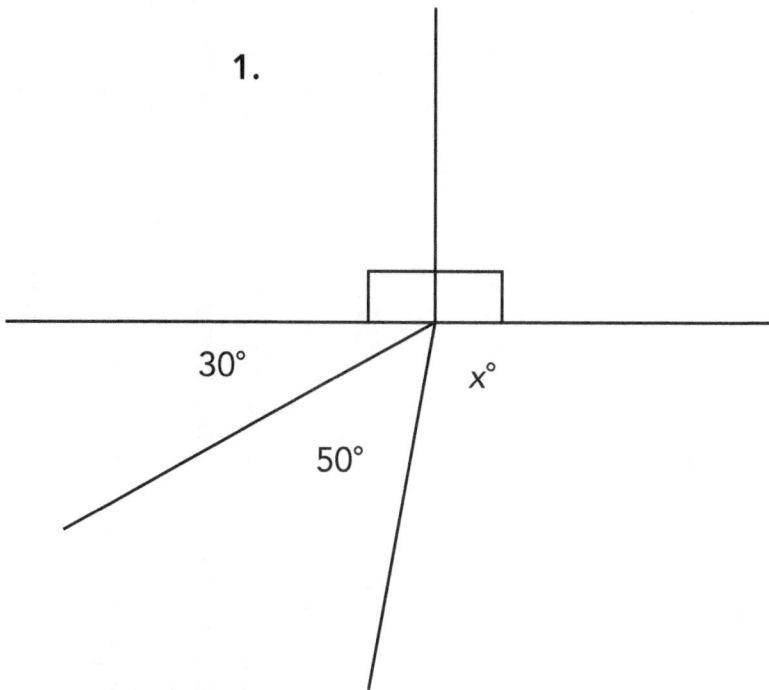

2.

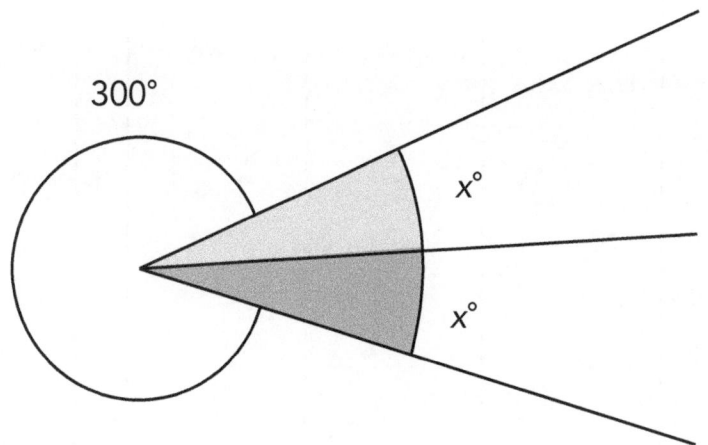

300°

3.

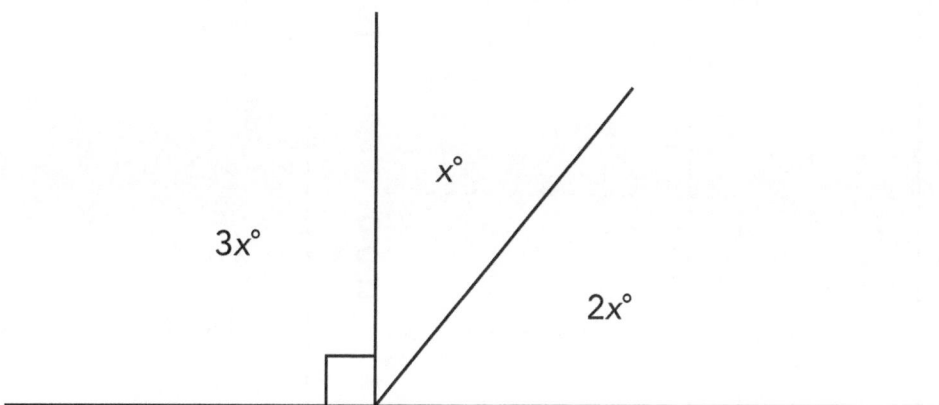

Resource 6.2.1a

Place value slider

- Cut along the dotted lines to create your place value slider.
- Now cut out the strips.
- Thread one strip through the slider and use this to write your number on.
- There are three strips, but you can always cut more or you could laminate one and use it again.

1000	100	10	1	0.1	0.01	0.001
Behind the strip	Behind the strip	Behind the strip	Behind the strip	Behind the strip	Behind the strip	Behind the strip

●

Which is larger?

Which of these calculations gives the greatest product?

0.8 × 3200	8 × 320	80 × 32	800 × 3.2

Explain how you know.

_____

_____

_____

_____

Write two more multiplications that could be a part of the set.

Resource 6.2.1c

Sliding

Where needed, fill in the numbers on the place value sliders to show the products.

$3 \times$ [☐ | 2 | 3 . | ☐ | ☐ | ☐] = [☐ | 6 | 9 . | ☐ | ☐ | ☐]

$3 \times$ [☐ | ☐ | 2 . | 3 | ☐ | ☐] = [☐ | ☐ | ☐ | 6 . | 9 | ☐]

$6 \times$ [☐ | 1 | 4 . | ☐ | ☐ | ☐] = [☐ | 8 | 4 . | ☐ | ☐ | ☐]

$6 \times$ [☐ | ☐ | 1 . | 4 | ☐ | ☐] = [☐ | ☐ | ☐ | . | ☐ | ☐]

$5 \times$ [1 | 3 | 5 . | ☐ | ☐ | ☐] = [6 | 7 | 5 . | ☐ | ☐ | ☐]

$5 \times$ [☐ | ☐ | 1 . | 3 | 5 | ☐] = [☐ | ☐ | ☐ | . | ☐ | ☐]

$4 \times$ [☐ | ☐ | ☐ . | ☐ | ☐ | ☐] = [9 | 2 | 4 . | ☐ | ☐ | ☐]

$4 \times$ [☐ | ☐ | 2 . | 3 | 1 | ☐] = [☐ | ☐ | ☐ | . | ☐ | ☐]

$5 \times$ [1 | 0 | 4 . | ☐ | ☐ | ☐] = [☐ | ☐ | ☐ | . | ☐ | ☐]

$5 \times$ [☐ | ☐ | 1 . | 0 | 4 | ☐] = [☐ | ☐ | ☐ | . | ☐ | ☐]

Resource 6.2.1d

Matching the questions

Cut out the cards and sort them into sets so that each set:
- shows a question
- the calculation needed to work it out
- the answer to the question.

One of the answers is missing, so you will need to make an extra card!

6×0.81	8 kg of apples are packed in a box that weighs 0.59 kg. What's the weight of the apples and the box?	8.59
A calculator costs £4.80. Amanda buys 3 calculators. How much does she spend?	0.3×16	4.8
4.72	$0.59 + 8$	3×4.80
A pencil costs £0.59. Fiona buys 8 pencils. How much does she spend?	A ruler is 0.3 m long. 16 rulers are set out end to end. How long are they in total?	0.59×8
4.86	An elastic band is 0.81 m long and is stretched so that it is 6 times its original length. How long is it?	

Points in different places

Fill in the blanks for each of these calculations.

1.

```
        3   2
  ×     5   9
  ─────────────
      ☐   ☐   ☐
    ☐   ☐   ☐   ☐
  ─────────────
    ☐   ☐   ☐   ☐
```

2.

```
          3     2
  ×   0 . 5     9
  ─────────────────
        ☐   ☐   ☐
      ☐   ☐   ☐   ☐
  ─────────────────
      ☐   ☐   ☐   ☐
```

3.

```
        3   2
  ×     5 . 9
  ─────────────
      ☐   ☐   ☐
    ☐   ☐   ☐   ☐
  ─────────────
    ☐   ☐   ☐   ☐
```

4.

```
    0 . 3   2
  ×     5   9
  ─────────────
      ☐   ☐   ☐
    ☐   ☐   ☐   ☐
  ─────────────
    ☐   ☐   ☐   ☐
```

5.

```
        3 . 2
  ×     5   9
  ─────────────
      ☐   ☐   ☐
    ☐   ☐   ☐   ☐
  ─────────────
    ☐   ☐   ☐   ☐
```

Missing digits

Fill in the gaps in these decimal multiplications.

1.

```
          3 . 0   1
  ×           __  8
  ─────────────────
      2  __ . 0   8
      6   0 . 2  __
  ─────────────────
      8   4 . 2  __
  ─────────────────
```

2.

```
          2 . 1   7
  ×            3  __
  ─────────────────
      1   0 . 8   5
      6   5 . 1  __
  ─────────────────
     __   5 . __ __
  ─────────────────
```

3.

```
          1 . 7
  ×           __
  ─────────────
         __ . 5
  ─────────────
```

4.

```
         __ . __  __
  ×             1   2
  ───────────────────
         __ . __   2
      4   8 . 6  __
  ───────────────────
     __  __ . 3  __
  ───────────────────
```

Number and word sentences

Cut out and match the number sentences and the word sentences.
Two of the number sentences give the same answer. Which two? Can you explain why?

$3 \times (2.1 + 5)$	$3 \times 2.1 + 5$	$3 \times 5 + 2.1$
Multiply 3 by 5 then subtract 2.1	Subtract 2.1 from 5 then multiply by 3	$3 \times 2.1 - 5$
Add 2.1 and 5, then multiply by 3	Add 5 and 2.1, then multiply by 3	$3 \times (5 - 2.1)$
Multiply 3 by 2.1 then subtract 5	$3 \times 5 - 2.1$	$3 \times (5 + 2.1)$
Multiply 3 by 5 then add 2.1	Multiply 3 by 2.1 then add 5	

Place the brackets

Some of these calculations are missing a pair of brackets.
Find these calculations and add brackets so that the calculations are correct.

1. $3.2 + 5 \times 1.7 = 13.94$

2. $26 \times 3.8 - 1.3 = 97.5$

3. $1.2 \times 2.3 + 1.5 - 0.2 = 4.32$

4. $5 - 1.7 + 3.2 = 0.1$

5. $3.2 + 5 \times 1.7 = 11.7$

6. $26 \times 3.8 - 1.3 = 65$

7. $1.2 \times 2.3 + 1.5 - 0.2 = 4.36$

Match the calculations

Each calculation has at least one card that describes it.

Group the cards together so that the descriptions and calculations are matched.

You will have two cards left. What calculations fit these cards?

$4 \times (1.4 + 0.7)$	0.7 is added to the product of 4 and 1.4. What is the result?	Apples cost £1.40 per kg. Sue buys 4 kg and Richard buys 0.7 kg of apples. How much do Sue and Richard spend on apples in total?
What is the result when 1.4 is multiplied by 4 then 0.7 is added?	Benny is making some shelves. He needs four 1.4 m long pieces of wood, and one 0.7 m long piece of wood. How much wood does he use?	What is 1.4 times the sum of 4 and 0.7?
$1.4 \times (4 + 0.7)$	Number A is found by adding 4 to 0.7. Number B is 1.4 times larger than number A. What is Number B?	$4 \times 1.4 + 0.7$
The sum of 1.4 and 0.7 is multiplied by 4. What is the product?	A bag of oranges weighs 0.7 kg and a bag of apples weighs 1.4 kg. What is the total weight of four bags of apples and one bag of oranges?	Two bags of apples weigh 1.4 kg and 0.7 kg. A box of pears weighs four times as much as the total weight of apples. How much does the box of pears weigh?
The decimal number that is 0.7 less than 1.4 is multiplied by 4. What is the result?	A chocolate bar costs £0.70 and a drink costs £1.40. Sarah buys a drink and a chocolate bar. She pays with £4. How much change does she get?	Mark is making some shelves. He needs a 1.4 m long and a 0.7 m long piece of wood for each shelf. How much wood does he use for 4 shelves?

Resource 6.2.3d

Different ways to say ...

Which of these statements means 6 − 0.3, which means 6 × 0.3, which means 6 + 0.3 and which doesn't fit into these categories?

Tick the correct box for each statement.

	6 − 0.3	6 × 0.3	6 + 0.3	None of these
What number is 0.3 more than 6?				
How much more than 0.3 is 6?				
What is the sum of 6 and 0.3?				
What is the product of 6 and 0.3?				
What number is 6 times more than 0.3?				
What is the difference between 6 and 0.3?				
Which is larger, 6 or 0.3?				
What is 0.3 multiplied by 6?				
What is 6 multiplied by 0.3?				
How many times larger is 6 than 0.3?				

Which way?

1. Which calculation do you think is easier?

$$3.5 \times 2 + 3.5 \times 8$$

OR

$$3.5 \times 10$$

2. Which calculation do you think is easier?

$$20 \times 2.1 \div 10$$

OR

$$20 \div 10 \times 2.1$$

3. Which calculation do you think is easier?

$$25 \times 3.14 \times 4$$

OR

$$100 \times 3.14$$

4. Which calculation do you think is easier? (Fill in the gaps.)

$$7 \times 7.2 + 3 \times 7.2$$

OR

$$\underline{\quad} \times 7.2$$

5. Which calculation do you think is easier? (Fill in the gaps.)

$$2 \times 1.7 \times 5$$

OR

$$\underline{\quad} \times 1.7$$

Resource 6.2.5a

Place value sliders – division

| | | 1 | 4 | . | | | | ÷ 2 = | | | | . | | |

| | | | 1 | . | 4 | | | ÷ 2 = | | | | . | | |

| | | 1 | 8 | . | | | | ÷ 3 = | | | | . | | |

| | | | 1 | . | 8 | | | ÷ 3 = | | | | . | | |

| | 2 | 1 | 4 | . | | | | ÷ 2 = | | | | . | | |

| | | | 2 | . | 1 | 4 | | ÷ 2 = | | | | . | | |

| | 1 | 8 | 9 | . | | | | ÷ 3 = | | | | . | | |

| | | | 1 | . | 8 | 9 | | ÷ 3 = | | | | . | | |

Double digits

Sarah uses this frame to calculate a quotient.

$$\boxed{}\boxed{}\boxed{} \cdot \boxed{} \div 5$$

Sarah puts in the digits 1, 2, 3 and 4 to create the calculation $123.4 \div 5 = 24.68$.
She notices that each digit in the quotient is double the digit in the dividend.

She tries again with $432.1 \div 5$.

Does the same thing happen?
Does it happen no matter what order the digits 1, 2, 3 and 4 are placed in the frame?
Why?

Does it happen with digits other than 1, 2, 3 and 4?
Why?

Matching the divisions

Cut out the cards and sort them into sets so that each set:

- shows a question
- the calculation needed to work it out
- the answer to the question.

One of the calculations is missing, so you will need to make an extra card.

$1.17 \div 3$	3.51 kg of cherries are put into three bags so that each bag has the same weight of cherries. How much does each bag weigh?	$168.3 \div 11$
15.3	$3.51 \div 3$	0.39
Number A is five times greater than Number B. If Number A is 9.1, what is number B?	$9.1 \div 5$	1.82
1.17	A bottle of water holds 1.17 litres. Three cups of water fill the bottle completely. How much does one cup hold?	11 times a number is 168.3. What is the number?
0.13	An elastic band is stretched so that it is 6 times its original length. The stretched band is 0.78 m long. How long is the band normally?	

Best buys

Which of these is the cheapest way to buy 1 litre of orange juice?

Arrange the prices in order, from the cheapest to the most expensive price per litre.

A

One 3-litre bottle for £1.86

B

Buy one 2-litre bottle for £1.68 and get another 2-litre bottle half price

C

One 2-litre bottle for £1.23

D

One 1-litre bottle costs £0.65

E

One 250 ml bottle costs £0.30

Resource 6.2.6

Division corrections

Tick the division calculations that are correct.

Write the correct version of each incorrect calculation.

1.

```
        9  5 . 7  0
   7 ) 6  6 . 9  9
       6  3
          3  9
          3  5
             4  9
             4  9
                0
```
☐

2.

```
        1  5 . 0  8
   3 ) 4  7 . 4
       4  5
          2  4
          2  4
             0
```
☐

3.

```
          1  5  0 . 7
   1  1 ) 1  7  2 . 7
          1  6  5
                7  7
                7  7
                   0
```
☐

4.

```
                8 . 6
   1  7 ) 1  4  6 . 2
          1  3  6
             1  0  2
             1  0  2
                   0
```
☐

Same value, different appearance

Draw lines to match all of the numbers that have the same value, even though they may look different.

1.900 000   1.90

$$\frac{19}{10}$$

1.0900   1.9

1.09

10.9

$$\frac{19}{100}$$

0.19

10.90

1.900

Extra zeros

1. $1.9 \div 4 = \boxed{}$

$$
\begin{array}{r}
0 \, . \, 4 \;\square\square \\
4 \overline{)\; 1 \, . \, 9} \\
1 \, . \, 6 \\
\hline
3 \;\square \\
\square\square \\
\hline
2\;\square \\
\square\square \\
\hline
0
\end{array}
$$

2. $2.2 \div 4 = \boxed{}$

$$
\begin{array}{r}
0 \, . \, 5 \;\square \\
4 \overline{)\; 2 \, . \, 2} \\
2 \, . \, 0 \\
\hline
\square\square \\
\square\square \\
\hline
0
\end{array}
$$

3. $2.3 \div 4 = \boxed{}$

$$
\begin{array}{r}
0 \, . \, 5 \;\square\square \\
4 \overline{)\; 2 \, . \, 3} \\
2 \, . \, 0 \\
\hline
3\;\square \\
\square\square \\
\hline
\square\square \\
\square\square \\
\hline
0
\end{array}
$$

4. $2.5 \div 4 = \boxed{}$

$$
\begin{array}{r}
0 \, . \, 6 \;\square\square \\
4 \overline{)\; 2 \, . \, 5} \\
2 \, . \, 4 \\
\hline
1\;\square \\
\square \\
\hline
\square\square \\
\square\square \\
\hline
0
\end{array}
$$

Number and word sentences

Match these cards first.

Then add these cards to the matched pairs.

Find the **product** of the **quotient** of 2.1 and 6 and the **sum** of 0.7 and 1.3.

Find the **quotient** of the **sum** of 2.1 and 6 and the **sum** of 0.7 and 1.3.

2.35

$(2.1 \div 6) \times (0.7 + 1.3)$

$(2.1 \times 6) \div (0.7 + 1.3)$

6.3

$(2.1 + 6) \div (0.7 + 1.3)$

$(2.1 \div 6) + (0.7 + 1.3)$

0.7

Find the **quotient** of the **product** of 2.1 and 6 and the **sum** of 0.7 and 1.3.

Find the **sum** of the **quotient** of 2.1 and 6 and the **sum** of 0.7 and 1.3.

4.05

Place value sliders – decimal division

The top slider shows that 47 ÷ 5 = 9.4.
Use this to complete the other calculations.

| | 4 | 7 | . | | | | | ÷ 5 = | | | 9 | . | 4 | | | |

| 4 | 7 | 0 | . | | | | | ÷ 5 = | | | | . | | | | |

| | | 0 | . | 4 | 7 | | | ÷ 5 = | | | | . | | | | |

| | | 0 | . | 0 | 4 | 7 | | ÷ 5 = | | | | . | | | | |

The top slider shows that 29 ÷ 4 = 7.25.
Use this to complete the other calculations.

| | 2 | 9 | . | | | | | ÷ 4 = | | | 7 | . | 2 | 5 | | |

| | | 2 | . | 9 | | | | ÷ 4 = | | | | . | | | | |

| 2 | 9 | 0 | . | | | | | ÷ 4 = | | | | . | | | | |

| | | 0 | . | 2 | 9 | | | ÷ 4 = | | | | . | | | | |

Changing divisors

Based on 54 ÷ 24 = 2.25, directly write the quotients of the divisions below.

54 ÷ 0.24 = _____   54 ÷ 2400 = _____   54 ÷ 240 = _____

54 ÷ 2.4 = _____   54 ÷ 0.0024 = _____   54 ÷ 0.024 = _____

Explain why these answers follow a different pattern to those in Question 1 in the Practice Book.

_____

_____

_____

_____

_____

_____

_____

_____

_____

_____

Resource 6.2.8c

How many times more?

Decide whether these quantities are 2 times, 2.3 times or 2.5 times greater than the original. Tick the correct boxes in the table.

	2 times greater	2.3 times greater	2.5 times greater
A chocolate bar weighs 36 grams. The extra large version of the bar weighs 72 grams. How many times heavier is the extra large bar than the standard bar?			
Ahmed draws two lines. On is 8 cm long and the other is 18.4 cm long. How many times longer is the second line than the first?			
A dog weighs 9.2 kg and a cat weighs 4 kg. How many times heavier than the cat is the dog?			
Sam's sports bag holds 10 t-shirts and Jack's holds 25 t-shirts. How many times more t-shirts does Jack's bag hold than Sam's?			
Sarah can jump 2 metres but Steph can jump 5 metres. How many times further than Sarah can Steph jump?			
Matilda is 1.36 metres tall. Robert Wadlow, the tallest man ever to have lived, was 2.72 metres tall. How many times taller was Robert than Matilda?			
A spring has a weight hung on one end and is 20.7 cm long. When the weight is taken off, the spring is only 9 cm long. How many times longer is the spring when it has the weight attached?			
Write your own *How many times …? question.*			

Calculator maze

1	8	2	.	1	=	5	.	5	2
.	3	×	=	7	×	÷	9	÷	5
7	3	×	8	÷	=	2	3	8	=
.	=	=	=	5	1	3	.	9	7
3	.	3	3	×	8	÷	1	×	5
÷	6	÷	×	=	÷	5	8	3	1
4	=	×	7	9	0	.	3	×	1
.	7	.	4	×	1	2	=	÷	2
5	3	×	5	×	3	5	1	÷	5
=	2	4	1	1	×	4	÷	2	=

Find a route through the maze by shading the calculator buttons you'd press to work out each of these calculations (the first is started for you). Then use a calculator to work out each answer.

1. $1.3 \times 2.1 =$ _____

2. $5.9 \div 5 =$ _____

3. $75 \times 1.32 =$ _____

4. $18 \div 0.3 =$ _____

5. $21 \times 4.7 =$ _____

6. $6.3 \div 4.5 =$ _____

Dividing by 37

Mandy says …

> If a 3-digit number is in the 37 times table then rearranging its digits will give another number that's also in the 37 times table.

Mandy gives the example:

- Start with $16 \times 37 = 592$.
- Rearranging 592 gives 925 which is 25×37 or I can rearrange it to give 259 which is 7×37.

Does this always work?

Does any rearrangement work or only certain rearrangements? Which ones?

Resource 6.2.9c

9s and 9s and 9s ...

Write down the 9 times table.

1 × 9 = _____   6 × 9 = _____

2 × 9 = _____   7 × 9 = _____

3 × 9 = _____   8 × 9 = _____

4 × 9 = _____   9 × 9 = _____

5 × 9 = _____

Now use a calculator to write down the 99 times table.

1 × 99 = _____   6 × 99 = _____

2 × 99 = _____   7 × 99 = _____

3 × 99 = _____   8 × 99 = _____

4 × 99 = _____   9 × 99 = _____

5 × 99 = _____

Now use a calculator to write down the 999 times table.

1 × 999 = _____   6 × 999 = _____

2 × 999 = _____   7 × 999 = _____

3 × 999 = _____   8 × 999 = _____

4 × 999 = _____   9 × 999 = _____

5 × 999 = _____

Did you use a calculator for all of the last set of questions, or did you spot a pattern?

Can you write down the 9999 times table without a calculator?

1 × 9999 = _____   6 × 9999 = _____

2 × 9999 = _____   7 × 9999 = _____

3 × 9999 = _____   8 × 9999 = _____

4 × 9999 = _____   9 × 9999 = _____

5 × 9999 = _____

Test your answers with a calculator. Were you right?

Rounding diagrams

1. Read the following and fill in the spaces.

> When 'rounding off' (or simply 'rounding') a decimal number to a certain place, if the digit in the value place to its right is _____ than 5, just drop off all the digits to its right. So, rounding 5.545 to the tenths place, the result is _____. If the digit is greater than or equal to 5, increase the digit in it by _____ and drop off all the digits to its right. So, rounding 10.257 to the hundredths place, the result is _____.

2. Circle the diagram you will use to help you round 5.386 to the nearest tenth.

A

1	.	$\frac{1}{10}$	$\frac{1}{100}$	$\frac{1}{1000}$
5	.	3	8	6

B

5.386

5.3   5.4

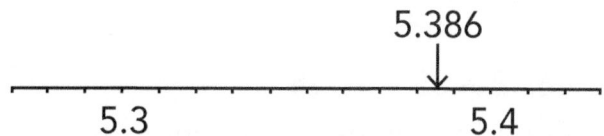

3. Circle the diagram you will use to help you round 4.93 to the nearest tenth.

A

1	.	$\frac{1}{10}$	$\frac{1}{100}$
4	.	9	3

B

4.93

4.9   5.0

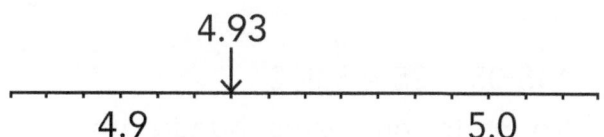

4. Which of the diagrams you've used so far will you use to help you round 5.06 to the nearest tenth?

Resource 6.2.10b

Rounding results

1. 0.37 × 38 = 14.06

   Round to the nearest tenth.

   Fill in the spaces with the answer.

   __ __ . __ | __ (Look at the digit after the line. How does that help you to round?)

   Write 14.06 to the nearest tenth here.

   __ __ . __

2. 2.34 × 1.07 = 2.5038

   Round to the nearest hundredth.

   Fill in the spaces with the answer.

   __ __ . __ __ | __ __

   Write 2.5038 to the nearest hundredth here.

   __ __ . __ __

3. 46.48 ÷ 35 = 1.328

   Round to the nearest hundredth.

   Fill in the spaces with the answer.

   __ __ . __ __ | __

   Write 1.328 to the nearest hundredth here.

   __ __ . __ __

4. 145.05 ÷ 25 = 5.802

   Round to the nearest hundredth.

   Fill in the spaces with the answer.

   __ __ . __ __ | __

   Write 5.802 to the nearest hundredth here.

   __ __ . __ __

5. 16.5 ÷ 6 = 2.75

   Round to the nearest tenth.

   Fill in the spaces with the answer.

   __ __ . __ | __

   Write 2.75 to the nearest tenth here.

   __ __ . __

Swapping digits

You have already calculated:

$0.31 \times 52 = 16.12$

$0.32 \times 51 = 16.32$

and

$0.32 \times 53 = 16.96$

$0.33 \times 52 = 17.16$

In both pairs of calculations, swapping the two decimal parts of the calculation gives results that:

- are 0.2 apart
- give the same result when rounded to the nearest whole number.

Do you think that this will always happen?

Try with these pairs of calculations:

0.33×54 and 0.34×53 _____

0.34×55 and 3.5×54 _____

0.35×56 and 0.36×55 _____

0.36×57 and 0.37×56 _____

0.37×58 and 0.38×57 _____

0.38×59 and 0.39×58 _____

Was your prediction correct?

Resource 6.2.11a

More blanks

We know that …

$2.3 \times 7 = 16.1$

$2.3 \times 7 \times 5 = 80.5$

$(2.3 \times 7) \times 5 = 80.5$

$2.3 + 7 + 5 = 14.3$

$(2.3 + 7) + 5 = 14.3$

So we also know that …

$7 \times \underline{\quad} = 16.1$

$5 \times 7 \times \underline{\quad} = 80.5$

$2.3 \times (7 \times \underline{\quad}) = 80.5$

$7 + \underline{\quad} + 5 = 14.3$

$\underline{\quad} + (7 + 5) = 14.3$

We know that …

```
      3  2
×     1  6
─────────────
   1  9  2
   3  2  0
─────────────
   5  1  2
```

```
      8  4  2
3 │ 2  5  2  6
   2  4  0  0
─────────────
      1  2  6
      1  2  6
─────────────
         0  6
         0  6
─────────────
         0  0
```

So we also know that …

```
      3 . 2
×     1   6
─────────────
   _   9 . 2
   3  2 . _
─────────────
   _   _   _
```

```
      _ . 4  2
3 │ 2  5 . 2  6
   2  4
─────────────
      1 . _
      1 . 2
─────────────
         0 . 6
         0 . _
─────────────
         0 . 0
```

Resource 6.2.11b

Tree stories

Alice buys 4 bottles of juice.

Each bottle costs £0.85.

She pays with a £5 note. How much change does Alice get?

Number sentence:

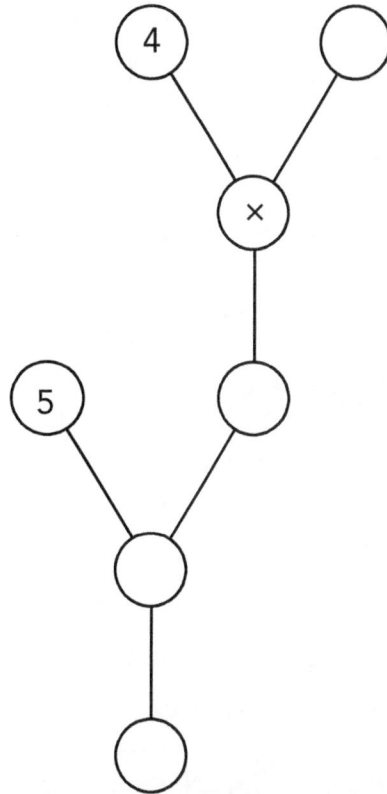

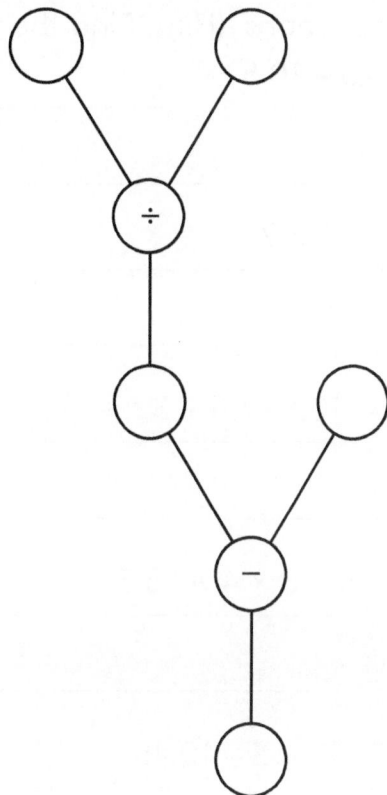

_____

Robyn has £15 which she shares equally among her four children.

One of her children, Willow, then spends 86 pence on some sweets.

How much money does Willow have left?

Number sentence:

_____

Find the values

1. Find the values of the letters in these sequences.

   a) 0, 1, 1, 2, 3, 5, A, 13, 21, 34, C, D

   A = ☐   C = ☐   D = ☐

   b) 1, 4, 9, E, 25, 36, F, 64, 81, G

   E = ☐   F = ☐   G = ☐

   c) 1, 2, 4, 8, H, 32, J, K, 256

   H = ☐   J = ☐   K = ☐

   d) L, M, 125, N, 27, 8, 1

   L = ☐   M = ☐   N = ☐

   e) 27, P, 16, 10.5, R, –0.5, S

   P = ☐   R = ☐   S = ☐

2. Solve these equations. (Hint: Find the value of each letter.)

   a) $A + 7.5 = 25 - 10.5$

   b) $X - 2.25 = 3.5 \times 7$

   c) $3 \times C + 4 = 100 - 7.5 + 3$

   d) $4 \div E + 25.5 = 3 \times 4 + 15.5$

   e) $2 \times 3 + 32 = 3 \times S - 10.45$

Resource 6.3.1b

True or false?

A

Decide if each of the following statements are true or false. Circle your answer.

a) $c + c + c + d + d = 2c + 3d$ True/False

b) $r + r + 3z = 2r + 3z$ True/False

c) $x + y + x + y = 2x + 2y$ True/False

d) $4r + t + t + t + t = 4r + 3t$ True/False

e) $2s \times y + s + y + s = 2sy + 2s + y$ True/False

f) $3rs + r + s = rs + rs + r + s$ True/False

B

Decide if each of the following statements are true or false. Circle your answer.

a) $7 \times (c + d) = 7(c + e)$ True/False

b) $c \times c + y + y + y = c^3 + y^3$ True/False

c) $d \div 2 + e \div 4 = 0.5d + 0.25e$ True/False

d) $d^2 + t(d + t) = d \times d + t \times (d + s)$ True/False

e) $5(d + e) + 0.5e^2 = 5 \times (d + e) + e \times e \div 2$ True/False

f) $3e^2 + d \times d + 0.125e = 3 \times e \times e + d^2 + e \div 8$ True/False

C

Decide if each of the following statements are true or false. Circle your answer.

a) $c \times c \times y + c^3 + c^3 - y \div 4 = yc^2 + 2 \times c^3 - 0.25y$ True/False

b) $d^3 \div 2 \div 2 + e \div 4 = 0.25d^2 + 0.125e$ True/False

c) $3d + 2t(d + t) = d \times d + 2 \times t \times (d + t^2)$ True/False

d) $25(d + e^3) - 0.1ed^2 = 25 \times (d + e \times e \times e) - ed \times d \div 10$ True/False

Correct the right-hand side of these statements so that they are true.

e) $7 \times (c^2 + d) + 0.125d^3 = 7(c^2 + d \times d) + d^3 \div 4$

_____

f) $0.01x^2 - 0.01ef = 0.001(x^3 - ef)$

_____

g) $d^3 \div 2 \div 2 \div 2 + e^2 \div 8 = 0.2d^3 + 0.125e$

_____

Resource 6.3.1c

Expressions matching

$c^3d^2 + 2c^2$	$7 \times (e+f) - 2 \times t \times t$	$3a^2b^3 - 2 \times a$	$3n$
$c \times c \times c \times d \times d + 2 \times c \times c \times c$	$7(e+f) - 2t^2$	$3 \times a \times a \times b^3 - 2a$	$n + n + n$
$3a^2 - 2t^3$	$5(t+s) + 0.25t^2$	$4a \div 2 + 1$	$7a^2 - 4 \times t$
$a^2 + a^2 + a^2 - t^3 - t^3$	$5 \times (t+s) + f \times f \div 4$	$0.5a + 1$	$7 \times a \times a - 4t$

Laws matching

Cut out the grid to make three sets of six cards.

Commutative law of addition	___ + 14 = ___ + 13	A + ___ = B + ___
Commutative law of multiplication	23 × ___ = 24 × ___	___ × H = ___ × G
Associative law of addition	(3 + ___) + 7 = ___ + (5 + 7)	(___ + Y) + ___ = X + (___ + Z)
Associative law of multiplication	(___ × 6) × ___ = 3 × (___ × 9)	(___ × B) × ___ = A × (___ × C)
Distributive law of multiplication over addition	3 × (14 + ___) = 3 × ___ + ___ × 24	___ × (G + ___) = F × G + ___ × H = F___ + FH
Distributive law of multiplication over subtraction	___ × (___ − 5) = ___ × 12 − 4 × ___	___ × (K + ___) = J × K + ___ × L = JK + J___

Pairing expressions

Using the same colour for each pair, shade the expressions that have the same meaning.
Correct any errors you find. Fill in the blanks.

$gf + gh$

$w \times y - (-2xy + y \times x \times y)$

$(e^3 \div h) \div (f^3 \div h)$

$s \times r \times s + 2 \times s^2 \times s$

$c - (d + e)$

$n^2 - 2f$

$x \div 6y$

$wy - y^2 - 2xy$

$(20 \div 4) \div (2 \div 4$

$b - c - d$

$s^2r^2 + 2s^3$

$20 \div 2$

$b - (c + d)$

$g(f + h)$

$14 - 6 - 2$

$n \times n - 2 \times f$

$c - e - d$

$5r + 5s - y^2 \div 2$

$e^3 \div f^2$

Spot the equation errors

Look at equations A and B below and circle any errors that you spot on the right-hand side of the equation. Explain how the errors should be corrected.

For example:

$3y + 2x - y^2 = y^3 - 2x + 2y$

The first y has been written as a cube. It should be $3y$. There is a minus sign in front of $2x$. It should be a plus sign. There is a plus sign in front of the 2. It should be a minus sign. There is a 2 in front of the y. It should be y squared.

1. $3(w + z) + y + x^2 = w^3 + z - y - 2x$

_____

_____

_____

_____

2. $y^2 \div 4 = y^2 \div (2 \div 4) \div 3$

_____

_____

_____

_____

Resource 6.3.2a

Matching terms and sequences

Using the same colour for each pair, shade the *n*th terms and their linear number sequences. Fill in any blanks with numbers or operations.

Fill in two of the blank shapes with your own sequences and pass to your partner to fill in the other blanks with their *n*th terms.

2, 5, 10, 17, ___, 37, ___, ___

$3n$ ___ 2

$0.5n -$ ___

0, 0.5, ___, 1.5, 2, ___, 3, ___

___$n - 4$

$2n -$ ___

1, 3, 5, ___, 9, ___, 13, ___

1, 6, ___, 16, 21, ___, ___, 36

5, ___, 11, ___, ___, 20, 23, 26

n^2 ___ 1

Word problems

A

For each of these problems, set out your calculations clearly. Use a separate sheet of paper if necessary.

1. On three mornings a week, Daniel goes to the gym. He spends 25 minutes doing *r* circuits, followed by *t* minutes on the rowing machine.

   a) How many minutes does Daniel spend at the gym per morning?

   _____

   b) How many minutes does Daniel spend doing circuits per week?

   _____

2. A construction firm plans to build *m* houses. It plans to build a house every *n* days. However, it takes *n* + 2 days to build each house.
   How long does it take to build all the houses?

   _____

B

1. Alison walks for *g* minutes every other day for 15 days. She cycles for *h* minutes on each of the other days. She says that she spends 15*g* + *h* minutes in total exercising. She is not correct. Why?

   _____

2. Sanjit decides to read a book that is *r* pages long. He plans to read *t* pages every day. However, as he starts, he only manages to read a quarter of what he wants per day.
   Sanjit still thinks he can complete the book in the amount of time he wants to.
   Can you help him decide?

   _____

Expressions spiders

A

Draw lines from each shape and write equivalent expressions at the end of them.

$4(a + 2b)$

$7a - 4b$

$2a + 3b + 4$

$15a \div 5 + 4b$

B

Find the errors in the right-hand side of the equations then add another correct equivalent expression.

$5(x - 3) + 3 \times 5s - 3x - 4x = 5x - 10 + 35s - 12x =$

_____

$12f^2 + g + 2f(f - 2) + 12f^2 \div 6 = 12f^2g + 2fg - 4 + 3 \times 3f + 3 =$

_____

Resource 6.3.3b

Expressions matching

$3n + n - 2n + 4p$	$(6 \div 1.5)\, p + 1.5n \div 0.5 - n$	$d(7a - 4) + 45a \div 3$
$15a - ad - 2d - 2d + 8ad$	$3(4x + 25y - 18y)$	$(42 \div 2 \times 3y \div 9) \times 3 + 4 \times 3x$
$4a \div 2 \times 11$	$6 \times 4a \div 8 + 19a$	$7(e + f) - 2f^2$
$7f + 0 \times 3e + 7e - 4f^2 \div 2$	$65x + 76x$	$10[7.6x + (0.5 + 6)x]$

Problem diagrams (1)

A

For each of these problems, draw diagrams to help you answer the questions. Set out your work clearly.

1. The length of rectangle D is g cm. Its width is half as long.

   The length of square E is twice the length of rectangle D.

   a) What is the total length of the two perimeters?

   b) What is the area of rectangle D?

   c) What is the area of square E?

2. Peter, Frank, Ann and Maria each swam s km last week on Monday, Tuesday and Wednesday.

   This week they each swam g km on four days of the week.

   What is the total distance they have swum altogether?

B

Look again at Question 2 of section A because the information is discovered to be wrong.

Last week, the four students each swam $s + 2\,\text{km}$ on Monday, Tuesday and Wednesday.

This week they swam $g - 3\,\text{km}$ on five days of the week.

Find out the correct total distance they swam altogether.

Problem diagrams (2)

A

For each of these problems, draw diagrams to help you answer the questions. Set out your work clearly.

1. Mint costs £0.25 per 12 g in the supermarket.

    How much does Alice pay for 54 g of mint?

2. Salad tomatoes cost £1.90 per kg in the supermarket.

    How much does Sarah pay for 1.5 kg of tomatoes?

3. Baby spinach costs £0.62 per 100 g in the supermarket.

    How much does Katie pay for 810 g of spinach?

4. Terry builds 5 toy cars in n hours and Mustafa builds g toy cars in 5 hours.
    How many toy cars do they each build each hour, on average?

5. Look again at Question 4. On average, how many hours do Terry and Mustafa each spend on one toy car?

6. David is 5 years older than his brother Samuel.

   y represents David's age and x represents Samuel's age.

   a) Express y in terms of x.

   b) Express x in terms of y.

   c) How old will David be when Samuel is n years old?

   d) How old will Samuel be when David is $2n$ years old?

B

Look again at Question 6 in section A because the information about David's age was recorded incorrectly.

David is 5.5 years older than Samuel.

How old will David be when Samuel is $n - 2$ years old?

How old will Samuel be when David is $2n + 1$ years old?

Resource 6.3.4a

Sequences and *nth* terms

A

Draw lines to connect the *nth* terms and their corresponding linear number sequences. Fill in any blanks with numbers.

$2n + 4$

$3\frac{2}{3}, 4\frac{1}{3}, \text{\_\_}, \text{\_\_}, 6\frac{1}{3}, \text{\_\_}$

$3n - 1$

$8, \text{\_\_}, \text{\_\_}, 23, 28, \text{\_\_}$

$5n + 3$

$2, 5, \text{\_\_}, \text{\_\_}, 14, \text{\_\_}$

$6, 8, \text{\_\_}, 12, \text{\_\_}, \text{\_\_}$

$\frac{2}{3}n + 3$

B

1. Mia wants to buy some toy cars priced at £3 each. The relation between the total price she pays, *s*, and the number of cars she buys, *t*, can be represented as $3t = s$. When $t = 1$, 4 and 11 what values does *s* represent, respectively?

2. Naomi swims 15 lengths every week. The relation between the total number of lengths, *P*, and the number of weeks, *q*, can be represented as $P = 15q$. When $q = 2$, 6 and 10, what values does *P* represent respectively?

C

Using the formulae, write the first five terms of each sequence.

1. $5(n - 2)$

2. $3n - 4$

3. $1.6n + 6$

4. $7 - 4n$

Word problems – applying algebra (1)

A

For each of these problems, draw diagrams to help you answer the questions. Set out your work clearly.

1. In the local bakery, *d* loaves were made every week for 3 weeks, then 30 loaves were made in the fourth week.

   a) Use an expression to express the number of loaves that were made altogether.

   b) If 75 loaves were made every week for the first 3 weeks, how many loaves were made altogether?

2. It rained every day for *r* minutes over a 12-day period. It then snowed every day for *s* minutes over a 10-day period.

   When $r = 12$ and $s = 13$, what is the total number of minutes?

3. An isosceles triangle has side lengths $3r$, $3r$, and $2s$.
   What is the perimeter of the triangle when $r = 4.5\,$cm and $s = 3.8\,$cm?

B

For each of these problems, draw diagrams to help you answer the questions. Set out your work clearly.

1. In the local gym, Amanda and Dave are using weights. Amanda lifts r kg for 12 days and Dave lifts s kg every day for 7 weeks.
   If $r = 15$ and $s = 2r$, how many kg did they lift altogether?

2. A design company makes picture frames. The length of the picture frame is $\frac{4}{3}$ the width of the picture frame.
   If the width is 105 mm, what is the length of the picture frame in centimetres?

3. What is the maximum area a picture could be for the picture frame in Question 2? Give your answer in mm².

Word problems – applying algebra (2)

For each of these problems, draw diagrams to help you answer the questions. Set out your work clearly.

1. A warehouse has tins, boxes of cereal and boxes of fruit. The tins are in t rows with 12 in each row, the boxes of cereal are in v rows with 14 in each row and the boxes of fruit are in $t + v$ rows, with 15 in each row.

   a) If $t = 15$ and $v = 16$, how many boxes and tins are there altogether?

   b) The warehouse reorganises the items. There is still the same number of items in each row, but they are now all in y rows, where $y = r + s$.
   Write an expression in terms of r and s to show the total number of items altogether.

   If $r = 30$ and $s = 45$, how many boxes and tins are there altogether?

2. A lorry travelled at v km per hour in the morning and 0.75v km per hour in the afternoon. It travelled 4.5 hours in the morning, stopped for 1.5 hours and then travelled d hours in the afternoon.

When $v = 80$ and $d = 3.5$:

How far did the lorry travel?

How many hours was the total journey?

What was the speed, on average, for the whole journey, not including stopping?

Resource 6.3.5

Establish equations

A

1. The sum of two cats' ages is 13. If *a* and *b* are their ages:

   a) Establish an equation with *a* and *b*. _____

   b) Complete the table below to list all the possible combinations of *a* and *b* that satisfy the equation. Use positive integers.

a	1	2	3	4	5	6	7	8	9	10	11	12
b												

2. The total length of two boats is 33 m. If *g* and *h* are the lengths:

   a) Establish an equation with *g* and *h*. _____

   b) Complete the table below to list possible combinations of *g* and *h* that satisfy the equation. Use positive integers.

g	22	24	26	28	30	32
h						

B

1. The sum of the heights of Sanjit and Pierre is 2.5 m. A fairground ride has a minimum height of 1.2 m.
   What are the minimum and maximum heights Sanjit and Pierre can be?

   _____

2. The difference of two dogs' ages is 12. The maximum age a dog will live to is 16. Find four different ages the dogs can be. Use positive integers.

   _____

3. A garage is 8.5 m long. A car is 1.5 m shorter than a van.

   What is the maximum length of car so that both car and van can fit together in the garage? Use examples to explain your reasoning.

Solve equations (1)

A

Find the solutions to these equations using bar models.

1. $H - 3 = 19$

2. $7 = b - 3.4$

3. $4 = 7 - x$

4. $25 - e = 18.2$

5. $W \div 4 = 11$

6. $2.5 = x \div 5$

7. $10 \div f = 2$

8. $0.5 = g \div 7$

B

1. Find the pairs of numbers that satisfy the equation $2x + y = 10$. Use positive integers.

_____

_____

2. Find the pairs of numbers that satisfy the equation $x + 4y = 18$. Use positive integers.

_____

_____

3. Find five pairs of numbers that satisfy the equation $3x - y = 15$. Use positive integers.

_____

_____

C

1. Find five pairs of numbers that satisfy the equation $2x - 3y = 12$. Use integers.

_____

_____

2. Find five pairs of numbers that satisfy the equation $0.5x - 2y = 6$. Use integers.

_____

_____

Solve equations (2)

A

Find the solutions to these equations. Set your work out clearly. The first one has been done for you.

1. $H + 5.4 = 11.2$

$H = 11.2 - 5.4$

$= 5.8$

Check: 5.8 + 5.4 = 11.2.
It checks.

2. $12.21 = 9.81 + D$

3. $34 = c - 7.4$

4. $18.4 - g = 5.6$

B

Find the solutions to these equations. Set your work out clearly.

1. $12.3 = 3f$

2. $0.5g = 4$

3. $x \div 3.4 = 5$

4. $7.5 \div r = 15$

5. $c \div 3.45 = 0$

C

Find the solutions to these equations. Set your work out clearly.

1. $4x \div 3.4 = 6$

2. $7.5 \div 2r = 15$

3. $3c \div 2.4 = 1$

Resource 6.3.6c

Equations match

$x \div 0.7 = 5$	3.5	$30.23 = 10.81 + f$
19.42	$11.6 = c + 6.8$	4.8
$w + 12.5 = 19.5$	7	$12.44 - g = 5.6$
6.84	$8.5 \div r = 17$	0.5

Equation problems

A

Solve the following problems carefully. Set your work out clearly.

1. Tim the tortoise is 15.5 years older than his sister Petra.
   Petra is y years old and Tim is 55. Write an equation and find the solution.

2. A taxi parked on the left is 85 cm shorter than a taxi parked on the right. The shorter taxi is v m long and the longer taxi is 350 cm long. Write an equation and find the solution.

3. Ahmed walked 16.8 km on the treadmill last week. He walked t km each day. Write an equation and find the solution.

4. S carrots are used by 45 students. They have exactly three carrots each. Andrew wants to know how many carrots there were. Can you help?

B

1. Look again at Question 3 from section A. Ahmed made a mistake. He actually walked 22.4 km on the treadmill last week. He also drove a total of 31.5 km to get to the gym.
   Can you help him find how many km he drove and walked each day?

2. Look again at Question 4 from section A. *D* pieces of fruit and *R* drinks were also used by the students. In total, 270 carrots, pieces of fruit and drinks were used by the students. Can you suggest what each student had? Explain your reasoning.

Connect equations and solutions

A

Draw lines to connect each equation with its solution.

$H + 5.5 = 17.8$

$9 \div x = 6$

$15 - x = 4.82$

11.22

0.5

$3.3h = 1.65$

$x + 4.2 + 3.8 = 38.25$

12.3

30.25

10.18

1.5

$j - 7.8 = 3.42$

B

1. $x + 4x - x = $ _____

2. $c - 4c + 6c = $ _____

3. $12v \div 4 = $ _____

4. $2j \times 4 - 5j \div 5 = $ _____

5. $30n \div 6 \times 2 - 4n = $ _____

6. $2f + 4f \times 5 + 3f \div 2f = $ _____

Solve the equations

$4r + 2 = 6$	$2v - 2 = 4$	$2q \div 3 = 6$
$s \div 2 = 6 - s$	$3x = 4 + x$	$t - 6 = 3 - t$

Find the solutions (1)

A

Find the solutions to these equations. Set your work out clearly.

1. $4H + 3.6 = 28$

2. $12.8 = 5b - 3.7$

3. $5 = 7 - x \div 4$

4. $25.4 - e \div 2 = 18.2$

5. $5 + 4x = 22 - 4.5x$

6. $6.8 - 0.2y = 2.8 + 0.2y$

7. $(5 + 1.4) \div f = 4$

8. $0.5 = (6.4 - 3.4) \div k$

9. $30 = 3(6 + h)$

10. $4(s + 3.2) = 26.8$

11. $(c + 6) \div 0.5 = 30$

12. $100 = (s - 5.5) \div 1.5$

B

David has written four solutions to equations:

3   3.5   4.2   1.2

What were his equations? Use examples from section A to help you.

Equations and solutions

A

Write equations for each problem, then find the solutions. Show your working clearly.

1. Sanjit bought *d* salads from the deli at £3 each. He paid with £50 and was given £8 change. Find *d*.

2. Samantha bought *s* cakes from the bakery with £30. Each cake cost £2.50. She had £10 left. Find *s*.

3. A company bought 8 pallets of paper with *x* kg on each pallet. 60 kg was used and 28 kg was left. Find *x*.

4. Pierre ran 4 km for *g* days. He ran 14 km then had 18 km left. Find *g*.

5. Amanda bought 5 presents at *r* pounds each. She paid £200 and got £14 change. Find *r*.

6. Sanjit bought *e* drinks from the supermarket at £1.50 each. He paid with £50 and was given £23 change. Find *e*.

7. A company bought 12 pallets of oranges with *x* kg on each pallet. 70 kg was used and 38 kg was left. Find *x*.

8. Petra bought *s* DVDs from a supermarket with £50. Each DVD cost £3.50. She had £18.50 left. Find *s*.

B

Fatima bought *d* salads costing £3 each and *e* drinks costing £0.80 each, from the deli. She paid with £50 and was given £8 change. How many different values for *d* and *e* can you find? Show all your working and explain your reasoning.

Find the solutions (2)

A

Find the solutions to these equations. Set your work out clearly.

1. $3c \div 3 - 6 = 10$

2. $4v \div 2 + 5 = 13$

3. $14.8 = 5b \div 4 + 5$

4. $7x + 1.5 - 2x = 2.2$

5. $8x - 3.5 - 5x = 5.8$

6. $0.5 = 3d - 5.5 + 5d$

7. $4(x - 2.5) + 2x = 5$

8. $6 = 3(x - 1.6) + 3x$

9. $6(y + 1.2) + 4y = 9$

B

David has written four solutions to equations:

4   1.5   4.6   1.85

What were his equations? Use examples from section A to help you.

Real-life problems (1)

A

Use equations to find the answers to these problems. Set your work out clearly.

1. There were 215 people on a ferry. When it docked, 137 people were left on the ferry.
   How many people got off the ferry?

2. Freda cycled 92 km over two days. On the first day she cycled 34 km.
   How many kilometres did she cycle on the second day?

3. A company bought 296 kg of paper. It was shared by 8 offices.
   How many kilograms of paper did each office receive?

4. There are 74 poodles in a dog show which is twice the number of labradors.
   How many labradors are there in the dog show?

5. Mohammed can do 92 press ups in 2 minutes. This is 7 more than Mark can do in 2 minutes.
How many press up can Mark do in 2 minutes?

6. The area of a town is 56 km². The length of the town is 7 km.
What is the width of the town?

7. Claire bought 1 sofa and 6 chairs at a cost of £736. The chairs were priced at £58 each.
How much did the sofa cost?

B

Use equations to find the answers to these problems. Set your work out clearly.

1. Last week 124 people attended the cinema. 76 people did not buy a programme.

    This week 2.5 times more people attended than last week and the same number of people did not buy a programme. How many programmes were sold this week?

2. At the gym last week, Gita spent 7 minutes on the rowing machine and the rest of time lifting weights. This week, she spent 11 minutes on the rowing machine and the rest of the time lifting weights. Over the two weeks she spent 90 minutes at the gym.

    Write an equation that represents Gita's time at the gym.

    For how long did Gita lift weights?

Complete the working

A

Find the solutions, or complete the working, for these problems. Set your work out clearly.

1. $8x - 9.3 = 7.5$

2. Complete the working.

$18.4 = 5g +$ _____

$5g =$ _____ $- 6.9$

_____ $g = 11.5$

$g = 11.5 \div 5$

$= 2.3$

Check: $18.4 = 5 \times$ _____ $+ 6.9$

It checks.

3. $357 \div 7 = 6x$

4. Complete the working.

$7x = 157.5 \div 3$

$7x =$ _____

$x = 52.5 \div$ _____

$=$ _____

Check: $7 \times 7.5 =$ _____ $\div 3$

It checks.

5. $4(x + 2.7) = 14.4$

6. $2.4 = 6(x - 0.4)$

7. Complete the working.

$12e \div 4 - e =$ _____

$3e -$ _____ $= 2.4$

_____$e = 2.4$

$e = 2.4 \div 2$

$=$ _____

Check: ___$e \times 1.2 \div$ _____ $- e = 2.4$

It checks.

8. $3.9 = 28x \div 7 + 2x$

B

Return to Questions 1 to 8 in section A.

Choose three questions from 1, 3, 5, 6 and 8.

For each one, change one of the numbers so that it is to two decimal places.

Find the new solutions.

Real-life problems (2)

A

Find the solutions to these problems. Set your work out clearly.

1. In a swimming club, the number of swimmers from town A equals the number of swimmers from town B multiplied by 4 then add 14.

   If 70 people are from town A, how many people are from town B?

2. A box of novels weighs 22 kg. This is 3.5 kg less than 1.5 times the weight of a box of comics.

   What is the weight of the box of comics?

3. A rubber costs £0.45 more than 4 pencils. The rubber is £0.85.

   What is the cost of a pencil?

4. The height of a mountain is 1500 m. This is 400 m shorter than twice the height of a small hill.

What is the height of the small hill?

5. A pair of trousers is priced at £82. This is £15 more than four times the price of a pair of shorts.

How much is the pair of shorts?

6. 25 people ran and 23 people walked in a race. In total, this was 4 times the number of people who watched the race.

How many people watched the race?

7. Last week, a car dealer bought 450 cars. This was 35 less than half the number in a car park. How many cars were in the car park?

B

1. In a swimming club, two times the number of swimmers from town C subtract 3 equals the number of swimmers from town D multiplied by 3 then add 15. If 60 people are from town C, how many people are from town D?

2. Last week, 3 rubbers cost £0.27 more than 6 pencils. A rubber was £0.65. This week, the price of a rubber is twice the cost of last week and a pencil is half the cost. What is the cost of a pencil and rubber this week?

Resource 6.3.10a

Match equations and solutions

$72.5 - e = 36.7$	35.8	$x \div 2.8 = 2.8$	7.84
$4f + 2.5 = 16.3$	3.45	$(5.7 + 1.3) \div y = 0.7$	10
$4(c + 2.5) = 10.8$	0.2	$4r + 2.5 \,(3r - 4) = 13$	2
$30t \div 1.5 - 15t = 6(t - 3)$	18	$(8z + 3.5) \div 3 = 54.5$	20

Resource 6.3.10b

Create expressions

Real-life problems (3)

A

Find the solutions to these problems. Set your work out clearly.

1. A warehouse received 120 kg of cereal. This was 40 kg more than 4 times the amount of sugar it received.
   How much sugar did the warehouse receive?

2. Ahmed ran 62 km last week. This was 8 km more than twice the amount Chris ran.
   How many kilometres did Chris run?

3. Peter's dad is 47 years old. This is 3 years more than 4 times Peter's age.
   How old is Peter?

4. There are 54 birds and some squirrels in a tree. There are 9 times as many birds as squirrels.
   How many squirrels are there?

5. The volume of a large motorbike engine is 1.1 litres. This is 400 ml less than 6 times the volume of a small motorbike engine.
    What is the volume of the small motorbike engine?

6. Diane is 3 times the age of Jenny. Diane is 28 years older than Jenny.
    What is the total age of Diane and Jenny?

7. A framing company bought 88 m of wood. This was the exact amount to make 40 small picture frames and 24 mirror frames. 0.4 m of wood was needed for each picture frame.
    How much wood was needed for each mirror frame?

8. Four years ago, a father was 7 times the age of his son. The father is 46 years old this year.
    What is the total age of the father and son this year?

B

1. On Monday, a warehouse received 135 kg of flour and W kg of washing up liquid. On Tuesday the warehouse received two thirds the amount of flour and four-fifths the amount of washing up liquid. The total received over the two days was 360 kg.
   How much washing up liquid did the warehouse receive altogether?

2. Sam walked A km every day during week 1. In week 2 he walked 1.5 times the total distance of week 1. In week 3 he walked twice the total distance of week 1. In total Sam walked 252 km over the three weeks.
   What is the value of A?

Perpendicular pairs

Mark right angles with the correct sign. Record pairs of perpendicular lines below the diagrams in the form **AB ⊥ CD**.

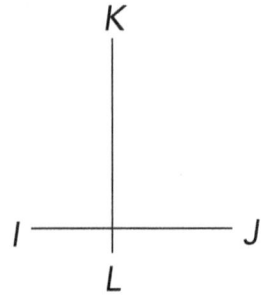

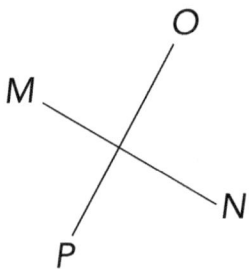

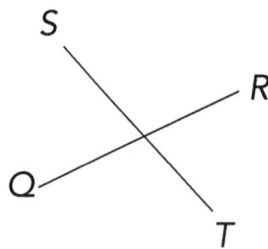

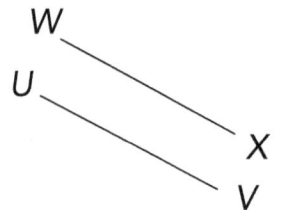

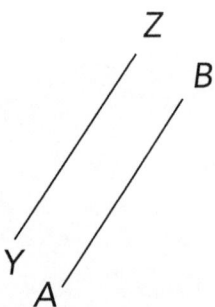

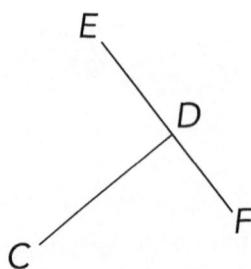

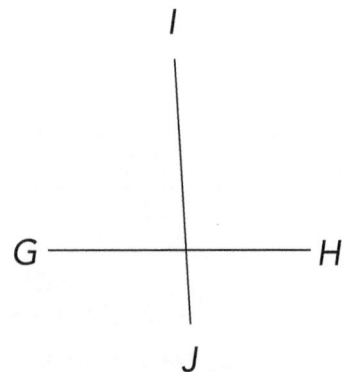

Paths of shortest distance

Mark a point *P* on a piece of paper. Draw three lines, *AB*, *CD* and *EF* at different distances from point *P* (see diagram below).

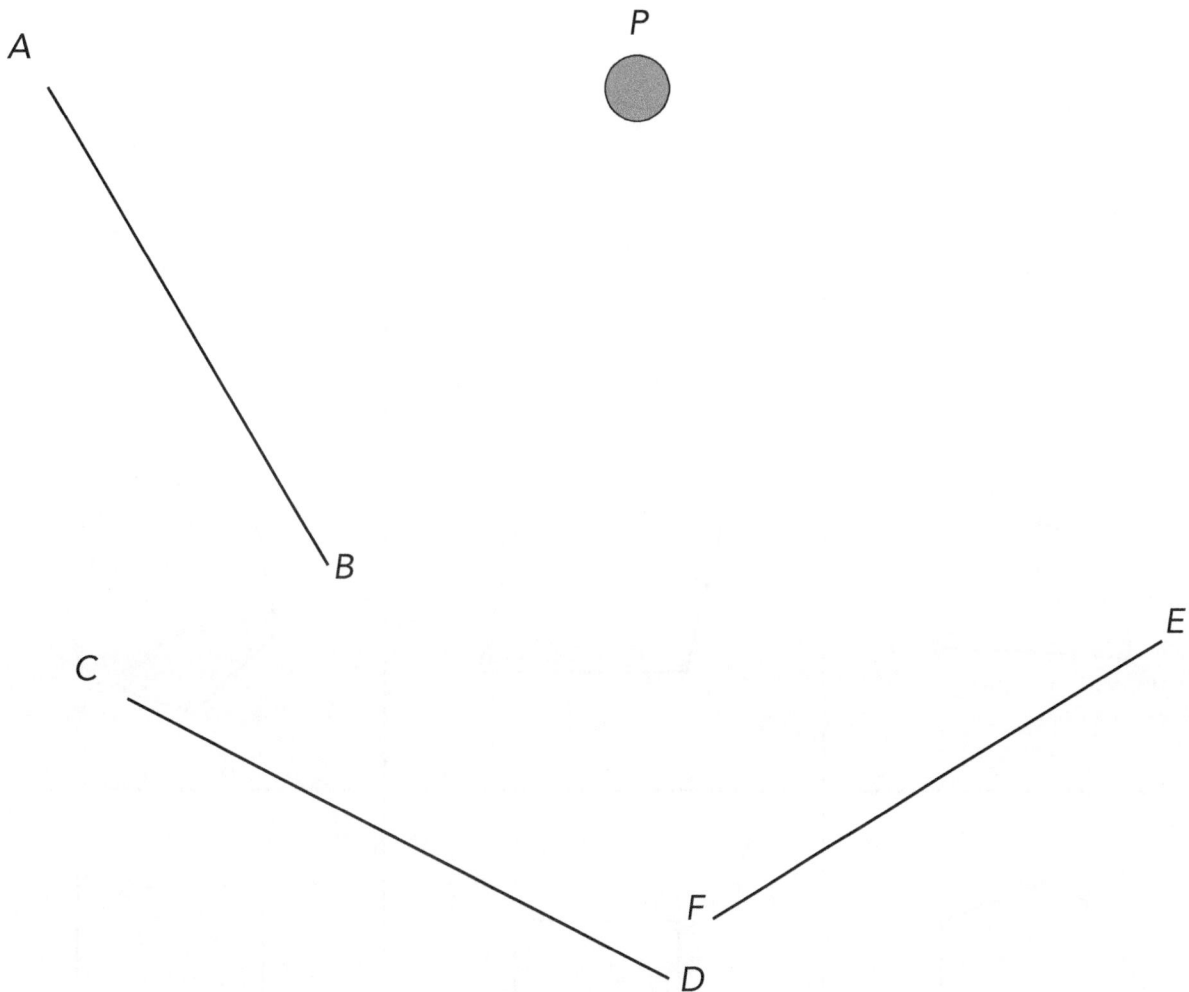

Draw a dotted line from each of the lines *AB*, *CD* and *EF* to *P* so that, in each case, the dotted line is the shortest possible distance between the line and the point.

Next, on the back of the sheet, draw another point and three lines for your partner, who must add the dotted lines to show the shortest distance between each line and the point.

Shapes

Cut out the shapes.

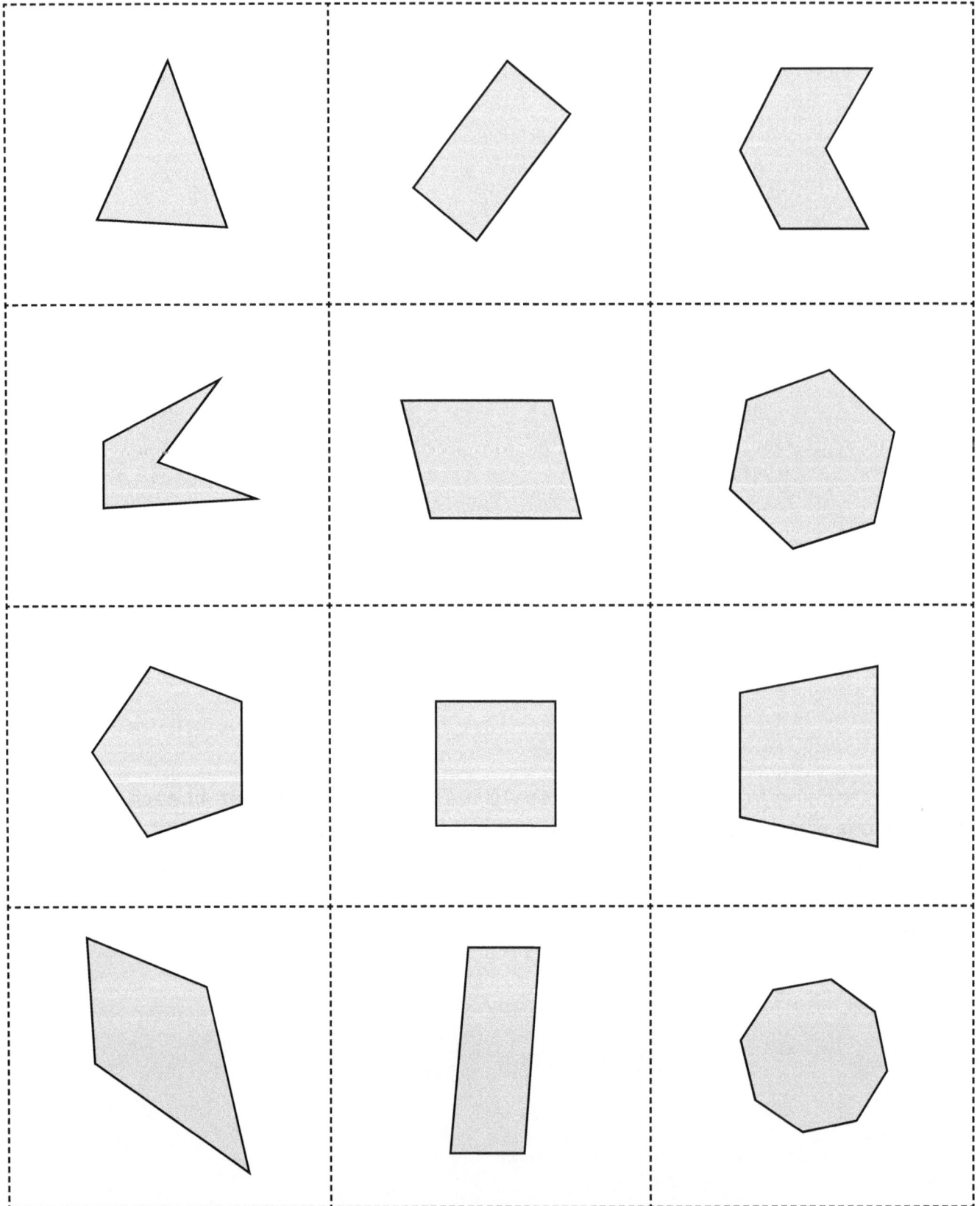

Parallel pairs

Circle the pairs of parallel lines.

1.

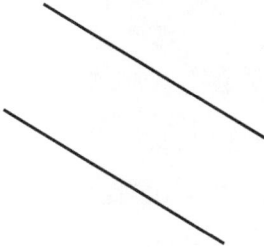

2.

3.

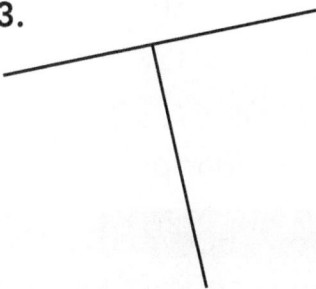

4.

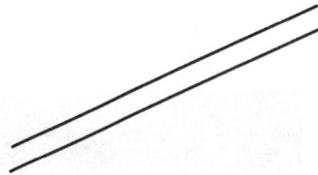

5.

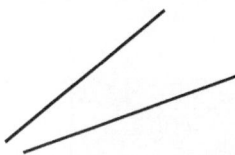

6.

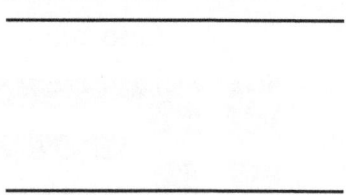

7.

8.

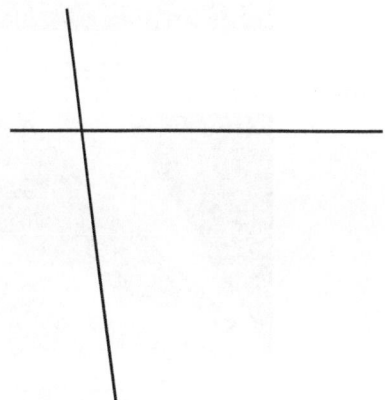

Flags

Use a highlighter pen to mark parallel and perpendicular lines.

Central African Republic

St. Kitts & Nevis

Syrla

Sao Tome & Principe

Georgia

Togo

Greece

Norway

Seychelles

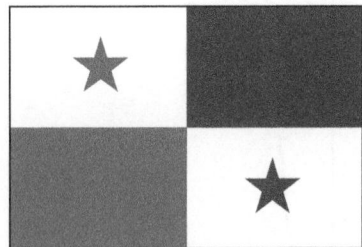

Panama

Parallelograms (1)

Count the squares up and across.

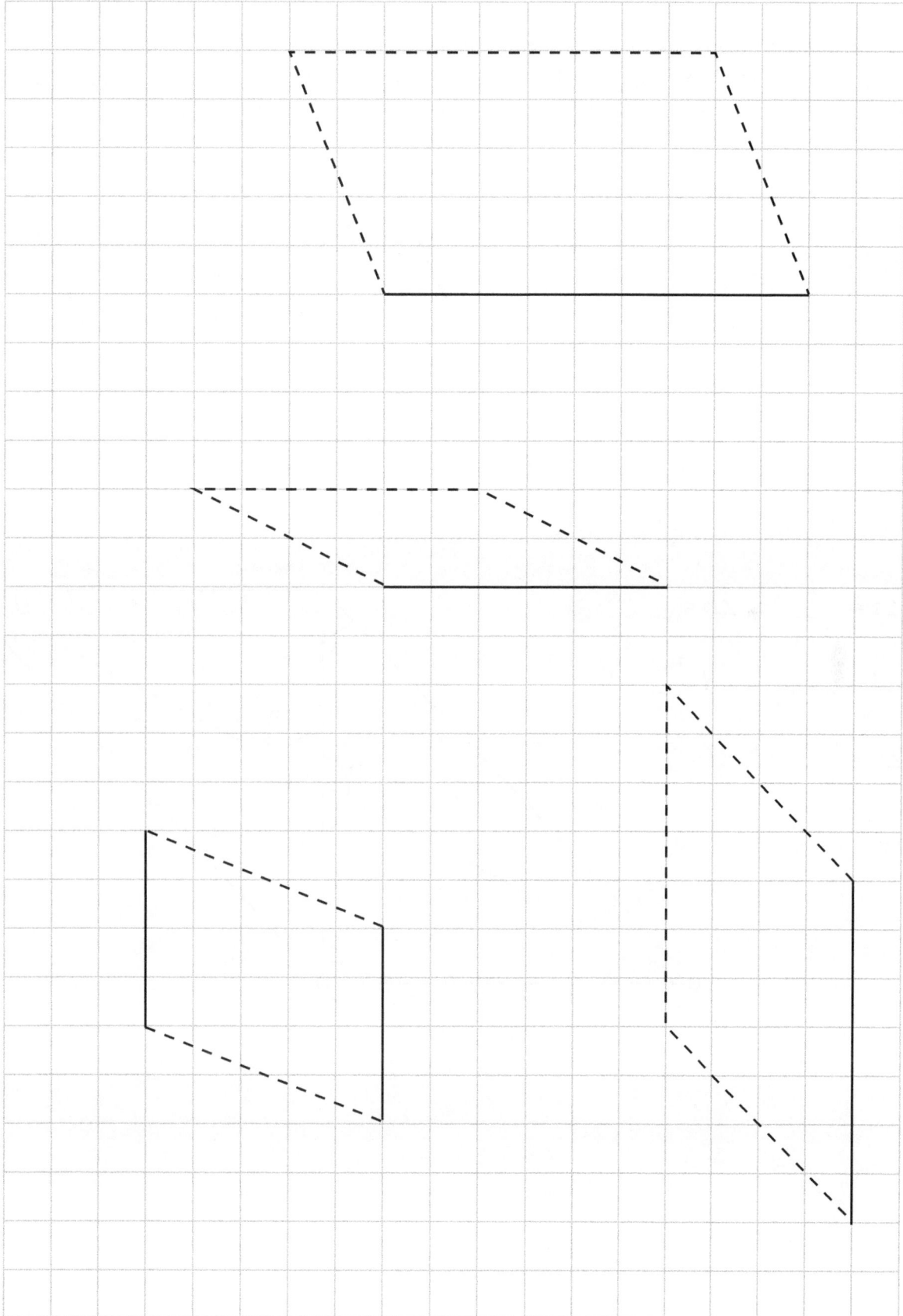

Missing angles

Work out the missing angles in each problem.

1. A parallelogram is cut along its diagonals to give two acute-angled triangles and two obtuse-angled triangles. If the acute angle of one of the triangles (∠AXD) is 63°, what size are the other three angles ∠AXB, ∠BXC and ∠CXD?

    ∠AXB = _____ °

    ∠BXC = _____ °

    ∠CXD = _____ °

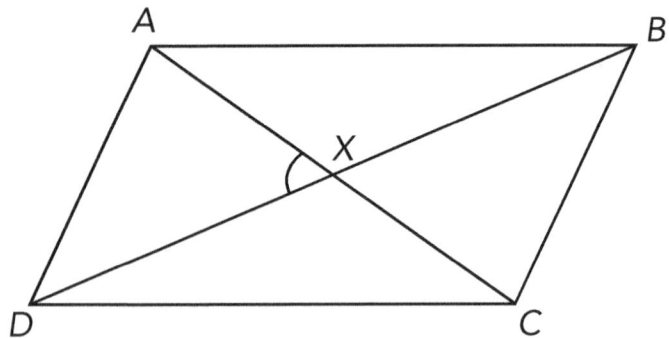

2. Find the missing angles a to g.

    ∠a = _____ °   ∠b = _____ °

    ∠c = _____ °   ∠d = _____ °

    ∠e = _____ °   ∠f = _____ °

    ∠g = _____ °

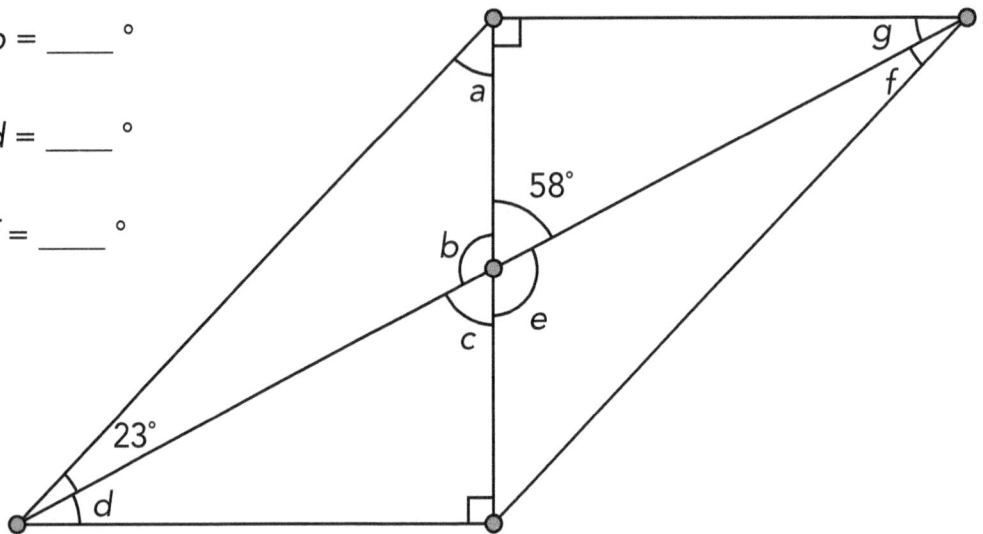

Parallelograms (2)

Cut out the parallelograms.

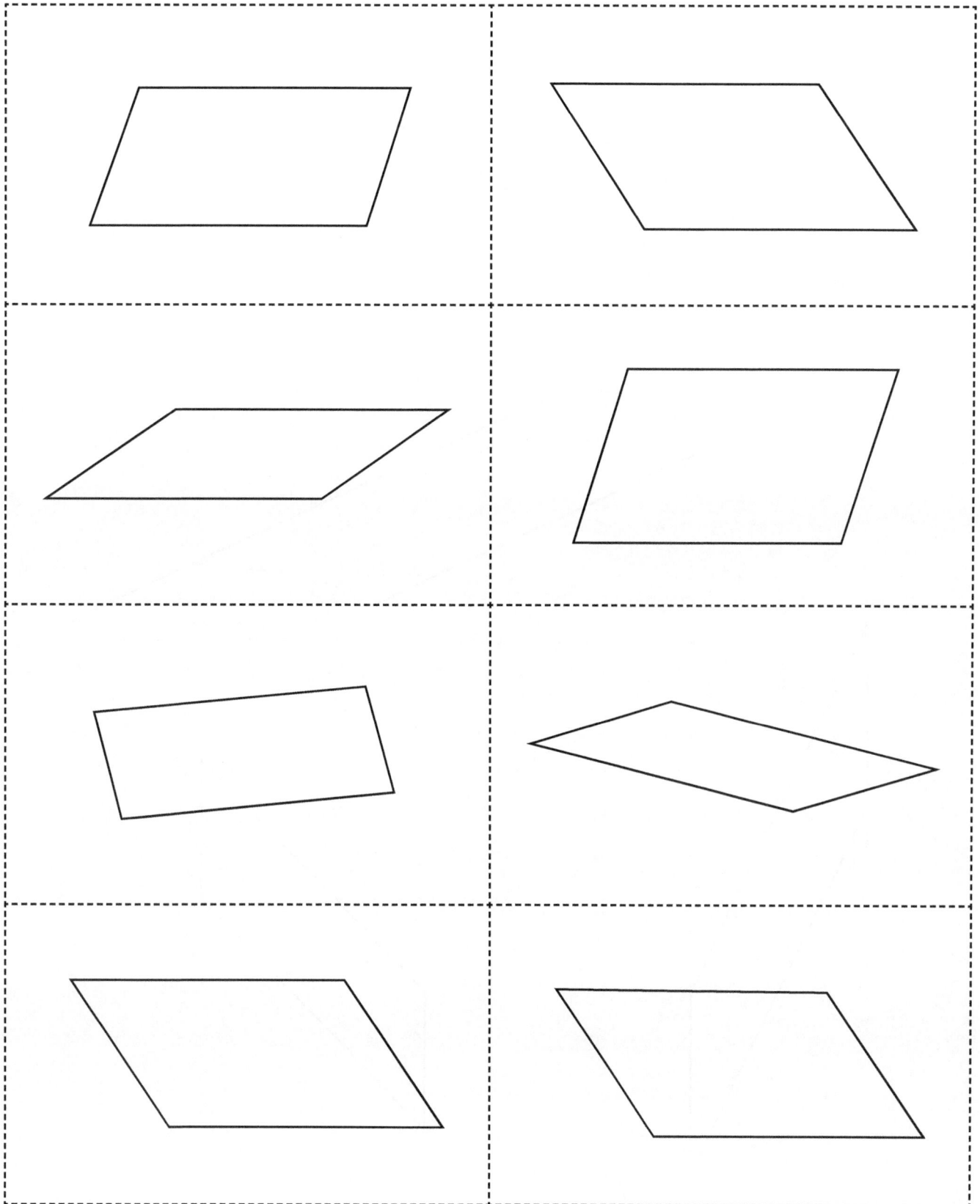

Height of parallelograms

Mark and label the height of each parallelogram. The base is drawn in grey.

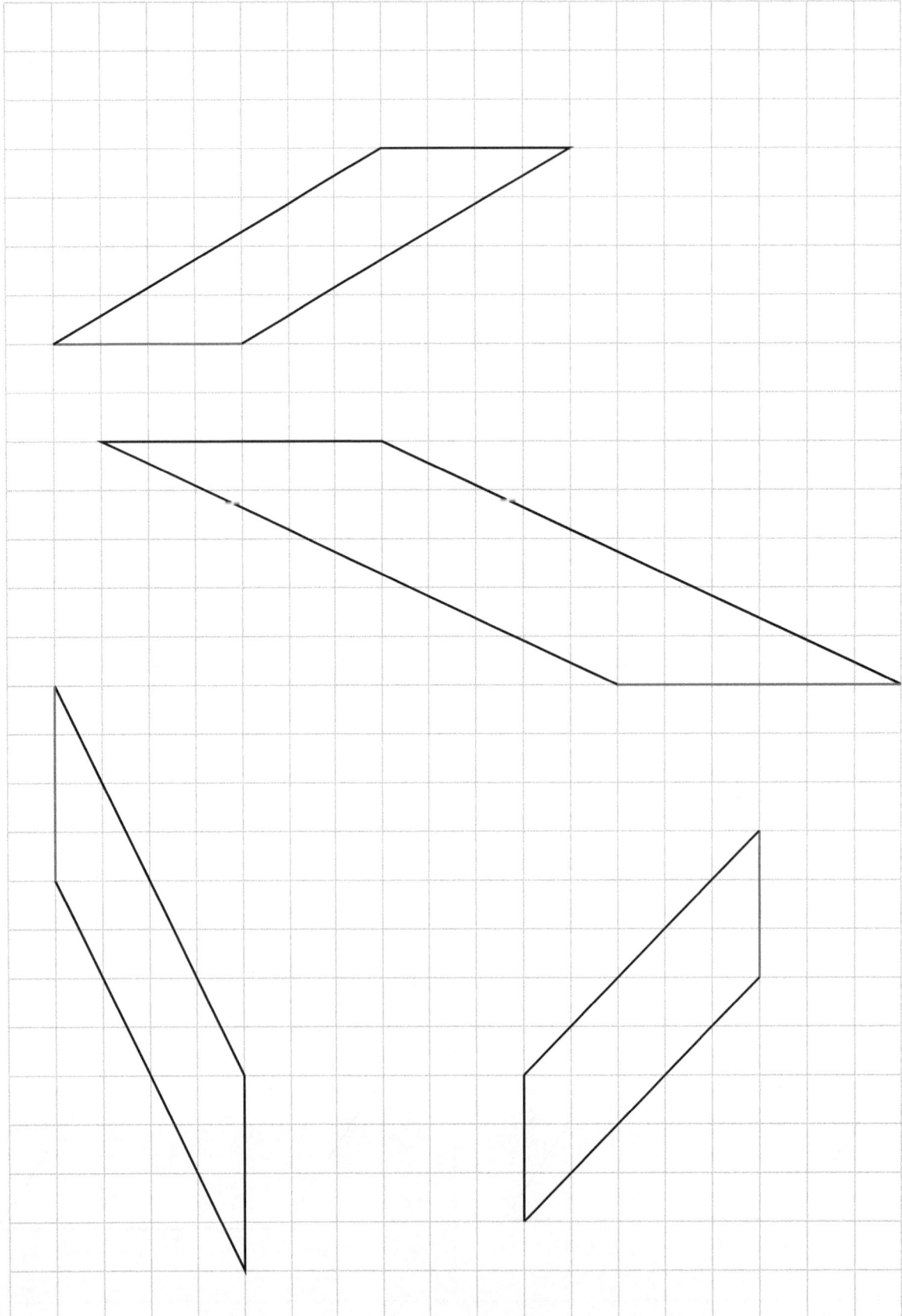

Parallelograms (3)

Draw parallelograms that have the same base and height as the shape given.

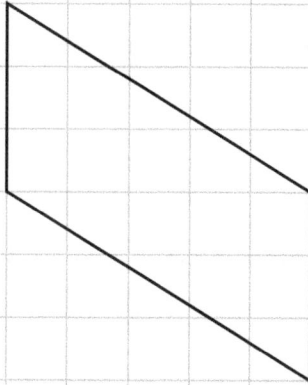

Resource 6.4.5a

Parallelograms (4)

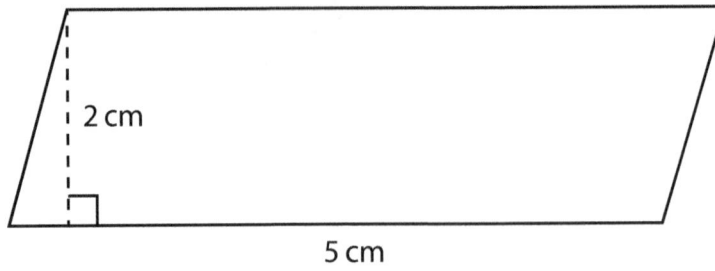

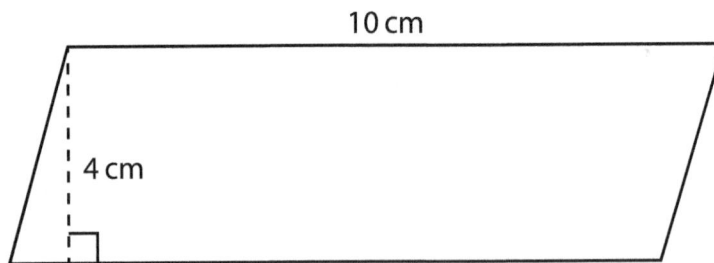

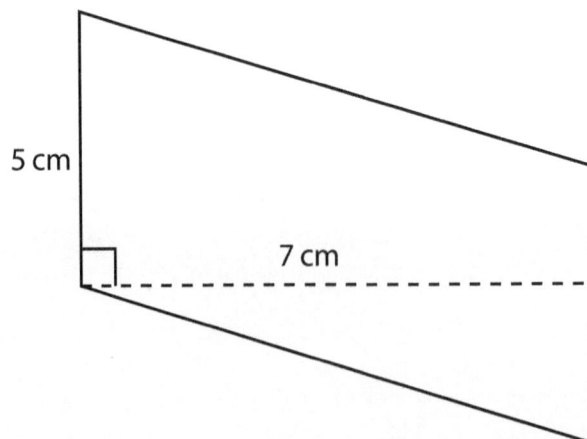

2 cm

5 cm

10 cm

4 cm

5 cm

7 cm

Parallelograms (5)

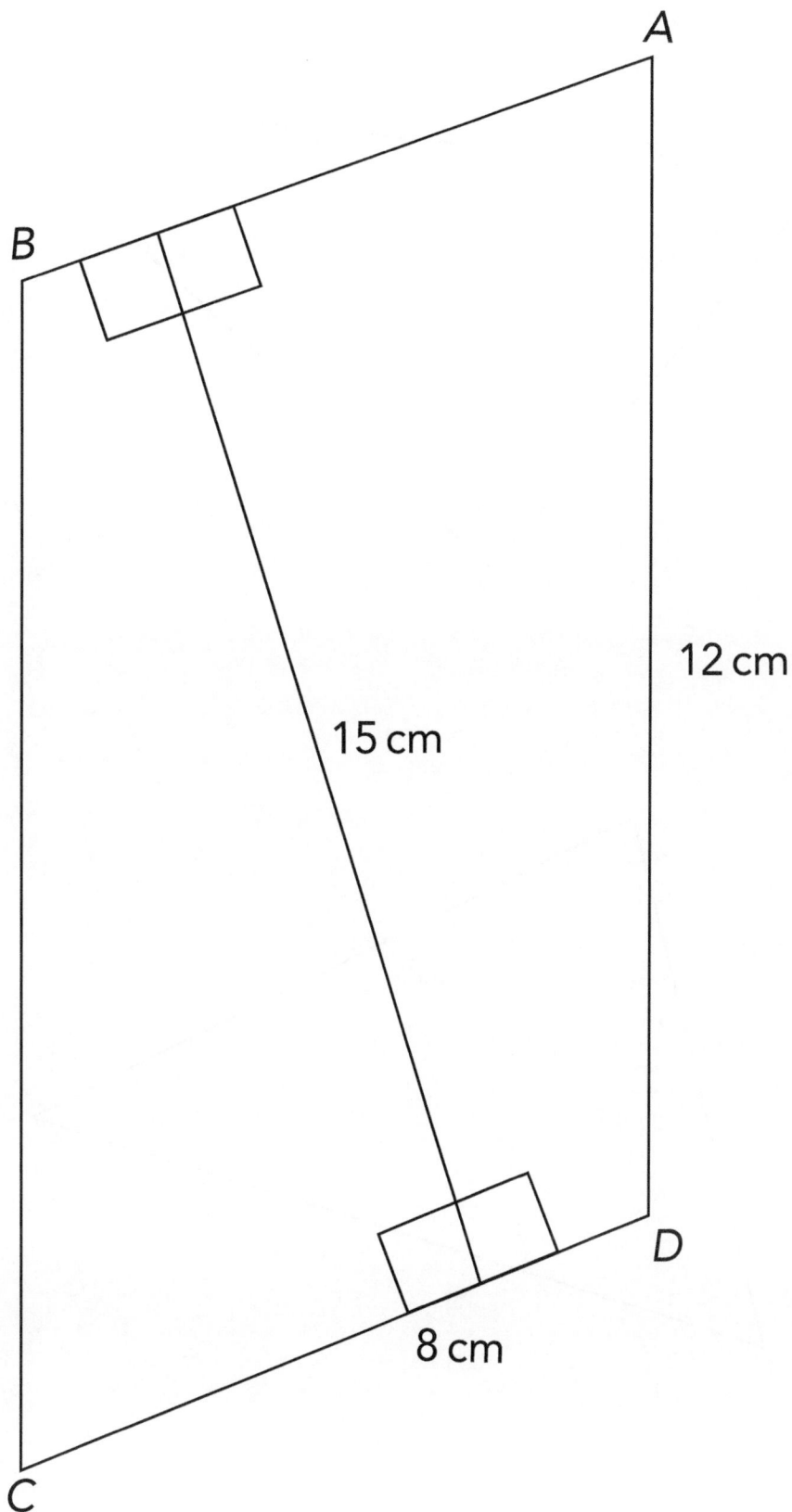

Heights of triangles

Use a set square to mark the three heights for each triangle.

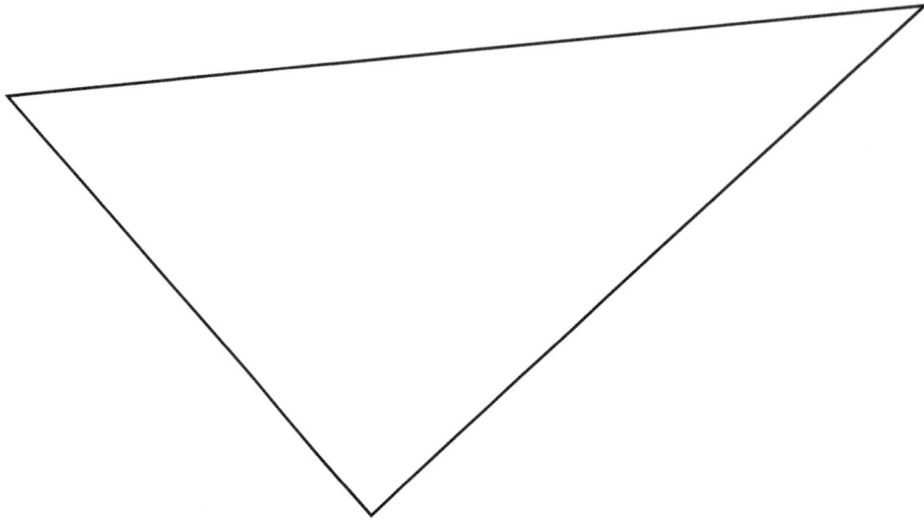

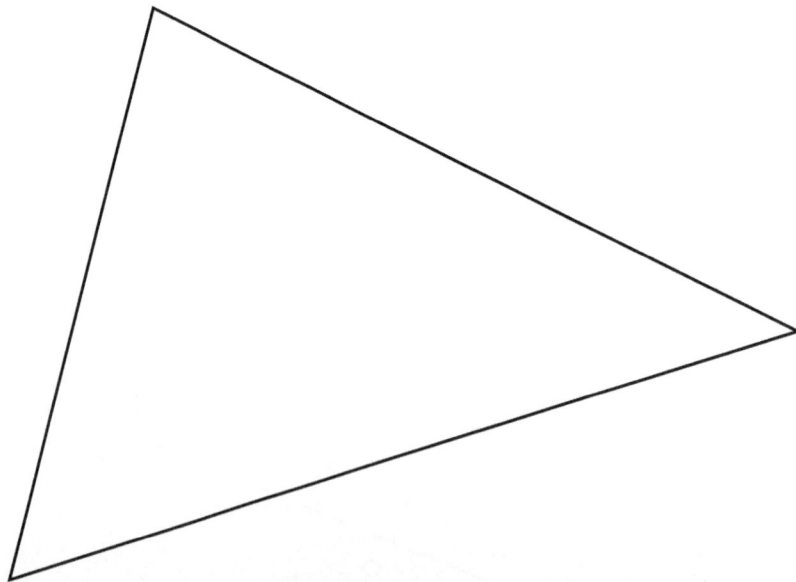

Making connections

Fill in the blanks to calculate the products.

1.

```
        3  1              3  1
   ×    1  5         ×    1 . 5
   ┌──┬──┬──┐        ┌──┬──┬──┐
   │  │  │  │        │←─┼──┼─→│
   ├──┼──┼──┤        ├──┼──┼──┤
   │  │  │  │        │  │  │  │
   ├──┴──┴──┤        ├──┴──┴──┤
   │  │  │  │        │  │  │  │
   └──┴──┴──┘        └──┴──┴──┘
```

2.

```
        9  0              9  0
   ×    1  3         ×    1 . 3
   ┌──┬──┬──┐        ┌──┬──┬──┐
   │  │  │  │        │←─┼──┼─→│
   ├──┼──┼──┤        ├──┼──┼──┤
   │  │  │  │        │  │  │  │
   ├──┴──┴──┤        ├──┴──┴──┤
   │  │  │  │        │  │  │  │
   └──┴──┴──┘        └──┴──┴──┘
```

3.

```
        2  7              2 . 7
   ×    5  5         ×    5 . 5
   ┌──┬──┬──┐        ┌──┬──┬──┐
   │  │  │  │        │←─┼──┼─→│
   ├──┼──┼──┤        ├──┼──┼──┤
   │  │  │  │        │  │  │  │
   ├──┴──┴──┤        ├──┴──┴──┤
   │  │  │  │        │  │  │  │
   └──┴──┴──┘        └──┴──┴──┘
```

4.

```
        6  3              6  3
   ×    1  1         ×    1 . 1
   ┌──┬──┬──┐        ┌──┬──┬──┐
   │  │  │  │        │←─┼──┼─→│
   ├──┼──┼──┤        ├──┼──┼──┤
   │  │  │  │        │  │  │  │
   ├──┴──┴──┤        ├──┴──┴──┤
   │  │  │  │        │  │  │  │
   └──┴──┴──┘        └──┴──┴──┘
```

Resource 6.5.2a

Tree diagrams

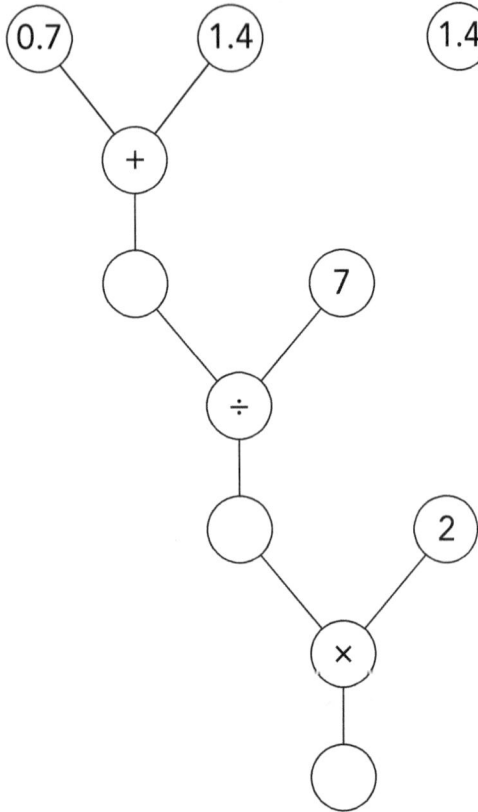

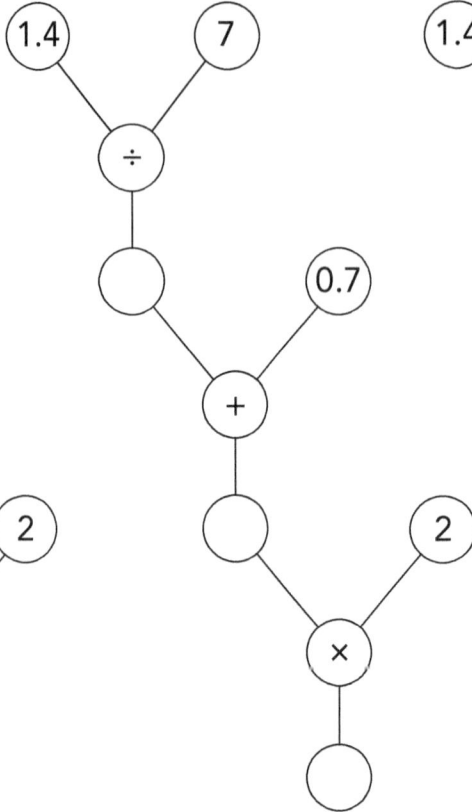

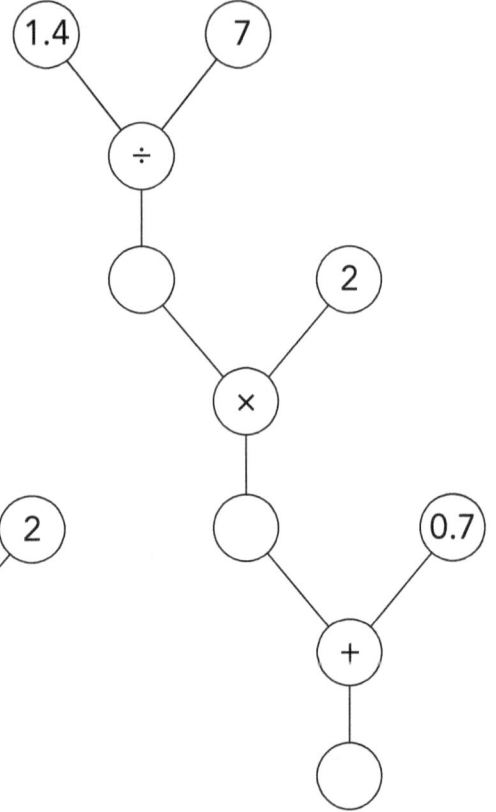

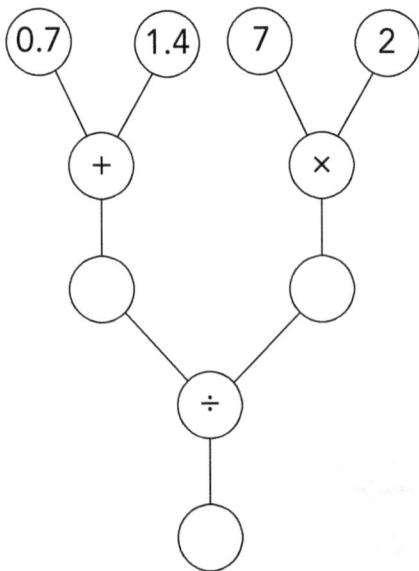

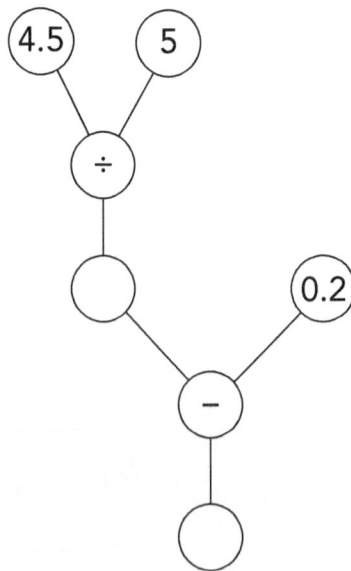

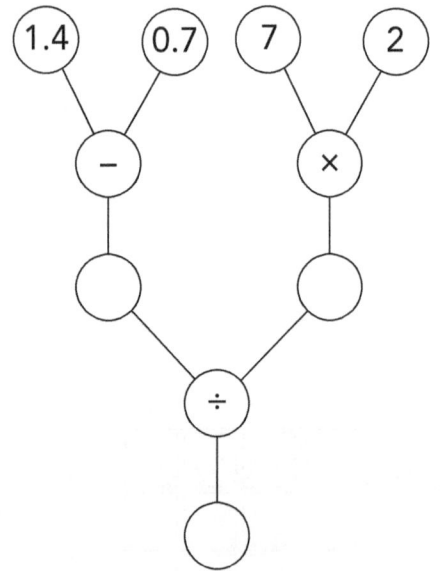

Resource 6.5.2b

Pairs

1. Which of these sets of calculations make a pair? Tick them.

   a) $3.2 \times 2 + 3.2 \times 7 + 3.2$ ☐

   b) 3.2×10 ☐

   c) $3.2 \times 2 + 3.2 \times 6$ ☐

   Why do they make a pair? _____

2. Which of these sets of calculations make a pair? Tick them.

   a) $4.67 + 2.96 + 1.04$ ☐

   b) $4.67 + 3$ ☐

   c) $4.67 + 4$ ☐

   Why do they make a pair? _____

3. Which of these sets of calculations make a pair? Tick them.

   a) $4.8 \div 2 + 4.8 \div 3$ ☐

   b) $4.8 \div 2 + 1.1 \div 2$ ☐

   c) $5.9 \div 2$ ☐

   Why do they make a pair? _____

4. Which of these sets of calculations make a pair? Tick them.

   a) $2.5 \times 1.7 \times 4 \times 2$ ☐

   b) $10 \times 2 \times 1.7$ ☐

   c) $2.5 \times 1.7 \times 6$ ☐

   Why do they make a pair? _____

Resource 6.5.3a

Match expressions

$3n + p - 2n + 4p$	$n + 5p$	$3(4x + 5y - 2y)$
$12x + 13y$	$4a \div 2 \times 11$	_____
$10 \times 4a \div 8 - 9a$	_____	$7e \times 5 - 3e$
$32e$	$2(4r + 2r - 4y \div 2)$	$\_(3\_ -y)$

374

© HarperCollins*Publishers* 2018

Find solutions

A

Find the solutions to these equations. Set your work out clearly, including checking the solution.

For the questions marked with a *, use two methods to find the solution.

1. $4j + 4.6 = 30$

2. $14 = 6b - 2.5$

3. $6 = 7 - x \div 5$

4. $8x \div 4 = 3.5*$

5. $14x - 28 = 4x$

6. $1 + 5x = 25x - 4 \times 3.5$

7. $8.8 - 0.4z = 2.8 + 0.4z*$

8. $(6 + 0.4) \div f = 4*$

9. $6(d - 2.5) = 2.5 \times 8 - 2$

10. $3 = 10(0.25 + h)$*

11. $3(2c + 2) \div 10 = 1.5$

12. $10 = 5(3s - 4.5) \div 1.5$*

B

David has written four solutions to equations:

        4   2.5   4.1   2.2

What were his equations? Use examples from section A to help you.

Equations and solutions

Using the same colour for each pair, shade or highlight the equations and their solutions.

$3(3H - 5) \div 8 = 1.5$

$9.6x \div 4 = 3.6$

$4 + 3b = 4b - 3.5$

3

$18(a - 1.5) = 27$

5

$4(2e - 1) = 2$

1.5

$4.5c = 13.5$

3

$d \div 2 \times 4 - 5.5 = 5.5$

5.5

3

7.5

$7.8 = 4f - 2 \times 6.1$

0.75

Problem solving (1)

A

Find the solutions to these problems. Set your work out clearly.

1. An office received 12 kg of paper on Wednesday. This was 4 kg more than two times the amount of paper it received on Tuesday.

   How much paper did the office receive on Tuesday?

2. Muhammed walked 55 km in January. This was 9 km less than two times the distance he walked in December.

   How many km did Muhammed walk in December?

3. A petrol station received 5000 litres of fuel on Thursday. This was 200 litres less than two times the amount of fuel it received on Tuesday.

   How much fuel does the petrol station have altogether?

4. A petrol station served 3400 motorists last week. This is 500 less than 1.5 times the number it served this week.

   How many customers were served altogether?

5. A road sweeper drove 25 km on Friday morning. This was 4 km more than half the distance it drove on Thursday.

How many km did the road sweep drive on Thursday?

6. A window cleaner worked for 45 hours this week. This was 20 hours more than half the amount he worked last week.

How many hours did the window cleaner work last week?

7. A courier drove 800 miles one week in February. This was 320 miles less than half the mileage for two weeks in March.

How many miles were driven altogether?

8. A recycling centre collected 2500 tonnes of rubbish in 2017. This was 1500 tonnes more than half the amount collected in 2018.

How many tonnes was collected altogether?

B

1. A recycling centre collected 2000 tonnes of rubbish in 2016 and again in 2017. In 2018 it collected 250 tonnes less than three quarters the total for 2016 and 2017.

   How many tonnes of rubbish were collected in 2016, 2017 and 2018 altogether?

2. A petrol station served 250 motorists every day last week. This week it predicts it will serve 1.2 times last week's total amount.

   If the prediction is correct, how many motorists would be served over the two weeks?

Card match

$32c \div 8 + 15 = 40$	$(5x + 7) \div 3 = 8$	$80 - 7(x + 1) = 20.5$	$8.2 \div (5x - 1.4) = 4.1$	$24e \div 6 + 15 = 60$	$60 - 3(2x - 4) = 7.8$
4.5	6.5	5.25	3.4	3.75	0.5

$2x - 4 = 5$	$52 - d = 7d$	$4(2x - 3) = 30$	$2(11x - 6x) = 34$	$42 - 8d = 12$	$8.1 \div (9x - 1.5) = 2.7$
10.7	6.25	3.4	7.5	0.68	11.25

Create equations

Problem solving (2)

A

Find the solutions to these problems. Set your work out clearly.

1. A bird flew 6.4 km in 0.3 hours.

   Based on this speed, how many hours will it take the bird to fly 16 km?

2. Andrew can run 1.4 km in 5.5 minutes.

   Based on this speed, how many minutes would it take Andrew to run 7 km?

3. A farmer sold 350 cows and some sheep at an agricultural show. The number of cows sold was 26 more than 1.5 times the number of sheep.

   How many sheep did the farmer sell?

4. A warehouse received some bread and cakes. The weight of the bread was 135 kg, which was 22.5 kg more than 1.8 times that of the cakes.

   How many kilograms of cakes did the warehouse receive?

5. Sarah bought roses and carnations. The number of roses was 175, which was 34 less than 1.9 times the number of carnations.

   How many carnations did Sarah buy?

6. There are two bags of wheat. The first bag weighs 145 kg. If 15 kg of wheat is taken out of the first bag and put into the second bag, then the remaining wheat in the first bag will be 15 kg more than the second bag.

   How many kilograms of wheat were in the second bag to begin with?

7. David and Sarah bought bags of sweets. The weight of David's bag was 250 g. When David gave 55 g of sweets to Sarah, his bag was 13 g lighter than Sarah's.

   How many grams of sweets did Sarah buy?

8. There are 8 boxes of nuts of equal weight. If 0.55 kg of nuts are taken out of each box, then the remaining nuts in the 8 boxes weigh 5.2 kg in total.

   How many kilograms of nuts were in each box to begin with?

9. A factory has 12 bags of sultanas of equal weight. If 125 g of sultanas are taken from each bag, then the remaining sultanas in the 12 bags weigh 1206 g in total.

   How many grams of sultanas were in each bag to begin with?

B

1. Peter can write 350 words in 10 minutes. To win a competition he has to be able to write at least 800 words in 25 minutes.

   Decide if Peter can win the competition, giving reasons for your answer.

2. Sanjit climbed a 5000 m high mountain. This was 352 m higher than 1.6 times the height of the mountain Angie climbed.

   How high was the mountain Angie climbed?

3. There are 2 bags of potatoes. The first bag weighs 30 kg. If 8 kg of potatoes is taken out of the first bag and put into the second bag, then the remaining potatoes in the first bag are 7 kg less than the second bag.

   How many kilograms of potatoes were in the second bag to begin with?

4. Four out of 6 bags of sweets are of equal weight. The other 2 bags are each half the weight of one of the 4 bags. If 25.5 g of sweets are taken from each of the first 4 bags, then the sweets in the 6 bags weigh 150 g in total.

   a) Write an equation that represents the problem.

   b) How many grams of sweets were in each bag to begin with?

Problem solving (3)

A

Find the solutions to these problems. Set your work out clearly.

1. Peter bought 5 books in a stationery shop with £60 and received £5 change. How much did each book cost?

2. Sanjit bought 8 paint brushes in an art shop with £25 and received £1.80 change. How much did each paint brush cost?

3. Samantha is thinking about buying 20 salads with £100, but she needs £10 more. How much does each salad cost?

4. Ayesha is thinking about buying 18 pizzas with £140, but she needs £3.82 more. How much does each pizza cost?

5. Sarah had £40 to spend. She bought a novel and then later she bought 2 magazines at £3.40 each.

   How much did the novel cost?

6. Sandra had £35 to spend. She bought an atlas and then later she bought 3 magazines at £3.25 each.

   How much did the atlas cost?

7. A company bought 15 small tables and 15 small lamps for £600. Each small table costs £19.

   How much did a small lamp cost?

8. A company bought 14 small cabinets and 11 small lamps for £1100. Each small cabinet costs £49.50.

   How much did a small lamp cost?

B

1. David bought 14 mirrors and Sarah bought 25 pictures. They spent £800 in total. Each mirror cost £23.50.

   How much did Sarah spend on the pictures?

2. Mo had £34.50 to spend on food but didn't want to spend more than £9.00 on any one item. He bought a salad, a cake and 2 pizzas at £8.99 each.

   a) Write an equation that represents the problem.

   b) Find three possible prices for the salad and cake, giving reasons for your choices.

Problem solving (4)

A

1. Angus drove 140 km this week, which is 50 more than 6 times the number of kilometres he drove last week.

   How many kilometres did Angus drive last week?

2. Mustafa employs 550 people, which is 60 more than 7 times the number of people Mustafa employed 6 years ago.

   How many people did Mustafa employ 6 years ago?

3. A farm has 256 sheep, which is 52 fewer than 4 times the number of cows the farm has.

   How many cows does the farm have?

4. A department store has 300 books, which is 48 fewer than 6 times the number of CDs the store has.

   How many CDs does the department store have?

5. The perimeter of a rectangle is 42 cm and its length is 8.5 cm.

    How long is the width of the rectangle?

6. The perimeter of a rectangle is 52 cm and its length is 7.6 cm.

    How long is the width of the rectangle?

7. Warehouse C has 140 pallets and warehouse D has 110 pallets. Warehouse C uses 16 pallets per day and warehouse D uses 11 pallets per day.

    After how many days will the warehouses have the same number of pallets?

8. Company E has 150 tonnes of steel and company F has 180 tonnes of steel. Company E uses 12 tonnes of steel per day and Company F uses 15 tonnes per day.

    After how many days will the companies have the same amount of steel?

B

1. Amy employs 1200 people which is 165 more than 1.5 times the number of people she employed 3 years ago.

   How many people did Amy employ 3 years ago?

2. A music store has 3395 DVDs and an online store has 4500 DVDs. The music store sells 15 DVDs per day and the online store sells 28 DVDs per day.

   After how many days will the music store and the online store have the same number of DVDs?

Resource 6.5.6

Triangles and parallelograms

Mark and label the height of each shape. The base is shown as a bold line.

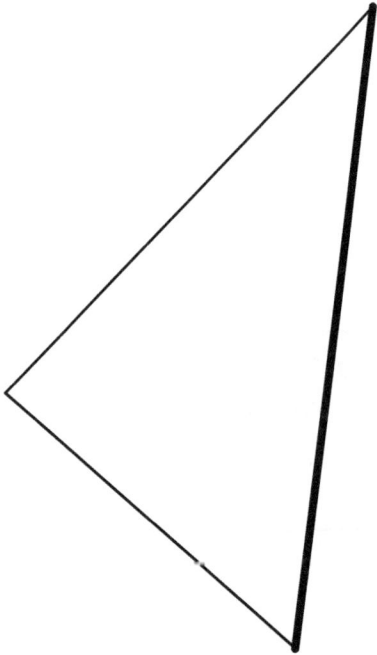

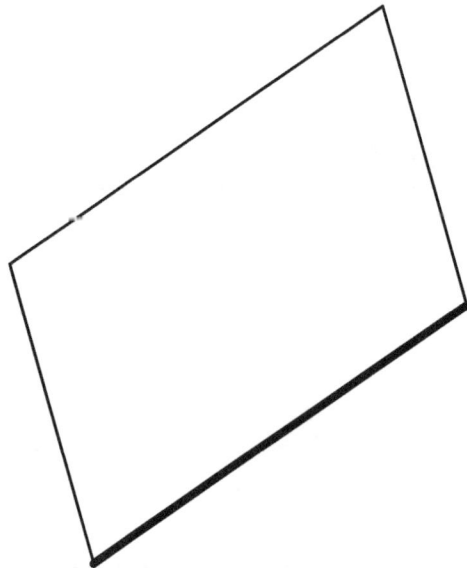

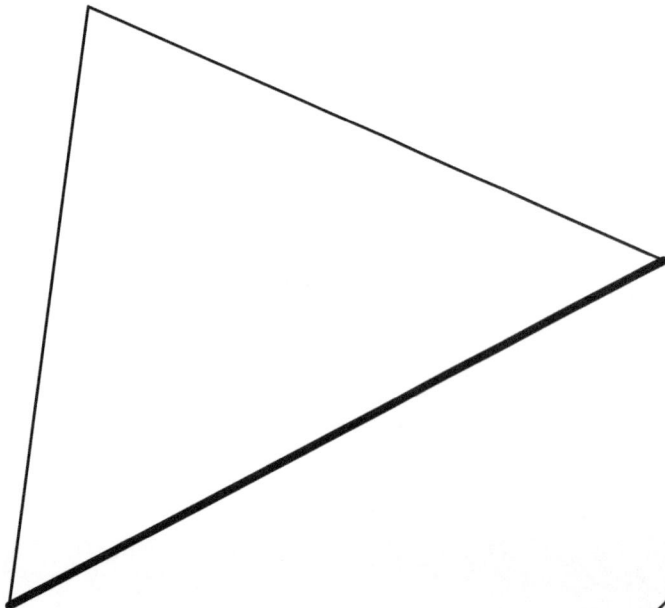

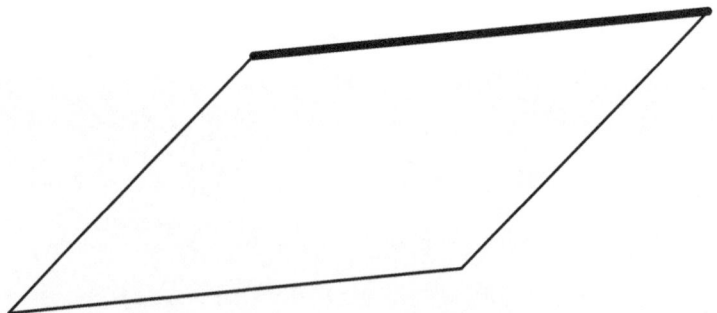

Think about duration

You will need an analogue clock with movable hands and a small group of friends to work with.

Instructions

One person in the group should choose a real-life situation where an activity or event might be timed, and give it a duration. For example:

- A bus journey that lasts 1 hour and 20 minutes.
- Someone cooking an apple pie for 55 minutes.
- A TV programme that is 2 hours and 8 minutes long.

1. The same person should use their clock face to model the start time of their chosen event.
2. The rest of the group should now have enough information to work out the end time. They should model the end time on their clock faces.
3. Compare your answers. Were they all the same?
4. Take it in turns to invent new problems. Try including problems where you give the end time and the duration and ask your friends to work backwards to find the start time.

Duration challenge!

You will need to cut out each of the following sets of cards:
- Time cards
- Duration cards
- Task cards

11:30 a.m.	4:02 p.m.	19:57	09:15	12:24 p.m.	5:46 p.m.
10:19	13:05	06:50	8:37 a.m.	7:12 p.m.	14:00

11:30 a.m.	55 minutes	1 hour 20 minutes	2 hours 5 minutes	1 hour 45minutes	90 minutes
135 minutes	76 minutes	1 hour 19 minutes	86 minutes	42 minutes	35 minutes

Your time is the time a train journey ended. Find the time it started.	Your time is the time a film ended. Find the time it started.	Your time is the time a lesson ended. Find the time it started.	Your time is the time a tennis match ended. Find the time it started.	Your time is the time a game of chess ended. Find the time it started.	Your time is the time a telephone call ended. Find the time it started.
Your time is the time a concert started. Find the time it ended.	Your time is the time a parade started. Find the time it ended.	Your time is the time an interview started. Find the time it ended.	Your time is the time a race started. Find the time it ended.	Your time is the time a chef started baking. Find the time they finished.	Your time is the time a journey started. Find the time it ended.

Instructions
1. Shuffle your cards and take one from each pile.
2. Using the information you have been given, can you work out the missing time?
3. Make up some problems of your own for your partner to solve.

Answers

Chapter 1 Revising and improving

1.1 Using symbols to represent numbers

1   (a) 14.4   (b) 5.6
    (c) 20   (d) 140
    (e) 9   (f) 32
    (g) 5   (h) 10.2
2   (a) 6   (b) 3
    (c) 3   (d) 6
    (e) 6   (f) 4
    (g) 3   (h) 5
3   (a) ★ = 17 ▧ = 33
    (b) ● = 7.1 ★ = 0.9
    (c) ▧ = 32 ★ = 256
    (d) ▲ = 1.3
4   (a) 6   (b) 4 to 11
    (c) 12   (d) 6
5   ● = 7 ▲ = 6
6   135; 9

1.2 Addition and subtraction of decimals (1)

1   (a) 20   (b) 0.63
    (c) 10   (d) 0.92
    (e) 12.64   (f) 20
    (g) 11   (h) 0.8
    (i) 19.8   (j) 1.5
    (k) 0.76   (l) 6
    (m) 0.36   (n) 10
2   (a) 101   (b) 2.07
3   (a) 67.6   (b) 12.8
4   (a) 14.5   (b) 10.9
    (c) 54.7   (d) 61
5   (a) B   (b) A
    (c) B   (d) A
6   (a) 1350   (b) 0.78
    (c) 15 400   (d) 30
    (e) 8   (f) 8.08
    (g) 4 200 000 (h) 500
    (i) 0.1   (j) 0.015
7   (a) 10 − 2.8 − 4.2 = 3 (metres)
    (b) 580 − 60 − 42.8 = 477.20 (pounds)
8   (a) 3.4 (b) 1.7

1.3 Addition and subtraction of decimals (2)

1   (a) 8.1 − 5.7 = 2.4; 7 − 2.4 = 4.6
    (b) 9.8 − 5.74 = 4.06; 4.06 + 3.28 = 7.34
2   Tree diagram correctly drawn. Number sentence: (80 − 8) ÷ 6 = 12 (years old)
3   (a) 9 − 1.73 = 7.27; 7.27 + 5.37 = 12.64
       or 9 − 1.73 + 5.37 = 12.64
    (b) 19.9 − 10.1 = 9.8; 9.8 − 5.45 = 4.35
       or 19.9 − 10.1 − 5.45 = 4.35
4   (a) 4.15   (b) 39
5   (a) 4 − 0.58 − 1.27 = 2.15 (m)
    (b) 1.42 + 0.05 + 0.03 = 1.5 (m)
    (c) 85.6 − 2.56 − 6.47 = 76.57 (tonnes)
       85.6 + 83.04 + 76.57 = 245.21 (tonnes)
6   The first basket: 48 ÷ 2 − 4.2 = 19.8 (kg).
    The second basket: 48 ÷ 2 + 4.2 = 28.2 (kg).

1.4 Decimals and approximate numbers (1)

1   (a) tenths; hundredths
    (b) less; 5.5; 1; 10.26
    (c) tenths
2

2	10	20	24
1.8	10.0	19.5	23.5
1.75	10.00	19.55	23.50

3   (a) 7.64   (b) 10.64
4   (a) 0.09   (b) 70.0
    (c) 0.06
5   (22.21 − 5.9) ÷ 100 = 0.1631 (m)
    ≈ 0.16 (m)
6   (a) 1.0; 0.001 (b) 29.500
    (c) 2.74; 2.65
7   He could have 4 combinations. The money left with each combination: headphones, washing machine and microwave: £460.02; headphones, washing machine and smart LED TV: £269.01; headphones, microwave and smart LED TV: £389.02; washing machine, microwave and smart LED TV: £258.01

1.5 Decimals and approximate numbers (2)

1   Rounding up method: £12.24, £8.00, £99.92, £35.01; Rounding down method: £12.23, £7.99, £99.91, £35.00
2   (a) 7.9   (b) 33.1
    (c) 102.0   (d) 82.0
3

11	2	1
11.9	2.5	1.1
11.94	2.49	1.06

4   (a) C   (b) B   (c) B
5   (200 − 27.6) ÷ 100 = 1.724 (m)
    ≈ 1.72 (m)
6   52 − 15.2 − (15.2 − 3.7) − (15.2 − 3.7 + 2.8) = 11 (m)
7   (a) 2.34; 2   (b) 3.13; 3.2
    (c) 0.953; 0.95
8   (a) 5 × 6 × 4 = 120 (combinations)
    (b) 5 + 6 + 4 = 15 (ways)

1.6 Revision for circles and angles

1   Circles correctly drawn
2   15
3   10; 20
4   100
5   30
6   Figures correctly drawn on the grid (Note: all the curved sides of the figures consist of quarter or half circles of different radius)
7   (a) 2
    (b) line correctly drawn
    (c) 45
    (d) circle correctly drawn

Chapter 1 test

1   (a) 0.86   (b) 1
    (c) 1   (d) 7.25
    (e) 52.3   (f) 9
2   (a) 23.7   (b) 35.22
3   (a) 185   (b) 7.19
4   (a) 6.68   (b) 41
    (c) 30   (d) 16
    (e) 82.24   (f) 3

5 (a) 1.4   (b) 1.95
   (c) 128.091   (d) 2
   (e) 90.46   (f) 10 7.95; 8.04
6 (a) D   (b) B
   (c) D; C   (d) C
7 (a) 7.80   (b) 4.10
8 (a) 280   (b) 0.138
   (c) 1.4256   (d) 1 520 000
   (e) 443   (f) 7 80

9 (a) 16; 37   (b) 13; 6
10 Circle correctly drawn
11 (a) 33   (b) 64   (c) 125
12 3.61 − 2.12 + 3.61 = 5.13 (hundred million km²)
13 7.25 − 1.2 + 1.45 = 7.5 (tonnes) 38 − 7.25 − (7.25 − 1.2) − 7.5 = 17.2 (tonnes)
14 2.84 − 0.55 + 0.17 = 2.46 (m)

15 880 − 80.5 − 102.9 = 696.6 (pounds)
16 8.4 − 2.8 − (2.8 + 1.9) = 0.9 (m)
17 (a) 8.68 + 9.8 + 4.5 = 22.98 (pounds)
   (b) 7.55 + 2.8 + 3.6 = 13.95 (pounds)
    Yes, it would be enough.
    15 − 13.95 = 1.05 (pounds)
18 (a) 6 8   (b) 5.9
   (c) 7; 1009   (d) 19

Chapter 2 Multiplication and division of decimals

2.1 Multiplying decimal numbers by whole numbers (1)

1 (a) Jason: 6; 48; 48
   (b) Tom: 580; 580; 4640
   (c) May: 58   464;   46.4; 464   10   46.4
2 (a) 256   10   25.6
   (b) 62   100   248   100   2.48
   (c) 9   135   1000   1215   1000   1.215
3 (a) Estimation: 8 × 1 = 8;
    Calculation: 7.52
   (b) Estimation: 9 × 7 = 63;
    Calculation: 63.35
   (c) Estimation: 111 × 3 = 333;
    Calculation: 332.1
   (d) Estimation: 280 × 9 = 2520;
    Calculation: 2560.95
4 (a) 3.68 × 4 = 14.72 (m)
   (b) 0.75 × 9 = 6.75 (pounds)
   (c) 4 + 3.6 × (6 − 1) = 22 (m)
5 less

2.2 Multiplying decimal numbers by whole numbers (2)

1

$$
\begin{array}{r}
4\ 2\\
\times 0.5\ 7\\
\hline
2\ 9\ 4\\
2\ 1\ 0\\
\hline
2\ 3.9\ 4
\end{array}
\quad
\begin{array}{r}
4\ 2\\
\times 0\ 5\ 7\\
\hline
2\ 9\ 4\\
2\ 1\ 0\\
\hline
2\ 3\ 9\ 4
\end{array}
$$

(×100 →, ÷100 ←)

2 (a) 174   (b) 1.74
   (c) 705   (d) 7.05
3 (a) 17.25   (b) 1.725
   (c) 0.1725   (d) 172.5
   (e) 1725   (f) 17.25
4 (b) 50.05   (c) 261
   (d) 7.65   (e) 550.8
   (f) 1180
5 (a) ✗ 4.5 × 8 = 36
   (b) ✗ 1.36 × 250 = 340
   (c) ✗ 3.14 × 1050 = 3297

6 (a) 39 × 0.16 = 6.24 (kg)
   (b) No, he doesn't have enough money.
    12.7 + 4.5 × 2 = 21.70 (pounds)
    £21.70 > £20
7 9.09
8 (a) 2   (b) 4.68   (c) 2.63

2.3 Addition, subtraction and multiplication with decimals

1 (b) 25 × (6.2 − 2.6) = 90
   (c) 34 × (0.45 × 1.2) = 18.36
2 (a) 9.62   (b) 14.56
   (c) 81   (d) 2.8
   (e) 6.79   (f) 441
3 (a) (7.8 + 1.2) × 0.6 = 5.4
   (b) (3.2 − 1.2) × 3.9 = 7.8
   (c) 10 × 0.44 − 2.5 = 1.9
   (d) (6.9 − 0.9) ÷ 2 = 3
4 (a) 2.08 × 3 + 2.08 = 8.32 (m)
   (b) 6 × 4.9 × 70 = 2058 (kg) = 2.058 (tonnes)
   (c) 4 − 8 × 0.32 = 1.44 (pounds)
   (d) Perimeter: 0.5 × 2 × 4 = 4 (m) Area: 0.5 × 0.5 × 4 = 1 (m²)
5 (a) (15.2 + 2.5) × 3 − 10.6 = 42.5
   (b) (30 − 11.8) × (2 − 1.5) = 9.1
   (c) 4.5 × (6.5 − 2.5) + 1.8 = 19.8

2.4 Laws of operations with decimal numbers

1 4 × 5.4 and 5.4 × 4; 4.6 × 9 + 5.4 × 9 and (4.6 + 5.4) × 9; 8 × (1.25 + 12.5) and 8 × 1.25 + 8 × 12.5; 6.7 × 4 × 2.5 and 6.7 × (4 × 2.5)
2 (a) ✗ (b) ✗ (c) ✔ (d) ✗
3 (a) 320   (b) 1.75
   (c) 10.89   (d) 57.6
   (e) 1125   (f) 50
   (g) 1100   (h) 7
   (i) 1748
4 (a) (12.5 + 10.99) × 320 = 7516.80 (pounds)
   (b) 12.5 × 16 × 2.5 = 500 (tonnes)

5 3.3; 125 (answer may vary)

2.5 Division of decimals by whole numbers (1)

1 (a) 1.4   84   14   14   1.4
   (b) 1.34   938   7   134   1.34
2 (a) 1.6   (b) 2.9   (c) 3.42
3 (a) 10.8   (b) 6.4   (c) 5.6
   (d) 5.46   (e) 6.4   (f) 7.64
4 (a) 128.4 ÷ 6 = 21.4
   (b) 2.28 − 2.28 ÷ 12 = 2.09
5 (a) 48 × 3.6 ÷ (3.6 + 0.4) = 43.2 (km/h)
 (b) (1.6 + 1.2) × 2 = 5.6 (m), 5.6 ÷ 4 = 1.4 (m), 1.4 × 1.4 = 1.96 (m²)
6 7 boxes £6.93; 14 packs £68.46; 42 £15.12; Total cost: £90.51

2.6 Division of decimals by whole numbers (2)

1 (a) 2.3   (b) 2.1   (c) 6.4
   (d) 6.6   (e) 0.7   (f) 7.4
   (g) 5.9   (h) 1.24
2 0; 9; 0.01; 0; dividend
3 (a) 0.83   (b) 1.93   (c) 0.048
   (d) 0.24   (e) 1.16   (f) 0.03
4 (a) 180 × 0.6 + 62.5 ÷ 25 = 110.5
   (b) (53.8 − 53.26) ÷ 54 = 0.01
5 (a) 9.9 ÷ 18 × 3 = 1.65 (tonnes)
   (b) 24.80 ÷ 8 = 3.10 (pounds) 24.80 ÷ (8 + 2) = 2.48 (pounds) 3.1 − 2.48 = 0.62 (pounds)
   (c) 3.25 ÷ 25 = 0.13 (tonnes) 0.13 × 40.5 = 5.265 (tonnes)

6

Plan	6-seater boat (No.)	4-seater boat (No.)	Cost (£)
1	1	11	185
2	3	8	180
3	5	5	175
4	7	2	170

Plan 4 is the cheapest with the total cost of £170 for seven 6-seater boats and two 4-seater boats. (Answer may vary.)

2.7 Division of decimals by whole numbers (3)

1   0.3; 0.375

2   (a) 1.95   (b) 4.35
    (c) 0.085   (d) 0.03
    (e) 0.115   (f) 0.175

3   (a) $7.2 \times 18 \div 4 = 32.4$
    (b) $800 \times 0.0125 - 1.04 \div 26 = 9.96$

4   (a) $100 \div 40 = 2.5$ (m)
    (b) $0.24 \div 4 = 0.06$ (m)
        $0.06 \times 4 = 0.24$ (m)
    (c) $2.88 \div 500 = 0.00576$ (pounds), $3.88 \div 800 = 0.00485$ (pounds), £0.00576 > £0.00485 Continental cookies are cheaper.

5   $28 \times 3 + 19 \times 2 = 122$ (pounds), maximum: $8 \times 3 + 5 \times 2 = 34$ (t-shirts)

6   Ms Smith had a better deal. Compare the unit price: $6.12 \times 3 \div 4 = 4.59$ (pounds), £4.59 < £5.45; compare the total price of 4 bottles: $6.12 \times 3 = 18.36$ (pounds), $5.45 \times 4 = 21.8$ (pounds), £18.36 < £21.8; compare the price of 1 litre: $5.45 \div 2 = 2.725$ (pounds), $6.12 \times 3 \div (2 \times 4) = 2.295$ (pounds), £2.295 < £2.725. (Answer may vary.)

2.8 Division of decimals by whole numbers (4)

1   (a) 0.0225   (b) 225
    (c) 22.5   (d) 0.225
    (e) 0.000 225   (f) 0.002 25

2   (a) 6.75   (b) 0.75

3   (a) 0.4   (b) 0.25
    (c) 0.08   (d) 0.375
    (e) 0.0625   (f) 4.25

4   (a) $65 \div 26 = 2.5$
    (b) $3 \times 0.5 \div 12 = 0.125$

5   (a) $4.5 \div 90 = 0.05$ (tonnes)
    (b) $306 \div 180 = 1.7$ (times)
    (c) $31.8 \div (9 - 5) = 7.95$ (pounds)
        $7.95 \times (9 + 5) = 111.30$ (pounds)

6   $6 \times 2 = 12$ (litres) = 12 000 (ml), $650 \times (6 \div 3) \times 2 = 2600$ (ml), 12 000 + 2600 = 14 600 (ml)

7   $3 + 0.25 + 144 \times 3 \div 150 = 6.13$ (pounds)

2.9 Calculation with calculators

1   (a) 284.7   (b) 35.208
    (c) 1541.12   (d) 37.3888
    (e) 4.45   (f) 29.58

2   (a) 36   (b) 4356
    (c) 443 556   (d) 44 435 556
    (e) 4 444 355 556
    (f) 444 443 555 556

3   (b) $0.\dot{2}$ (c) $0.\dot{3}$ (d) $0.\dot{4}$ (e) $0.\dot{5}$
    (f) $0.\dot{6}$ (g) $0.\dot{7}$ (h) $0.\dot{8}$

4   (a) $42\,371 \div 90 \div 60 = 7.846\,48\dot{1}\,5$ or $7.846\,48\dot{1}$ depending on calculator display
    (b) (i) $0.018 \times 365 = 6.57$ (tonnes)
        (ii) 6.57 tonnes = 6570 kg, $6570 \div 19 \approx 346$ (water tanks)
        (iii) $346 \div 3 \approx 115$ (months) $115 \div 12 \approx 10$ (years)

5   (a) 111 111 111   (b) 222 222 222
    (c) 333 333 333   (d) 444 444 444
    (e) 555 555 555   (f) 666 666 666
    (g) 777 777 777   (h) 888 888 888
    (i) 999 999 999

2.10 Approximation of products and quotients

1
	... to the nearest one	... to the nearest tenth	... to the nearest hundredth
3.409	3	3.4	3.41
16.032	16	16.0	16.03
5.697	6	5.7	5.70
29.993	30	30.0	29.99

2   (a) 362   (b) 27.95
    (c) 2.5   (d) 0.41

3   (a) $1.65 \times 18.5 = 30.525 \approx 30.53$ (pounds)
    (b) $39.75 \div 3 = 13.25 \approx 14$ (rounding up), 14 bottles are needed
    (c) (i) $12 \times 0.6289 = 7.5468 \approx 7.55$ (pounds)
        (ii) $980 \times 0.8372 = 820.456 \approx 820.46$ (pounds)
        (iii) $9995 \times 0.0996 = 995.502 \approx 995.50$ (pounds)

4   $0.1234\dot{5}$

5   4; 449

2.11 Practice and exercise (1)

1   (a) 7; 0.84   (b) 12.5; 3.28
    (c) 4; 4; 0.125; +; 2.5

2   (a) 0.2   (b) 0.5
    (c) 0.5

3   (a) $13.5 - 60.8 \div 16 = 9.7$
    (b) $14 \times (4.25 + 5.8) = 140.7$

4   (a) 6.12   (b) 18.352
    (c) 195   (d) 1
    (e) 135   (f) 70

5   (a) $27.9 \div (19.52 - 16.52) = 9.3$
    (b) $(3.6 + 4.4) \div 4 = 2$

6   (a) $38 \div 0.750 = 50$ (bottles) r 0.5 (litres)
    (b) $13.91 \div (6.5 \div 0.5) = 1.07$ (hours)
    (c) $73.8 \div 36 \times 56 = 114.8$ (kg)

7   (a) 44   (b) 5.91
    (c) >; <; <; >; >; <
    (d) 4.895; 4.904

8   A: 3.5; B: 3.05; C: 4.05

Chapter 2 test

1   (a) 12   (b) 0.188
    (c) 10   (d) 9.4

2   (a) 0.42   (b) 47.36
    (c) 0.44

3   (a) 720   (b) 125
    (c) 369.6   (d) 0.084

4   (a) $(4.8 - 0.6) \div 4 = 1.05$
    (b) $15 \times 0.24 \div (2.85 + 2.15) = 0.72$

5   $450 \div 2.5 - 96 = 84$ (km/h)

6   $9600 \div 750 = 12$ (bottles) r 600 ml

7   1 kg

8   3 times

9   420 (tiles)

10 (a) 1.25   (b) 12.5
    (c) 67.5   (d) 675

11 (a) >   (b) <   (c) =

12 100

13 7.04; 6.95

14 A

15 B

16 D

17 A

Chapter 3 Introduction to algebra

3.1 Using letters to represent numbers (1)

1   (a) 12   (b) 2
    (c) 5   (d) 5
    (e) 64   (f) 4; 25

2   (a) $8m$ (b) $3xy$
    (c) $6(9 + a)$ (d) $n + 0.5a$
    (e) a^3 (f) $3b + b^2$

3   (b) ac (c) c
    (d) +

4   (a) $180° - a° - b°$ (b) $180° - 2a°$
    (c) $C \div 4$ (d) $C \div A$
    (e) $S \div a$ (f) 3; 6; 12; n; $2n$; $4n$

5   $65t$ $210 \div v$ $s \div 6$; $480 \div x$ $x \div 25$ $30x$; $8.5b$ $x \div y$ $z \div a$

6   $a \div 3$; $a \div 3 - 2$; $a \div 3 + 2$

7 $A = 7$; $B = 6$; $C = 1$; $D = 8$

3.2 Using letters to represent numbers (2)

1 (a) C (b) D (c) B (d) C

2 (b) $5 \div x + n$ (c) $6s - 2$
  (d) $320 - 12m$ (e) $5(80 + b)$
  (f) $6(b + 90)$

3 (a) $50 + n$ (b) $m + 2n$
  (c) $50 + m + n$ (d) $2m + 3n$
  (e) $m - n$

4 (a) $85t$ (b) $m \div 6$
  (c) $24 - n$ (d) $3(a + b)$

5 (b) 20; 25; $5n - 5$ (c) 4; 5; $n - 1$
  (d) 8; 9; $n + 3$ (e) 53; 63; $10n + 3$

6 (a) $175a$ (pounds); $25a$ (pounds)
  (b) $[x \div (m + 2.5)]$ days

7 From left to right, they are: 1, 4, 9, 16, 25, 36; n^2; 4 072 324 (or 2018^2)

3.3 Simplification and evaluation (1)

1 (a) ✗ (b) ✗ (c) ✗ (d) ✗

2 (d) 0 (e) $12s + 20t$
  (f) $24x + 75y$ (g) $60a$
  (h) $4k$ (i) $9x$
  (j) $20y$ (k) $59x$
  (l) $18n$

3 (a) $3a$ (b) $2x + 3$
  (c) $10y + 5x$ (d) $11x$
  (e) $12a$; $6b$

4 (a) $50 - 9.6a \div 3a \times 10 = 18$ (pounds)
  (b) (i) $[(21 + n) \div 2]$ (paper flowers)
    (ii) $(21 \div m + n \div 2)$ (paper flowers)
  (c) $x + 6x + 6 = 7x + 6$
  (d) (i) $x + 4$
    (ii)

Mike's age: x	1	2	3	4	...	n	...
Rob's age: y	5	6	7	8	...	$n + 4$	...

5 The area: $15a$ cm². The perimeter: $2(15 + a)$ cm or $2(3a + 5)$ cm

6 $2a + 2b + 4(a - b) = (6a - 2b)$ cm

3.4 Simplification and evaluation (2)

1 4 8 12 16 20; 2 7 12 17 22;
  14 21 28 35 42; $2\frac{2}{3}$ $3\frac{1}{3}$ 4 $4\frac{2}{3}$ $5\frac{1}{3}$

2 7 21 35 49 63

3 (a) $(6c + s)$ m
  (b) 500 m

4 $4a$; a^2; 20; 25

5 (b) $24y$, 48 (c) $20m - 30n$, 26
  (d) $29a + b$, 15.1

6 (a) (i) $26x$ sycamores and cedars
    (ii) 520 sycamores and cedars
  (b) (i) $(4a + b)$ km
    (ii) 520 km

7 (a) $(3a - 4)$ pupils (b) 68 pupils

3.5 Simple equations (1)

1 (a) ✗ (b) ✔ (c) ✔ (d) ✗ (e) ✔

2 (a) C (b) D (c) C (d) B

3 $4y = 30$; $x + 8 = y$

4 (b) $45 - x = 15$ (c) $3x + 12 = 72$
  (d) $2(x + 3) = 48$ (e) $y \div 2 = 25$
  (f) $20 \div 10 + x = 8$ (g) $2x - 5 \times 3 = 1$
  (h) $4y - 15 \times 9 = 5$

5 (a) $x + y = 10$
  (b)

x	1	2	3	4	5	6	7	8	9
y	9	8	7	6	5	4	3	2	1

  (c) Tim: 8 years old; Jane: 2 years old

6 $2a = 3b$, $2(3a + b)$ cm or $2(a + 4b)$ cm, $2a(a + b)$ cm² or $3b(a + b)$ cm²
  $b = 4$ cm, 44 cm, 120 cm² or $4a + 5b$

3.6 Simple equations (2)

1 (a) solution (b) solution
  (c) $y = 15$ (d) $x = 1.4$

2 (a) D (b) A D (c) C

3 (b) $x = 35.8$ (c) $x = 4.8$
  (d) $x = 1.6$ (e) $x = 0$
  (f) $x = 6.76$

4 (a) $40 - x = 28$, $x = 12$
  (b) $y + 5 = 152$, $y = 147$
  (c) $7s = 2.8 \times 1000$, $s = 400$
  (d) $a \div 25 = 3$, $a = 75$

5 (a) $2x + 5y = 30$
  (b) two possibilities: $x = 5$, $y = 4$ and $x = 10$, $y = 2$

6 The shoes are packed in x boxes: $324 \div x = 72 \div 2$, $x = 9$. The store received 9 boxes.

3.7 Simple equations (3)

1 (a) $x = 28$ (b) $x = 4$
  (c) $x = 18$ (d) $x = 1$
  (e) x (f) $7x$

2 (b) $x = 16.8$ (c) $x = 9$
  (d) $x = 10$ (e) $x = 5$
  (f) $x = 2$

3 (a) $4x + 3.2 = 9.8$, $x = 1.65$
  (b) $5(12 - x) = 40$, $x = 4$
  (c) $3x - 102 = 78$, $x = 60$

4 (a) $50 - 8x = 2$, $x = 6$
  (b) $3x - 40 = 38$, $x = 26$
  (c) $3x + 8 = 200$, $x = 64$

5 $4x = x + 4.5$, $x = 1.5$; $3y = 4x$ or $3y = x + 4.5$, $y = 2$

3.8 Using equations to solve problems (1)

1 (a) $x = 55$ (b) $x = 0.5$
  (c) $x = 1.35$ (d) $x = 5$

2 (a) the quantity of pencils
  (b) The number of peach trees
  (c) work time
  (d) number of pupils in Class B

3 (b) $98 - x = 55$, $x = 43$
  (c) $480 \div x = 32$, $x = 15$
  (d) $64 \div x = 2$, $x = 32$
  (e) $86 - x = 8$, $x = 78$
  (f) $8x = 36$, $x = 4.5$ cm
  (g) $x + 6 \times 15 = 112$, $x = £22$

4 $6 + 4x = 20$, $x = £3.50$

5 $x - 3.5 = 4.5 \times 1.2$, $x = 8.9$ m

3.9 Using equations to solve problems (2)

1 (a) $x = 1.8$ (b) $x = 7.5$
  (c) $x = 0.9$ (d) $x = 1.6$

2 (a) $4x + 12 = 80$, $x = 17$
  (b) $1.5x - 3 = 18$, $x = 14$ kg
  (c) $3x + 0.3 = 1.5$, $x = £0.40$
  (d) $2x - 338 = 354$, $x = 346$ km
  (e) $2x + 14 = 78$, $x = £32$
  (f) $3x = 28 + 8$, $x = 12$
  (g) $x \div 2 + 25 = 375$, $x = 700$

3 $9x = 9 \times 15 + 4x$, $x = 27$ kg

3.10 Using equations to solve problems (3)

1 (a) $x = 11$ (b) $x = 2$
  (c) $x = 15$ (d) $x = 10$

2 (a) $3x - 30 = 150$, $x = 60$ kg
  (b) $2x + 8 = 56$, $x = 24$ tonnes
  (c) $3x + 2 = 35$, $x = 11$
  (d) $3x = 36$, $x = 12$
  (e) $5x - 250 = 2500$, $x = 550$ ml
  (f) $4x - x = 48$, $x = 16$, $4x = 64$
  (g) $20 \times 2.4 + 16x = 72$, $x = 1.5$ m
  (h) $6(x - 3) = 33 - 3$, $x = 8$

3 $6(x - 200) = x + 300$, $x = 300$

Chapter 3 test

1 (a) $x = 5$ (b) $x = 2.6$
  (c) $x = 34.4$ (d) $x = 4.6$
  (e) $x = 1$ (f) $x = 5.6$

2 (a) 6 (b) 24.5
  (c) 1 3 5 7 9; 5 8 11 14 17; 0 7 14 21 28;
    $1\frac{1}{2}$ 2 $2\frac{1}{2}$ 3 $3\frac{1}{2}$

3 (a) $2.5x + 5 = 25$, $x = 8$
  (b) $6.5x - 4x = 25$, $x = 10$
  (c) $8(x - 5) \div 3 = 120$, $x = 50$

4 $35 - 8x = 1.4$, $x = £4.20$

5 $3x - 14 = 55$, $x = 23$

6 $0.4 \times 8 - x \div 2 = 0.5$, $x = 5.4$ km

7 $20x = 5800 + 440, x = 312$

8 $x + 2x - 40 = 800, x = 280, 2x - 40 = 520$

9 If there are x tonnes of water in Pond A, and then there are $(40 - x)$ tonnes of water in Pond B, $x + 4 = 40 - x - 8$, $x = 14, 40 - x = 26$

10 $2.4 \div x$

11 $a + 3$

12 $a - 3$

13 $2x + 10$

14 $3a$; $8a$ pounds

15 $2x - 24$; 1280

16 $0.25a^2$

17 James

18 ✗

19 ✔

20 ✗

21 ✔

22 ✔

23 C

24 B

25 C

26 C

27 B

28 C

Chapter 4 Geometry and measurement (1)

4.1 Perpendicular lines

1 (a) perpendicular; perpendicular; perpendicular foot
   (b) angles; right angles; perpendicular
   (c) perpendicular; CD; AB; perpendicular; perpendicular
   (d) perpendicular
   (e) 3 or 9
   (f) right angles

2 (a) $AB \perp CD$ (b) $MN \perp OP$
   (e) $c \perp d$

3 PQ; perpendicular

4 Answers may vary

4.2 Parallel lines

1 B, D

2 (a) ✔ (b) ✗ (c) ✔ (d) ✔ (e) ✔

3 (a) $AB // DC$, $AD // BC$
   (b) $AD // BC$
   (c) $AF // CD$, $AB // ED$, $BC // FE$

4 (a) vertical; parallel; $a // b$; a is parallel to b
   (b) horizontal; parallel; $c // d // e$; equal

5 $2, 3, 4, n \div 2$

4.3 Parallelograms (1)

1 (a) AB CD; AD BC; parallel; parallelogram; diagonals
   (b) equal; equal
   (c) rectangle
   (d) square
   (e) rectangles; squares
   (f) 1 and 4

2 (a) ✔ (b) ✗ (c) ✗
   (d) ✗ (e) ✔ (f) ✗

3 Figures correctly drawn on the grid

4 (a) A, C, D   (b) A, B, C

5 18

6 7 cm; 1 cm and 6 cm; 5 cm; 2 cm and 3 cm

4.4 Parallelograms (2)

1 (a) height; base   (b) height
   (c) AF; BC; AD (d) equal
   (e) AC; DE (f) 2
   (g) rectangle; parallelogram

2 (a) B   (b) C   (c) D

3 Figures correctly drawn on the grid

4 A

5 10

6 20

4.5 Area of a parallelogram

1 $48\,m^2$, $1680\,cm^2$, $5\,mm$, $2.5\,cm$

2 (a) $180\,cm^2$ (b) $240\,cm^2$
   (c) $75\,cm^2$

3 (a) B   (b) C

4 (a) $10.8 \div 24 = 0.45$ (m)
   (b) $45 \times (45 - 1.3) = 1966.5$ (cm^2)
   (c) $28 \times 15 \times 4.5 = 1890$ (pounds)
   (d) $(36 \div 2 - 7.8) \times 5 = 51$ (cm^2)

5 B

6 ABFE, BCFE, CDFE, BFGE

4.6 Area of a triangle (1)

1 $90\,m^2$, $108\,cm^2$, $33\,m^2$, $22.5\,cm^2$

2 Figures correctly drawn

3 BE; BC; AB; CF

4 (a) $8 \times 5 \div 2 = 20$ (cm^2)
   (b) $15 \times 12 \div 2 = 90$ (cm^2)
   (c) $4 \times 3 \div 2 = 6$ (cm^2)

5 (a) ✗ (b) ✗ (c) ✔ (d) ✔

6 (a) $24 \times (24 \times 3 + 3) \div 2 = 900$ (cm^2)
   (b) $32 \times (32 - 7) \div 2 = 400$ (cm^2)
   (c) $0.18 \times (0.18 \div \frac{1}{5}) \div 2 = 0.081$($m^2$)

7 $6 \times 6 \div 2 = 18$ (cm^2)

8 $3.6 \times 4.8 \div 2 = 8.64$ (cm^2)

4.7 Area of a triangle (2)

1 (a) $7 \times 6 \div 2 = 21$ (cm^2)
   (b) $12 \times 5 \div 2 = 30$ (cm^2)
   (c) $12 \times 9 \div 2 = 54$ (cm^2)

2 (a) $20 \times 2 \div 8 = 5$ (cm)
   (b) $32.4 \times 2 \div 12 = 5.4$ (m)
   (c) $1536 \times 2 \div 64 = 48$ (cm)

3 (a) $18 \times (18 + 8) \div 2 = 234$ (m^2)
   (b) $(24 + 6) \times (16 + 3) \div 2 - 24 \times 16 \div 2 = 93$ (m^2)
   (c) $(6600 \div 60 - 40) \times 60 \div 2 = 2100$ (cm^2)
   (d) $(24 \times 2 \div 6) \times (6 + 5) \div 2 = 44$ (cm^2)

4 (a) 5   (b) 6   (c) 200   (d) 2.4

5 $30 \times 12 \div 2 = 180$ (cm^2)

6 $48 \div (2 + 1) \times 2 = 32$ (cm^2)

4.8 Practice and exercise (2)

1 (a) perpendicular
   (b) 2   (c) 0   (d) 4; 2   (e) $4a$

2 (a) D   (b) D   (c) D

3 $(40 - 2) \times (30 - 2) = 1064$ (m^2)

4 9

5 $101.25\,cm^2$

Chapter 4 test

1 (a) ✗ (b) ✗ (c) ✔
   (d) ✔ (e) ✗ (f) ✗; $c \perp d$; $e \perp f$; $m // n$

2 (a) B, C   (b) C   (c) B

3 (a) 67.5   (b) 38   (c) 4.8   (d) 4

4 (a) $63\,m^2$ (b) $720\,cm^2$

5 8 m

6 $(66 \div 2 - 18) \times 12 = 180$ (cm^2)

7 $120 \times (120 \div 3) \div 2 \times 75.8 \div 1000 = 181.92$ (kg)

8 $36 \times 25 \div 1.5 \times 2 = 32 = 37.5$ (cm)

9 $(100 \times 90) \div (6 \times 5 \div 2) = 600$ (triangles)

10 $3.6 \div (1.5 \times 2 \div 2 \times 2) = 1.2$ (kg)

Chapter 5 Consolidation and enhancement

5.1 Operations of decimals (1)

1. (a) 9.9   (b) 4.2
   (c) 21   (d) 1.6
   (e) 1.6   (f) 2.1
2. (a) 252   (b) 1426.8
   (c) 3.5   (d) 2.35
3. (a) 2.06   (b) 10
   (c) 1.2   (d) 480
4. (a) 1801.2; 23.7
   (b) 2 11; 5.6; 150; 50 6
   (c) D, A
   (d) 3.6
5. (a) A   (b) C
6. $18 \div (0.6 \times 60) = 0.5$ (km/minute)
   $(0.6 \times 60) \div 18 = 2$ (minutes)
7. (a) 23.3   (b) 131 r 6

5.2 Operations of decimals (2)

1. (a) 1.9   (b) 40.8
   (c) 0.52   (d) 7.2
2. (a) 19.45   (b) 9.34
   (c) 51.98   (d) 0.44
   (e) 19.13   (f) 4.05
   (g) 7.98   (h) 10.72
3. (a) 21.7   (b) 20
   (c) 100   (d) 100
   (e) 2.35   (f) 9.6
   (g) 450   (h) 50
4. $24 \times 12.5 \times 140 = 42\,000$ (suits); $42\,000 \div (12.5 - 2.5) \div (140 + 10) - 24 = 4$ (people)
5. (a) $(764 \times 0.4421) \div 3 \approx 112.59$ (pounds)
   (b) $(963 \times 0.1202) \div 3 \approx 38.58$ (pounds)
   (c) $(764 \times 0.4421) + (963 \times 0.1202) \approx 453.52$ (pounds)
   (d) Answer may vary.

5.3 Simplification and equations (1)

1. (a) $5a$ (b) $4y$
   (c) b (d) $5x$
   (e) $15x$ (f) $a - 12b$
2. (a) $x = 2$ (b) $x = 0.35$
3. (a) $x = 4$ (b) $x = 0.29$
   (c) $x = 9$ (d) $x = 4$
   (e) $x = 7.5$ (f) $x = 5$
4. (a) $3x \div 2 = 2.4, x = 1.6$
   (b) $5 \times (A + 1.28) = 19.25, A = 2.57$
   (c) $1.5 \times 12 = 24 \times (B - 2.25), B = 3$
5. (a) 850 (m²)   (b) 28 (basketballs)
6. (a) 5.6   (b) 28.125

5.4 Simplification and equations (2)

1. (a) 70   (b) 37.2
2. (a) $x = 2$ (b) $x = 4$
   (c) $x = 7$ (d) $x = 0.5$
   (e) $x = 3.75$ (f) $x = 19$
   (g) $x = 2.25$ (h) $x = 0.6$
3. (a) 1.5 (hours) (b) 164 (kg)
   (c) 80 (kg)   (d) 1 (kg)
4. $a = 5.5$
5. 28 (pupils)

5.5 More equation problems

1. (a) $x = 0.45$ (b) $x = 0.4$
   (c) $x = 6.1$ (d) $x = 0.4$
2. $50 - 4x = 6, x = £11$
3. $80x - 200 = 40, x = £3$
4. $6x + 40 = 1240, x = 200$
5. $3x - 32 = 370, x = 134$
6. $2(9.5 + x) = 32, x = 6.5$
7. $x + 2 \times 6.8 = 30, x = £16.40$
8. $16 \times 27.5 + 12x = 800, x = £30$
9. $148 - 18x = 112 - 12x, x = 6$ days
10. If the unit price of the chair is x pounds, then the unit price of the table is $(x + 10)$ pounds. $5(x + 10) + 8x = 375$, $x = £25$ (chair), $x + 10 = £35$ (table)

5.6 Calculating the areas of shapes

1. Figures correctly drawn
2. $14 \times 6 = 84$ (cm²); $14 \times 10.5 \div 2 = 73.5$ (cm²)
3. $36 \div 4.5 = 8$ (cm)
4. $6 \times 6 + 4 \times 4 - 6 \times 6 \div 2 - 4 \times (6 + 4) \div 2 = 14$ (cm²)
5. $24 \div 4 = 6$ (cm), $6 \div (2 + 1) = 2$ (cm), $2 \times 2 = 4$ (cm), $6 \times 6 - 6 \times 4 \div 2 - 6 \times 2 \div 2 - 2 \times 4 = 10$ (cm²)
6. $AE = 20 \div (3 + 1) = 5$ (cm), $DE = 5 \times 3 = 15$ (cm), $AF = 20 \div (4 + 1) = 4$ (cm), $BF = 4 \times 4 = 16$ (cm), $20 \times 20 - 20 \times 15 \div 2 - 20 \times 16 \div 2 - 5 \times 4 \div 2 = 80$ (cm²)

5.7 Mathematics plaza – calculation of time

1. (a) 22 minutes 30 seconds
   (b) 9 hours
   (c) 4 minutes 51 seconds
2. (a) 11:33 a.m.   (b) 8.30 a.m.

3. (a) $45 \times 4 + 20 + 30 = 230$ minutes = 3 hours and 50 minutes, 9:15 + 3 hours and 50 minutes = 13:05
   (b) 3 hours and 41 minutes
4. 38 minutes and 28 seconds
5. 8:20 − 6:30 = 1 hour and 50 minutes = 110 minutes, $110 \times 7 = 770$ (minutes) = 12 hours and 50 minutes
6. He should leave home at 18:35, and he will arrive home at 22:10
7. (a) 21:50
   (b) $600 - 100 = 500$ (people), $(8 \times 4 + 10 \times 3) \times 500 \times 7 = 217\,000$ (pounds)

Chapter 5 test

1. (a) 0.5   (b) 87
   (c) 1.6   (d) 6.25
2. (a) 419.92   (b) 5.66
3. (a) $x = 1$ (b) $x = 1.5$
4. (a) 5.4   (b) 0
   (c) 5   (d) 7.2
   (e) 0.5   (f) 56
5. $30 \times 40 \div (30 - 5) = 48$ (days)
6. $4x + 2 \times 7 = 30, x = £4$
7. $7x = 90 + 2 \times 480, x = £150$
8. $8x + 2 = 800 \div 16, x = £6$
9. (a) $10 + (8 - 3) \times 2 = 20$ (pounds)
   (b) $(30 - 10 - 2 \times 7) \div 3 + 10 = 12$ (km)
10. $3.5 \times 10 + 10 \times 8 \div 2 = 75$ (m²)
11. (a) a^2 $1.5a$ (b) 120; 48
12. B
13. B
14. D
15. D
16. (a) ✔ (b) ✘ (c) ✘ (d) ✘
17. 6.48; 0.18
18. 46
19. 72; 36; 81
20. $2m + 4$; 15